WRITING

A COLLEGE RHETORIC

WRITING

A COLLEGE RHETORIC

Brief Edition

LAURIE G. KIRSZNER

PHILADELPHIA COLLEGE OF PHARMACY AND SCIENCE

STEPHEN R. MANDELL

DREXEL UNIVERSITY

HOLT, RINEHART AND WINSTON

NEW YORK   CHICAGO   SAN FRANCISCO   PHILADELPHIA
MONTREAL   TORONTO   LONDON   SYDNEY
TOKYO   MEXICO CITY   RIO DE JANEIRO   MADRID

Publisher   Susan Katz
Editor   Charlyce Jones Owen
Developmental Editor   Cheryl Kupper
Special Projects Editor   Pamela Forcey
Production Manager   Annette Mayeski
Art Director   Louis Scardino
Cover Design   A. J. D'Agostino

Composition   York Graphic Services, Inc.
Printing and binding   Von Hoffmann Press, Inc.

Library of Congress Cataloging in Publication Data

Kirszner, Laurie G.
    Writing : a college rhetoric.

    Includes index.
    1. English language—Rhetoric.
I. Mandell, Stephen R. II. Title.
PE1408.K676   1985   808'.042
    84–22394

ISBN 0-03-001417-4

CBS COLLEGE PUBLISHING
Holt, Rinehart and Winston
The Dryden Press
Saunders College Publishing

ACKNOWLEDGMENTS

Excerpt from "The American T Party."
Copyright 1974 Time Inc. All rights reserved.
Reprinted by permission from *Time*.

Excerpt by Isaac Asimov. Copyright © 1981
by The New York Times Company. Reprinted
by permission.

Excerpt from "My Father Sold Chryslers" by
Ingrid Bengis. Copyright © 1980 by The New
York Times Company. Reprinted by permission.

Excerpt from "Bits 'n' Bytes About Computing." Reprinted with permission from *Personal
Computing*, September 1982. Copyright 1982,
Hayden Publishing Company.

Excerpt from "From New Game Firm" by
Michael Blanchet. Reprinted by permission:
Tribune Company Syndicate, Inc.

Excerpts from *Book Review Digest*. Copyright
© 1981, 1982 by The H. W. Wilson Company.
Material reproduced by permission of the publisher.

Capsule book reviews. Copyright © 1980 by
The New York Times Company. Reprinted by
permission.

Excerpt from "Rookie Misses No-Hitter in
Ninth" by Murray Chass. Copyright © 1981 by
The New York Times Company. Reprinted by
permission.

"Buffalo Bill" is reprinted from *Tulips and
Chimneys* by E. E. Cummings, by permission of
Liveright Publishing Corporation. Copyright
1923, 1925 and renewed 1951, 1953 by E. E.
Cummings. Copyright © 1973, 1976 by the

(continued on page 561)

PREFACE

Since we began teaching fifteen years ago, a lot has changed, but students coming to a college composition course still want to acquire, practice, and polish communication skills and techniques they can apply to *all* their college courses, not just English, and to their personal and professional lives as well. *Writing: A College Rhetoric* is a complete rhetoric for freshman composition. It treats writing as a process, places strong emphasis on thesis and support, and draws heavily on student writing from a variety of disciplines. The text moves logically from *prewriting* through *writing and arranging* to *revising*, covering the writing process in the first nine chapters, grouping special assignments (argumentation, business writing, the essay examination, the critical essay, and the library research paper) in the second half of the book. The special assignments are self-contained and may be introduced in any order.

The text's many innovative, yet practical exercises—particularly the "Working with Data" feature, the numerous student examples, and the separate chapters detailing and illustrating the process of drafting and revising—set it apart from most other books presently available. *Writing: A College Rhetoric* is comprehensive enough for a full-year course, yet in a one-semester or one-quarter course, the text is flexible enough to allow instructors to concentrate on Chapters 1–9 and to select whichever of the special assignments is important to them and to their students.

The first section of the book, "Prewriting," consists of two chapters. In Chapter 1, "The Writer's Boundaries," we consider the writer's purpose, audience, and occasion for writing, the length of the piece of writing, and the writer's knowledge. Special features of this section are a discussion of the writer's purpose based on the work of James L. Kinneavy and a detailed examination of the academic audience. We ask students to complete a variety of tasks that require them to react both to personal experiences and to a variety of materials such as newspaper articles, an editorial cartoon, a statistical chart, a list of facts, a set of student paragraphs, and capsule book reviews. We draw examples and exercises from subject matter as diverse as the Salem witchcraft trials, Dickens's *Hard Times*, organized religion, and toxic waste disposal.

Chapter 2, "Getting Started," begins with advice on using free writing to overcome writer's block and includes three free-writing exercises. We then show students how to use journalistic questions and more systematic questions to narrow a topic. The next section, "Finding Something to Say," helps students to see the limits of personal knowledge and how they can supplement their knowledge and experience by keeping a journal and by brainstorming. We continue the chapter with a discussion of how to find a tentative thesis and close with a comprehensive exercise that allows students to practice deriving a tentative thesis from material on the work of epidemiologists.

Section II, "Writing and Arranging," begins with Chapter 3, "Preliminary Shaping: The Rough Draft." After offering some introductory advice on how to prepare to write, we return to the student essay-in-progress, which was the focus of Chapter 2, and reproduce a rough draft of a student essay based on Chapter 2's scratch outline. We then present discussions and exercises on how to distinguish between strong and weak thesis statements, where to place thesis statements, and how to support the thesis. Here we reproduce a revised version of the student rough draft. The chapter concludes with exercises that ask students to draw original conclusions from a series of brief articles on business executives' summer jobs and to write a thesis-and-support essay.

Chapter 4, "Further Shaping: Patterns of Development," introduces students to five options for arranging expository material: *process, cause and effect, comparison and contrast, division and classification,* and *definition.* Each of the chapter's five sections includes a definition of the method of development, brief professional and student examples, tips on how to apply the pattern to typical assignments in various disciplines, information on how to organize an essay, and at least one annotated student essay followed by analysis. Each section concludes with a "Working with Data" exercise, a feature that permits students to use varied source materials provided in the text to help them write interesting, informative essays.

Chapter 5, "Writing Paragraphs," defines the paragraph as a unit of thought and illustrates its function as part of an essay and its nature as a group of sentences. We present the different patterns around which paragraphs may be structured, using Francis Christensen's rhetoric of the paragraph to demonstrate the criteria for effective paragraphs. We go on to discuss and illustrate different kinds of body paragraphs and introductory and concluding paragraphs.

Chapter 6, "Writing Sentences," presents the basic sentence pattern and ways to build simple, compound, and complex sentences through modification, coordination, and subordination, respectively. The chapter goes on to consider stylistic options that may be used to vary the basic sentence pattern. Here we discuss and illustrate cumulative, periodic, and parallel and balanced sentences.

In Chapter 7, "Writing: Words," we discuss the importance of using words accurately and effectively. We begin with an explanation of the difference between denotation and connotation and go on to consider the advantages of using specific and concrete diction and of using the kind of language the college audience expects. Next comes a section on choosing effective imagery and avoiding ineffective imagery. Finally, the chapter discusses the limitations of formal and informal diction (including slang).

Chapter 8, "Tone and Style," first examines the relationship between a writer's purpose and audience and the tone of his or her writing. It proceeds to consider the various levels of style—formal, popular, and informal—and the uses of each.

Section III, "Revising," consists of Chapter 9, "Revising Your Essay." Building on the research of E. D. Hirsch, Nancy Sommers, and Donald Murray, the chapter illustrates how students and professional writers revise and explains and illustrates three specific revision strategies: peer criticism, outlining, and checklists. Our emphasis is on revision as a process of moving from writer-based to reader-based prose.

Section IV, "Special Assignments," begins with Chapter 10, "Argumentation," which takes students through the process of writing an argumentative essay. The intent of this chapter is to teach argument as a series of rhetorical strategies. We first consider the difference between argument and persuasion. We then concentrate on choosing a topic, taking a stand, gathering evidence, considering an audience, being fair, and dealing with the opposition. In "Arranging Your Argument," we then explain how to structure deductive and inductive arguments, illustrating each with a student essay. The chapter closes with a "Working with Data" exercise.

Chapter 11, "Essay Examinations," analyzes pairs of paragraph- and essay-length examination answers (one strong, one weak) side by side—to point out specific strategies students can use to write clear, emphatic examination answers. Subjects include art history, sociology, and history, as well as literature.

Chapter 12, "Business Letters and Memos," covers the constraints governing the format, tone, and organization of the letter and the memo, approaching both in terms of student needs—for example, applications for part-time and full-time jobs (including résumé writing), letters to graduate and professional schools, letters requesting information for college papers and projects, and memos from a fraternity to the dean and from a library reference assistant to the librarian.

Chapter 13, "The Critical Essay," begins with an examination of critical writing in general terms, considering how it may be applied to non-literary subjects— ballet, restaurants, record albums, even video games. We go on to take a process approach to writing the critical literary essay. Poe's "The Cask of Amontillado" appears in the text along with exercises for prewriting, writing and arranging, and revising an essay about the story.

The last of the "Special Assignments" chapters, "The Library Research Paper," treats writing the research paper as an eleven-step process that includes choosing a topic, preliminary research, assembling a preliminary bibliography, concentrated reading and note taking, deciding on a thesis, making a working outline, writing the first draft, revising the first draft, documenting, preparing the final draft, and final editing. The treatment is thorough, and for this reason there is no need for a supplemental text that deals specifically with writing a research paper. We deal with students' and instructors' most pressing concerns: how to identify and avoid plagiarism, how to work source material into a paper, how to use quotations, and what to document. (Both MLA and APA formats are included). Exercises ask students to work with materials on the Ku Klux Klan, the origin of oral history, and Topeka, Kansas, before Brown vs. Board of Education. The chapter concludes with a thoroughly annotated student paper, "Civilian Control of Atomic Energy: Scientists' Bridge into Politics," complete with outline, selected note and bibliography cards, end notes, and bibliography.

The Instructor's Manual that accompanies this text includes answers to the exercises; a supplementary "Working with Data" exercise; suggested syllabi; blank form for peer revision; lists of writing topics; and a bibliography of helpful articles and books about writing as supplementary reading for students.

ACKNOWLEDGMENTS

Like most people who devote a lot of time and energy to a project, we have a long list of people to thank. Beginning at the beginning, we owe a good deal to Susan Katz, who first encouraged us to submit a proposal for *Writing*. We offer a special champagne toast to Nedah Abbott, our editor at Holt during the development of this text. And we are very grateful to Cheryl Kupper, whose work on the manuscript was truly wonderful, and whose patience and wit were always appreciated. We also thank Charlyce Jones Owen for making the transition between editors so smooth. Others at Holt who helped were Pamela Forcey, Karen Dubno, Anne Boynton-Trigg, Emily Barosse, and Susan Gowing.

We are grateful also to the reviewers who scrutinized each draft of our manuscript and offered suggestions for revision. They are: Bonnie Braendlin, Florida State University; Douglas Butturff, University of Central Arkansas; J. D. Daubs, University of Illinois, Urbana-Champaign; Jim Davis, University of Illinois, Urbana-Champaign; John Dick, University of Texas, El Paso; William D. Dyer, Mankato State University; Alice Gillam-Scott, University of Illinois at Chicago Circle; Patricia Graves, Georgia State University; Jeffrey T. Gross, Memphis State University; Nevin K. Laib, Texas Tech University; Andrea A. Lunsford, University of British Columbia; Walter E. Meyers, North Carolina State University; George Miller, University of Delaware; Nancy Sommers, Rutgers University; Christopher Thaiss, George Mason University; David Yerkes, Columbia University. A very special debt is owed to our friend and colleague Richard Elias of Ohio Wesleyan University for sharing with us the term paper and source materials in Chapter 14.

Meanwhile, back in Philadelphia, we wish to thank our students and colleagues, who freely volunteered materials and ideas; the staff of the Philadelphia Free Library; and Lee Endicott for truly professional typing services. We would also like at this time to acknowledge our gratitude for the little things—coffee and Chinese food, made-for-TV movies and call-waiting—that kept us going. Finally, we send our love to Mark and Demi and to our four terrific children, Adam and Rebecca Kirszner, and David and Sarah Mandell.

L.G.K.
S.R.M.

CONTENTS

IV *Special Assignments* *245*

Index to Reading Selections and Student Essays

I

Prewriting

One of the most important steps you can take toward becoming a good writer is to recognize that writing is a continuous process. Because so often we encounter writing as a "finished product"—something printed, bound, and separate—most of us are used to taking a reader's stance. We think of writing as something outside ourselves, something committed to paper and therefore complete. As readers we are passive. We learn to analyze, looking at a printed sheet and perhaps considering its audience and purpose, the pattern around which it has been organized and developed, the effectiveness of its paragraphs, or the stylistic choices its author has made. It is difficult, therefore, when we read the work of others, to see writing as

1

a dynamic, creative process, to see it from the writer's point of view.

But writing is a process of choosing—of selecting and rejecting, expanding and compressing, adding, deleting, and rearranging at every stage of the writing process. Learning to write well involves being aware of the options open to you and the choices you can make.

The writing process has three stages: (1) prewriting; (2) writing and arranging; and (3) revising. The process is not direct or linear—its stages constantly overlap—but we must treat these stages separately for clarity. In the *prewriting* stage, you talk to yourself and others, ask questions, wonder, and think. You also make lists and take notes and cross out unwanted items and think some more. You think about what you are supposed to be doing and why you are doing it in the first place, and you think about what your audience needs and expects. Bit by bit you consider your options, make decisions, and find answers, narrowing your subject and deciding on a topic and an angle from which to approach it. You begin to find material and to settle on a main idea that that material can support. Then, as you write the rough draft of your essay, you begin to shape your material.

During *writing* and *arranging* you continue to make choices, trying out ways to organize the material you have collected. You will probably write one or two—or several—more drafts as you try to get down on paper what you want to say the way you want to say it. You may find yourself making an outline or chart, or you may discover that your main idea or the material itself suggests a sensible organizing principle. Now you decide what information to put at the beginning, in the middle, and at the end. As you work on your various drafts, the shape of your essay will emerge more and more clearly.

Revising involves reseeing and rethinking and sometimes completely overhauling your work. (Recopying and proofreading, which you must do before handing in your paper, are not revising.) You may rethink concepts, rework paragraphs, recast phrases and sentences, and substitute words until you have a piece of writing that says what you want it to say. The important thing about revision is that it occurs at *every* stage of the writing process—not just when your essay is "finished."

At *any* stage you will find yourself making decisions: reassessing your purpose or the demands of your audience, reconsidering your main idea, deleting information, moving a sentence, substituting one word for another, correcting mechanical errors, refining your title, adding necessary links between ideas. You may even find yourself scrapping the whole project and starting over. What you will *not* do, however, is sail swiftly and confidently along from first word to last.

The writing process is actually a series of concerns, one or more of which dominate your writing at any given time. Each is "on hold" in the back of your mind, waiting to be called in when you need it. These concerns alternately surface and sink, come sharply into focus and go out of focus many times as you write. Thus as you narrow your subject (prewriting), you might also begin to find a pattern for your material (arranging); as you ar-range your ideas, you might also make changes in your main idea (revising); as you revise your essay, you might also continue to dis-cover new ideas (prewriting).

Writing, then, engages you, the writer, in a continuing series of conflicts with yourself. During the writing process, ideas spill out onto the paper or remain elusive; they suggest new ways of seeing and understanding, or they seem dis-connected and arbitrary. A word or phrase is "just right," or it sounds dead wrong. Or, worse, it seems, and remains, almost—but not quite—right. Whether writing is pleasant and exciting or tedious and frustrating depends on you, your subject matter, and the writ-ing task at hand. Whatever the case, you should always consider writing as work in progress; that is, it is constantly being changed and improved.

CHAPTER

1

The Writer's Boundaries

Everyone who sets out to write confronts a series of choices. Whenever you write, you make adjustments based on certain boundaries: your *purpose*, your *audience*, your *occasion* for writing, the *length* of your writing, and your *knowledge* of a subject. Each of these boundaries affects the others in different ways as your essay develops. For instance, your occasion for writing or your audience helps to determine your purpose; your purpose or your knowledge of the subject influences the length of your piece. A closer examination of these boundaries will enable you to make better choices as you write.

THE WRITER'S PURPOSE

Your purpose arises from the nature of your communication and from the communication process itself. All written communication has a writer who *sends* a message, a reader who *receives* a message, and a reality to which a message *refers*.

When a writer-sender emphasizes himself or herself, internal reality, then the purpose is *to express private feelings or attitudes*. The result is the introspective or meditative writing that appears in personal journals, diaries, autobiographical fragments, and occasionally letters. When a writer emphasizes outside facts or events, external reality, then the purpose is *to convey information* as accurately and as logically as possible. The result is the informational or expository writing that occurs in reports, news articles, encyclopedias, and textbooks. When a writer emphasizes the audience, then the purpose is *to convince or persuade*. The writer consciously tries to convince others that certain ideas or attitudes are worth listening to or believing. The result is the persuasive writing of advertising, proposals, editorials, sermons, and some business communications. Finally, when a writer emphasizes the internal ordering of the material itself, then the purpose is *to give pleasure*. The result is the creative writing of short stories, poems, novels, plays, and movies.

In the most general terms, then, writers write to express feelings, to convey information, to persuade, or to give pleasure. But writers may have other specific purposes as well. Under some circumstances writers may *evaluate*, assessing the validity or accuracy of certain information, as in book reviews, critiques, or recommendation reports. Writers may also write to *discover*, to gather ideas or record observations, as in a scientist's laboratory notes, a scholar's preliminary research, or a student's class notes. Or writers may *affirm*, expressing firmly held beliefs or strongly felt values, as in manifestoes, declarations, or statements of belief.

A writer's purpose can be complex, blending a number of these and other specific purposes. A police commissioner, for example, writes a passionate letter to the editor of a newspaper in favor of strict gun-control laws after returning from the funeral of an officer killed by a handgun. Why? To express anger and sadness; to change people's minds about gun control; to influence legislation on gun control; and, perhaps, to find justice and meaning in the officer's death.

EXERCISE

Read the following list of purposes you might have when you write. Look each word up in a dictionary, and jot down an assignment, situation, or task to which each of these words could apply.

analyze	advise	amuse	inform
consider	change	criticize	inflame
explain	convince	describe	inspire
speculate	influence	discredit	satirize
theorize	argue	motivate	speculate

In college writing, your usual purpose is expository, to convey information. Some special assignments, particularly in English composition class, ask you to persuade your audience, to entertain, or to evaluate. You might be asked to write an editorial, a humorous anecdote, or a critical essay. Just because you set out primarily to persuade, however, does not mean that you cannot present information, evaluate, or analyze; a good piece of writing often does all of these. The important thing is that having a clear sense of the purpose of your essay always helps you make sensible choices as you write.

Once you think you have your purpose, dig into your motives to see if you know just what made you decide to compose the piece you have in mind. Ask yourself if you have a strong opinion or if you are neutral. If you have a strong opinion, concentrate on the impressions or arguments you most want to convey to your reader, and why. Finally, take into account how the needs of your audience affect your purpose. Remember, your purpose does not have to remain constant; you are not locked into the purpose you had in mind when you began. As you revise, you may change your assessment of your purpose, and this shift will require you to make corresponding changes in your paper's style, structure, format, and emphasis.

EXERCISES

1. Read the following selections carefully. Try to put yourself in the writer's position and determine the purpose or purposes each had in mind when writing the paragraphs. More specifically, consider each writer's motive: why did each write as he or she did?

a. The underground is forty miles of dismal platforms, intimidating concourses, slippery steps, stagnant puddles, befouled air, poorly lighted waiting areas, graffiti-covered walls, out-numbered cops, juvenile wolf packs, daily racial confrontations and cattle-car rolling stock . . . . (*Philadelphia Magazine*)

b. A medium-fast computer can add one million times faster than a person, and a fast computer can add 1,000 times faster still. As Donald Knuth of Stanford University explains, comparing the calculating speeds of computers and humans is like comparing the fastest airplane to the pace of a snail. ("Trial-and-Error Game that Puzzles Fast Computers," *Smithsonian*)

c. Of course, short people have been looked down upon for years. In the matter of language, for example . . . one does not wish to be found short-tempered, short-winded or shortsighted. One does not wish to be left with the short end, caught short-handed or given short shrift. Shortages, short circuits and shortfalls are universally deplored. On the other hand, one takes pride in filling a tall order, gapes at the tall ships, admires a tall tale and—out here in the Wild West—sits tall in the saddle. Although brevity is the soul of wit and one strives to make a long story short, this quality is not equally appreciated when manifested in human form. Just as we habitually use the masculine gender to denote all people, we use tallness to measure height. Thus there are those who say they are "4 feet tall" when they are clearly 4 feet short. (Beth Luey, "Short Shrift," *Newsweek*)

d.

1980 Register & Tribune Syndicate

"Our theory is that nobody knows it's here, and what nobody knows can't hurt 'em."

e.   Radio began with the transatlantic "wireless" communication of Guglielmo Marconi (1874–1937) in 1901 and the development of the vacuum tube in 1904, which permitted the transmission of speech and music. But it was only in 1920 that the first major broadcasts of special events were made in Great Britain and the United States. Lord Northcliffe, who had pioneered in journalism with the inexpensive, mass-circulation *Daily Mail,* sponsored a broadcast of "only one artist . . . the world's very best, the soprano Nellie Melba." Singing from London in English, Italian and French, Melba was heard simultaneously all over Europe on June 16, 1920. This historic event captured the public's imagination. The meteoric career of radio was launched. (McKay, Hill, Buckler, *A History of Western Society,* Vol. II)

2.   The following article, from the September 21, 1980, *New York Times,* primarily presents information. How would you change it to convince your reader that people would rather have jobs than be on welfare? Would you omit any information? Would you reorder any details? Would you add anything?

Officials Say 26,200 Applied for 75 Jobs in Baltimore

BALTIMORE, Sept. 20—At least 26,200 persons have picked up application forms for the 75 entry-level positions offered this week with the Social Security Administration here, officials said today.

The total is more than double the first-day turnout of 12,000 persons who lined up Monday at three separate Federal office buildings, some waiting up to three hours, to get the applications. The salaries will range from $7,210 for clerical work to $11,565 for warehouse duties.

Jim M. Brown, a spokesman for the agency, said officials had been overwhelmed by the turnout of applicants, most of whom were black. "What this proves is what black leaders have been saying for years—people would rather have jobs than be on welfare," he said.

However, it will be the lucky few who get these jobs. A lottery system, using the last two digits of a person's Social Security number, will be used in the next three months to draw applications from the vast pool. Mr. Brown said once drawn, those forms will be reviewed for qualifications, such as high school diploma and citizenship.

For each vacancy only three persons will be interviewed, a total of 225, and veterans will receive preference, following standard Federal hiring policies. In addition, although the jobs do not require special skills or testing, those who do have experience will be given preference. Those not hired but who qualify for jobs will be put on a waiting list.

The applications for the jobs were to have been mailed by yesterday or left at one of the two Social Security offices or the Federal Building downtown, Mr. Brown said.

People interviewed in the long lines on Monday morning indicated most had heard about the jobs by word of mouth.

Unemployment for Baltimore in July, the latest month for which figures are available, was 9.9 percent, as against the national rate of 7.8 percent for July and 7.6 percent for August.

The most recent data on Baltimore's nonwhite unemployment rate from the Federal Bureau of Labor Statistics included only figures for 1979, which showed a level of 17.9 percent. For 16- to 19-year-olds, the figure rose to 51.5 percent.

3.   The table on page 10 is from a college-level economics textbook. Study the facts and use the information as source material for three paragraphs.

    a.   In the first, summarize the information *in your own words.*

    b.   Next, write a paragraph in which your primary purpose is to suggest, in a humorous manner, that West Germany will disappear by the year 2000.

c.   Finally, write a paragraph in which you use the information to try to persuade your audience that the contrast between the birth rates in so-called developed and underdeveloped countries has alarming implications.

TABLE 13-4   Birth Rates per 1,000 People, Selected Countries, 1970

Developed countries	Births per 1,000 people	Underdeveloped countries	Births per 1,000 people
Israel	26.8	U.S. Virgin Islands	49.5
New Zealand	22.1	Mexico	43.4
Australia	20.6	Algeria	40.9 (1968)
Japan	18.8	El Salvador	40.0
Netherlands	18.3	Guatemala	39.0
United States	18.2	Madagascar	38.6 (1969)
Canada	17.5 (1969)	Libya	37.9 (1968)
USSR	17.5	Dominican Republic	37.1 (1969)
Italy	16.8	Panama	37.1
France	16.7	Egypt	36.9 (1969)
Norway	16.6	Tunisia	36.2
Bulgaria	16.3	Jamaica	34.4
United Kingdom	16.2	Costa Rica	33.8
Czechoslovakia	15.8	Paraguay	33.4
Switzerland	15.8	Thailand	32.6 (1969)
Austria	15.2	Portuguese Guinea	30.2
Belgium	14.7	Guam	28.8
East Germany	13.9	Taiwan	28.1
Sweden	13.7	Lebanon	27.3
West Germany	13.3	Chile	26.6 (1968)

Sources: Monthly Bulletin of Statistics, *Vol. XXVI, No. 7 (July 1972), pp. 6–7; Statistical Office of the United Nations, Department of Economic and Social Affairs,* Demographic Yearbook, 1970. *New York: 1971, pp. 619–27.*

(William C. Blanchfield and Jacob Oser, *Economics: Reality Through Theory*)

THE WRITER'S AUDIENCE

The act of writing is a solitary one, and when you are in your own private world staring at a blank sheet of paper you can easily forget about your audience. Some writing, of course—diaries and journals, for instance—does remain private. And, in the stages that lead up to *any* writing, you probably feel that you're only talking to yourself. When you begin a paper or letter or report, you do scribble down ideas, make notes or journal entries, ask questions, or engage in discussions about your topic without any thought to your eventual reader. At this stage, your writing may seem to be very private, with little relationship to outside concerns.

But writers almost always write for an audience. In a letter to a friend, you take into account the experiences you share, your friend's interests, and how much you need to explain. In a letter of complaint, you try to marshal the evidence that will convince your reader that your complaint is justified. In a job-application letter, you decide how to make your reader see you in the best possible light. And this is true of all the other writing you do in your daily life.

At work the demands and expectations of your audience shape your writing even more dramatically. Whether you write for your peers, your immediate super-visor, your subordinates, or the public, you aim your style and content directly at them. In each case you ask yourself what information your audience needs and what language and format will communicate this information to them most effec-tively. The art of arranging words, sentences, and ideas to influence an audience is called *rhetoric*. And it is on these rhetorical concerns that this book focuses.

Most of your writing as a student, of course, also has an audience. Whether that is an audience of one, as in the case of a midterm examination, or an audience of many, as in the case of an article for your school newspaper, the challenge remains the same—trying to communicate ideas or information to readers in a way they will believe. Your relationship with your audience determines how you treat your subject—what words you use, how much detail you go into, and what evi-dence you muster.

Early in the writing process, you should begin to envision the final written product, and you should design this product with a certain audience in mind. The decisions you make about the audience's interests, level of education, prejudices, and expectations determine the information you will cover. If you judge your audience correctly, the response you want—interest, praise, or action—will follow.

Professional writers rarely, if ever, get direct feedback from their audiences. Student writers, however, almost always receive feedback from their teachers—their job is to criticize—and you can (and should) make the most of this. Incorpo-rating your instructors' suggestions into your writing process and adjusting your presentation to their reasonable demands will take you a long way toward becom-ing a forceful and effective communicator.

UNDERSTANDING YOUR AUDIENCE

Let's try to bring the audience for your college work into focus. To be realistic about it, your audience is your instructor, although in some courses you may write for a group of instructors or students. You actually write for a different audience in each of your courses because each of your instructors has different areas of interest and expertise, different concerns and standards. But ending our discussion of your college audience here would mislead you. In fact, whenever you write in an academic setting, you address a generalized, representative reader. In addition to being a unique person, your instructor is a representative reader who applies the standards of a wider world of academic writing in a fairly predictable way. In college writing you must learn to know what this representative reader, whom you should see as a critic and collaborator, needs and expects.

Although college teachers do have different specialties and fields of interest, all of them share a commitment to helping you produce high-quality written work. They expect you to work hard at achieving it. Every instructor looks for correct information, standard grammar and spelling, logical organization, and a measure of stylistic fluency.

Your instructors are trained as careful readers and demanding critics. They require precisely defined terms and carefully qualified generalizations supported with data. They expect you to show how your observations lead to a general statement, and they expect a high degree of precision and accuracy in reporting. Like any demanding reader, they want to know what you know, and they want to see you express what you know clearly and accurately. They construct written assignments to see how well you can think, and so the way you organize and present your ideas is just as important as the ideas themselves.

Given that this generalized college audience shares certain standards and expectations, particular instructors have special knowledge or interests that also influence the material you write about and the way you write about it. You should consider, for instance, how much your reader knows about your subject.

You can assume that all of your instructors are well-versed in their areas of interest, and when writing for them you treat them as specialists. You need not provide long summaries of background information, involved overviews, or discussions of self-evident points. Outside their areas, however, most instructors are just general readers. You may know more about your subject than your instructor does. So, when you write a paper on fusion research for your journalism class, give your instructor the basic comparisons and examples and the general background and definitions you would give to any intelligent generalist. Even an uninformed reader, however, expects an interesting, thoughtful paper. Don't make the mistake of thinking that a basic paper must be simple-minded.

Assessing the interest of your audience in your subject is at least as important as judging their knowledge of it. Whether or not your academic audience is interested in your subject determines how you present your material. For instance, if you were writing a paper on "A Major Social Impact of Twentieth-Century Engineering" in your engineering ethics class, you could assume audience interest. You don't have to bring on a marching band, because you don't need to arouse interest. But if you were writing that same paper for your freshman composition class, you'd want to do something to make sure your instructor didn't lose interest.

WRITING FOR THE COLLEGE AUDIENCE

Considering the interests and abilities of your readers carefully helps you make the right writing choices. After all, you must tailor your purpose for different audiences, and your purpose controls your selection of material. Suppose, for instance, you planned to write a short paper about the seventeenth-century Salem, Massachusetts, witchcraft trials. The facts are these:

> In 1692, an epidemic of an epilepsy-like condition swept through the town of Salem. When doctors proved unable to halt the spread of the disease, the townspeople began to believe that evil spirits—specifically, witches—were responsible for the epidemic. In their sermons, clergymen—especially Cotton Mather, one of the most famous ministers of his time—encouraged this belief. Eventually nineteen persons suspected of being witches were hanged and another one hundred fifty jailed. An additional fifty-five were forced by fear or torture to confess their guilt. At this point distinguished citizens of Salem also encouraged the persecution by sanctioning court proceedings. Only after some of these prominent citizens, including the governor's wife, came to be suspected of being witches did the witchcraft hysteria die down.
>
> Adapted from the *Oxford Companion to American Literature*

In an American history course, you can safely assume that your instructor knows the situation. You won't need an overview of the facts, but you might want to show how the witchcraft trials grew logically out of the world view held by the citizens of seventeenth-century Salem. You might choose to emphasize the parallels between the witchcraft trials and the persecution of the Jews in Nazi Germany. For a literature course, you would quickly summarize the facts about Salem before discussing Arthur Miller's 1953 play *The Crucible*, which uses the trials to comment upon the McCarthy era in America. Your literature instructor does not need a long plot summary, but if none of your classmates has read *The Crucible*, they need overviews of both the play and the historical event. For a class in religion, a historical summary could lead into a discussion of the role of seventeenth-century Calvinism in the persecution. For a class in public health, you could examine the epidemic and the controversial theory that it was connected with ergot poisoning, which produces hallucinations like those of LSD. For psychology, you could analyze ways in which hysteria spread among the population.

In every case, your academic audience expects a certain quality to your work, and those demands provide general guidelines. But beyond that, you must base your choices of what to include and how to present it on how you assess your audience's background, needs, expectations, knowledge, and interest. In the two paragraphs below, two different students treat Charles Dickens's novel *Hard Times*. At left is part of a long paper on characterization in Dickens, written for a course in Victorian literature. The right-hand paragraph, about Dickens's treatment of grammar-school education in England, comes from a paper written for a course in educational methods.

I

Throughout his work, Dickens used exaggerated physical traits to comment on character. In *Hard Times*, for instance, Gradgrind's physical appearance is described in mechanical terms that parallel and enhance the rigidity of his personality. Over and over again Gradgrind is described as "square," with a "wide, thin, and hard set" mouth to complement his "inflexible, dry and dictatorial" voice. Gradgrind is a "man of realities. A man of facts and calculations," and Dickens's physical descriptions of him as "a cannon loaded to the muzzle with facts" and "a galvanizing apparatus" reinforce this mechanical, unyielding personality.

II

Perhaps nowhere are the Victorian era's dehumanizing methods of educating its young people more vividly presented than in a work of fiction, Charles Dickens's *Hard Times*. With its obvious parallels to life in the factories, life in the schoolroom is shown to be harsh, with lessons learned mechanically under the direction of the rigid Mr. Gradgrind. The emphasis here is on facts, not feeling, on discipline, not creativity, and the outlook for the children in this "model" school is every bit as bleak as it is elsewhere in the industrialized society.

Before they began to write, both student authors considered their audiences. The result is two quite different paragraphs. Paragraph I, written for an English literature professor, focuses on Dickens's use of caricature. The author expects her audience to know a good deal about Dickens as a craftsman and as a social critic. She need not create interest or summarize the plot, and she starts by mentioning already familiar characters. The student who wrote paragraph II, about Dickens's portrayal of Victorian education, does not assume that his audience knows or cares much about Dickens or his novel, and so he devotes much of the paragraph to creating interest by illustrating the relevance of the topic. Mr. Gradgrind, the schoolmaster, is identified and placed in context. Throughout the rest of the essay, the writer included summary sections to establish his topic and maintain interest.

EXERCISES

1. Reread paragraph II above and answer these questions about the author's strategy.

    a.   What audience is the author writing for?

    b.   What is the principal similarity between this paragraph and paragraph I?

    c.   What is the central focus of this paragraph? How do you know?

    d.   What details are included here that are not included in paragraph I? What details are omitted? Why?

    e.   What prior knowledge does this author expect his audience to have? How can you tell?

    f.   What interests does this author expect his audience to have? How can you tell?

    g.   Is this paragraph appropriate and effective for its audience? Explain.

2.	The notes that follow are adapted from the articles "A Time of Renewal for U.S. Churches" and "Spread of 'Alternate Religions'" in the April 11, 1977, issue of *U.S. News and World Report* and "Stepchildren of the Moral Majority" by Daniel Yankelovich in the November 1981 issue of *Psychology Today*. Assume that you have been assigned to consider the topic "Some Developments in Organized Religion in America in the Last Ten Years" in classes in economics, composition, sociology, and psychology. Choose one course and, using the discussion on pages 10–14 as a guide, analyze your audience and determine your probable approach. What information would you include or exclude? Would your audience need an overview? How might you begin your paper? What would your major concern be?

Notes

○ The recent decline in church membership seems to be reversing itself; now some churches and synagogues report "modest gains."

○ ". . . Americans remain one of the world's most religious people in purpose if not always in practice," with 56 percent considering religion "'very important' in their lives" and 94 percent believing in God.

○ "Well over 30 million Americans, many of them members of established religions, are engaged in offbeat spiritual pursuits that range from studying horoscopes to worshipping the Devil."

○ 20 percent of all Americans believe in astrology, while 4 percent of those questioned in a Gallup Poll follow Transcendental Meditation, 3 percent yoga, 2 percent "charismatic" Christianity, 2 percent mysticism, and 1 percent Eastern religions.

○ The San Francisco Bay area is host to as many as 125 new religious movements, including Sufi Muslims and Satanists.

○ Some religious groups, such as Reverend Moon's Unification Church and the Hare Krishna movement, have been accused of "mind control."

○ Ecumenism's former goal—to create "one big denomination for everybody"—has been replaced by new goals: to reaffirm basic differences and at the same time build "friendship, respect, and cooperation" among religions.

○ Clergymen are seeking ways to strengthen links between religion and the family and to increase the appeal of religion to the young.

○ Sales of religious books are booming.

○ Congregations are moving firmly away from their bland 1950s role; they are no longer willing to function as civic clubs.

○ The search by Americans for a politician worthy of their trust may explain the election of President Reagan, a man known to the public for his strong moral and religious convictions.

○ The Moral Majority, led by the Reverend Jerry Falwell, claimed to have registered 3 million new voters in the 1980 Presidential election.

○ The Moral Majority's Coalition for Better Television tries to make TV programs conform to fundamentalist standards and values.

○ The Moral Majority also opposes abortion, homosexuality, busing, the ERA, pornography, premarital sex, and divorce.

○ The Moral Majority supports "prayer in the schools, community censorship of textbooks, capital punishment, military superiority over the Soviet Union, a strong and traditional family."

3. Consider your experience in the working world: all the jobs (paid or unpaid, full- or part-time) you have held.

> **a.** Write a two-page journal entry (for your eyes only) in which you explore these experiences.
>
> **b.** Write several paragraphs explaining the different kinds of jobs you have had to your English composition instructor.
>
> **c.** Try to identify the most striking differences *in content* between the two pieces of writing you have just produced.

4. Consider how the paragraphs you have just written might be changed if you were going to write:

> **a.** a short paper for a course in management in which the focus is on employer-employee relationships;
>
> **b.** a letter of application for a job;
>
> **c.** a short paper for a speech class in which the topic is job interviews;
>
> **d.** an editorial on the availability and quality of student employment.

Who would your audience be in each case? What would you be likely to know about this audience? What guidelines would you use to plan your strategy? Use the considerations on pages 10–14 to help you with this exercise.

5. Rewrite your original discussion for one of the four situations listed above.

OCCASION, LENGTH, KNOWLEDGE: OTHER CONSIDERATIONS FOR THE COLLEGE WRITER

OCCASION

Another boundary that all writers must deal with is the *occasion* for which they are writing. Different writing situations may have different purposes and different audiences. These in turn call for different styles, different formats, different content, and different emphases, and you must be in control of these variations as you compose. An explanation of the mechanism of a self-developing camera, for instance, has very different requirements depending on whether it is to go into an instruction booklet for the owner, an encyclopedia article, a basic science magazine, a text for a course in chemical engineering, or an advertising brochure. In each case, language, content, detail, structure, and emphasis all differ.

Before you begin any assignment, you, like all writers, should consider the different kinds of formats, style, content, and emphasis appropriate to your writing occasion. Even within one course—and even when your audience and purpose are identical—your presentation varies with the occasion. An impromptu in-class essay, a quiz or a final exam, a book report, a summary, scientific observations and notes, a report based on statistical data, a letter, a memo, a technical report—each of these situations demands different conventions of style, organization, and emphasis.

Even when your audience and purpose are similar, occasion can dictate two very different discussions—of F. Scott Fitzgerald's novel *Tender Is the Night,* for example. A student preparing a *book report* in an American literature class might present a brief plot summary and then go on to evaluate the novel, but in an essay on the *final examination* she would not summarize the plot but answer the question, comparing and contrasting, analyzing plot and character, and so on. A *biography* of Fitzgerald's wife, Zelda, would undoubtedly emphasize the similarities between Zelda and the fictional Nicole Diver, while a *critical discussion* of Fitzgerald's work might concentrate instead on analogies between *Tender Is the Night* and his other novels. Different situations, then, demand different treatments of the same general subject.

Different writing occasions require different strategies: to determine the appropriate strategy, you must understand your writing occasion. Most important, consider your assignment. What, exactly, is the assignment your instructor has given you? The assignment should make your writing occasion clear. (Don't hesitate to ask questions if it is not clear.) Next, decide whether the occasion requires a specific format, and make sure you know what that format is. Does this format have special stylistic or organizational conventions associated with it? Will you be writing in class or at home, and how much time will you have to write? Answers to these questions tell you whether your writing occasion is *formal,* as is a term paper or report, or *informal,* as is an essay on the same subject written in class. Finally, does your occasion suggest a certain emphasis for your writing? Perhaps certain points or features are particularly appropriate—or inappropriate—for your writing occasion. Your paper's audience and your purpose also figure in your decision.

EXERCISES

1. Each of the paragraphs below, on the general subject of Bernard Malamud's short story "A Summer's Reading," was written to fulfill a different assignment for a course in modern American literature. The first paragraph is part of a précis which summarized the story's plot. The second was written in response to the examination question "In what ways does Mr. Cattanzara serve as a father figure to George Stoyonovich in 'A Summer's Reading'?" The last paragraph comes from a short critical paper on Malamud's short stories. Read the three paragraphs and be prepared to discuss how the different occasions for which they were written influenced the writers' treatments of their common subject.

a.   From a précis of "A Summer's Reading"

George Stoyonovich quit high school when he was sixteen. This was an impulsive move that left him nowhere. He wasn't able to obtain a decent job because he lacked a decent education, and having so much time on his hands left him to wander about the streets at night. George's mother was dead, and his father and older sister worked at menial jobs for menial pay. The family was just able to get by. The only contribution George was able to make was to keep the house clean; otherwise, he was just another useless body that took up needed space. All this made George feel he was of no importance to anyone, and yet he wanted to be liked and respected by his family and the community. So he decided to tell people he was going to read 100 books by the end of the summer, hoping he could in this way gain the respect he wanted so badly.

b.   From an answer to the examination question "In what ways does Mr. Cattanzara serve as a father figure to George Stoyonovich in 'A Summer's Reading'?"

George is an aimless young man, a high school dropout who spends his days lying on his bed and his nights wandering around the neighborhood. His father works hard to support the family and is unable to exert any significant influence on George. After George makes his reckless—even desperate—announcement about his summer's reading, Mr. Cattanzara begins to emerge as his conscience. Mr. Cattanzara, a change maker in the subway who used to give George nickels when he was a little boy, also takes long walks around the neighborhood. His frequent questions about the progress of George's reading show George that he hasn't fooled the older man. Mr. Cattanzara's concern makes George see that he is playing a child's game even though he is no longer a child. His longstanding affectionate relationship with the older man, his present discomfort under Mr. Cattanzara's scrutiny, and his desire to make Mr. Cattanzara proud of him show the reader that the older man serves as a father figure to George.

c.   From a short critical paper on Malamud's short stories

Sidney Richman, in a chapter on Malamud's short story in *Bernard Malamud and the Critics*, classifies "A Summer's Reading," along with "The Prison," as one of the "New York tales without Jews." Finding these two stories very different from others, like "The Loan" or "The Bill," Mr. Richman attributes this to the lack of a central Jewish character. This difference, Richman notes, "accounts precisely for what the stories lack: the sense of the pertinacity of spirit, an indefinable aura of 'goodness' which . . . transforms the most extreme of failures into a sad redemption." Richman considers "A Summer's Reading" to be less a fable than a "naturalistic tale."

2.   Take as your general subject any essay you have read in your English class. Assuming that you are writing for your composition course and for essentially the same purpose and audience, explain how you would develop your piece of writing differently for each of these four occasions:

a.   a journal entry recording your impressions of the essay (the journal will be read by your instructor);
b.   an examination that asks for an analysis of the essay's theme;
c.   a summary of the essay;
d.   a section of a report in which you are asked to evaluate the essay's arguments.

LENGTH

The length of the piece you are preparing also helps to determine your composition strategy. A business executive includes a good deal more information and analysis in an annual report than in a memo. A news reporter doing a capsule update on an earthquake in Italy cannot provide much background information, detail, or speculation about possible effects. A longer article, of course, would give space to all this—and more.

In college writing, your instructor's word or page limit sets an important boundary for you. Your assignment may define limits from a sentence or paragraph on a test to ten pages for a term paper. On an art history examination, for instance, you might see a series of slides to identify in one-sentence, one-paragraph, or essay-length answers. In the first case, you simply identify the slide in question. Your sentence names the work, the artist, the artist's school of painting and, perhaps, the approximate date of the work. A one-paragraph identification would include all these elements with two or three points of major importance about the work. You might mention the most striking features of the painter's technique and the work's composition, using this information to justify your identification. An essay-length response would go into greater depth, bringing in supporting information about influences on the painter, a more detailed analysis of the artist's technique, and a discussion of similarities between this and other paintings as well as the periods the painter went through.

Remember, before you begin any writing assignment, be sure you know how long your response *is supposed to be*. If a word or page limit has been set, consider just how much information you can present within those limits and then decide which material takes precedence. If you have no limit, set one yourself: your purpose or occasion should suggest how many words or pages it will take to fulfill the demands of your assignment.

EXERCISES

1. Read the capsule reviews from the *New York Times Book Review* reprinted below. In each case, the author was limited to perhaps one hundred words and so included only essential information.

a. What, according to the writer, constitutes essential information (that is, what features do *all* the reviews contain)?

b. In each case, speculate about what kind of information would be included in a review three or four times as long. List additional topics that might be explored in each review.

c. Find a longer review of any of these books in a newspaper or magazine. What kind of additional information actually goes into a longer review?

THE OLD PATAGONIAN EXPRESS, by Paul Theroux. (Pocket, $3.50.) Paul Theroux, who made a notable trip around the world in "The Great Railway Bazaar" (Ballantine, $2.50), continues his train-borne adventuring, this time from Boston to southern Argentina's Patagonia. Like all fine travel writing, this combines vivid narrative and perceptive comment about things observed and people talked with. Especially memorable is an encounter with the celebrated writer Jorge Luis Borges.

THE FAMILY CRUCIBLE, by Augustus Y. Napier and Carl A. Whitaker. (Bantam, $3.95.) In alternating chapters, two University of Wisconsin psychiatrists report on a series of interviews with members of a family troubled by a rebellious teen-age daughter and offer an overview of the psychological theories they consider relevant to such situations. Lay readers will find it a clearly written introduction to complex problems that are common in contemporary society.

ON A CLEAR DAY YOU CAN SEE GENERAL MOTORS, by J. Patrick Wright. (Avon, $2.95.) Following his resignation in 1973 as a General Motors vice president, John Z. DeLorean, a 48-year-old engineer who seemed a likely candidate for the corporation's presidency, told what he knew and felt about his former employer to J. Patrick Wright, a Business Week correspondent. Mr. Wright's name appears on the title page of this sharp indictment of the practices of big business in general and G.M. in particular, but its first person voice is Mr. DeLorean's.

HUMBUG MOUNTAIN, by Sid Fleischman. (Scholastic, $1.25.) As their Pa frequently gets "the yonders," it falls to 13-year-old Wiley and his 10-year-old sister Glorietta, who live on the Missouri River at the time it was the frontier, to cope with an invasion of gold seekers, a petrified man and a ghost who haunts the old beached ship that their family lives in. The story's surprising twists and turns and the Mark Twainish dialogue will please readers 7 to 10.

PORTRAITS FROM LIFE, by Ford Madox Ford. (Houghton Mifflin, $4.95.) Profiles and critiques of Henry James, Stephen Crane, W. H. Hudson, Conrad, Hardy, H. G. Wells, Galsworthy, D. H. Lawrence, Turgenev, Dreiser and Swinburne by a British man of letters who knew most of them personally. When Ford Madox Ford (1873–1939) published this collection two years before his death, our reviewer called it "reminiscent and reflective to just the right degree, racy, flavorous and full of charm."

2.   Consider how you would treat each of these subjects in one sentence, one paragraph, and a five-hundred-word essay. List the specific kinds of information you would include in each case.

- Dissecting a shark
- TV commercials
- Poetry
- Writing a business letter
- How inflation affects college students
- Life on Mars
- The Miss America pageant
- Extinct animals

What might you add in each case if you were planning to treat the subject in a twenty-page paper?

KNOWLEDGE

Naturally you try to write about something you know about—or at least something you would *like* to know about. Your knowledge, or the knowledge you can reasonably expect to acquire before the assignment is due, establishes another boundary.

When you write a term paper, for instance, the choice of a topic is frequently left up to you, and one of the ways you decide on a topic is to define your own areas of knowledge, interest, and potential expertise. If you have a good background in or understanding of a particular issue, or if you have access to a good deal of helpful material, you ought to start with that subject, at least. If it doesn't work out, you can deal with that later.

Suppose that your class in environmental biology is assigned a term paper on toxic waste disposal. You could explore the logistical problem of transporting toxic wastes to dumping sites, consider trends in state and federal legislation regarding chemical dumping, deal with birth defects that threaten the offspring of women exposed to chemical wastes, discuss the effect of chemical dumping on air and water quality, or consider the need for stricter health and safety regulations for industrial workers. Dozens of other topics would also be appropriate for your audience, purpose, and occasion. At this stage, you may be tempted to base your choice solely on what interests you, and naturally your paper will be easier to write if you like your subject. You are bound to know more about topics that fascinate you than about those that leave you cold. But think, too, about what is possible. What do you already have some grasp of? What reference materials can you put your hands on? What subject will be most congenial to read about and assimilate when you do research?

If, for example, you happen to live around Niagara Falls, New York, perhaps you could interview people who were directly affected by the Hooker Chemical Company's dumping of waste in the Love Canal. You may have easy access to local newspapers, community newsletters or leaflets—even personal letters. This kind of direct knowledge might suggest an angle for a paper on toxic waste disposal. Even without first-hand knowledge, of course, you could still write about Love Canal. You may have not only a high interest in these events, but also a basic familiarity with the situation and some ideas about where to look for further information. In either case, you have a better start on this paper than you would have, say, on a paper about the possible effects of dumping radioactive wastes on Mars.

EXERCISES

1. Choose as your topic any sport or game in which you have experience as a spectator or amateur player. Write a paragraph on any aspect of that sport or game— rules, players, advantages, drawbacks, history, or controversies, for example.

2. Interview an "expert"—a friend who knows more than you do about the sport or game. Sticking to the aspect you focused on in your own paragraph, see what additional information you might acquire from your expert source. Revise the paragraph you wrote, incorporating this new information.

3.   Do some light reading on your topic in a general-audience magazine—*Sports Illustrated* or *Games,* for instance—or on the sports page of a daily newspaper. Still focusing on the aspect you wrote about in paragraph 1, see what additional information you can come up with and revise your paragraph again.

4.   Finally, take your topic one step further by looking at relevant headings in the library card catalog or in the *Readers' Guide to Periodical Literature.* Without consulting any of the books or articles, list other kinds of information you might acquire from research but not from personal experience, interviews, or casual reading.

As you can see, each of your boundaries runs into all the others. Each choice you make in one area influences all the others. Your boundaries are simply parts which interact to determine the shape of the whole.

Let us say it one more time. When you write, you don't consider each of these boundaries one at a time. In the actual process of writing, things are all too often chaotic, and choices you make at one stage may very well change at another stage. You are constantly rethinking and sifting your choices, reconsidering audience, purpose, format, sentences, and words until you blend them together to form the finished whole that is your essay. A certain amount of disorder is natural and even desirable whenever you make choices about writing. So stop thinking about writing as if it happened in some clear, correct way and begin thinking about it as a process in which a multitude of choices have to be made over and over again.

CHAPTER

2

Getting Started

Many people think that writing should come naturally, that good writing flows freely in an uninterrupted stream from pen to paper. Nothing could be farther from the truth. Writing is hard work. No matter what you've heard, most writers spend a good deal of time staring at a blank sheet of paper trying to decide what to write about.

When asked what it's like to "sit in solitude and face that blank page," Thomas Berger, author of ten novels, replied "By now that's no longer a problem. But at the beginning of my career I prepared myself for each session of writing by whimpering all afternoon, watching television all evening, and, after throwing up at midnight, fastening myself to the desk with shackles, to remain there till dawn." This initial uncertainty, while frustrating, is part of the writing process. Not knowing where to begin or what to write about is natural when you try to come to terms with a specific writing task.

OVERCOMING WRITER'S BLOCK: FREE WRITING

Occasionally writing flows easily, almost effortlessly, but more often than not, the words and ideas just don't come. When writing comes in fits and starts—or not at all—we call it "writer's block." Science-fiction writer Ray Bradbury attributes it to lack of stimuli or lack of knowledge about the subject; novelist Frank Yerby, accepting the inevitable, says "only amateurs believe in inspiration."

Writer's block can happen any time, but students most often complain that they have difficulty getting started. When faced with a writing assignment, they stare at the blank paper in front of them, getting more and more frustrated until they freeze solid. Experienced writers know that the ice will thaw, and in the meantime they respond to writer's block in different ways. Some sit at the typewriter and type words; others doodle. But at some point, you have to begin writing something—anything. This technique, called *free writing,* often gets you moving.

Free writing means just what it says. Fix your mind on a specific topic and write nonstop for a certain period of time—five minutes, ten minutes, you decide. Don't worry about punctuation, spelling, or grammar; just loosen up and let your thoughts go where they may. If your mind wanders or your focus shifts, don't fight it. Some of your best ideas may emerge this way. But you must continue to write without stopping for the predetermined time—even if you say nothing important. The secret of free writing is that *just by writing* you force your mind to focus on a subject, almost in spite of yourself. Your mind makes connections and generates ideas that you may not even be aware of. So you must keep writing without stopping to correct yourself or to think critically. If you run out of things to say, record your frustration or describe things you see around you until you pick up your subject again. Free writing like this will get whatever is blocking your writing off your mind. With the anxiety gone, your confidence returns and you can get to the business at hand.

After completing your free writing, read what you have written and isolate material that you can use. You can often arrive at a workable topic for your essay by summing up in a sentence the essence of what you have just written. The most important result of free writing, however, is that you overcome your fear of having nothing to say. You have begun writing. At the beginning, in the middle, or at the end of the writing process, free writing can give you the push you need to get moving.

Here is a ten-minute piece of free writing that a student, Kim Soltzner, did to help her get started on the topic "Keeping Fit":

Keeping fit — keeping fit — 8 o'clock and he wants me to write — for this I work in the library. Keeping fit — nothing — crack in the board — never noticed. Library — library — Complete Book of Running — started jogging a week ago — not really enough time — What the heck — Only subject. Running — running — running — Bought shoes the other day — expensive shorts — shirt — Odd bunch of people —

Always talking about running. Salesman nice — knew a lot — Can't write on this — this — this — keep writing — keep fit — Ha! Could write about preparing to run — buying shoes, clothes, etc. Better work — no other ideas. Isn't 10 minutes up yet??? Never knew it could be so important — Nike? Padded heel important — knee bandage — keep in shape — Help circulation etc. —

First Kim struggled to focus on her topic. Eventually she succeeded and her ideas began to emerge. After reading what she wrote, Kim noticed that certain ideas came up again and again and that each of those ideas could be expanded into an entire essay. Kim could, for example, write about her trip to a sporting-goods store or her difficulty deciding what equipment to buy. She could also write an essay on jogging shoes, outlining the different types available and the kind she eventually decided to buy. After some thought, she decided to write about the problems a beginning runner can have when buying jogging shoes. The following phrase summed up her thoughts, and it made an excellent starting point for an essay.

Deciding what kind of jogging shoes to buy

More free writing would have yielded more ideas about her topic.

EXERCISES

1. Choose one of the following subjects and free write for ten minutes in a direction it suggests. After completing your free writing, sum up its essence in a single sentence. Don't stop to think about corrections; keep writing until you are able to focus on your subject.

Money   Recreation
College   Movies

2. Do another ten-minute free writing focusing on the topic that emerged from the first exercise. Try to generate as much information as you can about your subject. Read your free writing and underline the ideas that you could use in an essay.

3. Write several paragraphs discussing how much or how little free writing helped you to start writing and to arrive at a workable topic.

LIMITING YOUR SUBJECT

Most of the writing you do in college is assigned by your instructors. Very rarely do you have to think of a subject entirely on your own. These assignments are usually general—a subject area, a type of essay to write, or a list of subjects to choose from—so you have a good deal of freedom to decide what you want to write about.

The following are typical writing assignments:

Political Science	In a five-page paper, explore a political event that took place during the past thirty years. (specifies subject area)
Freshman Composition	Write a five-hundred-word narrative essay about an experience that had a profound effect on you. (specifies type of essay)
Early Childhood Education	Choose one of the following subjects and write a thousand-word essay about it. —Children and divorce —Only children —Twins —Sibling rivalry —One stage of child development (presents list of subjects to choose from)

But writing about any of these subjects in their present form would be impossible. What, for instance, *is* the experience that had a profound effect on you? *What* political event are you going to explore? A thousand-word essay on "Children and Divorce," say, would be much too general. It would take more than one book to treat subjects as general as these adequately, but exactly how narrow your topic needs to be depends, to a great extent, on the boundaries of your assignment. The identity of your audience, the purpose and occasion of your writing, the length of your paper, and how much you know about your subject are all factors you must consider as you narrow a general subject into a workable topic. All general subjects must be limited considerably before you can begin to decide what you want to say about them.

General subject	Possible narrowed topics
In a five-page paper, explore a political event that took place during the past thirty years.	The nuclear test ban treaty The formation of the Trilateral Commission
Write a five-hundred-word narrative essay about an experience that had a profound effect on you.	The death of my grandfather Evening college
Choose one of the following subjects and write a thousand-word essay about it: Children and divorce	The benefits to the child of shared custody
Only children	The drawbacks and benefits of being an only child

Twins   A case study of separated twins
Sibling rivalry   Sibling rivalry in college-age women
One stage of child development   The first three months of life

---

EXERCISE

Which of the following are general subjects and which are narrowed topics? Be prepared to discuss your answers.

1. Football

2. Injuries caused by high school sports

3. Crime rates before and after legalized gambling in Atlantic City

4. New finds in archeology

5. Disease and civilization

6. The effects of the 1918–1919 flu epidemic on Philadelphia

7. The role of women in the Catholic Church

8. The pricing policies of oil companies in 1984

9. The decline in quality of American life

10. Discrimination in health care

You can use a number of techniques to narrow your general subject to a limited topic. Sometimes, of course, a likely topic may just come to you. But many times it will not, and you will have to go through a systematic process to limit your subject. In short, you will have to work at it.

Of course, no writer uses all of the following techniques, but many use more than one. Don't make the mistake of skipping this stage of the writing process, hoping that ideas will come to you as you write. A haphazard approach can be time-consuming, unproductive, and frustrating. No single method of limiting your subject suits all writing situations, so experiment and find out what works best for you.

THE JOURNALISTIC QUESTIONS

The journalistic questions are a formal method of discovery that enables you to probe your general subject in an organized way. There are six of them: Who? What? When? Where? Why? How? Beginning newspaper reporters learn that the lead, or opening paragraph, of a newspaper story should answer these questions, ensuring that the reader has enough information to understand the main points of a story. This formula, although not as universally applied as it once was, is especially effective in telling about something that has happened. Notice how the two short opening paragraphs in this article from *New York* magazine answer most of these questions:

> Some of us have the good fortune to see our projects succeed and others have the good fortune to know they have failed. Either way there is the freedom of certainty. But for Herbert Terrace [who?] neither is true.
>
> For the past four years [when?], Terrace, a professor of psychology at Columbia University [where?], has been on a peculiarly hazardous intellectual quest: He has been trying to demonstrate that a chimpanzee can be taught to use a human language [what?].
>
> "Nim Chimpsky and How He Grew," *New York*

The rest of the article concentrates on the "why" and "how" of Herbert Terrace's endeavor.

If you expand the questions a little, you can state them in ways that emphasize their relationship to one another.

○ *What* occurred?

○ *Who* caused it to occur?

○ *How* did it occur?

○ *Why* did it occur?

○ *Where* and *when* did it occur?

By concentrating on each of the questions, you can form a number of more specific questions, some of which can be good paper topics. Not all of these questions will apply to a single subject, but enough will to make using them worthwhile. This discovery technique allows you to probe a subject quickly and systematically, and it is especially useful when time counts—as for in-class essays and examinations.

Paula Samansky, a student in an introductory political science course, used this discovery method to generate the following topics for a short paper on the general subject, "recent immigration." She felt that she didn't know enough about her subject to rely on free writing, so she used some of the journalistic questions to help her examine her subject from a number of different angles.

○ *What occurred?*
  What are the immigration policies of the United States?
  What are the laws or quotas?

○ *Who caused it to occur?*
  What countries are responsible for the influx of new immigrants?
  What countries discriminate against minorities?
  What is Fidel Castro doing to encourage emigration from Cuba?

○ *How did it occur?*
  How do immigrants get out of their countries?
  How do they get to the United States?
  How do Vietnamese and Cambodian refugees get to the United States?
  How do Haitian refugees get to Florida?

   ○ *Why did it occur?*
    From what countries do immigrants come?
    Do these countries have things in common?

When she read over this list, Paula saw that several topics exceeded the boundaries of the assignment. Paula decided to answer the question about the plight of Haitian refugees in Florida. She felt confident that she could treat the topic adequately in a three-page, or 750-word, paper, and because she had four days to prepare the assignment, she had the time to review her class notes and look up other information.

EXERCISES

1. Choose one of the general subjects listed below and apply the journalistic questions to it. What topics do these subjects suggest? What conclusion can you draw about the merits of this invention technique in relation to the topic you chose and to your own preferences as a writer?

○ The Louisiana Purchase	○ Teachers
○ High school English	○ Inflation
○ Small cars	○ Local history
○ Pornography	○ Discrimination
○ Solar power	○ Nuclear weapons

2. Assume you have been given a choice of the following general subjects for a take-home examination in American history. Choose two of them, and use the journalistic questions to generate five topics for each that you could discuss within the boundaries of the assignment.

○ Mercantilism	○ Labor unions
○ The frontier thesis	○ Slavery
○ Expansionism	○ The Midwest
○ Tariffs	○ Industrialism
○ The Spanish-American War	○ The Robber Barons

The journalistic questions have advantages and disadvantages. They are a quick way of carrying out an organized examination of a general subject. Their major disadvantage, however, is that they provide only a limited view of your assignment. When time is not a factor, as with at-home assignments and research papers, consider probing your topic using a more expansive list of questions.

QUESTIONS FOR PROBING

Like the journalistic questions, questions for probing give you a number of fixed
angles from which to view your subject. This method of narrowing also involves
asking a number of questions about your subject. But these questions reflect the
way your mind actually operates—dividing, classifying, comparing and contrasting, defining—in other words, *seeing relationships*. By running through these questions systematically, you can make a well-planned, in-depth search of your subject.

Ask one question at a time, taking care to jot down and think hard about your
answers. If a question doesn't work with your subject, don't worry. Move on to one
that does. Not all questions apply to every subject, but be careful not to dismiss a
question before you try it. Sometimes a question that seems useless suggests an
exciting topic that never occurred to you before.

These questions are not meant to be memorized. They are useful in situations
where you have the time and opportunity—usually at home—to explore your
subject thoughtfully and at some length.

Narration	What happened? When did it happen? Where did it happen?
Description	What does it look like? What are its characteristics?
Exemplification	What are some typical cases or examples of it?
Process	How did it happen? What makes it work? How is it made?
Cause and effect	Why did it happen? What caused it? What does it cause? What are its effects?
Comparison and contrast	How is it related to something else? How is it like other things? How is it different from other things?
Division and classification	What are its parts or types? How can its parts or types be separated or grouped? Do its parts or types fit into a logical order? Into what categories can its parts or types be arranged? On what basis can it be categorized?
Definition	What is it? How does it resemble other members of its class? How does it differ from other members of its class? What are its limits?

Questions for probing help you to explore seemingly complex or unpromising general subjects. They offer you a wider range of rhetorical options than the journalistic questions. Naturally the method you choose to limit a topic depends on your personal preference, your subject, the type of assignment you have, and how much time you have, but these questions for probing can help you generate a long list of topics. Joan Renier, a student in a freshman research-paper course, used this method to limit her subject, "The Holocaust." Because a book she had read—Elie Wiesel's *Night*—dealt with Hitler's persecution of Jews, Joan had some knowledge of her subject. But she still found her subject a bit overwhelming. To organize her own thoughts and to uncover new ideas, she applied the questions for probing and came up with the following more limited questions.

- What factors caused the Holocaust?
- How was the Holocaust carried out?
- What was the scope of the Holocaust?
- How did the persecution of the Jews differ from the persecution of other groups?
- What were the phases of Hitler's persecution of the Jews?
- How were the children of survivors affected by the Holocaust?
- How was Hitler able to carry out his persecution?
- What form did the persecution of the Jews take?

With this list in hand, Joan was not afraid to discard those possibilities that seemed weak—topics that were too general, or would take too much work, or did not interest her. Joan had plenty to consider, and she decided to write about how the children of Holocaust survivors reacted to their parents' experiences. Her interest in early childhood development and her reading on the subject made her choice a good one, but she had not thought of it until she applied the questions for probing.

This method of discovery also has its problems, however. Probing a subject in great depth takes time and effort. The amount of information that results may seem overwhelming. The questions themselves can seem ponderous and complicated until you get used to using them. If you take the time to master the process, however, you'll be surprised at the results. Properly used, questions for probing can provide you with insights and ideas for any subject you may want to write about.

EXERCISES

1. Choose one of the following general subjects and explore it using questions for probing. Answer each appropriate question in writing and be prepared to discuss your responses with the class.

- Sex education
- Professional sports
- Single parents
- Drugs

- Cars
- Smoking
- Affirmative action

- Rock music
- Conservation
- Jogging

2. Choose one of the following general subjects and apply the journalistic questions. Then narrow the same subject using the questions for probing. Which method of narrowing your subject did you find most helpful? How can you account for this?

- Organized crime
- College cafeterias
- Genetic engineering
- Astrology
- Religion

- Ecology
- Teenage drinking
- Abstract art
- The 1984 presidential election
- Unemployment

FINDING SOMETHING TO SAY

Once you have limited your subject and decided on a topic, you must think of something to say about it. Information comes from two sources—you and your reading. Most of you already know a great deal about a number of topics. Your life experiences, your conversations, your observations, your casual reading have put a storehouse of information at your disposal. This knowledge is all you need to write some interesting and detailed essays. In other situations, however, you may have to review your textbooks and class notes, or do library research (see Chapter 14). As in other stages of the writing process, finding something to say is easier if you proceed in an organized manner. Let us now examine some of the ways that successful writers commonly generate material.

THE LIMITS OF PERSONAL KNOWLEDGE

William Faulkner, speaking to students at the University of Virginia in 1957, expressed his strong feelings about the value of personal knowledge and experience to the fiction writer, saying,

> Of course the writer collects his material all his life from everything he reads, from everything he listens to, everything he sees, and he stores all that away in a sort of filing cabinet. I believe that he thinks either of an anecdote concerning people or a character which is moving enough to be worth writing about and then when he begins to write, the character demands that he be shown in certain lights so the writer simply hunts around in his filing case—in my case it's not anything near as neat as a filing case, it's more like a junk box—and he digs out something that he has read or seen to throw the flashlight on the particular moment. But he doesn't get out and do any research. I think if he does that, he is not really a fiction writer. He becomes something else.

Faulkner in the University

No matter how uneventful our lives may seem to be, we all read and observe and experience. We all make judgments about what we see and hear, we consider the relative merits of different alternatives, and we find analogies among the things we know. All this influences our writing. But in your academic career, you will need to supplement your knowledge and experience by discovering new information and new ways of looking at familiar things. Your personal knowledge may not carry you through an assignment, but it gives you a starting point on which to build.

KEEPING A JOURNAL

Many professional writers keep journals. They make a habit of writing daily, whether or not they have a specific project in mind. What may start as personal writing often ends up in work written for a general audience. The essayist Joan Didion explains how her notebooks nourish her writing:

> *How it felt to me:* that is getting closer to the truth about a notebook. I sometimes delude myself about why I keep a notebook, imagine that some thrifty virtue derives from preserving everything observed. See enough and write it down, I tell myself, and then some morning when the world seems drained of wonder, some day when I am only going through the motions of doing what I am supposed to do, which is write—on that bankrupt morning I will simply open my notebook and there it will be: a forgotten account with accumulated interest, and passage back to the world out there. . . . I imagine, in other words, that the notebook is about other people. But of course it is not. . . . *Remember what it was to be me:* that is always the point.
>
> Woman as Writer

Joseph Conrad wrote every day in his journal. When he was in Africa, he made the following entries:

> *Thursday, 3rd July.* Left at 6 A.M. after a good night's rest. Crossed a low range of hills and entered a broad valley . . . with a break in the middle. Met an officer of the State inspecting. A few minutes afterwards saw at a camping place the dead body of a Backongo. Shot? Horrid smell.
>
> *Friday, 4th July.* Left camp at 6 A.M. after a very unpleasant night. Marching across a chain of hills and then in a maze of hills. At 8:15 opened out into an undulating plain. Took bearings of a break in the chain of mountains on the other side. Bearing N.N.E. Road passes through that. . . . Saw another dead body lying by the path in an attitude of meditative repose.
>
> The Congo Diary

Eventually Conrad used these journal accounts in writing his well-known short novel *Heart of Darkness.*

Many scientists also keep journals to record their observations and their reactions to them. During his first voyage, on a map-making expedition, Charles Darwin kept a journal. Published as *The Voyage of the "Beagle,"* this work provided invaluable data when Darwin later formulated his theory of evolution in the *Origin of Species.*

April 27, 1834

This day I shot a condor. It measured from tip to tip of the wings, eight and a half feet, and from beak to tail, four feet. This bird is known to have a wide geographical range, being found off the west coast of South America, from the Strait of Magellan along the Cordillera as far as eight degrees N. of the equator. The steep cliff near the mouth of the Rio Negro is its northern limit on the Patagonian coast; and they have there wandered about four hundred miles from the great central line of their habitation in the Andes. Further south, among the bold precipices at the head of Point Desire, the condor is not uncommon; yet only a few stragglers occasionally visit the sea coast. A line of cliffs near the mouth of the Santa Cruz is frequented by these birds, and about eighty miles up the river . . . the condor reappears. From these facts it seems that the condors require perpendicular cliffs. In Chile, they haunt . . . the lower country near the shores of the Pacific, and at night several roost together in one tree. . . .

You too can record your observations and reactions in a journal. Don't simply record your daily activities, but your thoughts, your reactions to things you hear or read, and your interpretations of your experiences and observations. Not only is keeping a journal a good way to practice writing, it provides you with a fund of information to fall back on when an assignment calls for introspection or self-examination. Bill Leska, a composition student, used this journal entry as a source for an essay.

December 26

Yesterday my family went to my grandmother's for Christmas dinner. Traditionally we all meet at her house, where she lives with my two aunts. There are always cakes, cookies, and holiday bread in the oven. This year, however, things were a bit different. My grandmother is slipping—weakening. She developed diabetes a couple of years ago, so she wasn't allowed to eat sugar—which of course was in everything she baked. We couldn't stop her from baking but we had to watch her so she wouldn't cheat. She was hospitalized twice for a high sugar count, but it didn't really teach her a lesson. After recovering and getting her strength back, she continued her same routine of baking, cleaning, and gardening. But I could tell yesterday how much she has slipped—she kept forgetting to set the oven—and she looked so tired.

In the following essay, Bill used this journal entry as well as several others. Notice how his journal provided him with a record of his thoughts and a description of an incident that played an important part in the essay.

My Grandmother

When I was a child, my grandmother Mary used to tell me stories of her girlhood in Poland. She'd tell me about how she and her sisters, Claire and Alicja, had learned to do fancy embroidery and to bake, and about the pillowcases and napkins they'd collected for their hope chests. And she'd tell me about how her father, my great-grandfather Jan Kalicki, had been killed in a hunting accident when she was a little girl. When I grew older, my grandmother taught my sister Jane what her mother had taught her: she taught her to do needlework and to bake. We used to love visiting her, sitting in the kitchen, watching her take tray after tray of cookies out of the oven. In the past two years, though, my grandmother began a steady decline, and I started to worry that she wouldn't be with us much longer.

My first clue that something was wrong came two years ago, when my cousin's baby was christened. The baby was my grandmother's first granddaughter (after five grandsons), and at first she was very excited. But during the ceremony itself she was restless and jumpy, and at the party afterward she was still fidgety and distracted. She didn't want to hold Marie, the baby, and she kept calling her "Alicja," her own dead sister's name. Worst of all, she kept talking about her parents as if they were still alive. But after the christening she seemed fine—for a while.

Another thing that worried me was a sudden month-long lapse about a year later. She stopped going out, even to church, and my mother had to take food to her and even help her get dressed while my aunts and uncles were at work. If she didn't, my grandmother would stay in her housecoat all day, looking out the window and drinking tea. Then she started losing weight, and little by little she began neglecting her appearance. She stopped combing her hair, the hair she always wore in a long braid wrapped around her head, and she stopped bathing. Eventually she developed diabetes and had to be hospitalized twice for a high sugar count. After about two months, though, she managed to recover her strength and get back to her daily routine— baking, cleaning, and even gardening.

But last Christmas dinner things were bad again. Traditionally we all meet at my grandmother's, and this year was no exception. Just as in past years, there were cakes, cookies, and holiday bread in the oven. But now my grandmother's diabetes meant she wasn't allowed to eat sugar—which of course was in everything she baked. We couldn't stop her from baking, but we had to watch her so she wouldn't cheat— and she hated that. And I could tell how much she had slipped, because she kept forgetting to set the oven, and she looked so tired.

In the weeks after Christmas I was busy with my own life, and I didn't see my grandmother much. My mother and my aunts and uncles took care of her, giving her insulin, doing her shopping, tidying up her room. She didn't seem to need much. But by February she had stopped getting out of bed, and in March she died.

Bill's journal entries served as the kernels around which he illustrated his grandmother's decline in his essay. In addition to adapting full entries, he used different fragments from other journal notes to help him recall details about his grandmother. When he sat down to write his essay, he took notes and reviewed them several times before he chose the most pertinent material.

When you begin to keep your journal, try to write a page or so each day. Regular writing works better than trying to play catch-up at the end of a week. You want to get into the habit of writing and to discipline yourself to do it regularly— whether you feel like it or not. Some days you will have little to say, and that's all right. Describe what you did in school or what you heard on the radio. Other days you will have a lot to say, and your writing will flow easily. The important thing is that your journal can be a source of pleasure to you and a ready source of material for your essays.

EXERCISES

1.   Keep a journal for one week, making sure you write at least a page every day.

2.   Read through the journal you have kept, and see how many of the following topics your journal material would help you to discuss.

- One thing in my life I would change
- My finances
- My job
- My prejudices
- People who bother me

- My philosophy
- My best or worst day
- My parents
- Something that makes me happy
- My friends

3.   Using your journal as a resource, write a two-page essay on one of the above topics. Be sure to submit your journal entry along with your finished essay.

BRAINSTORMING

Brainstorming helps you turn up usable new ideas about a topic. When you brainstorm, you write down everything you can think of about a topic in rapid-fire succession. You can do this alone, or—if your instructor breaks the class into small groups—you can collaborate with others. Like free writing, brainstorming uses free association to unlock your mind and release information that you didn't know you had. But by the time you use it you usually have a topic in mind, so brainstorming is more focused than free writing.

Jot down your limited topic at the top of your page and set an arbitrary time limit—say, five minutes. This forces you to write nonstop without pausing or worrying over a single item. Your notes can be single words, phrases, or complete sentences, and you should proceed without regard to spelling, punctuation, or grammar. Your goal is to get down as much useful information as you can. Some of your ideas might come from class notes or assigned reading; others might occur to you as you brainstorm; still others might come from your journal, conversations with friends, newspaper or magazine articles you've read, or programs you've seen on TV.

A prospective biology major, Aaron Zino, came up with the following brainstorming notes when his freshman composition teacher asked him to write a five-hundred-word theme explaining how some past experience had helped shape his career goals.

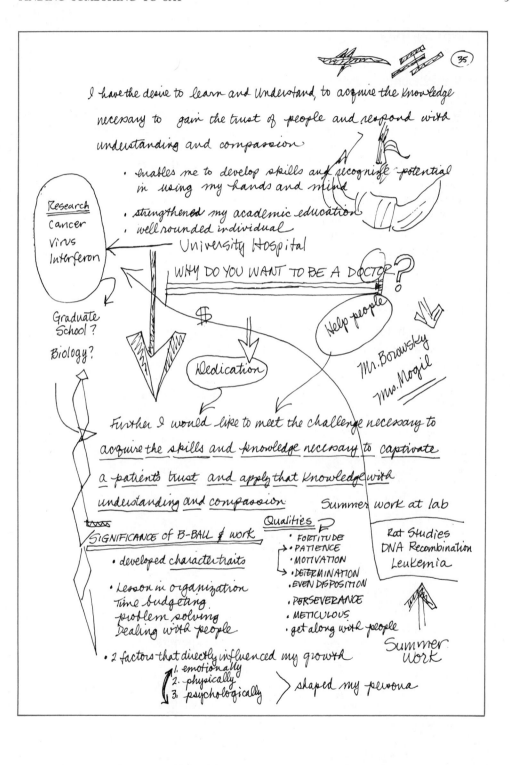

(35)

I have the desire to learn and understand, to acquire the knowledge necessary to gain the trust of people and respond with understanding and compassion

- enables me to develop skills and recognize potential in using my hands and mind
- strengthened my academic education
- well rounded individual

Research
Cancer
Virus
Interferon

University Hospital

WHY DO YOU WANT TO BE A DOCTOR?

$

Graduate School ?

Biology ?

Dedication

Help people

Mr. Borowsky
Mrs. Mogil

Further I would like to meet the challenge necessary to acquire the skills and knowledge necessary to captivate a patient's trust and apply that knowledge with understanding and compassion

Summer work at lab

Rat Studies
DNA Recombination
Leukemia

SIGNIFICANCE OF B-BALL & work

Qualities

- developed character traits

- Lesson in organization
Time budgeting.
problem solving
Dealing with people

- FORTITUDE
- PATIENCE
- MOTIVATION
- DETERMINATION
- EVEN DISPOSITION
- PERSEVERANCE
- METICULOUS
- get along with people

Summer Work

- 2 factors that directly influenced my growth
1. emotionally
2. physically
3. psychologically
> shaped my persona

GROUPING IDEAS

Aaron's notes show that he was at no loss for good ideas. But none of his material was in usable form. It was jumbled and disorganized. Now he had to choose the points to *focus* on in his essay. He considered the boundaries of his assignment. The paper was due the next day and limited to five hundred words, so he would have time neither to explore "cancer research" or "interferon," which would call for library work, nor to delve into his childhood. His audience would not understand a complicated technical discussion of his hospital experience. He needed to concentrate on the subjects he could discuss most easily and which most clearly showed how particular experiences shaped his career goals.

His next step was to group the material he selected from his brainstorming notes. He began by jotting down the three key concepts he saw there—high school science, summer job, basketball—and drew a *topic tree* to help him visualize his ideas. He broke the key ideas into narrower subdivisions, consulting his notes again. His tree looked like this:

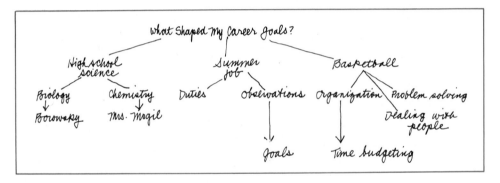

This diagram showed Aaron the hierarchy of his ideas—which points were dominant and which subordinate.

Before beginning to write his essay, Aaron arranged the points on his topic tree in a *scratch outline* he could follow as he wrote.

How My Experiences Shaped My Decision
to Become a Doctor

High school science courses
  - Bio: Mr. Borowsky
  - Chem: Mrs. Mogil
Summer work - lab
  - Duties: bottlewasher, "gofer"
  - Observations: teamwork, rat studies
  - Goals: research (cancer)
Basketball
  - Organization / time budgeting
  - Problem solving
  - Dealing with people

EXERCISES

1. Look through the want ads in your Sunday paper and pick a job that you could apply for. Brainstorm to generate a list of your qualifications and select your strongest to present in a letter of application.

2. Your composition teacher has asked you to write a five-hundred-word in-class essay in which you describe your neighborhood, city, or town. Brainstorm to generate notes on the things you want to describe and choose the best three or four to use in the essay. Be prepared to discuss the reasons for your choices.

3. Assume that you're a high school senior filling out an application to your college or university. Part of the application asks applicants to write a short essay outlining their reasons for wanting to attend the school. Brainstorm to determine your reasons, group your points, and arrange the four best ones in a scratch outline.

FINDING A TENTATIVE THESIS

As he looked over his scratch outline, Aaron could see where his ideas led. Now he wanted to express this direction in a tentative *thesis:* a single sentence, which he could refine later, that would keep him centered on the points he wanted to discuss. Here is the tentative thesis he arrived at:

> My high school science courses, my summer work, and my experiences playing bas-
> ketball showed me that I could succeed as a doctor.

Aaron didn't know what the structure of his finished essay would be, but his tentative thesis gave him the focus for his first draft. This statement not only expressed the central concerns of his scratch outline; it also indicated the order in which he would consider them.

Your tentative thesis should develop out of your data or observations. Sometimes your tentative thesis can be relatively easy to see, especially when it makes a point about your own experience. When you are familiar with a topic, you don't have to sort through a lot of complicated information to find a focus. At other times finding a tentative thesis can be difficult—especially if you are working with information from textbooks, class notes, articles, questionnaires, or surveys. The process is the same, but the amount of information you have to deal with may confuse you. Even so, a systematic and methodical approach will lead you to a good tentative thesis.

The point at which you formulate your tentative thesis depends on your own method of writing, your knowledge of your subject, and your assignment. Some writers like to wait until after they have reviewed all their prewriting notes before they think about a thesis. Others, especially if they are well acquainted with their

subject, like to formulate a tentative thesis right after they limit their topic. Occasionally an assignment suggests a thesis—"Examine *three effects* of rat population
overcrowding." Whatever the case, a tentative thesis before you actually begin
writing your essay provides you with the direction you need to write a coherent and
focused draft.

Remember that as you write you will constantly be changing and sharpening
your thesis. It is entirely possible, then, that you could begin your essay with one
thesis in mind and end up having said something else. As you proceed through the
writing process, you will arrive at new insights about your material, and the final
version of your thesis, and your paper, will be the better for it.

EXERCISE

Suppose that for a class in public health you are asked to write a short paper on the
general subject of what you consider the most important weapon used to fight disease
in the last fifty years, and why. You have been doing some light reading on this subject
in newspapers and magazines, you have a special interest in this area, and you have
just finished reading a book called *The Medical Detectives,* so you decide to narrow
your topic to a discussion of the work of epidemiologists, perhaps focusing on the
work of the National Centers for Disease Control (CDC) in Atlanta, Georgia.

The boundaries of your assignment give you some valuable information about your
paper. Since you will be presenting your paper orally to the class, your audience consists not only of your professor (who is likely to be familiar with the CDC's operations)
but a class of students with many different majors. Your purpose has not been speci-
fied, but the wording of the assignment suggests that you should emphasize the value
of epidemiology in the fight against disease; thus your general purpose will be to
inform and persuade. More specifically, this paper should show why the work of epidemiologists is just as important a weapon in disease control as more conventional weapons like new medical and surgical techniques. The paper is to be written at home and
to be about five pages long. You can supplement personal experience and observations
with some informal research, but your instructor has said that you are *not* to search
scientific or medical texts for information. Instead, you may read in general-interest
magazines or newspapers; perhaps consult a good encyclopedia, an almanac, or a
similar general reference work; and carefully consider class notes and discussions. The
paper should reflect an opinion of your own based on information from these sources.

Study the brainstorming notes below, and try to sort the information into logical
groups, discarding any material that seems irrelevant. When you have arranged the
items in categories that make sense to you, try to formulate several different thesis
statements that this information could support.

Brainstorming notes

Definition of disease? Definition of epidemiology?

National Centers for Disease Control—when founded? Why? How big? Chain of command?

Local Departments of Health? Medical examiners?

    Epidemics: Black Death, 1340s—25 million dead?

                    Cholera, 1840s and 1880s—millions dead worldwide.

                    Influenza (1917–19)

Mysterious diseases—Legionnaire's disease (1976), "Lyme disease" (1975), hemorrhagic fevers (Lassa fever, etc.), infant botulism

Poisoning—botulism, salmonella

Reye's syndrome—usually in children—may follow minor illness like chicken pox—Barbara's cousin (11 years old) died before he could be diagnosed—physicians must be trained to recognize symptoms—role of CDC in education?

Rabies—bats, squirrels, dogs

        new inoculation procedures? (less painful)

        woman contracted rabies through cornea transplant

CDC tried to find common denominator in "epidemic" of murders of Atlanta children (1980)

Advertisement for Roueché's *Medical Detectives* notes it's like a mystery story—possible parallels with Sherlock Holmes? (Methodology: deduction; Conan Doyle was M.D.)

General weapons against disease—diet, sanitation, new surgical procedures, early diagnosis, equipment (x-rays, CAT scanners), drugs (nuclear medicine, cancer chemotherapy)

Background—Early weapons against disease:

                Jenner—smallpox antitoxin (1796)

                Lister—surgical antisepsis (1865)

                Reed—yellow fever (1901)

                Wassermann—test for syphillis (1906)

                Fleming—discovery of penicillin (1928)

        —Weapons of last 50 years:

                Domagk—use of sulfa drugs (c. 1932)

                Waksman—discovery of streptomycin (1943)

                Polio vaccine—Salk (1954), Sabin (1955)

"New" diseases—toxic shock syndrome. Reporting of cases increasing. Search of medical literature suggests it may have been around since the 20s. Dr. Bolognese says *Lancet* reported first case in England in 1978. FDA's role in TSS? Role of manufacturers? Role of CDC?

                —AIDS. Affects male homosexuals, Haitian immigrants, intravenous drug users, hemophiliacs. CDC initially slow to become involved. Current role?

Epidemiologists' contributions: Found link between smoking and cancer, make diagnoses that puzzle other doctors (e.g., botulism), determine what food is responsible in cases of food poisoning.

Interview with Berton Roueché, author of *Medical Detectives, in New York Times* notes parallels between doctors and detectives—uses phrases like "medical sleuthing."

Medical Detectives focuses on cases of rabies, trichinosis, anthrax, etc. One chapter, "The Case of the Eleven Blue Men" (1940s)—group of derelicts turned blue after eating oatmeal. New York City Health Department epidemiologists found out sodium nitrate had been substituted for salt in cafeteria where they ate.

Long-range impact of CDC and other medical sleuthing?

Lives saved?

II

Writing and arranging

The moment you begin writing an essay you also begin shaping it. As you write your rough draft, you take some steps toward drawing your ideas together under your tentative thesis. As you write later drafts of your essay, you begin to realize the shape of your ideas. Finally, after a good deal of work, you move with confidence, feeling that you are in control of your material. Certainly this orderly progression somewhat misrepresents the repetitious and random nature of the writing process. But this picture also holds some truth. Most writing takes shape only after it appears on paper. Often students make the mistake of trying to do too much in their heads, only to find out that their short-term memory is not up to handling the complex relationships that characterize most writing. Only by writing several drafts and by trying out several approaches can one organize one's thoughts and discover the most effective way of presenting them.

You can shape your ideas in a number of ways. By telling how something looks, feels, tastes, smells, or sounds, you can *describe* it. By arranging events in a chronological sequence, you can *narrate* them. You can use these ways of writing to express feelings, to explain, to persuade, or to give pleasure. For instance, you could describe a pond to tell how you felt as you looked at it, to explain the effects of pollution, to argue against chemical dumping, or to introduce a short story.

We said in Chapter 1 that the primary purpose of most college writing is to convey information, and we concentrate on that in this section. The patterns of process explanation, cause and effect, comparison and contrast, classification and division, and definition are associated primarily with *expository*, or informational, writing. To flesh out our examination of writing and shaping, we also look at different options for creating and reworking the paragraphs, sentences, and words in an essay. Revising, an ongoing and inseparable part of the writing process, is treated in the section that follows.

CHAPTER

3

Preliminary Shaping:

The Rough Draft

Once you have a tentative thesis, you must make your observations, notes, and ideas into an essay by writing a rough draft. The purpose of a rough draft is to get your thoughts down on paper so you can react to them, and often it focuses only on the middle paragraphs of your essay. This is as it should be. Students who struggle to write the "perfect" introduction often find that they discard it in later drafts when their ideas take shape.

WRITING YOUR ROUGH DRAFT

Here are some things that you should keep in mind when you write your first draft. (More specific advice appears in Chapter 9, Revising Your Essay.)

1. *Prepare your work area* Once you begin to write, you won't want to stop

because you need pencils, paper, notes, or anything else. Unscheduled stops can break your concentration and make writing your rough draft difficult.

2. *Get your ideas down on paper as quickly as you can* Don't worry about style, diction, sentence structure, or spelling. Get your points down on paper and make tentative connections between them. Your rough draft not only helps you judge ideas you already have; it also helps you discover new ones.

3. *Take regular breaks as you write* Try writing one section of your paper at a time. When you complete a part of your draft, take a break and do something else. Many people find that while they do other things, their unconscious mind still focuses on their writing. After this incubation period, their writing often flows more easily.

4. *Free write at any point where ideas will not flow* Because your rough draft provides the raw material for future drafts, ideas—even those you get by free association—may prove useful. At this stage you are talking to *yourself*, so your ideas need not make sense to a reader.

5. *Leave yourself enough time to revise* Many inexperienced writers think that they can complete a piece of written work in a single draft, and they don't leave themselves enough time to revise. You should understand that almost all writing benefits from careful revision. Even when time is short, as on midterm and final examinations, you should allow time to reread your work.

Aaron Zino, the student we discussed in Chapter 2, wrote the rough draft shown on page 51. His paragraph divisions loosely correspond to the points in his scratch outline and to the first level of branches in his topic tree, and he begins with his tentative thesis. Even though Aaron revised this draft extensively, it provided much of the information he used in his finished paper, and it helped him start to shape his ideas.

EXERCISE

1.   Reread Aaron's brainstorming notes on page 39 and his draft carefully. What material from his notes did he use in his draft? What did he omit? Why? What information did he add as he wrote? Why?

2.   What ideas in his rough draft do you think Aaron could develop? What part do you think he could discard? Be prepared to discuss your answers in class.

CONSTRUCTING AND FINE-TUNING YOUR THESIS

Once your first draft is down on paper, you should see whether your tentative thesis accurately represents your ideas. Your first draft has probably taken you in

> My high school science courses, my summer work, and my experiences playing basketball showed me that I could be a doctor.
>
> ~~My high school~~
>
> ~~My high school teachers helped me decide get interested in it in high school. There were a number of Borowsky my high school biology~~
>
> My high school biology teacher, Mr. Borowsky, got me interested ~~on~~ in biology. I dissected various things—frog—worm—fish—in his class. ~~He~~ Mr. Borowsky made it easy for me to see how knowing biology could help me with medicine. ~~Other teachers helped me too. Mrs. Mogil helped me.~~ ~~She was my chemistry teacher in 11th grade.~~ Mrs. Mogil my chemistry teacher helped me too. She tutored me after school. ~~I found working in the lab~~ I found I liked the precision and sense of discovery.
>
> My job pushed me toward pre med. ~~I did a lot but it was boring sometimes. Working at the hospital was good though. I met a lot of doctors and got to talk to them.~~ Even though my duties were limited, I did get to see a lot. There was some high level cancer research being done—and I got to observe. I knew this was the kind of setting I belonged in.
>
> My basketball team helped me to ^decide to^ become a doctor. It's odd—for the first time I really worked hard to get what I wanted. I was ~~certain~~ captain. ~~The game with George Washington high I kept one~~ helped me grow.
>
> All these things helped me make up my mind.

some unexpected directions. You may have departed from your scratch outline and added, deleted, or rearranged material. There is nothing wrong with this—re-thinking is part of the writing process. But if your direction has changed, your thesis must change too.

WHAT SHOULD YOUR THESIS DO?

Your thesis should always do three things: it should take a stand, be clear, and give your readers a good idea of what your essay is about.

First, a good thesis tells your readers what you think and how you feel about your material, so it must be more than a title or an announcement of the subject. As your central idea, it presents the stand you will take in your paper.

Title
Fairy Tales and Human Behavior

Announcement

In this paper I will discuss the relationship of fairy tales and early childhood.

Neither statement gives enough information to qualify as a thesis. The following statement leaves no doubt about the writer's position.

Thesis

Not just empty stories for children, fairy tales shed light on the psychology of young children.

Second, your thesis should be clear. Neither you nor your readers should have any doubt about what you are going to discuss. Don't use vague or confusing words or leave questions unanswered.

Unclear

Although the timber wolf is a timid and gentle animal, it is being systematically exterminated. (*Why* is the timber wolf being exterminated?)

Unclear

The timber wolf is being systematically exterminated because people believe it is a fierce and cold-blooded killer. (*Is* the timber wolf a killer?)

Clear

Although the timber wolf is actually a timid and gentle animal, it is being systematically exterminated because people wrongfully believe it to be a fierce and cold-blooded killer.

The first two versions of the thesis raise as many questions as they answer. The third puts the issue into perspective and clearly presents the main idea.

Third, a good thesis accurately represents what you intend to discuss in your essay. It makes no promises you do not intend to fulfill. If you want to discuss some effects of a rise in the prime interest rate, don't write:

Inaccurate

Although not all economists would agree, there are three causes of a high prime interest rate.

This thesis distorts your purpose and misleads and confuses your audience. You want to stress some *effects* of a rise in the prime interest rate, so don't talk about *causes*. A more accurate thesis is:

Accurate

Because of an unusually high prime interest rate, more and more people are getting mortgage money from sources other than banks.

This revised thesis limits the scope of your discussion and gives your audience an accurate idea of what you will examine.

EXERCISES

1. Analyze the following statements and determine why none of them qualifies as a good thesis. Be prepared to explain your criticisms.

   a. The rise of the space shuttle.
   b. Union organizers are devoting many hours to the Houston Organizing Project.
   c. In the pages that follow, I will compare and contrast several versions of the Arthurian legend.
   d. Both the Phillies and the Mets made dramatic gains from their prior underdog status.
   e. Radio City Music Hall is more than fifty years old.
   f. Pornography: pro and con.
   g. Many advertising slogans are very clever, but others are dull.
   h. Gothic novels, science fiction, westerns, and mysteries are read by millions of Americans each year.
   i. Deep sea fishing can be exciting, but there is another sport I prefer.
   j. Cable TV has become a major industry in recent years.

2. Read the following quotations and decide how effective each would be as a thesis statement for a short essay. In each case consider the following:

○ Does the statement take a stand?

○ Is the statement clear?

○ Could the statement clearly establish the focus of an essay?

   a. In many a fin and reptile foot I have seen myself passing by—some part of myself, that is, some part that lies unrealized in the momentary shape I inhabit. (Loren Eiseley, *The Immense Journey*)
   b. From the present point of view, child rearing may be regarded as an educational process in which the child is taught what games to play and how to play them. (Eric Berne, *Games People Play*)
   c. Each of us has to do his little bit toward transforming this spirit of the times. (Albert Einstein, *Ideas and Opinions*)
   d. It had been my accidental reading of fiction and literary criticism that had evoked in me vague glimpses of life's possibilities. (Richard Wright, *Black Boy*)
   e. One's reaction to the photographs Roman Vishniac took in 1938 of daily life in the ghettos of Poland is overwhelmingly affected by the knowledge of how soon these people were to perish. (Susan Sontag, *On Photography*)
   f. As you know, any plain person you chance to meet can prove to be a powerful immortal in disguise come to test you. (Maxine Hong Kingston, *China Men*)
   g. Throughout the inhabited world, in all times and under every circumstance, the myths of man have flourished; and they have been the living inspiration of whatever else may have appeared out of the activities of the human body and mind. (Joseph Campbell, *The Hero with a Thousand Faces*)
   h. The data strongly imply that changes need to be made in the way composition is taught in American secondary schools. (Janet Emig, *The Composing Process of Twelfth Graders*)

WHERE SHOULD YOU STATE YOUR THESIS?

Your thesis also helps keep your readers on track. Most often you should place your thesis at the *beginning* of your essay, especially when you want your readers to know immediately what the essay is about. This is certainly true with midterm and final examinations and short thesis-and-support essays. At other times you may *delay* your thesis. If your essay is about a controversial subject or a subject that needs preliminary explanation or definition, you may decide to postpone your thesis. In this case, the background material sets the stage and encourages your readers to accept your thesis when it finally appears. You may also decide to place your thesis at the *end* of an essay. This builds suspense or creates a mood. When your thesis finally appears, it has added impact and effect on your audience. You see this strategy in essays in which an author draws an unexpected conclusion or has an unusual reaction to an event.

Not every thesis needs to be explicitly stated. *Implying* your thesis lets your readers discover your intent as they read. With controversial issues or in personal-experience essays, for example, this technique is often effective. If you do decide to imply a thesis, you must make certain that your central idea is clear. An implied thesis should be as obvious as an explicit thesis.

Whether you want an explicit or implied thesis depends on the boundaries of your assignment. In academic writing, your general audience in most cases is your instructor and your purpose is to convey information. Examine your specific motive—why you are writing—to determine which kind of thesis you need. Carol Sterns decided to use an implied thesis in this introduction to a personal-experience essay:

> The skyscrapers loomed around me as I munched on the last bite of a bagel smothered in cream cheese that I had picked up at the New York train station. My eyes bulged as I watched merchants pushing huge racks of clothes in every direction down the sidewalks, a scene so typical of the city's famous garment district. Thinking of my already aching feet as I scurried to keep up with my cousin Joanna, I wondered if New York consisted of anything but concrete and cement. I had no idea what that hot July day had in store for me.

Although Carol does not say so explicitly, she leaves little doubt that her paper is about her visit to a cousin in New York City. The assignment was to write about a personal experience—to tell a story. Readers don't expect a story to take a stand, but even so, Carol's paper has an unstated thesis—that her trip to New York's garment center helped her decide to major in fashion and design. A more structured paper, though, would demand a different approach.

Steven Erb used an explicit thesis to begin his answer to an examination question. The question was "Choose one of the short stories we have read this semester and discuss how the central character is like or unlike the author."

"A & P" is a short story that takes place in a small town in Massachusetts similar to the one the author, John Updike, grew up in. The central character of the story is Sammy, a cashier at a local supermarket. He is nineteen years old, cynical, and, above all, observant. *It is through Sammy that readers learn about the town, the people, and ultimately the author's view of working-class America.*

Steven's purpose was to demonstrate his knowledge of the course material, so he needed a clear, explicit answer to the question. He introduces his thesis quickly, at the end of a short introduction. In the introduction, Steven briefly connects the town in the story to the town Updike grew up in, establishes the importance of the central character, and then states his thesis in the last sentence.

Not everything you write needs or should have a thesis. Beginning a case study or a trip report with some arguable point would just be misleading. Opening a lab report with "synthesizing dinitrobenzene can be an exciting and interesting experience" distorts your purpose, which is simply to report your observations, not your opinion of them or your feelings about them.

SUPPORTING YOUR THESIS

Although you arrive at new insights as you write it, your rough draft is not as unfocused as you may imagine. You write your rough draft with your tentative thesis in mind, and you structure it using your scratch outline. Even in the rough-draft stage, then, you begin to see the shape that your material suggests. Many of your assignments will require you to support your thesis with specific examples or evidence. It will help if you are familiar with one of the most common ways of presenting information, *thesis and support.* Knowing the basic structure of a thesis-and-support paper helps you with both the preliminary shaping of your essay and the revising you do later.

In a *thesis-and-support* paper, your *introduction* states your thesis. The *body* of your paper presents examples that support the assertions you make in your thesis. And your *conclusion* restates your thesis or the major points that you want your audience to remember.

When you write a thesis-and-support paper, consider your audience as skeptical readers who must be convinced that what you say is valid. Expect your readers to be asking "Why should I accept this statement? What evidence is there to support this point?" Your examples are the evidence for your case. Enough of the right examples and a sufficient variety of them will prove your case. Remember that only concrete evidence will do. Empty generalizations and unsupported opinions undermine your credibility and detract from your presentation.

To illustrate what we mean by "thesis and support," let's look at a revision of the rough draft by Aaron Zino that you saw on page 51.

Working Toward a Goal

Introduction

Thesis

I have wanted to be a medical doctor ever since I can remember. It was during high school, though, that a combination of experiences helped to confirm my choice. *My science courses, my summer job, and my experiences playing basketball showed me that I have the ability to become a doctor.*

Body ¶ (Gives two examples that support the thesis)

Although I was never particularly interested in science before high school, two gifted teachers motivated me. My biology teacher, Mr. Borowsky, showed me the intricacy of the different systems in the human body. In his class I did my first dissection and realized how fascinating biological processes can be. Mr. Borowsky encouraged me to see the parallels between human and animal life and encouraged me to pursue a career in medicine. My chemistry teacher, Mrs. Mogil, also became a kind of mentor for me. She gave me the opportunity to spend time after school working on experiments on my own. Always challenging me to do better, she made me realize how much I like precision and a sense of discovery. Mrs. Mogil also helped me get a summer job as a laboratory assistant at University Hospital.

Body ¶ (Another example to support the thesis)

My job in the laboratory pushed me further toward medicine. Even though my actual duties were limited to "bottle washing" and cleaning up, I got to see a lot. Some high-level cancer research was being done in the lab, and I got to help with it. I observed the researchers and technicians as they worked with animals, recorded data, and discussed preliminary results. I found it exciting to witness this kind of endeavor. By the end of the summer, I knew that medical research was the path I wanted to follow.

Body ¶ (Final example to support the thesis)

In an indirect way, my experiences on the basketball team also helped me decide to become a doctor. Basketball convinced me that I could work hard to achieve a goal. I played basketball for all four years in high school, earning a starting position in my sophomore year. Being a student athlete forced me to make many adjustments. I spent many hours studying by flashlight while traveling in the team van. I also had to mature and learn to put group goals above my individual goals. During my last year I was captain and was responsible for molding individual players into a winning team.

Conclusion (Restatement of the major ideas of the essay)

When I look back over my high school years, it is not hard to see how different experiences influenced my decision to become a medical doctor. I enjoyed my biology and chemistry courses, and I feel that they prepared me for the courses I will take in college. My work at University Hospital showed me that I like research, and my participation on the basketball team gave me confidence to pursue this goal.

Aaron's paper examines the high school experiences that influenced his career choice. He introduces his subject and states his thesis: "My science courses, my summer job, and my experiences playing basketball showed me that I have the ability to become a doctor." The thesis occurs early enough to alert readers to the points that he will consider in his body paragraphs. Although the thesis is not controversial, it does make an assertion with which some readers could disagree.

Once Aaron presents his thesis, he then must support it with evidence. He must convince his readers that what he is saying is valid. "How did your science courses help you make up your mind? How did your summer job and your experience playing basketball make you think you could become a doctor?" The essay's three body paragraphs answer each of these questions with examples. In paragraph 2, Aaron considers the influence of two gifted science teachers; in paragraph 3, he discusses how a job in a hospital laboratory led him to focus on medical research; and in paragraph 4, he explains how playing basketball helped him develop qualities that he could use to reach his goal.

The last paragraph, Aaron's conclusion, sums up his thesis and the nature of the evidence. As he again considers how three different experiences guided him toward a career in medicine, he convinces his readers that his thesis is supported by more than personal opinion.

An important point to remember is that "thesis and support" is just a general structure. The way you present your support—the reasons, examples, and arguments you use in the body paragraphs—can take many different forms. The next chapter introduces some of the strategies you can use to support your thesis. As you practice writing, you will learn to recognize these patterns and to use them to your advantage.

EXERCISES

1.   Read this thesis-and-support essay and label the introduction, body, and conclusion. Then construct a scratch outline, like the one on page 40, indicating the major points as well as the supporting details.

The Good Things: Duke on America
John Wayne

It's no real chore for me to write about "The Good Things" of America, although I wondered for quite a while as to why it was so hard to start. Then it came to me loud and clear. There are so many good things about America, I found myself trying to eliminate hundreds of them that I might at least not write a book on the subject. It was then that I decided to dwell upon facets of America that in each case cover a sea of individual "Good Things."

Therefore, I suppose that my number one topic should be my job. It's the one thing that takes up most of my time. It's something I'm grateful for because it's a job I love to do. If any youngster should ask me for advice on that subject, I'd have to tell him that he must find out what he really wants to do with his life. Take a long hard look and make darn sure that it's what you really, really want. Then jump in feet first and give it all you have. The chances are you'll succeed, for success is not measured in your wealth but in your worth. A person who is eager to go to his job every day is a happy man, and that's success.

The major factor is our free-enterprise system. Under that system you are free to pursue whatever career suits you and you have 50 states to find it in. Yes, a "Good Thing" in our country is that right to decide what you want to do with your life and where you want to do it. Free enterprise means "do your own thing," and if you really put your heart and soul in it, you'll have a pretty fair shot at the good life.

In many parts of the world, even though you may be a national of a particular country, you have to have visas to travel in your own nation. One of our "Good Things" lies in the fact that although we solidly back states' rights in America, every citizen can be as much at home in one state as he can be in any other. A Texan can't get by pretending that he's from New York, but he can live there with the same total rights any New Yorker has. A Minnesotan doesn't speak with a Mississippi drawl, but he can move to Tupelo and not create a single wave.

Our country thrives on change. In nature nothing is permanent. So it stands to reason that as laws change, ideologies and mores change so that society changes and that is good. When America moves slowly to a change of long duration, that change has to be for the good of the majority. If it isn't, we just rare up and the next time Election Day rolls around and we want to alter that situation, our representatives start paying attention.

No guns or bombs or Army coups. Just the biggest and best weapon of them all, our right to vote. X's on paper. The ballot box, a "Good Thing."

Let's take a look at our religious beliefs. While the majority of Americans embrace Christianity, every religion of the world has found its way to our shores. Certainly we have our share of fanatics but the preponderance of Americans have a deep-rooted respect for the beliefs of their fellow man. After all, was not one of our Founding Fathers' prime considerations freedom from persecution and freedom of religion?

Here all the world's religions have gathered under the vast canopy of America's skies to live and to let live in harmony. In my opinion that's a mighty "Good Thing."

Under the umbrella of all these "Good Things" an American can live an exciting and a full life. You may vote for whom you want, pray to whatever deity pleases you, work at whatever trade or profession you really desire and live in a country that affords you every type of terrain in the world.

Day after day in America, people enjoy the good life. It's solid and it's real. There's so much here it's easy to take it for granted and to become alarmed at the headlines that shout out disasters in bold print. Just remember that the bad news makes up less than 2 percent of our nation's activities. The other 98 percent—a man towing a stranger's car to a garage, a neighbor caring for a sick child or a minister making a call to a dying parishioner in a driving rain—doesn't make the headlines because it won't sell papers. But "Good Things," we have them, here in America. (*Saturday Evening Post*)

2.   This exercise asks you to write your first thesis-and-support paper. In it, support your thesis with several examples that will prove your point to your audience. Using the same topic Aaron Zino wrote on—"How Have Your Experiences Helped to Shape Your Career Goals?"—brainstorm to come up with some ideas you can use. Then use those ideas to develop a scratch outline and arrive at a tentative thesis. Finally, write a draft of a five-hundred-word essay with an introduction, body, and conclusion.

3.   For additional practice in writing thesis-and-support essays, choose one of the topics listed below and develop it into a five-hundred-word essay.

- Living in a dormitory
- TV soap operas
- Cheating on campus
- How technology is changing our lives
- Violence in horror movies
- Commercials that seem to work
- How TV portrays minorities

4.   In the pages that follow, four business executives describe summer jobs they once held. Read these pieces and try to draw some general conclusions from the writers' experiences. How, for instance, might these early jobs have helped to give them a start in business? How could these jobs have helped to mold the characters of these executives-to-be or have helped them decide on a future career? Develop several different thesis statements based on your conclusions, making sure that each thesis can be supported with information drawn from these remembrances. Finally, write a five-hundred-word essay supporting one of the thesis statements.

Helen Meyer

72, Editorial Consultant to Doubleday Inc., New York; Former Chairman, Dell Publishing Company.

After graduating from Bushwick High School in Brooklyn, where I was a student in an experimental commercial course and planning to continue my education in the fall, I thought I would try to get a summer job. This was some time late in July and somehow I knew, possibly through a girlfriend, of an employment agency called Hamilton, at Church Street in Manhattan.

I was sent out for an interview to two companies. One was National Biscuit Company and the other was Popular Science-McCall Distributing Company, the distributor for those two magazines, which is now called Select Distributing Company. I was hired by the distributor at $15 a week as an adjustment clerk. I became so infatuated with my work that I decided not to go back to school. Instead I took various courses at night: English and commercial law, that I felt would help me in my work. After spending more than a year there, I was offered a job at Dell through someone who had worked with me at Popular Science-McCall. And I continued with Dell for over 50 years, from clerking to chairman of the board.

Walter Hoving

81, Chairman, Tiffany & Company, New York (1978 sales: $73.25 million).

I always believed in summer jobs because I think it's a very good way for young men and women to test out their abilities and their interests. One summer job that I had when I was at school was with a big insurance company downtown, and I was one of the file clerks. I was about 13.

I think I got paid $3.50 a week; this was some time ago. The files were on one floor which was almost a block square, and it was a cement floor. The files hadn't been arranged, so the A's were in some place and the B's were in another place and then there'd be more A's. They hadn't bothered to put all the files for one letter together in the same area.

After I'd worked there about six weeks, I made a little map of what I thought they should do to rearrange those files. Then I went up to the straw boss who sat in one of the corners. It didn't seem to me that he was doing much work. But anyway, I said, "Sir, here's a little plan of how you can make it easier for these boys to do the filing. Also, because it's a cement floor, if you put the boys on roller skates you could probably do the filing with half the force that you have now." And he looked at this thing and then he looked at me, and then he said, "Look, Hoving, you think you're too goddamn smart. You're fired."

Years later, when I joined Montgomery Ward in Chicago, I found that the clerks who pulled the stock that had to be sent down a chute in a basket to be sent to customers were all on roller skates. It took me 18 years to discover that that was not too bad a suggestion.

Mary Kay Ash

(A great-grandmother who says, 'Any woman who would tell her age would tell anything'), Co-founder and Chairman, Mary Kay Cosmetics Inc., Dallas, Tex. (1978 net sales: $53.75 million).

At the age of 16 and during the height of the Great Depression, I found employment with the Tabernacle Baptist Church, which was located in the fifth ward of Houston, Tex. I worked seven days a week for the Reverend Lewis B. Quarrels, an enthusiastic individual who was determined to rebuild the Tabernacle Baptist Church from near bankruptcy, as well as sizeably increase the number of members in the congregation. I assisted Mr. Quarrels in his endeavors along with performing various clerical duties, and I took my hard-earned yet minimal wages straight home to my mother, since this income was essential to the support of my family.

During the time I was employed at the church, Mr. Quarrels succeeded in expanding Sunday service attendance to over 900 members, from almost nothing. An administrator as well as a minister, Mr. Quarrels accomplished this through such methods as rewarding consistent thirteen-week attendance with the presentation of a small white Bible. I was among those who helped him implement this and other such programs, including contacting families through-out the area to encourage them to participate in Church activities.

Though my job was extremely demanding, I discovered a true sense of personal achievement and contribution to a greater cause as the church substantially increased its membership. The fundamentals of various promotional and organizational techniques that I learned from Mr. Quarrels proved invaluable to me when I later embarked on my direct selling career.

Victor H. Palmieri

49, Chairman, Victor Palmieri & Company Inc., a Los Angeles and Washington D.C.-based asset management firm.

It was the summer of '52. I had just graduated from Stanford and had been admitted to the law school. I was dead broke, however, and my chances of making it to law school depended on what I could earn that summer.

The Korean War was underway and the newspapers told of a huge construction boom and fabulous wages in Anchorage. Alaska was clearly the answer to my financial problem.

Anchorage that summer was like Dodge City a century earlier. Drifters, misfits and hard cases from all over the world had collected there to prey on the construction workers. We lived in a giant tent camp, rose at dawn and spent the days lifting 50-pound concrete blocks up to the scaffold platforms and then scampering around setting concrete forms 6 or 7 stories above ground.

After a little experience with camp life I decided I might as well work nights also, and so I hired on as a bar waiter in the Village Barn, Anchorage's toughest bar. When the construction job shut down at 4 in the afternoon, I washed up, headed for town and was ready for action, bar tray in hand, when the construction workers hit Main Street and the Village Barn became a madhouse.

All that summer I worked those two jobs, sleeping 4 hours a night and earning $600 a week. I came back to Stanford Law School in the fall rock hard, 20 pounds heavier and with enough money for the school year. I also came back with one other thing—a lifelong aversion to physical labor.

CHAPTER

4

Further Shaping:

Patterns of

Development

As you think about your subject and as you write, your mind works in characteristic ways. You examine how things work, you look for causes and effects, you compare and contrast, you divide and classify, and you define. Even if you are not aware of these mental operations, you carry them out every time you write. Within a general thesis-and-support approach, each specific pattern represents a basic way of thinking about a subject, and each involves a strategy, a series of decisions about structure. If you learn to arrange and revise your essays in terms of these patterns, you can convey information more effectively.

Naturally you won't start out saying, "I'm going to write a classification essay," or "I think I'll support my thesis with a definition pattern this time." Your strategy evolves out of your material; it is never imposed on it. As you prepare to write, you may notice that your assignment calls for classification. Or your essay may naturally take the shape of definition. Sometimes just a sentence or two of your rough draft indicates the particular pattern that you should use. These strategies, therefore, help you when you first spell out your ideas and when you revise them.

Practicing these patterns at this stage makes you aware of how your mind works and trains you to work in new ways. It also helps you revise and tighten the logical structure of your writing. We consider each pattern separately, even though you will combine these patterns in much of your writing.

PROCESS

When you write a set of instructions or explain how something works, you are presenting a process explanation. Like narration—that is, telling a story—process pays careful attention to sequence. But unlike narration, process explanations and instructions maintain strict chronology—that is, they present each step of the process in the order it occurs, describing a sequence of steps or stages that can be repeated with the same results. Because sequence is at the heart of any process, those words that enable your readers to keep track of the sequence—transitional signals like "first," "second," "next," "after this," and "now"—are extremely important.

You also need good analytical skills, for you must be able to see the correct divisions, or stages, of the procedure, not just the order in which they occur. Some steps can be naturally grouped together or summarized; others may need to be isolated and explained thoroughly.

INSTRUCTIONS VS. PROCESS EXPLANATION

Instructions and process explanations are similar, but they have several notable differences. Instructions or directions enable readers to *perform* the process. Typically, you use commands (the imperative mood) and the present tense, second person, and active voice. ("Next, [you] attach the shelf at point B.") A process explanation, however, helps readers *understand* the process. You do not expect them actually to carry out the process. You use either the first or third person ("Now I attach [the technician attaches] the shelf at point B") and either past or present tense, depending on whether the process is one that has been completed ("Then, I attached the shelf at point B") or one that occurs regularly ("At this time one usually attaches the shelf at point B"). You may also use the active voice ("I [he, they] attached the shelf . . .") or the passive ("The shelf was attached").

The following two paragraphs illustrate these differences. Sue De Corte wrote the first for a freshman composition class. Her set of instructions makes use of the second person, the present tense, and the imperative mood to outline the steps in making a milk shake.

Making a milk shake may seem to be a simple task; however, several different steps are involved in the procedure. First, you must assemble the necessary equipment: a special metal container which has two distinct lines marked on the inside, and the ingredients. The first ingredient is the ice milk. (Ice cream cannot be used, or the milk shake will be a cream shake!) Place two and a half scoops of ice milk in the metal container for a regular shake (three and a half for the extra-thick shake). Then, add milk until the mixture reaches the second line on the inside of the container. Now, add the flavoring: three squirts for cherry, strawberry, or vanilla but only two for chocolate or the milk shake will be too chocolatey. Once you have put the ingredients into the container, attach it to the machine which thoroughly mixes it. (If it is not left on the machine long enough, all of the ice milk will remain on the bottom). When the mixture is ready, pour it into a large wax-coated paper cup, topped with a lid, and hand it to the customer with a straw and a smile.

Sue's purpose was to tell her readers how to make a milk shake themselves, so she cast the process as a set of instructions. She begins by telling her readers what equipment they need and continues by listing the steps in the order that they should be performed. Transitional words such as "then" and "now" help her to make the sequence clear.

In her book *A Distant Mirror,* the historian Barbara W. Tuchman describes the education of a young boy from a noble family in the fourteenth century.

A boy of noble family was left for his first seven years in the charge of women, who schooled him in manners and to some extent in letters. Significantly, St. Anne, the patron saint of mothers, is usually portrayed teaching her child, the Virgin Mary, how to read from a book. From age eight to fourteen the noble's son was sent as a page to the castle of a neighboring lord, in the same way that boys of lower orders went at seven or eight to another family as apprentices or servants. Personal service was not considered degrading: a page or even a squire as a grown man assisted his lord to bathe and dress, took care of his clothes, waited on him at table while sharing noble status. In return for free labor, the lord provided a free school for the sons of his peers. The boy would learn to ride, to fight, and to hawk, the three chief physical elements of noble life, to play chess and backgammon, to sing and dance, play an instrument, and compose, and other romantic skills. The castle's private chaplain or a local abbey would supply his religious education, and teach him the rudiments of reading and writing and possibly some elements of the grammar-school curriculum that non-noble boys studied.

Tuchman's purpose was simply to tell her readers how a typical boy's education proceeded, not how to get such an education themselves, so she used the devices of process explanation, using third person, the past tense, and, occasionally, the passive voice.

THE THESIS STATEMENT

Frequently a process explanation has no explicit thesis because it is designed to inform, not to make a point. If the purpose of your paper is simply to tell your readers how to program a computer in PILOT, for example, no thesis is necessary. At other times, however, a process essay may have a thesis—for instance, when your purpose is to convince your readers that a process is particularly complex or difficult, or that one method of carrying out an operation is better than another. Such a process paper could have a thesis statement like "For educational purposes, PILOT is superior to LOGO because it is easier to use."

APPLYING PROCESS

Academic situations frequently call for process explanations and sometimes for instructions. In scientific and technical writing you may describe how an apparatus works or how a procedure is carried out. Occasionally you may even write a set of instructions telling your readers how to duplicate your procedure. In the humanities you might have to write a proposal for a library paper in which you describe how you intend to carry out your research. Here are some typical assignments that call for process explanation.

○ Explain how an amendment is added to the Constitution. (Political science quiz)

○ Review the stages each of the Old English long vowels went through during the great vowel shift. (Examination in history of the English language)

○ Outline the steps in the process of mitosis. (Biology lab quiz)

○ Present a set of instructions that you would give to patients to instruct them in cardiopulmonary resuscitation. (Nursing education quiz)

○ Discuss the residence histories that most American families follow. (Sociology paper topic)

ORGANIZING PROCESS

The level of your audience, what they know and don't know about your subject, determines how much detail you must include. To tell an uninformed reader how to change a faucet washer, you would have to list—and perhaps describe—the exact tools needed. If you cannot decide what information to present, find a friend who is unfamiliar with your subject and ask him or her.

In general, process explanation has a relatively straightforward structure. In your introduction, present an overview of your subject. Next, itemize the information your readers need to understand your discussion and, in the case of instructions, describe any equipment or tools required. In the body of your essay, list the steps of the procedure in the order in which they occur. Finally, conclude by summing up the steps and considering the significance of the process as a whole.

The scheme of a process essay looks like this.

Introduction   Name the process, explain why it is being performed, and provide an overview.

Body	Present the steps of your procedure.
	Step 1
	Step 2
	Step 3
	Step 4 . . .
Conclusion	Review the process and note its significance.

Richard Patrone, a student in a course in animal biology, submitted the following laboratory report. He gathered his material, arranged it in a workable order, and, after his rough draft, he revised to make sure that his steps represented what actually occurred. In writing up his experiment he provides an exact record of what he did and gives his readers enough information to understand his procedure.

Introduction

Based on the postulation that pollen contains an anticarcinogenic principle that can be added to food, an experiment was set up in which female mice, fed with pollenized food, were checked for delays in the appearance of spontaneous mammary tumors. Mice used in the study were bred from a subline of the C_3H strain, which develop palpable tumors at between 18 and 25 weeks of age.

Procedure

Steps in the process

First, 10 mice were set aside as controls, to be fed only unpollenized food (Purina Laboratory Chow). Next, the pollen suspension was prepared by grinding one gram of bee-gathered pollen and mixing it with 50 ml of distilled water. Two different mixtures were then prepared using this pollen suspension. One mixture consisted of 6 lb of food with a 36 ml dosage of pollen suspension (1 part pollen per 3800 parts food), and one consisted of 6 lb of lab chow with an 8 ml dosage of suspension (1 part pollen per 120,000 parts food). Each of these two mixtures was then fed to a different group of 10 mice. The mice were weighed weekly, and the amount of food eaten was recorded. As soon as estrus began, vaginal smears of each mouse were made daily and examined microscopically for the presence of cornified cells.

Results

Conclusion

The experimental results indicated that the development of mammary tumors in C_3H mice was delayed 10 to 12 weeks with the ingestion of pollenized food.

Richard gives an overview of his experiment in his introduction. In "Procedure" he presents the steps he followed. Because he wants to explain how he carried out the experiment rather than to tell someone else how to do it, he uses the third person and the past tense. The passive voice emphasizes the experiment itself rather than his own role. He adheres to chronology and uses transitions like "next," "then," and "as soon as" to make the order clear.

Richard reports his conclusions under "Results." Notice that this lab report contains no thesis—its purpose is simply to report what happened.

WORKING WITH DATA: PROCESS

Write an essay based on the following cartoon in which you give a set of instructions for assembling the components of the cigarette extinguisher. Use present tense, second person, and imperative (command) mood. Then rewrite your essay as a process explanation.

SUGGESTED TOPICS FOR PROCESS ESSAYS

1.   Write a short essay describing your writing process. Then "translate" the explanation into a set of instructions.

2.   Write a detailed set of instructions for playing pinball, Pac Man, or any other game whose rules you know well.

3.   Think about a time when you had to complete a complicated transaction that involved dealing with bureaucratic red tape—applying for a student loan, getting your driver's license, or opening a charge account, for instance. List the steps you went through, and then write an explanation of the process.

CAUSE AND EFFECT

Like process, cause-and-effect writing involves the movement of events in time. But instead of focusing on their *order*, cause-and-effect explores the *reasons behind* the events and their *consequences*.

Cause-and-effect relationships are often complex: one cause may have many effects, and a single effect may have several causes. And because their relationships are subtle, you may fail to distinguish the more obvious *immediate* causes from the less visible—but perhaps more important—*remote* causes. For instance, your grades are slipping, and you at first attribute this to the difficulty of your courses. But a closer look may reveal other causes—personal problems, a demanding part-time job—which affect your grades even more. Or you may confuse *primary* (most important) and *secondary* (less important) causes. Or you may commit what is known as the post hoc fallacy—you assume that just because one event preceded another, it caused the other. Just because "Ping-Pong diplomacy" preceded improved relations between the United States and China, for instance, doesn't mean that Ping-Pong had any impact, good or bad, on politics. Finally, you may fail to see that an effect is also a cause—as in a *causal chain,* in which each event in a series causes the next. For instance, a chance meeting can result in a summer job, which in turn can bring about a new career direction.

Because cause-and-effect relationships are often so complicated, you should take care when you use this pattern to distinguish causes from effects, immediate from remote causes, and primary from secondary causes. Transitional elements ("Another cause," "Further affecting the situation," "A more important result," "Because of this," and so on) can help you identify these distinctions. Of course, just putting in a "because" or a "therefore" won't create a causal relationship where none exists; you must take care that you actually have a cause-and-effect connection before you give those signals to your readers.

DESCRIBING EFFECTS

Cause-and-effect writing focuses either on finding causes or on describing effects. This paragraph from John Brooks's *The Telephone: The First Hundred Years* considers the wide-ranging *effects* of the invention of the telephone on our lives.

What has the telephone done to us, or for us, in the hundred years of its existence? A few effects suggest themselves at once. It has saved lives by getting rapid word of illness, injury, or famine from remote places. By joining with the elevator to make possible the multistory residence or office building, it has made possible—for better or worse—the modern city. By bringing about a quantum leap in the speed and ease with which information moves from place to place, it has greatly accelerated the rate of scientific and technological change and growth in industry. Beyond doubt it has crippled if not killed the ancient art of letter writing. It has made living alone possible for persons with normal societal impulses; by so doing, it has played a role in one of the greatest social changes of this century, the breakup of the multigenerational household. It has made the waging of war chillingly more efficient than formerly. Perhaps (though not provably) it has prevented wars that might have arisen out of international misunderstanding caused by written communication. Or perhaps—again not provably—by magnifying and extending irrational personal conflicts based on voice contact, it has caused wars. Certainly it has extended the scope of human conflicts, since it impartially disseminates the useful knowledge of scientists and the babble of bores, the affection of the affectionate and the malice of the malicious.

Brooks answers his opening question by presenting—in no particular order—some of the most obvious effects of the telephone. His use of phrases like "made possible," "bringing about," and "played a role" makes his focus on effects clear. The cause-and-effect relationships are complex, and as we can see, one cause—the telephone—can have many effects.

FINDING CAUSES

This excerpt from Lester C. Thurow's essay "Why Women Are Paid Less Than Men" emphasizes causes.

> Back in 1939 it was possible to attribute the earnings gap to large differences in educational attainments. But the educational gap between men and women has been eliminated since World War II. It is no longer possible to use education as an explanation for the lower earnings of women.
>
> Some observers have argued that women earn less money since they are less reliable workers who are more apt to leave the labor force. But it is difficult to maintain this position since women are less apt to quit one job to take another and as a result they tend to work as long, or longer, for any one employer. From any employer's perspective they are more reliable, not less reliable, than men.
>
> Part of the answer is visible if you look at the lifetime earnings profile of men. Suppose that you were asked to predict which men in a group of 25-year-olds would become economically successful. At age 25 it is difficult to tell who will be economically successful and your predictions are apt to be highly inaccurate.
>
> But suppose that you were asked to predict which men in a group of 35-year-olds would become economically successful. If you are successful at age 35, you are very likely to remain successful for the rest of your life. If you have not become economically successful by age 35, you are very unlikely to do so later.
>
> The decade between 25 and 35 is when men either succeed or fail. It is the decade when lawyers become partners in the good firms, when business managers make it onto the "fast track," when academics get tenure at good universities, and when blue collar workers find the job opportunities that will lead to training opportunities and the skills that will generate high earnings.
>
> If there is any one decade when it pays to work hard and to be consistently in the labor force, it is the decade between 25 and 35. For those who succeed, earnings will rise rapidly. For those who fail, earnings will remain flat for the rest of their lives.
>
> But the decade between 25 and 35 is precisely the decade when women are most apt to leave the labor force or become part-time workers to have children. When they do, the current system of promotion and skill acquisition will extract an enormous lifetime price.

After dismissing two possible secondary causes for the gap between what men and women earn, Thurow focuses on what he considers the primary cause—the fact that women are more likely than men to reduce their workload during the crucial decade between the ages of twenty-five and thirty-five. This may be a less obvious cause than the others, but Thurow feels it is the most significant, or primary cause.

THE THESIS STATEMENT

Each of these selections has a strong thesis: Brooks's point is that the telephone has had a major impact on our lives; Thurow's is that educational inequities can no longer account for women's lower earnings. Your thesis must always tell your readers whether you are focusing on *effects*, as Brooks does, or on *causes*, like Thurow. In addition, as in other kinds of essays, the thesis of a cause-and-effect paper must be clearly written and clearly arguable. "The decline in student enrollment has caused many universities to eliminate unpopular departments" simply states a fact. "The decline in student enrollment has caused many universities to eliminate unpopular departments, unfairly depriving today's students of opportunities in many fields of study" states an arguable thesis.

APPLYING CAUSE AND EFFECT

Many of your course assignments call for writing that examines causes, predicts effects, or both. Language like "How did X affect Y," "What were the contributing factors," "Describe some side effects," "What caused X," "What were the results of X," and "Why did X happen" suggests cause-and-effect writing. Here are some typical assignments:

- Explain some contributing factors to the recession of 1975. (Economics essay)
- Describe some of the possible side effects of dialysis. (Nursing examination)
- How have geologic changes affected the productivity of Pennsylvania soil? (Agronomy project)
- What factors led to the Eastern European exodus to this country at the turn of the century? (American history examination)
- How did Ernest Hemingway's experiences in World War I influence his writing? (Literature paper)

ORGANIZING CAUSE AND EFFECT

The structure of an essay using a cause-and-effect pattern generally follows one of two designs. If your purpose is *to ascertain causes,* you begin by identifying the effect you want to examine and perhaps summarize its causes. The body presents each cause separately, or it groups several related causes in each paragraph, usually working from least to most important cause. The conclusion reviews the causes and firmly establishes their relationship to the effect in question.

Introduction   Identifies effect; states thesis

Body   Cause 1
                Cause 2
                Cause 3
                Cause 4 . . .

Conclusion   Reviews causes; establishes their relationship to effect

If your purpose is *to consider effects,* you begin by identifying the cause and perhaps give an overview of the effects. The body takes up each effect in turn, perhaps grouping related causes together, building up to the most significant. The conclusion reconsiders the effects the essay considers, carefully connecting them to the cause under discussion.

Introduction   Identifies cause; states thesis

Body   Effect 1
                Effect 2
                Effect 3
                Effect 4 . . .

Conclusion   Reconsiders effects; connects them to cause

Michael Liebman wrote the essay that follows for a class in elementary education. The assignment was "Identify the causes of a social problem of concern to both parents and educators, and analyze the effects of this problem, making some recommendations about how the problem can be solved." Michael examines the positive and negative effects on children of being left on their own after school. When revising his rough draft, he made sure that the causal connections between his ideas were clear and that he accurately differentiated causes and effects.

The Latch-Key Children

Introduction
(States primary
cause: working
parents)

    In the past ten years, the inflationary economy and wider employment opportunities for women have combined to lead more and more mothers of school-aged children to return to work. In fact, more than half of the mothers of school-aged children are now employed, and the two-paycheck family is rapidly becoming the norm. As a result, hundreds of thousands—perhaps millions—of children are now left unsupervised between 3 and 6 P.M. every day. The lack of much-needed after-school programs has left many families in cities and suburbs alike with no other alternative but to leave the children on their own and hope for the best. Luckily, many of the children manage extraordinarily well.

Negative effects

    The negative effects of the latch-key trend are fairly easily perceived. Many parents' firm rules—don't use the stove, don't open the door to anyone, don't let telephone callers know you are alone—have reportedly made some children (especially those without siblings) fearful and jittery. These children may also become very lonely in an empty house or apartment. Since many working parents do not allow their children's friends to visit when no adult is present, their children may spend hours with no company but the television set. A lonely, frightened child turning to the TV for comfort and companionship is a common stereotype of the latch-key child—fortunately, it is for the most part not an accurate one.

Other possible negative effects

The latch-key phenomenon has the potential to have some even more disturbing effects on children. Parents and teachers have voiced fears that unattended children will be more vulnerable to violent crimes, especially sexual assaults and kidnapping. They also fear the children will be unable to protect themselves in case of fire or other disaster. Parents have been concerned as well that young adolescents left alone will be free to experiment with sex, drugs, and alcohol. But these fears have not been substantiated by statistical data.

First positive effect

Surprisingly enough, in fact, many positive results have actually been observed—positive both for the children and parents involved and for our society as a whole. One such positive result has been the response of the many schools across the country which have instituted courses in "survival skills." In these courses, boys and girls as young as 10 learn skills such as cleaning, cooking, and sewing; consumerism; safety and first aid; and how to care for younger siblings. The focus of the home economics courses in these schools has changed as the students' needs have, and the trend toward these "domestic survival courses" seems to be spreading.

Second positive effect

Perhaps the most significant effect has been a rather subtle one: the emotional strengths so often observed in the latch-key children. As they learn to fend for themselves, and take pride in doing so, their self-esteem increases. Educators cite these children as more self-reliant, more mature, more confident; parents add that they are also more cooperative around the house. Of course it is still too early to tell whether the latch-key trend will produce a generation of more independent, self-reliant adults, but it is certainly a possibility.

Conclusion

Clearly, the latch-key syndrome has negative as well as positive results, but the answer is not to have parents leave the work force. For the majority of working parents, especially in single-parent families, working is an economic necessity. Parents should be able to remain employed, and most of their children will benefit—though some, inevitably, will suffer. The best solution would be the development of government-sponsored programs to meet the needs of the latch-key child. Most important among these would be supervised after-school programs, perhaps utilizing school buildings and facilities. The community and private industry can also

contribute—the former by establishing networks of "block parents" and information and referral services, the latter by offering
"flex-time" as an option for working parents. Most latch-key children are managing quite well, but their lives and their parents'
lives can—and should—be made a lot easier.

Michael's assignment told him to note the cause of a social problem and analyze its effects. He begins his essay by clearly identifying the problem (latch-key
children) and its cause (working parents) and goes on to present his four effects—
two negative and two positive. Each of Michael's body paragraphs begins with a
sentence that uses the word "effect" or "result" and indicates whether the topic is
negative or positive.

Michael's introduction briefly explains the primary cause of the latch-key
trend—the economic pressures and new employment opportunities for women
that have caused many mothers of school-aged children to go back to work. If his
focus were on causes, he would have had to specify others.

WORKING WITH DATA: CAUSE AND EFFECT

Read "A Graduate Who Says He Can't Read" by Edward B. Fiske (*New York Times*)
and write an essay in which you explain *why* Edward Donohue was able to graduate
from high school even though he is illiterate. You will probably want to begin by
reading the article over carefully, underlining important points, perhaps *listing* the
reasons he was able to remain in school.

A Graduate Who Says He Can't Read
Edward B. Fiske

When 18-year-old Edward Donohue walked through the door of the Lindenhurst Diner on
Long Island one day recently he had already decided that he would order a cheeseburger.

"When you can't read a menu," the unemployed carpenter said, "you have to know what
you want."

Mr. Donohue is not alone in having a serious reading problem. The United States Office of
Education estimates that there are 23 million American adults who are unable to perform basic
coping skills, such as reading a train schedule.

Mr. Donohue's case is notable, though, in one important respect: last month it was announced that he and his family were suing the Copiague Union Free Schools for $5 million on
the ground of "educational malpractice."

In a notice of claim, which is the first step in a civil suit against a government body, the 1976
graduate of Copiague High School charged that the school system had failed to educate him
properly and had left him "unable to cope properly with the affairs of the world."

The reaction in the predominantly blue-collar Copiague community of 20,000 has been
vigorous and sometimes bitter. Letters to the editor in local newspapers have been overwhelm-

ingly critical of Mr. Donohue's parents, both for bringing the suit and for allegedly neglecting their son's education, and Margaret Donohue, Edward's mother, said that she had been harassed by late-night phone calls with nobody on the other end.

"One woman threatened to run me off the road," she said in an interview. "Another man threatened to sue us if the publicity hurt the value of his property."

On the advice of counsel, school officials have declined to discuss the "Donohue case." N. Paul Buscemi, the superintendent, declared simply, "I'm fully confident that when we get to court, we will be vindicated." Several teachers declined to discuss the matter because they said that they feared retaliation by school administrators, and a reporter interviewing students at Copiague High School was ordered off the grounds by the principal.

The suit comes at a time when new questions are being asked about the accountability of school officials and when educators and politicians are showing increased concern for matters of basic literacy.

More than two dozen states either have adopted, or are adopting, "minimum competency" requirements for high school graduation. Last month New York State began formal administration of a new test of applied math and reading skills to the class of 1979, which is the first to be affected by its new competency law.

Because of such developments, the Copiague situation is being closely watched by school officials across the country.

Edward Donohue is a tall, quiet youth who lives in the "American Venice" section of Lindenhurst, which is in the Copiague school district. His mother, who was born in Ireland and came to this country as a teen-ager, is a practical nurse at a local hospital. His father, Francis, works for the telephone company.

Like his six brothers and sisters, Edward Donohue attended local public schools, and, although temporarily held back on several occasions, he graduated from elementary, junior high and senior high school with his class.

Last June he received a diploma from Copiague High School that describes his major field as "Vocational Technical Courses." He says that he cannot read the document. The unofficial transcript in his possession of his high school record reveals that he failed seven of the 23 courses he took and received minimal grades of 65 or 70 on most of those that he passed.

Teachers and others who have examined the document have expressed surprise at some of the information it contains. Mr. Donohue accumulated 17 academic points in the courses he passed, which teachers say is one more than the New York State minimum but one less than the 18 points that Copiague High School normally requires for a diploma.

With the exception of carpentry, which he took at the local B.O.C.E.S., Mr. Donohue failed all of his courses in his junior year. Without having passed either sophomore or junior English, he was admitted to senior English the following year. Graduation was apparently assured by the fact that during his senior year he took three English courses and passed them with grades of 65, 65 and 68.

School officials, citing the litigation, declined to discuss their decisions regarding Mr. Donohue's promotion and graduation.

In interviews Mr. Donohue said that he was aware at an early age that he had a reading problem. He said that he used to have to build model airplanes without reference to the instructions and that as a paper-boy he used to keep his customers' accounts in his head because "I couldn't keep a notebook."

When he was in the fifth grade at the Scudder Avenue School, he recalled, his teacher used to give him less difficult spelling lists than she gave the rest of the class. "I guess she was trying to build up my confidence," he said.

Mr. Donohue said that being functionally illiterate in modern American society posed continual, and often embarrassing, problems. He reported that he failed the test for his driver's license the first time because he couldn't handle the written segment and passed the second time only because the examiner "read it to me."

When shopping for clothes he has to ask the clerk to read the cleaning instructions on the label, he said, and when applying for jobs he normally brings the application forms home for his mother to fill out.

Illiteracy affects personal relationships. "If you can't read books and newspapers, what do you have to talk about?" said Mr. Donohue. "All you know is what everyone else knows." Some months ago when the high school graduates were signing one another's yearbooks, he said, "I just walked away—a lot of my friends got aggravated because I didn't write anything."

Among those willing to discuss Mr. Donohue's situation there seems to be general agreement that he has faced a genuine and long-standing learning problem.

Some believe that he has a "learning disability," the term used to describe the inability of otherwise normal persons to perform certain specific tasks, such as sounding out an unfamiliar word. Others suggest that he is among a minority of students who do not learn well under the "phonics" approach to reading that is normal in most elementary schools, including those in Copiague today.

Whatever the problem Edward Donohue may or may not have, one of the allegations being made in the legal action is that the school system failed to administer tests that might have provided information on why he was doing poorly.

Most local citizens seem to blame Edward Donohue and his parents for his situation. One anonymous letter received by them, for example, begins, "You and only you are responsible for the fact that your child is uneducated. It seems that you were too wrapped up in your own business (personal) until now to pay attention to what your son was doing."

Students at the high school, sensitive to how the publicity surrounding the case could affect the value of their diplomas, also tend to be critical. "I think he wants the money," said Robert Durgin, a senior. "Why else would he be suing the school?"

Mrs. Donohue replied that at all three levels of schooling she had inquired about her son's poor grades and had repeatedly been assured that he was getting sufficient help. "They said he would snap out of it," she stated.

Others, including some teachers, put the blame on Edward Donohue's own attitude toward school. They note that he was suspended twice in the eighth grade for fighting and similar incidents, and he acknowledges that his high school attendance record left something to be desired, especially during the 10th grade.

Mr. Donohue goes on to add, though, that by the time he reached high school he had come to regard formal instruction as a meaningless and often humiliating experience. When a teacher called upon him, he said, he would often pretend that he was looking out the window in the hope that the teacher would move on to someone else.

The young man stated that it was only after he began working with a private tutor at the end of his senior year and in the months since then that his attitude toward learning changed.

"I always thought that it was my fault," he said. "I just figured I couldn't learn. Then I realized that the reason I can't read is not because of me but because I was taught wrong. I always thought that other people were better than me. Now I know we are the same."

Mr. Donohue said that since completing high school his reading had improved under the guidance of a tutor. He produced a stack of "flash cards" and noted that whereas eight months ago he was working on recognition of words like "let," "at" and "four," his tutor now had him doing words like "opposite" and "electric."

The youth and his family reject charges that the problem lies with them and argue that the schools should have paid more attention to diagnosing and treating his learning problems.

Mr. Donohue acknowledged that as early as the second grade he was put into small groups for help in reading and speech and that such attention also continued, at least some of the time, at Copiague Junior High School. At the high school, he said, he received individualized tutoring, primarily from supervisory personnel, in social studies and English in the last few months before his scheduled graduation.

The Donohues argue, however, that such attention was insufficient and constitutes ground for a claim of negligence.

There is also, however, a widespread belief among teachers at Copiague High School that the policy of the district is to move children with problems out of the system as soon as possible. Virtually all of those interviewed, for instance, reported that there was an "unwritten rule" that no more than 15 percent of a teacher's grades would be failures.

"No one ever tells you anything," said William Levien, the high school social studies teacher who is president of the Copiague teachers association. "But when you hand in your distribution sheets, a high number of failures will come back circled. You know that it came to someone's attention."

Mr. Donohue maintains, and some teachers agree with him, that his rather bizarre senior-year program reflected a desire to push him out of the system. He said that he sensed this during his tutoring in social studies shortly before graduation. "When I realized that they were going to pass me anyway," he said, "I didn't do any more work."

SUGGESTED TOPICS FOR CAUSE-AND-EFFECT ESSAYS

1. Write an essay describing the likely effects on your present life of one of the following situations: losing your scholarship, loan, or job; becoming a parent; failing a course; inheriting five thousand dollars.

2. The rights of adopted children is a topic under a good deal of discussion lately. Although information about parentage has traditionally been denied, many people think adoptees should have the right to know the identities of their biological parents. Write an essay in which you explore the possible effects of opening adoption files on *one* of the following: adoptive parents, parents who give their children up for adoption, or adopted children.

3. What caused you to come to the college you now attend? Consider both immediate and remote causes. For instance, were you influenced by the school's size, location, or course offerings? By your friends' choices? By your parents' wishes? By your financial situation?

COMPARISON AND CONTRAST

One of the clearest ways of explaining something is to show how it is like or unlike something else—that is, by comparison and contrast. A *comparison* stresses either similarities or differences, while a *contrast* emphasizes differences. In the following paragraph of a physical geography paper, Mary Collier uses comparison and contrast to develop her ideas:

> The largest body of salt water on our planet is called an ocean; the largest body of fresh water is called a lake. They are both considered nondirectional; that is, they do not flow in one direction like a river. The ocean, however, is very large and salty; the lake is much smaller and contains no salt. The ocean has a tide moving in and out, and waves constantly churn its surface. The lake's surface is smooth, and any rise and fall of its level is due to heavy rainfall. The salts and constant motion keep the ocean from freezing over, but in winter time a lake can freeze over its entire surface. Although both are bodies of water, the ocean and the lake are only superficially alike.

This paragraph compares two bodies of water, oceans and lakes. Mary's discussion lists a number of similarities and differences between the two, and she ends with her main idea that even though they are superficially alike, oceans and lakes are fundamentally quite different.

BASIS OF COMPARISON

Before you compare two things, you should be sure they have elements in common. Without some shared qualities there is no basis for comparison or contrast.

In addition to establishing common elements, a comparison must go beyond the self-evident. You could, for instance, compare two museums, the National Gallery in London and the Pompidou Center in Paris. Both have excellent, extensive art collections, and both are world-famous. But a paper saying just this would not hold anyone's interest for long. By focusing on the architecture of the two buildings, however, you could examine the different attitudes toward art that each structure reflects. The classical lines of the National Gallery emphasize solidity and endurance. The strikingly modern Pompidou Center, as one critic says, looks as if the builders finished it and forgot to take down the scaffolding.

In a short office report comparing two automatic typing systems, you would not say that both have keys and run on electricity. You would stress instead the factors that would be of interest—that one typing system is self-correcting and stores information on magnetic discs, for example, while the other does not.

In this paragraph from his essay "Grant and Lee: A Study in Contrasts," Bruce Catton goes beyond obvious similarities and selects as his basis of comparison the fact that both Grant and Lee, despite their many differences, were ideal champions for their respective causes.

So Grant and Lee were in complete contrast, representing two diametrically opposed elements in American life. Grant was the modern man emerging; beyond him, ready to come on the stage, was the great age of steel and machinery, of crowded cities and a restless burgeoning vitality. Lee might have ridden down from the old age of chivalry, lance in hand, silken banner fluttering over his head. Each man was the perfect champion of his cause, drawing both his strengths and weaknesses from the people he led.

POINTS FOR COMPARISON

Once you have decided on your basis of comparison, determine which specific points you will use. With comparison and contrast, you must discuss *the same points* for each subject. If you are comparing the potential economic growth of two cities, New York and Dallas, you could consider *both* cities in terms of the following specific points:

New York	Dallas
Population profile	Population profile
Unemployment	Unemployment
Business climate	Business climate

People often make the mistake of discussing different points for each subject. This obscures your comparison and confuses your readers. New York and Dallas, for example, could *not* be logically or convincingly compared this way:

New York	Dallas
Population profile	Home building
Unemployment	Investment opportunities
Business climate	Rental market

THE THESIS STATEMENT

A comparison-and-contrast paper provides information or makes judgments, or both. Comparisons intended to inform, to present items side by side without commenting on their relative merits, may have no thesis. They may rely on a unifying idea for coherence. Their purpose is to give readers enough data to draw their own conclusions. Judgmental comparisons, however, always have a thesis, stated or implied. The writer takes a stand and asks readers to accept that his or her conclusions are reasonable.

In most of your college writing, a clear thesis statement will make your comparisons clearer and stronger. Your thesis should clarify your intentions—whether you are stressing similarities, differences, or both. The way you structure your thesis statement helps you emphasize your priorities. Stating your purpose in the main clause rather than in a subordinate clause provides you with a definite structure for your discussion.

Focus on differences

Even though Aristotle was Plato's student, he did not agree with his teacher concerning the relation of form to matter.

Focus on similarities

Despite being separated by several decades, Stephen Crane and Ernest Hemingway are surprisingly similar in their word choice and subject matter.

Focus on similarities

Although Egyptian and Aztec cultures were quite different, they both had religions that suggested the fall and eventual salvation of humankind.

Each of these statements indicates the subject to be discussed and establishes a basis of comparison and a structure for the essay that follows.

APPLYING COMPARISON AND CONTRAST

Instructors often ask you to use comparison and contrast in answering examination questions.

◦ Compare and contrast the Neoclassic and Romantic views of nature. (English)

◦ Discuss the similarities and differences of the insanity defenses for murder under the M'Naghten test and the Durham rule. (Criminology)

◦ What are the advantages and disadvantages of load and no-load mutual funds? (Personal Finance)

◦ Examine the benefits and liabilities of team-taught and individual teacher-centered classrooms. (Educational Methods)

◦ How did Darwin and Lamarck differ on the subject of mutability of the species? (Biology)

Each of these assignments provides you with cues that tell you how to treat your material. Certain words and phrases—"compare and contrast," "similarities and differences," "advantages and disadvantages," and "benefits and liabilities"—indicate that you should use the methods of comparison and contrast when you write your answer. Many other situations also call for comparison and contrast. For example, if your supervisor on a work-study project asked you to write a short report discussing the feasibility of two types of insulation, cellulose and urethane foam, you would use comparison and contrast to organize your ideas.

ORGANIZING COMPARISON AND CONTRAST

When your thesis suggests a comparison-and-contrast pattern, you have two options for arranging your material. You can discuss each subject separately, devoting a section to subject A and then giving the same treatment to subject B. Or, you can make your first point of comparison between both subjects A and B and then examine each subsequent point, considering both A and B, until you have completed all your points. Each method has strengths and weaknesses.

☐ SUBJECT-BY-SUBJECT COMPARISON

In subject-by-subject comparison, you treat each of the subjects you are comparing separately. You present all you have to say about subject A and then you go on to discuss subject B, using the same criteria and organization. No matter how long your discussion, remember (1) that each part of your treatment should be self-contained, and (2) that you must consider the same points for each subject. The following scheme illustrates this method of arrangement.

Paragraph 1
Introduction—Thesis: If you are building a new home you should consider installing either a passive or active solar energy system.

Paragraph 2
Passive Solar System
  Operation
  Advantages
  Disadvantages

Paragraph 3
Active Solar System
  Operation
  Advantages
  Disadvantages

Paragraph 4
Conclusion—Restatement of Thesis

In this subject-by-subject comparison, the thesis identifies the subject and states the basis of the comparison, thereby linking the two parts of the discussion. Each part of the comparison treats the same points in the same order. The conclusion reunites both parts of the comparison in a new and richer sense.

Subject-by-subject comparisons work best for shorter discussions. A long paper organized in this way asks too much of an audience: it requires them to remember all of the points from the first section while they read through the second section. Then, too, a long subject-by-subject comparison tends to look like two essays connected only by a flabby transition.

☐ POINT-BY-POINT COMPARISON

For longer comparisons, a point-by-point discussion is easier to follow. With this method of organization, you treat subjects A and B individually but alternately, in pairs. The advantage of a point-by-point arrangement is that you repeatedly link your subjects under each point of comparison, reinforcing your comparison as you go. The following scheme illustrates this pattern:

Paragraph 1
Introduction—Thesis: Scientists have long debated how the world will end, and so far evidence suggests the universe is open, but a growing number of scientists are supporting a closed picture of the universe.

Paragraphs 2–3
Spatial Geometry
   Open Universe
   Closed Universe

Paragraphs 3–4
Spatial Density
   Open Universe
   Closed Universe

Paragraphs 4–5
Ultimate Fate
   Open Universe
   Closed Universe

Paragraph 6
Conclusion—Restatement of Thesis: A growing number of scientists now agree that the universe will collapse in upon itself and form a massive black hole.

A point-by-point comparison requires a writer to exercise a great deal of control. Poorly done, it can end up just a list of loosely related points. Your thesis must also be especially strong if it is to guide you as you write.

Notice how Alan Escobero, a self-professed expert on arcade games, uses a point-by-point comparison to present his ideas.

Arcade Wars

Introduction   Long ago, in a time more innocent than ours, pinball aficionados were content to while away the hours watching silver balls bounce frenetically through a maze of bumpers and flashing lights. That, of course, was in the pre–Space Invader era, before solid-state technology revolutionized the coin-operated game industry and challenged pinball machines with computerized video games.

Currently, pinball and video games are locked in deadly combat in arcades across the country for dominance of a multimillion-dollar market. How this battle will be won or lost depends, to a great extent, on how enthusiasts react to two entirely different game formats.

Pinball machines have a long history. They can be traced back to a popular nineteenth-century game that was played on a table and was similar to pool. The original pinball game, a board with a coin chute and variations on the placement of holes, went through a swift period of change. New machines had ingenuity in operating and in new scoring and play attraction features. Pinball games as we now know them got their start in the late nineteen thirties and within a few years developed into the array of flippers, bumpers, and wires we know today.

Video games had their start in the solid-state technology that was a spinoff of the space program and computer research. Experts generally give Nolan Bushnell, the founder of Atari, the credit for inventing the first video game in 1972. The game, called Pong, had a television screen and a few hand-held controls. This simple machine, which at first was viewed by pinball manufacturers as a curiosity, eventually revolutionized the industry and prepared the way for the games that followed. Current video games combine intellectual strategies with elaborate visual effects.

Pinball games mainly attract males between twelve and sixteen years old. Players who talk about how they feel playing pinball say that they get great satisfaction from beating the machine. Some say that pinball challenges their skill and enables them to beat a machine on its own terms. Obviously the game provides a release of frustration, a challenge, and an opportunity to win—all very important. It also stimulates the senses with an array of buzzers, gongs, and electronic sounds. Perhaps one habitual player sums up the attraction of pinball games when he says, "When you play, nothing else counts. It's just you and the machine."

Computerized video games attract a different type of player, as a trip to a downtown arcade any weekday at lunch time will show. Standing beside the usual crowd of teenagers are groups of young executives. As one stockbroker said, "I'd rather play these games than eat." And no wonder, for new video games draw you into a world that lets your imagination run wild. They can give a player the sense of piloting a starship or the thrill of maneuvering a tank through a realistic battle setting. The most popular—Centipede, Pac Man, and Zaxxon—allow you to work out your most violent and aggressive fantasies.

It is too soon to tell who will win the technological war that is presently being fought in arcades. The stakes are big, for a good machine can take in over five hundred dollars a week. Presently, both pinball and video game designers are planning new and spec-

(marginal labels)

Thesis

History (Pinball machines)

History (Video games)

Players (Pinball machines)

Players (Video games)

Restatement of thesis

Concluding summary

tacular games. But even the most ardent of pinball loyalists believe that video games will eventually triumph. Pinball is still a game of silver balls being bounced by flippers and bumpers. Video games are new and take advantage of computer technology. Possibly the most important factor is that when you play a pinball machine, you only push around a ball, but when you play a video game, you fight for a galaxy.

Alan's thesis emphasizes that his composition conveys information rather than opinion or evaluation. The outcome of the battle for the marketplace, he says, depends upon how enthusiasts react to two very different game formats. His introduction establishes his subject, its importance, and the basis of comparison. Using a point-by-point organization, Alan then compares his two topics—the history of pinball and video, and the consumers who play these machines. Strong topic sentences and clear transitions indicate his points:

Paragraph 2
Pinball machines have a long history.

Paragraph 3
Video games had their start . . .

Paragraph 4
Pinball games mainly attract males . . .

Paragraph 5
Computerized video games attract a different type of player . . .

In his conclusion Alan restates his thesis, summarizes his major points, and ends with his own prediction about how the competition will turn out.

WORKING WITH DATA: COMPARISON AND CONTRAST

Study the two pictures reproduced opposite and the accompanying notes below and on page 86 adapted from the *Encyclopedia Americana*. Jot down any notes or observations of your own—questions that occur to you about the paintings, any detail you find unusual or notable.

○ Homer—1836–1910

○ nineteenth-century naturalist

○ post–Civil War—scenes of idyllic country life

○ 1881–1882: lived in English fishing village on North Sea and painted scenes of this life

○ 1883: settled on Maine coast for rest of life; painted sea, forest, mountains and "hardy lives of outdoor men"

Winslow Homer. *The Gulf Stream*. 1899. Metropolitan Museum of Art, New York (Wolfe Fund, 1906).

Andrew Wyeth. *Christina's World*. 1948. Museum of Modern Art, New York.

Your own notes might include: Who is this man? Why is he alone on a stormy sea? What is he looking toward? What do the sharks suggest? Why is the lower left-hand part of the picture darker than the rest?

○ Wyeth—born 1917

○ paints rural countryside near Chadds Ford, Pennsylvania, and "seashore, island, and bleak houses" near his summer home in Maine

○ "at 16, Wyeth first saw the work of Winslow Homer and discovered a kindred spirit"

○ influence of Homer in choice of subject—"simple, often somber landscapes and . . . unpretentious spare people"—but increasingly Wyeth used tempera rather than watercolor

Your notes might include: Who is this woman? Why is she alone in the open field? What is she looking for? What could the house represent for her?

Now assume that you are a student in an introductory art history class. You are assigned a paper in which you must compare and contrast these two paintings. Your instructor has made it clear that she is less interested in techniques and movements in art than in the sensitivity and perceptiveness of your reactions to the two paintings. Ask yourself how the two painters are alike and different, then how their creations are similar and different in subject matter and in form. Taking the thesis, "Although these pictures portray obvious differences in subject matter, they show some striking similarities in arrangement," write an essay of five hundred words.

SUGGESTED TOPICS FOR COMPARISON-AND-CONTRAST ESSAYS

1.   Compare any two athletes, movie or TV stars, writers, or musicians with whom you are familiar. Brainstorm about their differences and similarities in order to formulate a tentative thesis.

2.   Write a comparison-and-contrast essay about a disillusioning experience you have had. Contrast your original view of what you expected with your view after you were disillusioned.

3.   Think of the best and worst classes or teachers you have had in your academic career. Write a comparison-and-contrast essay in which you account for the differences between the two.

DIVISION AND CLASSIFICATION

Dividing and classifying information is central to the writing process—in fact, it is central to the way we think. When we *divide*, we begin with a whole, a complete body of information or one idea, and break it into its parts: thus a whole manuscript can be divided into chapters, or a large tract of land divided into half-acre lots. When we *classify*, we begin with many small observations and sort them into categories on the basis of their similarities: thus notes on a brainstorming list may be earmarked for one paragraph or another, or books unpacked from a carton assigned to different shelves in the library according to subject matter.

Most of the time, classification and division are closely related processes. You use classification or division as a pattern of development to find order and coherence in the chaos of a mass of seemingly unrelated material. These systems not only organize information, they may also suggest points of comparison or contrast between categories. In classification essays, you often devote equal attention to each category. This parallel treatment highlights the similarities and differences among subtopics. Transitions should clearly indicate when a new category is under discussion.

In the following paragraph from the book *The Development of Modern English*, Stuart Robinson introduces a section in which he uses division and classification. He begins by dividing the English language into three major categories, then goes on to discuss the arbitrariness of these categories. He concludes his paragraph with a list of the categories—periods in this case—that he will go on to discuss.

> Languages are studied historically according to the "periods" of their development, during which they exhibit distinguishing characteristics; thus, English is divided into the Old, Middle, and Modern periods. Obviously, such a division, while convenient, is arbitrary, since people do not leave off speaking one form of a language one night and start speaking another form the next day. Though it does not go always at the same pace, language development is continuous. The division into periods is made when the historical linguist, looking backward, sees that by about a certain date the gradual changes have mounted up until the language as a whole is decidedly different, or has entered a new phase of development. We shall date the periods of English as follows:
>
> > Old English—450–1100
> > Middle English—1100–1500
> > Modern English—1500–the present

The following excerpt from an article in *Redbook* uses classification.

> Some substances, called teratogens, from the Greek "teras," meaning "monster," are dangerous only after the sperm has fertilized the egg. The drug thalidomide is a good example of a teratogen. If taken by a pregnant woman between the twentieth and thirty-fifth day after conception, it almost always will cause serious defects in the growing embryo.
>
> The "transplacental carcinogens" make up a second group of harmful substances. These (DES, for one) cross the placenta of the pregnant woman, pass into the blood stream of the fetus and create conditions for the later development of cancer. Since the cancer takes years to develop, it is difficult to foresee which substances will have this effect.
>
> Both teratogens and transplacental carcinogens affect the fetus directly. But a third category of dangerous substances—mutagens—causes mutations, or changes,

in the genes and chromosomes of the germ cells—the egg and the sperm—from which the fetus is formed. Such mutations result in stillbirths, miscarriages, retardation and deformity, and are at least as likely to occur in the father's sperm as in the mother's egg.

The author describes three categories of harmful substances, treating each in a parallel fashion. First the substance is named and defined; then its method of affecting fetal development is explained.

THE THESIS STATEMENT

The thesis statement of a division and classification essay should do two things: it should tell your readers whether you will divide or classify (or both) and let them know what point you are making by doing so. If your purpose is simply to point out that there are three general classes of rocks or that blood is composed of red and white cells, platelets, and plasma, you need not have a thesis at all. But if you are classifying or dividing for another purpose—to demonstrate, for instance, that the number or kind of categories is significant or that one category is somehow notable—your essay will have a thesis: "Without borrowings of Dutch, Indian, and Spanish words, English would not have so rich a vocabulary" or "The course offerings in the business school are more practical than those open to liberal arts or engineering students."

APPLYING DIVISION AND CLASSIFICATION

You divide and classify information every time you write an academic paper. You divide your subject into possible topics, you group your brainstorming notes into categories, and you divide your paper into paragraphs.

When you study a laboratory animal, you may divide your observations according to the animal's systems: digestive, circulatory, nervous, and so on. When you write a book review, you may classify your information into sections devoted to plot, the author's previously published works, and your evaluation of the book you are reviewing. Assignments like these are typical of many that call for classification and division:

  ◦ The English language is constantly in the process of acquiring new words. Write an essay in which you classify some of the many examples of these coinages and adaptations into at least five distinct categories. (History of Language midterm)

  ◦ "Recurrent themes in James Baldwin's novels, short stories, and essays" (American Literature term paper)

  ◦ Analyze the workings of the federal court system, paying special attention to the relationship between the lower courts, the appellate courts, and the Supreme Court. (Take-home examination in American Government)

  ◦ Write a detailed report analyzing the possible roles of each member of the management team during the proposed reorganization of the credit department. (Business Management report)

    ◦ Explain in general terms how the most common orchestral instruments are classified, making sure you provide examples of instruments in each group. (Introduction to Music quiz)

ORGANIZING DIVISION AND CLASSIFICATION

Essays based on division and classification have a straightforward structure. Your introduction tells what categories you are going to discuss and presents your thesis or unifying idea. In the body of your essay you consider each category and justify your system of classification. With your conclusion you restate or reevaluate your major points and clarify the relationship of your categories to one another. A complete essay using division and classification can be arranged like this:

Introduction   Names the categories; states thesis.

Body   First category
              Second category
              Third category
              Fourth category . . .

Conclusion   Reviews categories; clarifies their relationship to each other.

    In this student essay, written as part of a geology examination, Robin Twery uses division and classification to give structure to her answer. The question— "Discuss the three different types of rocks in terms of their origin and composition"—clearly indicated that she should use this pattern. The question also told Robin to treat the three categories in parallel terms.

    Robin put together a scratch outline before writing, and this enabled her to arrange her categories and to address both origin and composition of the different types of rocks.

Classes of Rocks

Introduction (Lists categories)

    Rocks are divided into three general classes: igneous rocks, sedimentary rocks, and metamorphic rocks.

First category

    The first group, igneous rocks, were once molten rock; now they have cooled down and solidified. Igneous rocks may be intrusive or extrusive. Intrusive igneous rocks, in their molten state, forced their way into other rocks and cooled and hardened there, sometimes forming very large masses called batholiths. These batholiths are frequently made up of granite, a crystalline rock. Some other intrusive igneous rocks can form between other rocks in the form of sills or dikes. Other igneous rocks are extrusive; that is, they are formed when molten rock is driven out onto the surface of the earth to cool and harden. The molten rock that flows along the earth's surface is lava. The bits of molten rock that are extruded into the air solidify in the air and fall to the ground in the form of volcanic ash and cinder.

Second category

Sedimentary rocks are formed when other rocks break apart. Pieces of rock, borne by water or wind, are deposited in the form of sediments. After a time, these particles are consolidated into rock. Sedimentary rocks may be classified according to the size of the grains of which they are composed, ranging from coarse gravel to finer sand, silt, or clay to fine lime and marl. Sedimentary rocks are usually deposited in layers (strata), with the oldest sediments on the bottom and the most recent on top.

Third category

The final category, metamorphic rock, has been subjected to great heat and pressure. Metamorphic rocks have been buried under other rocks so that their structures and their mineral components have been altered by the weight of the layers above and the high temperatures to which they are exposed under the earth. An example of a metamorphic rock is the crystalline rock gneiss.

Because this is an examination, Robin does not attempt to attract attention with an interesting introduction. (Nor does she need a concluding paragraph.) Her overview names the three categories right at the beginning. Because her purpose is to convey information, Robin states facts but includes no thesis. Her opening sentence does, however, provide a unifying idea.

In response to the examination question, Robin carefully considers how each kind of rock developed and what each is composed of. To show her instructor that she has treated all three categories, she begins each new paragraph with a topic sentence that specifies the kind of rock under discussion.

WORKING WITH DATA: CLASSIFICATION

Read the following list, reprinted from *The Book of Lists,* and write a five-hundred-word essay on what kinds of books have the power to "change the world." Classify some or all of the titles on this list into groups and use the resulting categories to support your thesis.

Robert B. Downs's 16 Books That Changed the World

1. *The Prince* (1517) by Niccolò Machiavelli

In its 26 chapters, this political treatise studies power—how to get it and how to keep it. Rulers of the past are used as examples, and Cesare Borgia is cited as a model prince. A realist, Machiavelli tells his reader that it is more important to retain power than to be loved, that virtue is commendable but it may not be practical. In sum, the end justifies the means.

2. *De Revolutionibus Orbium Coelestium* (1530, 1543) by Nicolaus Copernicus

The Polish astronomer laid the groundwork for modern astronomy when he upset the Ptolemaic teachings. *On the Revolution of Heavenly Bodies*—finished in 1530, but not published until

1543—theorized that the earth was *not* the center of the universe. In fact, the earth and all the other planets revolved around the sun in separate orbits, meanwhile rotating on their axes, said Copernicus. Theologic opposition to this theory was immediate and violent since man could then no longer be viewed as the ultimate creation.

3. *De Motu Cordis* (1628) by William Harvey

Published in 1628, this treatise explained a discovery that Harvey had made in 1616: that the blood in animals circulates. This was a major step forward in the study of physiology and anatomy.

4. *Principia* (1687) by Sir Isaac Newton

Newton divided his work into three parts: "The Motion of Bodies," "The Motion of Bodies in Resisting Media," and "The System of the World." He advocated reasoning by use of physical events, and he also proposed a new law of gravitation. Hence the book marked the start of the age of scientific exploration and experimentation.

5. *Common Sense* (1776) by Thomas Paine

This outspoken pamphlet—bought by over 100,000 colonists in the first few months following its publication—advocated separation from England and helped set the scene for the Declaration of Independence. Tried in absentia for treason by the English, made an honorary citizen by the republican government of France, British-born Paine died in the newly formed U.S. in poverty and obscurity.

6. *Wealth of Nations* (1776) by Adam Smith

In this important work on economics, Smith proposed the laissez-faire system, one embracing a totally free economy, for modern governments.

7. *Essay on the Principle of Population* (1798) by Thomas Robert Malthus

The same year that he became a curate of the Church of England, Malthus put forth his now famous doctrine that population increases in a geometric ratio while food supplies, etc., increase arithmetically. Also he suggested that the evils of society—crime, pestilence, war—are needed to hold down the increase in population. In 1803, as an afterthought, Malthus proposed moral restraint as an additional check for population growth.

8. *Civil Disobedience* (1849) by Henry David Thoreau

This essay is the source of the familiar statement: "That government is best which governs least." Thoreau also put being true to oneself above being loyal to a man-made government. Among his famous followers was Mohandas K. Gandhi, whose version of civil disobedience became known as "passive resistance" and was reimported into the U.S. as "sit-ins."

9. *Uncle Tom's Cabin* (1852) by Harriet Beecher Stowe

Subtitled *Life Among the Lowly,* the book is remembered today for the Yankee overseer Simon Legree, the death of Little Eva, and the flight of Eliza over the ice. Actually, the book was a fairly balanced treatment of the southern slave problem. Mrs. Stowe expressed admiration in it for the humane slaveholder, and her villain is a displaced northerner from Vermont. Although the book was *not* written by God—despite Mrs. Stowe's claim—it contributed substantially to the abolitionist movement.

10. *Origin of Species* (1859) by Charles Darwin

A revolutionary theory in its day, the theory of evolution is now accepted by most people. Darwin proposed that species evolve from earlier species, and that evolution is controlled or

determined by natural selection. That is, the plant or animal that adapts through positive muta-
tion to its surroundings is the one most likely to survive and reproduce its kind.

11. *Das Kapital* (1867–1895) by Karl Marx

Written in London, Volume I of *Das Kapital* was Marx's major work. (Volumes II and III were
completed by Friedrich Engels from Marx's notes.) A study of capitalistic society, the book went
on to espouse dialectical materialism. Marx believed in class struggle as the basic force in shaping
history, and that the world's increasing industrialization—controlled by the capitalists—would
inevitably lead to overt revolution of the proletariat and a classless society.

12. *The Influence of Sea Power upon History* (1890) by Alfred Thayer Mahan

Written by an American naval officer/historian, this book sought to prove the importance of
naval power in a nation's defenses. Mahan was a lecturer in naval tactics at Newport War
College. His ideas were influential in shaping naval policy in the U.S., England, and Germany.

13. *The Interpretation of Dreams* (1900) by Sigmund Freud

An early report on Freud's findings, after his long study of the subconscious. Dream
interpretation was one of the tools Freud used in analysis. A patient recounted his dreams and
they were explored for their symbolic meanings. Freud thought that these dreams reflected
repressed emotions, which in turn caused neuroses.

14. ''The Geographical Pivot of History'' (1904) by Halford J. Mackinder

Mackinder, a geopolitician in later life, encouraged the revival of interest in geographical
learning in Britain while he was still at Oxford. After establishing geography as an academic
subject when he taught at the University of London, he became director of the London School of
Economics. ''The Geographical Pivot of History'' was a 24-page paper later developed into a
book, *Democratic Ideals and Reality* (1919), which viewed Eurasia as the ''geographical pivot''
and the ''heartland'' of history. The U.S. and Great Britain ignored this theory before W.W. II, but
Germany used it to support Nazi geopolitics.

15. *Relativity: The Special and General Theories* (1905, 1916) by Albert Einstein

A German-Swiss-U.S. physicist, Einstein proposed his special theory of relativity in 1905, his
general theory of relativity in 1916. While these complicated theories made possible the splitting
of the atom and the atomic bomb, they did not win a Nobel prize for Einstein.

16. *Mein Kampf* (1925) by Adolf Hitler

This autobiography was dictated to Rudolf Hess while Hitler and Hess were imprisoned following the Beer Hall Putsch in 1923. The unsuccessful uprising in Munich had sought to over-
throw the Bavarian government. In addition to being an autobiography, *Mein Kampf* (My Struggle) outlined Hitler's plan to achieve political control of Germany.

SUGGESTED TOPICS FOR DIVISION AND CLASSIFICATION ESSAYS

1.   Every social group is governed by a hierarchy, a system whereby individuals or
groups of people are ranked at different levels according to their relative importance in
the group. Choose one group you know well—your extended family, the population

of your college or university, the people on your street, fellow members of a special interest group you belong to, coworkers at your place of employment—and write a classification and division essay placing groups of people within the hierarchy. Explain why each group ranks where it does according to your scheme.

2.   Itemize the contents of your desk, the surface as well as the drawers. Study your list and classify the items on it into categories. Now, write a few paragraphs describing an ideal organization pattern for a college student's desk, adding any items you think are needed in each category.

DEFINITION

Definition, as a strategy for development, provides an answer to the question "What does [something] mean?" We are not talking here about a formal definition of a term, the kind you see in the dictionary, although that may appear within a longer, extended definition. Extended definitions are usually vital to any writing task, and they can even provide the structure for a complete paper.

Formal definitions include the term itself, the class to which it belongs, and the details that distinguish it from other items in its class.

term   class to which it belongs
Democracy is a government

distinguishing details
in which the supreme power is vested in the individual.

   term   class to which it belongs
A frisbee is a piece of sports equipment,

distinguishing details
saucer-shaped and made of plastic,
which is thrown among two or more players.

term   class to which it belongs
Sociometry is the study and measurement

distinguishing details
of interpersonal relationships in a group of people.

   term   class to which it belongs
A puffin is a sea bird

distinguishing details
with a short neck and deep grooved parti-colored compressed bill.

An extended definition builds on this basic format and uses one or more of the most common patterns of development to expand the original definition. Unlike the other patterns of development we have considered, definition does not have its own structural arrangement. Extended definitions take their structure from any combination of expository patterns. You can define a subject in a number of ways:

- By telling how something works: process
- By telling what causes something or results from it: cause and effect
- By explaining what something is like or unlike: comparison and contrast
- By dividing something into its parts: division and classification

And, like other kinds of exposition, a definition essay can also support its thesis by

- Telling a story: narration
- Telling what something looks like: description

   Extended definitions also use other, special techniques. Definitions often provide the background or origin for a term or concept. For instance, you might note that the slang term "snafu," meaning a confused or chaotic situation, was coined during World War II from the first letters of "Situation Normal: All Fouled Up." A term may be defined by negation, by telling what it is not ("A snafu is not just a minor hitch in plans"). Or, a term may be defined with synonyms ("A snafu is a total muddle").
   Here are some of your options for expanding formal definitions.

DEFINING WITH EXAMPLES

In a definition of homesickness for an essay in freshman composition, Peter Reilly gives a series of familiar examples:

> A child in a hospital bed, alone after visiting hours, begins to cry for her parents; a family moving into a new house is silent and depressed; a college freshman in his dorm room feels sick and has trouble concentrating. All these people are experiencing homesickness. Homesickness is a longing to go back to some old, familiar thing you are leaving behind. It's that gnawing feeling in your stomach when you try to eat some institutional food that just can't be compared to "Mom's home cooking." Or that feeling of loss and loneliness you get when you see a family together and yours is two thousand miles from where you're standing. Or remembering it's your father's birthday and you won't be there to help celebrate the occasion. It's that feeling of knowing where you are now and where you would like desperately to be—and that is home.

DEFINING WITH DESCRIPTION

In a *Vogue* article about how clothing reveals information about a person's politics, Gloria Emerson describes an item of clothing in order to define a cultural attitude toward women. After the definition, she goes on to interpret its political significance.

It is not much, only a wide belt of black cotton cloth, silk for those who are very rich, lacking buttons, snaps, hooks, or fastenings of any kind so the woman must hold it with her arms and hands for it must never slip. It is the "veil," the chador, the shapeless head-to-ankle covering for Moslem women conforming to the orthodox Islamic custom that a woman's hair, arms, and legs cannot be revealed. The chador is a sign of her smallness in the Moslem world.

DEFINING WITH COMPARISON AND PROCESS

In this selection from the book *Arts and Ideas,* William Fleming defines the term "concrete music" by using both *comparison* (what it is like) and *process* (how it is made).

Concrete music is the term used to identify one aspect of contemporary composition. It involves using the tape recorder to capture everyday sounds and manipulate them on magnetic tape. The procedure might be compared with the way Robert Rauschenberg puts together one of his assemblages. . . . The artist selects some random objects—Coke bottles, a bird cage, bedsprings, old newspaper clippings—and then combines them into a three-dimensional collage, even painting some sections.

The composer of *concrete music* finds sounds and noises all around—the clanking of trash cans, the whine of jet engines, the roar of city traffic, the sirens of fire trucks. Once recorded, these environmental sounds can be edited, the sequence controlled, and the tape run at varying speeds, spliced or scrambled, and played backward. The material can also be filtered by eliminating overtones, with feedback added or subtracted, and certain sounds may be isolated, fragmented, and broken down into separate components. The possibilities are far-ranging.

The first two sentences provide the formal definition of concrete music. The third sentence extends the definition, comparing this music to an analogous technique in art, and the fourth sentence describes that technique. The second paragraph extends the definition further, describing the process of composing concrete music.

THE THESIS STATEMENT

The thesis of a definition essay must explain why the paper is presenting the definition. The thesis must be arguable, not just a statement of fact, so "Dyslexia is a perceptual disorder" cannot be a thesis for an essay. However, "If dyslexia is viewed correctly as a perceptual disorder instead of as a form of mental retardation, dyslexics and their families will be less reluctant to seek the help they need" would make a good thesis. Similarly, "*Marbury v. Madison* changed the American court system by establishing the concept of judicial review" would be an effective thesis; "*Marbury v. Madison* established the concept of judicial review" would not work because it is not debatable.

APPLYING DEFINITION

You must always define your terms in academic writing to prove to your audience that you know what you are talking about. Within longer essays, papers, or reports, whatever their pattern of development, brief or extended definitions are almost always necessary to clarify a crucial concept or term. Definition can also provide the structure for a complete piece of writing.

Some typical assignments calling for definition include the following:

○ "The WPA: History, Operation, and Contributions" (American History paper)

○ "The Villanelle in French and American Poetry" (Comparative Literature paper)

○ Distinguish between the organic and international schools of modern architecture. (Architecture exam)

○ What is a colluvial soil? (Agronomy quiz)

○ Define the school of painting known as Fauvism, paying particular attention to the early work of Matisse. (History of Art midterm)

○ In a few sentences, identify four of the following dysfunctions: anorexia, autism, schizophrenia, agoraphobia, paranoia, manic depression, dyssymbolia. (Psychology quiz)

ORGANIZING DEFINITION

Most frequently, definitions appear as sections of longer pieces of writing. Sometimes, however, a definition serves as the basic framework for an entire piece of writing, as it would in the last three topics on the list above. In such cases a typical structure might be organized something like this. The introduction presents the term to be defined, offers a brief formal definition and perhaps a discussion of the term's origin, and states the essay's thesis. The body expands the basic definition, using a pattern or patterns of the writer's choice. Finally, the conclusion may sum up the term's significance, make predictions or recommendations, or drive home the thesis.

Introduction	Includes term to be defined, formal definition, and thesis.
Body	Expands the basic definition.
Conclusion	Sums up, makes predictions or recommendations, or restates thesis.

In response to the examination question "Choose *one* early twentieth-century American social or political movement and briefly discuss its purpose, its leading supporters, and their contributions," Suzanne Bohrer chose to write on the muckrakers. In defining the term "muckraker," she decided to include a formal definition, provide a brief explanation of the term's origin, and expand the basic definition to discuss the movement's role in American social and political history.

Even though this was an examination, Suzanne had time to rework her answer. As she reread it, she saw that she needed a brief definition of the term "muckraker" and that she needed to explain more about one of her examples, Upton Sinclair's novel, *The Jungle*. After adding this information, she recopied her rough draft and handed in the following essay.

Introduction (Includes formal definition and origin of term)

Muckrakers were early-twentieth-century reformers whose mission was to look for and uncover political and business corruption. The term "muckraker," which referred to the "man with a muckrake" in John Bunyan's *Pilgrim's Progress,* was first used in a pejorative sense by Theodore Roosevelt, whose opinion of the muckrakers was that they were biased and overreacting.

Thesis

The movement began about 1902 and died down by 1917. Despite its brief duration, however, it had a significant impact on the political, commercial, and even literary climate of the period.

First point— influence reflected in magazines

Many popular magazines featured articles whose purpose was to expose corruption. Some of these muckraking periodicals included *The Arena, Everybody's, The Independent,* and *McClure's.* Lincoln Steffens, managing editor of *McClure's* (and later associate editor of *American Magazine* and *Everybody's*) was an important leader of the muckraking movement. Some of his exposés were collected in his 1904 book *The Shame of the Cities* and in two other volumes, and his 1931 autobiography also discusses the corruption he uncovered and the development of the muckraking movement. Ida Tarbell, another noted muckraker, wrote a number of articles for *McClure's,* some of which were gathered in her 1904 book *The History of the Standard Oil Company.*

Second point—influence reflected in fiction of D. G. Phillips

Muckraking appeared in fiction as well. David Graham Phillips, who began his career as a newspaperman, went on to write muckraking magazine articles and eventually novels about contemporary economic, political, and social problems such as insurance scandals, state and municipal corruption, shady Wall Street dealings, slum life, and women's emancipation.

Third (and most important) point— influence reflected in *The Jungle*

Perhaps the best-known muckraking novel, however, was Upton Sinclair's *The Jungle,* the 1906 exposé of the Chicago meat-packing industry. The novel focuses on an immigrant family and sympathetically and realistically describes their struggles with loan sharks and others who take advantage of their innocence. More important, Sinclair graphically describes the brutal working conditions of those who find work in the stockyards. The main character's work in the fertilizer plant is particularly gruesome; at the novel's end, this man turns to socialism.

Conclusion

With the muckrakers featured prominently in fiction, magazines, and newspapers—especially the New York *World* and the Kansas City *Star*—some results were forthcoming. Perhaps the most far-reaching was the pure-food legislation of 1906, supposedly a direct result of Roosevelt's reading of *The Jungle*. In any case, the muckrakers helped to nourish the growing tradition of social reform in America.

Suzanne's essay begins with a formal definition to introduce the movement she has decided to discuss. A brief explanation of the origin of the term suggests the political context of the movement. Her thesis statement—that the movement had a great impact on contemporary life—follows, and the rest of her definition paper gives examples that support the thesis.

Suzanne expands her definition by presenting a series of examples of well-known muckrakers and their most influential writings. These examples answer the need for a discussion of the movement's leading supporters and their contributions.

WORKING WITH DATA: DEFINITION

You are going to write a letter to your school newspaper in which you discuss dyslexia, a condition characterized by perceptual difficulties. You want to convince your readers that the school should begin a program to train teachers to treat dyslexic children.

Review the following objective, neutral articles to help you formulate your definition essay. The purpose of each is simply to provide information, not to convince the reader of anything. Although you may begin your letter with a "dictionary definition" taken from the source material, your assignment is to create an *extended* definition, using any or all the modes of development that you think appropriate.

Everyone on campus, from your peers to the dean of the School of Education, reads the paper, so be very careful to support your assertions with specific facts. You may want to quote a particularly forceful or unusual statement; otherwise, be sure to put the information into your own words and to acknowledge borrowed material as such. (In an informal letter, footnotes are not necessary, but you can—and should—note in parentheses, or in the text of your letter, the names of your sources. You might, for instance, say something like "*The Encyclopedia Americana* notes possible causes of dyslexia. . . .") In constructing your extended definition, do *not* deal with each article in turn. Rather, try to combine information from each source as you make your own points.

DYSLEXIA, dis-leks'ē-ə, a marked difficulty in learning to read. The term "dyslexia" is often applied to persons who habitually reverse the letters of words, reading "saw" for "was," for example; or reverse the letters themselves, reading "b" for "d" and "p" for "q." These people may also perceive words upside down as well as backward. For example, they may read the word "OIL" as the number "710."

Dyslexia is regarded by some authorities as a definite neurological or psychological disorder with characteristic symptoms and specifiable causes. Most of these authorities include the combination of illegible handwriting and poor spelling, together with average or above average intelligence, among the symptoms of dyslexia. Some include general dyssymbolia, the inability to formulate thoughts into language, as a symptom of dyslexia, and others limit dyslexic symptoms to problems of translating and combining symbols into concepts. Still others include as dyslexics poor readers who also have difficulties with hand-eye coordination. This poor coordination, they feel, accounts for the distorted handwriting, poor spelling, and evidence of neurological disorders that may be associated with dyslexia.

Among the causes suggested for dyslexia are brain damage and inherited neurological abnormalities not associated with brain damage. Environmental factors, such as poor teaching, are also regarded as possible causes.

Many researchers and practitioners question the use of the term "dyslexia." While they agree that individual symptoms and combinations of symptoms may exist in both good and poor readers, they still refuse to use the term for two reasons. First, few professionals seem to agree on the proper use of the term, and second, even when there is agreement, the term has little or no relevance to treatment. S. ALAN COHEN, *Yeshiva University*
(Encyclopedia Americana)

Dyslexia
(Congenital Word Blindness; Primary Reading Disability)

A condition in which an individual with normal vision is unable to interpret written language and therefore is unable to read. Educationally, the term is applied when a child of normal intelligence is 2 or more yr behind his expected grade level in reading. A family history of language disorders is common, and boys are affected more often than are girls. The cause is unknown, but a CNS [central nervous system] defect in the ability to organize graphic symbols has been postulated.

Alexia is a similar condition that develops later in life because of a neurologic lesion.

Symptoms and Signs

Dyslexic children are usually of normal or better intelligence. Their inability to read is inconsistent with their achievement in other school subjects, such as arithmetic. Spelling ability may or may not be impaired. Sensory deficits and neurologic impairment are absent. The child may be left-handed, right-handed, or ambidextrous, or dominance may be mixed.

Confusion in orientation of letters is the prime characteristic. This is manifested in reading from right to left, failure to see (and sometimes to hear) similarities or differences in letters or words, or inability to work out the pronunciation of unfamiliar words. Attempts to read or write are characterized by letter and word reversals (e.g., "p" for "g," "saw" for "was") that are typical of normal 1st- and 2nd-graders, but persist in the dyslexic child. A better-than-normal facility at mirror-reading or -writing is common.

In attempting to satisfy demands that he read, a dyslexic child may make up a story if the text contains a picture or may substitute words for those he cannot read. He may be able to vocalize words; i.e., to read aloud but without comprehension.

Symptoms of frustration are inevitable. The reading disability and its effects on learning and school performance may lead to behavioral problems, delinquency, aggression, withdrawal, and alienation from other children, parents, and teachers.

Diagnosis

Before dyslexia is diagnosed, the child with a reading problem must have thorough ophthalmic, auditory, psychologic, and neurologic examinations to verify that his poor reading is not due to some other disorder. Early diagnosis is important since the prognosis is much better if the defect can be identified and treated before a pattern of frustration and failure is established.

A battery of psychologic tests are used to provide a profile of the child's abilities and deficits. Commonly used tests include (1) the Illinois Test of Psycholinguistic Abilities (ITPA), which analyzes comprehension ("decoding") and use ("encoding") of auditory and visual symbols; (2) the Marianne Frostig Developmental Test of Visual Perception, which uses drawings to test and train eye-motor coordination and perception of figure-vs-ground, configuration, and spatial relationships; (3) the Wechsler Intelligence Scale for Children (WISC), which divides intelligence into verbal and performance aspects; and (4) the Durrell Analysis of Reading Difficulty, which tests numerous aspects of reading ability.

Treatment

Treatment is by remedial education since there is no known way to correct perceptual deficits. The psychologic test results help to identify the child's areas of strengths and weaknesses so that a suitable teaching program can be designed. Remedial steps are aimed at teaching around the problem, using the child's abilities and unimpaired capabilities to compensate for his areas of weakness. Thus, auditory perception may be emphasized for a child who has difficulty in comprehending purely visual symbols, for example by having him name and pronounce letters aloud as he traces them and, later, by having him read aloud instead of silently. (*The Merck Manual*, 13th ed.)

Dyslexia (from the Greek, *dys,* faulty, + *lexis,* speech, cognate with the Latin *legere,* to read), developmental or specific dyslexia as it's technically called, the disorder I suffered from, is the inability of otherwise normal children to read. Children whose intelligence is below average, whose vision or hearing is defective, who have not had proper schooling, or who are too emotionally disturbed or brain-damaged to profit from it belong in other diagnostic categories. They, too, may be unable to learn to read, but they cannot properly be called dyslexics.

For more than seventy years the essential nature of the affliction has been hotly disputed by psychologists, neurologists, and educators. It is generally agreed, however, that it is the result of a neurophysiological flaw in the brain's ability to process language. It is probably inherited, although some experts are reluctant to say this because they fear people will equate "inherited" with "untreatable." Treatable it certainly is: not a disease to be cured, but a malfunction that requires retraining.

Reading is the most complex skill a child entering school is asked to develop. What makes it complex, in part, is that letters are less constant than objects. A car seen from a distance, close to, from above, or below, or in a mirror still looks like a car even though the optical image changes. The letters of the alphabet are more whimsical. Take the letter *b.* Turned upside down it becomes a *p.* Looked at in a mirror, it becomes a *d.* Capitalized, it becomes something quite different, a *B.* The *M* upside down is a *W.* The *E* flipped over becomes Ǝ. This reversed *E* is familiar to mothers of normal children who have just begun to go to school. The earliest examples of art work they bring home often have I LOVƎ YOU written on them.

Dyslexics differ from other children in that they read, spell, and write letters upside down and turned around far more frequently and for a much longer time. In what seems like a capricious manner, they also add letters, syllables, and words, or, just as capriciously, delete them. With palindromic words (was–saw, on–no), it is the order of the letters rather than the orientation they change. The new word makes sense, but not the sense intended. Then there are other words where the changed order—"sorty" for story—does not make sense at all.

The inability to recognize that g, *g*, and G are the same letter, the inability to maintain the orientation of the letters, to retain the order in which they appear, and to follow a line of text without jumping above or below it—all the results of the flaw—can make of an orderly page of words a dish of alphabet soup.

Also essential for reading is the ability to store words in memory and to retrieve them. This very particular kind of memory dyslexics lack. So, too, do they lack the ability to hear what the eye sees, and to see what they hear. If the eye sees "off," the ear must hear "off" and not "of," or "for." If the ear hears "saw," the eye must see that it looks like "saw" on the page and not "was." Lacking these skills, a sentence or paragraph becomes a coded message to which the dyslexic can't find the key.

It is only a slight exaggeration to say that those who learned to read without difficulty can best understand the labor reading is for a dyslexic by turning a page of text upside down and trying to decipher it. (Eileen Simpson, *Reversals: A Personal Account of Victory over Dyslexia*)

SUGGESTED TOPICS FOR DEFINITION ESSAYS

1.   Select a term or concept that is central to an understanding of a unit of study in one of your courses other than English composition. Write a five-hundred-word definition essay explaining the term to someone who has not yet taken the course.

2.   Choose a word that has a strong emotional meaning for almost everyone—a word like "patriotism" or "communism"—and interview five people from different age groups and backgrounds, asking each what the term means. Use their responses to write a definition essay developed by a series of examples.

CHAPTER

5

Writing
Paragraphs

A paragraph is a unit of thought composed of sentences, smaller units of thought, that relate to a single topic. Paragraph divisions serve two very useful functions. First, they provide readers with breaks which relieve the tedium of page after page of unbroken text. Second, well-conceived paragraphs group sentences into easily understood units. In an essay, sentences are organized in paragraphs, each of which presents one segment of a general controlling idea. Because each paragraph covers a recognizable unit of thought, paragraphing serves as an important signal to your readers. On the other hand, rambling paragraphs, erratic paragraphing, or pointless single sentence paragraphs confuse your readers and obscure your ideas.

THE PARAGRAPH AS PART OF AN ESSAY

One way of looking at a paragraph is to see it as part of a longer piece of writing. With the exception of those written to express private feelings, most essays explain or present information to a reader. These essays require a constant interplay between your thesis, which presents the central statement of your paper, and your body paragraphs, which enable you to explore the promise of your thesis. Making sure that this interaction takes place helps you write a clear and internally consistent essay.

Let's examine an essay, "The American T Party." Notice how the thesis presents the main idea of the essay and how each body paragraph explores an idea related to the main topic.

The American T Party

1   From Waikiki to Wall Street, men, women and children of all vintages, shapes and inclinations are finding a new way to get something off their chests—by putting it on them. They are doing so decked out—and frequently spaced out—in versions of the old World War II T shirt. Underwear elevated to glamour, the current Model T has suddenly become the hottest fashion trend in the U.S. It might be called the dress-to-express vogue.

2   In infinite variety, the new T shirts are printed to order by the thousands with a picture or slogan that reflects the wearer's whims and wheezes, concerns, complaints, sentiments (SHARING MAKES YOU SMILE INSIDE), politics, and anything else he or she may want to proclaim, profess or promote. Thanks to novel techniques, notably a fast-heat pressure press that can transfer to a T shirt any picture, design or message in full color, major department stores such as Manhattan's Macy's and Chicago's Carson Pirie Scott and hundreds of small T shops across the country let buyers pick from an almost limitless selection of designs and sayings—or fashion their own.

3   On a beach in Long Island's with-it Hamptons, one comely lady last week sported a shirt labeled simply VAN CLEEF & ARPELS—a Fifth Avenue gem dispensary—explaining that her husband had bought it in place of "other merchandise from there." Superstar Paul Newman's T advises: DRINK WET CEMENT . . . GET REALLY STONED. Indeed, with the likes of Joanne Woodward (wearing husband Paul's face centered on her front), Yoko Ono, Carly Simon and an Alabama comedienne and L.A. talk-show regular who cottons to a replica of a fried egg on each well-poached breast, show-biz bashes these days seem mostly T parties.

4   The biggest influence in the shirt spurt is a year-old Manhattan company cryptically called J.B.T.* Chroma. Through thousands of stores, it has sold more than 1.5 million pop shirts. Like other companies in the business, J.B.T.C. sells shirts, equipment and several hundred heat transfers to stores. Customers can choose for their chests old magazine covers, orange-crate labels from the '20's (JUCIFUL), paintings,

---

* Named "for good luck" after John Beresford Tipton, the character in the 1950s *The Millionaire* TV series who gave away $1 million a week.

cartoons, 1940s line drawings of stars Charles Boyer, Judy Garland and Errol Flynn and any number of messages that invite massage, including a picture of a stallion labeled STUD. And there are Ts for two: couples may wear matching shirts, or proclaim their love with HIS and HERS (or even more visibly in San Francisco, HIS and HIS).

5   Why the vogue for underwear turned outer? For one thing, Ts are relatively cheap (ranging from $3.25 to a top of $14.95); they also eliminate ties and the button crunching of laundries. And as Eloise Laws, 28, a black show-biz beauty shopping on Long Island, put it, "I chose the design, the color, the style. I feel like I created this one myself."

6   A passing fad? Not according to the Gimbels chain (67 stores), whose main Manhattan store sells more than 1,000 imprints a week. The chain, says one executive, will stay with the T "forever." Fashions are never forever, but this one, while it lasts, should have a run of fun.

Time Magazine

The relationships among ideas in this essay become clear when you isolate the specific assertions made in each paragraph.

¶ 1   *Thesis:*   The T shirt has suddenly become the hottest fashion trend in the United States.

¶ 2   *Supporting idea plus examples:*   T shirts can be printed in infinite variety to express any idea.

¶ 3   *More examples:*   Support for the idea in paragraph 2 (woman with Van Cleef & Arpels shirt, Paul Newman, Joanne Woodward, Yoko Ono, etc.).

¶ 4   *Another supporting idea plus examples:*   J.B.T. Chroma is the biggest influence on the market.

As this brief analysis illustrates, the paragraphs in an essay are not separate units of thought. The first body paragraph develops one element of the thesis and sets the stage for the material in the following paragraph. Each paragraph extends the ideas that came before it, and each foreshadows the ideas that come after it. Paragraphs in essays are units of thought that overlap and interact with one another in specific ways to present information. Each paragraph contributes something to the overall message of the essay.

Often the first words of each paragraph indicate the relationship of that paragraph to the overall idea. They link the paragraphs together. Such phrases include:

The first reason . . .	The point is . . .
The second reason . . .	But of course . . .
The third reason . . .	For this reason . . .
Finally . . .	A number of people . . .
Now . . .	On the one hand . . .

Then . . .   On the other hand . . .
In the future . . .   Therefore . . .

(For more on linking ideas within and between paragraphs, see "Coherence,"
page 112.)

THE PARAGRAPH AS A GROUP OF SENTENCES

You can also see a paragraph as a group of sentences, all of which focus on a single
subject. The main idea of the paragraph often appears in a *topic sentence*, usually
located at or near the beginning of the paragraph.

> *A Hindoo temple is a conglomeration of adornment.* The lines of the building are
> completely hidden by the decorations. Sculptured figures and ornaments crowd its
> surface, stand out from it in thick masses, break it up into a bewildering series of
> irregular tiers. It is not a unity but a collection, rich, confused. It looks like some-
> thing not planned but built this way and that as the ornament required. The convic-
> tion underlying it can be perceived: each bit of exquisitely wrought detail had a
> mystical meaning and the temple's exterior was important only as a means for the
> artist to ascribe thereon the symbols of the truth. It is decoration, not architecture.
>
> Edith Hamilton, *The Greek Way*

Hamilton begins with a topic sentence asserting that a Hindu temple is elaborately
adorned. The rest of her paragraph supports this with a series of descriptive examples.

You can examine the ebb and flow of ideas in a paragraph by charting them. As
you look at the paragraph's underlying structure, you can see how each sentence
contributes to the central idea. Put the topic sentence of a paragraph first and
mark it with a "1." Then read each of the other sentences. If a sentence has the
same weight of ideas or the same level of generality, assign it the same level and
number. If a sentence contains more specific ideas, indent it and give it a "2." If
a sentence has even more detailed content, indent it further and give it a "3." And
so on. Do this for every sentence in the paragraph.

The following student paragraph illustrates the way you set up this kind of
paragraph analysis.

1 There are a number of characteristics that most games have in common.
   2 Most games are engaged in freely and are not obligatory.
   2 They exist within time and space limits that are defined in advance.
   2 The course of a game is uncertain, allowing for player initiative and innova-
      tion.
   2 Games are unproductive, creating no new elements of any kind, just resulting
      in the exchange of property among players.
   2 Games are make-believe and are set against the conventions of real life.
   2 Finally, games are governed by rules that suspend ordinary rules of behavior.

Stephen Lerner

We see that this paragraph has a *coordinate pattern* of development—all of the sentences after the first carry the same weight and stand in the same relation to one another. The topic sentence (level 1) introduces the general idea, and each succeeding sentence (level 2) offers specific, equal instances or illustrations of that idea.

Paragraphs may also use a *subordinate pattern;* that is, each sentence may be subordinate to the one immediately preceding it. The following paragraph illustrates this pattern:

1 Supporters of the powerful landowners called themselves "samurai."
  2 This term can be roughly translated as "those who serve."
    3 "Samurai" comes from the verbs "samurau" or "saburan" which mean "to serve."
      4 The original meaning of "samurai" may seem to have no military connotation, but the definition of the word changes considerably through Japanese history.

S. R. Turnbull, The Samurai

In this paragraph the topic sentence presents the main idea. The next sentence (level 2) is subordinate to the first, translating the term "samurai," which is used in sentence 1. The following sentences, levels 3 and 4, zero in further on this term. Number 3 tells what verbs "samurai" comes from, and number 4 gets even more specific, commenting on the original meaning of the word.

But many times ideas do not fall into neat packages, and paragraphs cannot be purely coordinate or subordinate. Instead you *mix these patterns,* as this student does in a job application letter.

1 I would like to be considered for the position of computer operator you advertised in the *Philadelphia Inquirer* on Sunday, July 28.
  2 I have relevant knowledge of several computer languages.
    3 During the past three years I have taken courses in COBOL and FORTRAN.
    3 Presently I am developing proficiency in APL, BAL, and Assembler language.
  2 My employment experience also qualifies me for this job.
    3 I am currently employed by the Philadelphia National Bank as a lead operator.
    3 Prior to this I worked as an operator for Electronic Data Systems, Camp Hill, Pennsylvania.
      4 Here I obtained a wide variety of JCL experience on the IBM 370/3033 MVS.
        5 This experience prepared me for the time I spent as a JCC analyst and a shift supervisor.

Franklyn Williams

Checking the structure of your paragraphs helps you uncover sentences that stray from your logic. By charting these patterns, you can identify problems that may escape you if you just reread your paragraphs. Franklyn, for example, could easily have gotten sidetracked discussing his courses in COBOL. But any departure from the logic of his presentation would have become apparent when he charted his paragraph pattern.

WRITING EFFECTIVE PARAGRAPHS

As our discussion so far indicates, paragraphs can vary quite a bit. Even so, all effective expository paragraphs have three characteristics in common:

- They are unified.
- They are coherent.
- They are complete.

UNITY

To be effective and easily understood, a paragraph should focus on a single idea and develop it. Without such focus, without being about one clear thing, a paragraph drifts apart in loosely related sentences.

In stating the main idea of your paragraph, your *topic sentence* acts as a constant reminder of your main idea. It makes your intention clear to yourself and your readers. Our advice to you as beginning writers is to lead off your paragraphs with strong topic sentences. Using your topic sentence as a guide, you can make sure that all of the sentences in your paragraph connect to your central idea. Notice how this focus is achieved in the following paragraph.

> *Gutenberg, who is credited with inventing the printing press, was not the first to grasp the need for, and the potentialities of, large-scale production of literature.* On the contrary, his invention was largely prompted by the fact that the multiplication of texts was not only a general want but had, by the middle of the fifteenth century, become a recognizable and lucrative trade. Professional scribes catered for the wealthy collector of classical manuscripts as well as for the poor student who needed his legal and theological handbooks. The Florentine bookseller Vesagasiano de Bisticci employed up to fifty scribes at a time; in the university towns, of which Paris was the most important, the copyists were numerous enough to form themselves into guilds. The religious congregation of the Brethren of the Common Life in Deventer specialized in copying philosophical and theological books for which they established a market all over northern Europe. Diebold Lauber ran a veritable "book factory" in the Alsatian town of Hagenau; he, like any later publisher, produced books for the open market; "light reading" was Lauber's specialty, and illustrations, also produced by rote, added to the popular appeal.
>
> S. H. Steinberg, *Five Hundred Years of Printing*

The topic sentence of this paragraph sums up in advance the ideas that the paragraph develops. After saying that Gutenberg was not the first to think of the need for large-scale production of the printed word, the paragraph goes on to present supporting data. Each sentence expands the initial assertion by giving examples of other fifteenth-century book producers who catered to the public's desire for books. None of the sentences in this paragraph distracts readers with irrelevant information. The unity of the paragraph comes from the direct connection of each individual sentence to the topic sentence.

When you reread and revise your paragraphs, you must edit out sentences that do not have the same focus as your topic or that do not fill in or advance the idea of your paragraph. Digressions, fuzzy thinking, and wrong connections tell your readers that you don't know what you want to say. A number of sentences in the following paragraph wander off the topic.

> (1) *Nuclear power is the third major source of energy that can be substantially increased in the next twenty years.* (2) The amount of nuclear capacity that can be installed is fairly certain. (3) Building nuclear installations in some countries requires only half the time we require in the United States. (4) There is no reason why nuclear construction here could not proceed faster. (5) Even taking safety factors into consideration, we could cut construction time in half by eliminating much of the red tape that is part of the Nuclear Regulatory Commission's procedure. (6) There is much more exploration for uranium going on now at price levels of $40 per pound than there was when the price was $6 per pound. (7) These increased reserves, combined with self-generating breeder reactors, could do a lot to ensure that we will have enough domestic power to make us energy independent within the next fifty years.

This paragraph begins by saying that nuclear power can be substantially increased in the next twenty years. The second sentence continues this idea, saying that the amount of increase is fairly certain. Sentence 3, however, shifts to the problem of constructing nuclear reactors. This digression continues in sentences 4 and 5. Sentence 6 shifts the focus again to uranium reserves, and this idea is developed further in sentence 7. Because the paragraph lacks unity, it is extremely difficult to follow.

When you chart the underlying structure of this paragraph, its problems become quite clear.

1 Nuclear power is the third major source of energy that can be substantially increased in the next twenty years.
  2 The amount of nuclear capacity that can be installed is fairly certain.
1 Building nuclear installations in some countries requires only half the time we require in the United States.
  2 There is no reason why nuclear construction here could not proceed faster.
    3 Even taking safety factors into consideration, we could cut construction time in half by eliminating much of the red tape that is part of the Nuclear Regulatory Commission's procedure.

1   There is much more exploration for uranium going on now at price levels of $40 per pound than there was when the price was $6 per pound.
2   These increased reserves, combined with self-generating breeder reactors, could do a lot to ensure that we will have enough domestic power to make us energy independent within the next fifty years.

This paragraph has *three* topics, not one. Each level 1 sentence represents a topic that should be developed in its own paragraph. The writer has made a series of false starts, or departures from the main idea of the paragraph. As readers progress, they sense this lack of unity and wonder just what the main idea is.

Careful revision brings the ideas of this paragraph into focus. The student has to decide which of his three separate ideas should be his main idea. If, for instance, this paragraph is about the fact that nuclear power can be increased over the next twenty years, then all its sentences should focus on that idea. Talk about nuclear construction and breeder reactors must come out, and only details relevant to the central idea should stay in. A revision of this paragraph would look like this:

Nuclear power is the third major source of energy supply that can be substantially increased in the next ten to twenty years. The amount of nuclear capacity that can be installed is fairly certain. For example, increasing capacity up to the limits of our production would allow us to double our energy-generating capability within ten years. At this rate, we would be able to generate a substantial amount of our electrical power requirements by the year 2000. Research is now going forward on ways of increasing reactor safety and efficiency, so we can assume that these predictions could be conservative. For the sake of accuracy, however, we will limit our discussion to technology that is already in hand. It is fair to say that even with the figures we have just quoted, nuclear power can help the United States maintain its leadership role in the world and have a positive effect on the balance of payments.

A paragraph without a topic sentence must also be unified. The following paragraph has no topic sentence, but it consistently develops the point that Julius Caesar was an extraordinary person who could do many things at once. Notice that each sentence contributes to this central idea by adding new examples of Caesar's versatility and talent.

In light, four-wheeled carriages, bumping and jolting along highly imperfect roads and tracks, Caesar would cover a hundred miles a day, twice the pace of an average traveller. And while he was on his way he did not just look out at the countryside; for he composed a two volume work *On Analogy* during a crossing of the Alps, and a poem "The Journey" on an exhausting twenty-seven-day land journey from Rome to southern Spain. These works, if he wrote them down in person, had to be composed in daytime, since the light cannot have been good enough to write after dark. But perhaps he dictated them, because he often spent the nights in his carriage or litter, so as to be able to get on with his work. "I have heard," reported the elder Pliny, "that Caesar was accustomed to write or dictate and read at the same time, simultaneously dictating to his secretaries four letters on the most important subjects or, if he had nothing else to do, as many as seven." He also spent a great deal of time on his judicial duties, administering justice with the utmost conscientiousness and strictness. And yet . . . he also managed to make himself as accessible as he could.

Michael Grant, The Twelve Caesars

EXERCISES

1. Read each of the following paragraphs and determine whether it is unified. Decide what the central idea of the paragraph is, and determine whether all of the sentences in the paragraph relate to that idea. Be prepared to discuss your conclusions.

a. The best way to inform our stockholders of a decrease in dividends is to inform them of our need for new well and storage facilities. The existing sources are now insufficient for our future needs and have to be increased. By the next decade we will have an increased demand for fuel and wells pumping at 50 percent of their present rate. Ground-water studies have shown that deeper sources exist, and our engineers feel that the cost of drilling would be more than offset by the future cost of water. Therefore it would be to the advantage of our stockholders to absorb a short-term decrease in profit for a long-term increase in dividends. (Rose Sulbiger, student)

b. The boardwalk, one of Atlantic City's chief attractions, was inspired by a hotel owner who was tired of having his hotel dirtied by bathers returning from the beach. The first Easter parade was held in 1876. In 1944 a hurricane with eighty-five-mile-an-hour winds washed away most of the boardwalk. The constant friction of feet plus sand erosion can wear out a section of boardwalk in twelve years. (Thomas Carr, student)

c. These sprays, dusts and aerosols are now applied almost universally to farms, gardens, forests, and homes—nonselective chemicals that have the power to kill every insect, the "good" and the "bad," to still the song of birds and the leaping of fish in the streams, to coat the leaves with a deadly film, and to linger on in soil—all this though the intended target may be only a few weeds or insects. Can anyone believe it is possible to lay down such a barrage of poisons on the surface without making it unfit for all life? They should not be called "insecticides," but "biocides." (Rachel Carson, Silent Spring)

d. They stood on the deck as the ancient, rusty ship that had been their home and ark for seventeen days wore into Ellis Island—shoulder to shoulder, cheek to jowl. Everyone was on deck, the old and the young, screaming children, weeping babies, the silent, the terrified, the sick, the hopeful, nationalities and tongues in a flux of tears and laughter. The great lady of hope welcomed them, and this they had been waiting to see. The Eighth Wonder of the World. "Give me your tired, your poor, your huddled masses yearning to breathe free." In five tongues the statistics floated over the babble of sound. She is a hundred and fifty-two feet high and she weighs two hundred and twenty-five tons. Yes, you can stand up there in the torch at the very end of her arm. Across the water, there was the mass of buildings on the Battery, but the lady of liberty was something else. (Howard Fast, The Immigrants)

e. Henry James's story The Turn of the Screw has baffled many critics. The story focuses upon the efforts of a governess to save her charges, Miles and Flora, from the ghosts of a former governess and her lover. Moved by her concern for the children, the governess throws herself like a screen between the children and the ghosts. It is debatable whether the children are indeed possessed. The boy, Miles, dies (presumably of fright) and the girl, Flora, is driven into a delirium which threatens her health and sanity. Even so, the governess can be seen as an agent of good setting herself against unmitigated evil. (Carol Browne, student)

2.   Choose two of the above paragraphs and chart the underlying structures of each. See if the conclusions you reached in exercise 1 are borne out.

COHERENCE

Just as topic sentences help readers follow your ideas, other signals also help them understand what you have to say. Beginning writers often disregard the need to signal relationships between their sentences. But it is up to you as a writer to make the connections between your ideas clear to your readers. When you write and when you revise, look for the areas that seem choppy or unconnected—that lack coherence. You can establish better coherence by using the following devices: *pronoun reference, repetition,* and *transitional devices words and phrases.*

☐   COHERENCE THROUGH PRONOUN REFERENCE

Because pronouns refer back to their antecedents, they establish bridges from one sentence to another. Well-placed, clear pronoun references serve as guideposts that lead readers through your paragraphs. Notice in the following paragraph how pronouns referring to their antecedents draw the sentences of the paragraph together and emphasize major points in the discussion.

> Clearly, if smallpox had not come when it did, the Spanish victory could not have been achieved in Mexico. The same was true of Pizarro's filibuster into Peru. For the smallpox epidemic in Mexico did not confine its ravages to Aztec territory. Instead it spread to Guatemala, where it appeared in 1520, and continued southward, penetrating the Inca domain in 1525 or 1526. Consequences there were just as drastic as among the Aztecs. The reigning Inca died of the disease while away from his capital on campaign in the North. His designated heir also died, leaving no legitimate successor. Civil war ensued, and it was amid the wreckage of the Inca political structure that Pizarro and his crew of rough-necks made their way to Cuzco and plundered its treasures. He met no serious military resistance at all.
>
> William H. McNeill, Plagues and People

The use of pronouns which point back to their antecedents creates coherence in this paragraph. "The same" in line 2 refers to the part smallpox played in the Spanish victory in Mexico and connects this idea to Pizarro's conquest of Peru. Throughout the rest of the passage, pronouns tie sentences together and make the connections between ideas clear to readers.

When you revise a paragraph for coherence, you should make sure that pronouns tie together major points in your discussion. Some words of caution are in order, however. Pronoun reference works only when it is not ambiguous. Inexact references confuse your readers and make your writing incoherent. Make sure that your pronouns refer clearly to a single antecedent. For example, when using the pronoun "this," include a word that specifies its antecedent: "this *situation*," "this *person*," or "this *place*." And make sure that no pronoun is separated from its antecedent by more than one sentence and that you don't use a pronoun over and over again without periodically restating its antecedent. Remember, you cannot expect your readers to keep the antecedent of a pronoun in mind indefinitely. Without repetition and reinforcement, they will lose sight of it.

☐ COHERENCE THROUGH REPETITION

The repetition of certain words and phrases can effectively create a pattern of reader expectation. Carefully used, repetition emphasizes important ideas in your paragraph. In the following paragraph from his speech "I Have a Dream," Martin Luther King, Jr., repeats the phrase "one hundred years later" to emphasize important ideas. In using this device, he underscores conditions that he feels define the lives of blacks in America.

> But one hundred years later, we must face the tragic fact that the Negro is still not free. One hundred years later, the life of the Negro is still sadly crippled by the manacles of segregation and the chains of discrimination. One hundred years later, the Negro lives on a lonely island of poverty in the midst of a vast ocean of material prosperity. One hundred years later, the Negro is still languishing in the corners of American society and finds himself an exile in his own land.

When we chart the sentences in this paragraph, we see how repetition relates the examples in the paragraph to the topic sentence.

1   But *one hundred years later,* we must face the tragic fact that the Negro is still not free.
   2   *One hundred years later,* the life of the Negro is still sadly crippled by the manacles of segregation and the chains of discrimination.
   2   *One hundred years later,* the Negro lives on a lonely island of poverty in the midst of a vast ocean of material prosperity.
   2   *One hundred years later,* the Negro is still languishing in the corners of American society and finds himself an exile in his own land.

Repetition doesn't have to be this dramatic or this obvious to work on your reader. In this journalistic paragraph, for instance, the careful repetition of key words like "architect" and "museum" helps the audience follow the line of thought without calling attention to the writer's strategy.

> As a supreme test of the *architect,* the American *museum* now ranks with the cathedral and the skyscraper. Since the end of World War II, American *architects* have probably designed and built more *museums* than ever before existed in the entire world. The "public" *museum* is a comparatively recent phenomenon, dating only

from the French Revolution when the new government invited the people in to look at the royal art treasures. Following that example, the first *museums* in Europe were mainly reconverted palaces. In the United States, however, the *museum* became something else—a Hydra-headed civic monument. The *architect* was asked to provide at once a dignified external presence, radiant interior galleries, restaurants, bookstores and theaters. In the 1960s and '70s, when "image" counted most of all, the cream of America's *architects*—Marcel Breuer, I. M. Pei, Kevin Roche—turned out one such dramatic monolith after another, from the massive Whitney *Museum* of American Art in New York to the spectacular East Wing of the National Gallery in Washington, D.C.

Newsweek

This device of repeating key words or phrases, whether used subtly or emphatically, can be extremely helpful in linking sentences and giving coherence to a particular paragraph. But repetition is only effective when it highlights your main ideas and makes your reader's job easier. Careless repetition, repetition without a purpose, clutters your writing with useless words and phrases. In unskilled hands, repetition probably creates more problems than it solves. As a beginning writer, you should use this technique very carefully—possibly only with your instructor's help.

□ COHERENCE THROUGH TRANSITIONAL WORDS AND PHRASES

Transitional words and phrases show the relationship of one sentence or clause to another. These signals speed up your reader's understanding and tie together ideas before your reader has a chance to forget them. Here is a list of some commonly used transitional expressions.

Words that signal addition

and	moreover
again	next
also	one . . . another
besides	last
finally	in addition
furthermore	

Words that signal time

at first, second, etc.	former—latter
soon	afterward
before	at length
after	immediately
finally	meanwhile
then	in the meantime
later	until
next	

Words that signal comparison

however	instead
but	on the one hand . . .
yet	on the other hand
still	in contrast
nonetheless	although
on the contrary	meanwhile
nevertheless	

Words that signal examples

for example	to illustrate
for instance	the following example

Words that signal conclusions or summaries

in summary	consequently
in conclusion	in other words
to conclude	thus
therefore	as a result

Words that signal concession

although it is true that	although you could say that
granted	of course
naturally	

Consider the following paragraph:

> The boat Baddibu vibrated upriver, with me acutely tense: Were these Africans maybe viewing me as but another of the pith helmets? We put in at James Island, for me to see the ruins of the once British-operated James Fort. Two centuries of slave ships had loaded thousands of cargoes of Gambian tribespeople. The crumbling stones, the deeply oxidized swivel cannon, even some remnant links of chain seemed all but impossible to believe. We continued upriver to the left-bank village of Albreda, and there put ashore to continue on foot to Juffure, village of the *Griot* [oral historian]. We stopped for me to see *Toubob Kolong,* "The White Man's well," almost filled in, in a swampy area with abundant, tall, saw-toothed grass. It was dug to "17 men's height deep" to insure survival drinking water for long-driven, vanishing coffles of slaves.

Although the main idea of this paragraph is clear—it describes a trip up an African river—the sequence of events is not. The sentences offer no signals to establish relationships among events. In many respects this paragraph reads like a list. Of course a reader could, with some difficulty, guess at the connections between ideas. But in effective writing, you must anticipate your reader's needs and meet them before they arise. The following version of this passage provides the cues that signal the sequence of events in time.

The boat Baddibu vibrated upriver, with me acutely tense: Were these Africans maybe viewing me as but another of the pith helmets? *After about two hours,* we put in at James Island, for me to see the ruins of the once British-operated James Fort. *Here* two centuries of slave ships had loaded thousands of cargoes of Gambian tribespeople. The crumbling stones, the deeply oxidized swivel cannon, even some remnant links of chain seemed all but impossible to believe. *Then* we continued upriver to the left-bank village of Albreda, and then put ashore to continue on foot to Juffure, village of the *Griot. Once more* we stopped, for me to see *Toubob Kolong,* "The White Man's well," *now* almost filled in, in a swampy area with abundant, tall, saw-toothed grass. It was dug *two centuries ago* to "17 men's height deep" to insure survival drinking water for long-driven, vanishing coffles of slaves.

Alex Haley, "My Furthest Back Person: The African"

This paragraph illustrates how transitional words and phrases establish coherence between sentences. Words and phrases like "after about two hours," "here," "then," "once more," "now," and "two centuries ago" provide the links that set a chronological pattern for the passage.

☐ COHERENCE BETWEEN PARAGRAPHS

The same three methods that establish coherence within paragraphs can also help you link separate paragraphs together. Pronoun reference, repetition of key words and phrases, and transitional devices also work to establish coherence between paragraphs in an essay. The following three paragraphs use these strategies well:

1   Those of us who grew up in the fifties believed in the permanence of our American-history textbooks. To us as children, those texts were the truth of things: they were American history. It was not just that we read them before we understood that not everything that is printed is the truth, or the whole truth. It was that they, much more than other books, had the demeanor and trappings of authority. They were weighty volumes. They spoke in measured cadences: imperturbable, humorless, and as distant as Chinese emperors. Our teachers treated them with respect, and we paid them abject homage by memorizing a chapter a week. But now the textbook histories have changed, some of them to such an extent that an adult would find them unrecognizable.

2   One current junior-high-school American history begins with a story about a Negro cowboy called George McJunkin. It appears that when McJunkin was riding down a lonely trail in New Mexico one cold spring morning in 1925 he discovered a mound containing bones and stone implements, which scientists later proved belonged to an Indian civilization ten thousand years old. The book goes on to say that scientists now believe there were people in the Americas at least twenty thousand years ago. It discusses the Aztec, Mayan, and Incan civilizations and the meaning of the word "culture" before introducing the European explorers.

3   Another history text—this one for the fifth grade—begins with the story of how Henry B. Gonzalez, who is a member of Congress from Texas, learned about his own nationality. When he was ten years old, his teacher told him he was an American because he was born in the United States. His grandmother, however, said,

"The cat was born in the oven. Does that make him bread?" After reporting that Mr. Gonzalez eventually went to college and law school, the book explains that "the melting pot idea hasn't worked out as some thought it would," and that now "some people say that the people of the United States are more like a salad bowl than a melting pot."

Frances FitzGerald, History Revised

These paragraphs form a very tightly knit unit. Each topic sentence includes a variation of the phrase "history textbooks," which appears in paragraph 1. In addition, transitional words at the beginning of paragraphs 2 and 3 ("*one* current . . . history"; "*another* history text"), along with repeated words and phrases, tell you that the author is presenting a series of examples. By setting up a pattern of expectation and by repeating key concepts, FitzGerald leads her readers through her discussion.

¶ 1   Those of us who grew up in the fifties believed in the permanence of our American-history *textbooks*.

¶ 2   *One* current junior-high-school American history *begins with a story*. . . .

¶ 3   *Another* history text—this one for the fifth grade—*begins with a story*. . . .

Not only does the repetition of key words keep readers focused on the topic, the transitional phrases that signal examples remind readers of the essay's pattern.

EXERCISES

---

1.   Read the essays you have written so far and choose a paragraph in which you have used transitions. Underline all the transitional elements, and rewrite it, if necessary, to improve coherence.

2.   Rearrange the following sentences into a coherent paragraph. Add a topic sentence and supply transitions. Remember, your topic sentence should provide a focus, and your sentences should reflect this focus.

Live machine-gun bullets are no longer used in basic training.
The bayonet, which caused training injuries, is a thing of the past.
Trainees use ear plugs to protect them from noise during shooting practice.
K.P., a standard form of punishment years ago, has passed out of existence.
Civilian contractors are hired to do dirty work.
Barracks life is tolerable.
Recruits live in carpeted cubicles with only three men or women for each latrine.
There are free washing machines in the barracks.
New uniforms require no ironing.

3.   Read each of the following paragraphs carefully. Then, identify the principal device or devices that make each paragraph coherent. Finally, underline the specific words or phrases that contribute to each paragraph's coherence.

a.   From despotisms like the Soviet Union the only voices that tell one anything are the voices of private life. These distinguish the sporadic correspondence of Olga Freidenberg with her first cousin Boris Pasternak between 1910 and 1954. She was in Leningrad, he mostly in Moscow. Forty-five years of this harassed exchange of news and affection come out of their cold envelopes and bring us close to the dire and confusing realities of their time. The cousins were born in 1890 in distinguished and cultivated families who were assimilated Jews. (One can guess at their hopeful childhood and youth in Pasternak's early writings.) We see them first in 1910 and—after the long gap of the First World War—in touch with each other again through the Second World War and the Stalinist terror, until 1954, the year before she died. (V. S. Pritchett, *New York Review of Books*)

b.   Law is never so necessary as when it has no ethical significance whatever, and is pure law for the sake of law. The law that compels me to keep to the left when driving along Oxford Street is ethically senseless, as is shown by the fact that keeping to the right answers equally well in Paris; and it certainly destroys my freedom to choose my side; but by enabling me to count on everyone else keeping to the left also, thus making traffic possible and safe, it enlarges my life and sets my mind free for nobler issues. Most laws, in short, are not the expression of the ethical verdicts of the community, but pure etiquet and nothing else. (George Bernard Shaw, *The Sanity of Art*)

c.   It is time for the baby's birthday party: a white cake, strawberry-marshmallow ice cream, a bottle of champagne saved from another party. In the evening, after she has gone to sleep, I kneel beside the crib and touch her face, where it is pressed against the slats, with mine. She is an open and trusting child, unprepared for and unaccustomed to the ambushes of family life, and perhaps it is just as well that I can offer her little of that life. I would like to give her more. I would like to promise her that she will grow up with a sense of her cousins and of rivers and of her great-grandmother's teacups, would like to pledge her a picnic on a river with fried chicken and her hair uncombed, would like to give her *home* for her birthday, but we live differently now and I can promise her nothing like that. I give her a xylophone and a sundress from Madeira, and promise to tell her a funny story. (Joan Didion, "On Going Home")

COMPLETENESS: PROVIDING ENOUGH SUPPORT

One of the basic ways we have of explaining a concept or proving a point is to illustrate it with examples—specific points that make a general statement clear. Examples also add interest and persuade an audience that what you are saying is reasonable or valid. The way you support your assertions enables your readers to understand exactly what you are trying to say. Your paragraphs should be complete enough to explain and justify your topic sentences and to support the thesis of the whole essay. Consider the following paragraph.

> Those who have not grown up with computers generally find them more frightening than those who have. The growing use in North America of small computers has helped reduce this sense of strangeness. In another decade, however, computers will be a perfectly natural part of our lives.

The writer says that computers are intimidating to those who are not familiar with them. He alludes to the fact that people use computers more and more, but he doesn't develop this idea. He says that soon computers will be a part of people's lives, but he doesn't explain how or how much. Now look at this version of the paragraph:

> Those who have not grown up with computers generally find them more frightening than those who have. The legendary manic biller who will not take no—or even yes—for an answer, and who can be satisfied only by receiving a check for zero dollars and zero cents is not to be considered representative of the entire tribe; it is a feeble-minded computer to begin with, and its mistakes are those of its human programmers. The growing use in North America of integrated circuits and small computers for aircraft safety, teaching machines, cardiac pacemakers, electronic games, smoke-actuated fire alarms and automated factories, to name only a few uses, has helped greatly to reduce the sense of strangeness with which so novel an invention is usually invested. There are some 200,000 digital computers in the world today; in another decade, there are likely to be tens of millions. In another generation . . . computers will be treated as a perfectly natural—or at least commonplace—aspect of our lives.
>
> Carl Sagan, *The Dragons of Eden*

Sagan uses examples to support his main idea that the growing use of computers in this country will help reduce their strangeness. His details are well-chosen, calculated to convince a general audience that his conclusions are reasonable. This paragraph not only develops its main idea adequately; it also contributes to Sagan's larger thesis that computers, despite their capabilities, are nonetheless just extensions of the human mind. Notice also that even though Carl Sagan is a scientist and probably knows a great deal about his subject, he has not provided too much information. He realizes that for his readers an overabundance of detail could be as troublesome as too little.

Unfortunately, no hard-and-fast rule defines what is "enough" support. Whether you use one or a number of examples depends on how much or how little you have claimed in your topic sentence. Sometimes a single *extended example* provides all the information or insight you need to make your point. In the following paragraph the writer employs an extended example to illustrate his assertion that the influence of aggressiveness on hormone secretion and sexual behavior reaches its peak in the case of a certain tropical fish. Notice that, in this paragraph, a single example gives us sufficient detail to accept the author's limited contention.

> The influence of aggressiveness and dominance on hormones and sex reaches its peak in the case of a small tropical fish called "cleaners," which feed off parasites that they remove from the skin of other fish. One species, studied on the Australian Great Barrier Reef, lives in groups of one male with a harem of three to six females; the male dominates the females, and the larger, older females dominate the smaller, younger ones. If the male dies or is removed from the group, the largest of the females almost immediately begins to act like a male, carrying out typical male aggressive displays toward the other females. And within a couple of weeks *she*

actually turns into a male, producing sperm instead of eggs! I am not suggesting, of course, that anything of the sort could occur in primates or other mammals; for one thing, most or all cleaner-fish females possess rudimentary testes, as mammalian females do not. Nonetheless, I find rather mind-blowing the fact that a female can change into a male simply by acting like one.

Robert Claiborne, "Evolution and Evil"

More often, you need more than one example to illustrate an idea. In the following paragraph the writer uses several short examples to support his general assertion.

Movies have come a long way from the early days, when cameras were as big as pianos and film emulsions captured only the most basic images, to the present-day lightweight portability of most equipment and the fastest emulsions and processing techniques. Today, kids experiment with super 8mm cameras in their back-yards. College students major in film courses on a countrywide basis, where only a few years ago serious film study was limited to a few campuses, and even then was further limited by a dying industry in which few students could expect employment and by equipment which had still not sufficiently advanced to afford the portability so necessary to the amateur film industry. Now the independent film industry is growing in rather unpredictable ways and some of its products which reach the screen bear about as much resemblance to the early Hollywood features as the Edison Kinetoscope bears to today's portable 16mm camera with sound-on-film recording equipment small enough to carry on the camera operator's back.

Richard Barson, *The Non-Fiction Film*

Barson knows that a single example could never support the claim in his topic sentence. So he supports his main idea with examples of film making by children, college students, and independent film makers.

Determining just how many examples you have included in a paragraph isn't always easy. Often what appears to be a new example is actually a more specific version of a previous example. In cases such as these, charting the structure of your paragraph helps you decide if you have included enough different examples.

EXERCISES

1.   Read each of the following student paragraphs and decide if they contain enough specific detail. If a paragraph is incomplete, tell what information the writer needs to add.

   a.   Researchers found that a good package should attract a shopper like a flame dancing in front of a moth. They designed packages with pictures of rich desserts, sizzling steaks, and sumptuous meals. The idea was to sell the allure of the product, not the product itself. Further research showed that color could create the desired effects. A woman's eye, for instance, is most quickly attracted to red packages, while a man's is most quickly attracted to blue. In addition, studies showed that packages placed at eye level sold significantly more than those placed either on top or bottom shelves.

b. Summer is a special time in the city. I remember the special joy of running through the jet of an open fire hydrant or walking down the avenue relishing a cherry water ice. Sometimes we would play stickball or kick-the-can, games that would result in heated neighborhood rivalries.

c. There have been a number of Europeans who have attempted to analyze the nature of democracy in America. In 1831 Alexis de Tocqueville began a journey that resulted in the publication of his book entitled *Democracy in America*.

d. Walking dogs as a part-time job is not only physically exhausting, it can also be hazardous. Every day I walk, or rather am dragged, approximately a mile and a half by six dogs. For this service I am paid ten dollars per dog each week. On many occasions I have been bitten by my charges, once severely enough to require a doctor's attention.

e. From an engineering standpoint, alcohol could easily be substituted for diesel fuel. All engineers would have to do is implement several simple engine modifications.

2. Choose three of the following statements as topic sentences and write paragraphs for them. Be sure your paragraphs contain enough examples to prove your point.

- Every time I take a test I have the same problems.
- There was one movie I saw this year that I liked a lot.
- Life at this college would not be bad if the food were better.
- There are a few things that students can do to defray their expenses at college.
- If two people want to make a relationship work, they have to work hard.
- The transition from high school to college can be a difficult one.
- Despite the quality of imports, there is one American car that beats them all, hands down.
- My parents did one thing to help me mature.
- My favorite place to go on weekends is _____.
- No matter how old I get, I will always be afraid of going to the dentist.

KINDS OF PARAGRAPHS

The paragraphs in an essay serve three principal functions: most of them support your thesis, while specifically constructed ones introduce that thesis and state your conclusions.

BODY PARAGRAPHS

The paragraphs in the middle section of an essay carry the information that supports and develops the thesis. Because these body paragraphs present the facts and examples which convince your readers that your assertions are valid, you must take care to use clear patterns of development. Knowing your alternatives helps. Many of the patterns of development correspond to the patterns we discussed in connection with whole essays. Because these patterns reflect the way people think, this should come as no surprise.

Of course, many paragraphs don't rely on a single pattern of development. You will often want to mix two or more patterns to make a point. At this stage in your writing, however, practicing each pattern separately helps you learn paragraphing skills. After you have more confidence, you can try mixing and matching.

☐ NARRATION

Narrative paragraphs use sequence, usually chronological sequence, to tell a story. Often narrative paragraphs do not have topic sentences. But they always have a unifying idea—what happened—that draws events together, and they have clear transitions that signal sequence. In this narrative paragraph, a student author recalls his first year of school. He begins by setting the scene and proceeds by filling in the details of the incident.

> Most of my first year of school is lost to me. Bits and pieces remain—a sliding board, big wooden blocks, and a tall, rather dark presence—but I have forgotten the rest. One rainy afternoon, however, does stand out vividly in my imagination. It was the day my mother came late to pick me up from school. Every day at twelve o'clock I would eagerly anticipate my mother's arrival. She would meet me in the school yard and pretend that she had forgotten to bring me a snack. Finally, after my mock pleading and searching, she would laugh and take the precious cookie or piece of candy from her pocket and we would both laugh. But that day she never came. Looking at the empty rain-soaked spot where she usually stood, I felt momentarily abandoned. But I knew the way home, so fighting back my tears I gathered up my canvas school bag and began the walk home.
>
> James Donze

Details are everything to a narrative paragraph. They provide the touches that make your reader see, hear, and otherwise feel that your story rings true. In the following narrative paragraph, details enrich an account of how Elizabeth Kingsley, originator of the Double-Crostic, came to invent that popular puzzle.

> Elizabeth Seelman Kingsley was born in Brooklyn in about 1878 and grew up working scrambled-word puzzles in *St. Nicholas* magazine; after graduating from Wellesley in 1898, she became an English teacher until her marriage. During the national crossword-puzzle binge of the 1920's, she worked several crosswords and then remarked: "How futile! There is a certain fun in the thrill of the puzzle, to be sure, but what is the goal?" A few years later, at a Wellesley reunion, she became so disturbed at the undergraduates' enthusiasm for James Joyce and Gertrude Stein that she determined to do something about it. "Suddenly it dawned upon me," she said years later, "that a puzzle which stimulated the imagination and heightened an appreciation of fine literature by reviewing English and American prose masters would be a puzzle *with* a goal." Thus was born the first Double-Crostic, and in 1934 Mrs. Kingsley sold her first puzzle—and the rights to the name—to the *Saturday Review of Literature*.
>
> Nora Ephron, *Scribble, Scribble*

In this paragraph, Ephron supplies details that introduce her readers to Mrs. Kingsley. Her information is solid and concrete and includes names, dates, and places. The two quotations Ephron includes make Mrs. Kingsley's motivation believable and clear to the reader.

□ DESCRIPTION

Description is another way of analyzing experience. To describe something you have to see it, and to see it, you have to consider it in its separate elements, much the way you look at one thing, then another, when you see a painting or a photograph. In a descriptive paragraph you present these elements so that they form a pattern for your audience, and you arrange the elements so that you control the impression that they convey.

Usually you arrange the elements in a descriptive paragraph according to the way you view a subject, moving from near to far, right to left, or top to bottom, for example. Here is a descriptive paragraph written by a student describing the interior of The Breakers, a mansion in Newport, Rhode Island.

> The interior of The Breakers is as exquisite as the exterior. As you walk in the front door, you enter the Great Hall, or reception room, which is also decorated with intricately carved stone and marble. The Great Hall rises nearly fifty feet and is the largest room in any of the Newport mansions. Its ceiling is covered with geometric patterns of fourteen-karat gold gilding that run rectangularly over the entire surface. There are eight chandeliers, each suspended by a single metal rod. The second story of the room is an open balcony with a black wrought-iron railing that repeats the scrollwork motif of the entrance gates. The railing is divided into sections by two-story-high, square stone columns with Ionic capitals. The Greek Ionic column is the same as those used on the exterior of the mansion. The railing continues along the side of the royal-red carpeted stairs to the first floor. Surrounding the room is a series of arches, each situated between two of the two-story-high columns. Floor-length royal-red tie-back draperies hang inside the arches. The wood parquet floor is covered with Persian area rugs, and potted ferns at the base of each column add a touch of greenery to the room.
>
> Barbara Quercetti

The organizing principle of this paragraph is simple yet effective. We move from outside to inside; more specifically, it is as if we walked through the front door into the great hall, then looked around, noticing nearby, then far-away, details. Barbara includes a lot of specific detail in her description: The Great Hall rises nearly *fifty feet;* its ceiling is covered with *geometric patterns;* there are *eight chandeliers;* the room is surrounded by *two-story-high columns.* Barbara keeps her description coherent with transitional words and phrases. Throughout the paragraph she emphasizes locations and relationships: "As you walk in the front door," "The second story of the room," "Surrounding the room."

☐ PROCESS

Some paragraphs use chronological organization to explain a *process*. The topic sentence identifies the process, and the rest of the paragraph presents the parts of the process in order. Throughout, words like "first," "second," "next," and "then" can be used to signal the chronological organization. The following paragraph uses this pattern to outline the development of a White Dwarf star.

> What about the White Dwarf stars? Very bright stars, as time goes on, will burn up more and more of their hydrogen, and eventually they will be left without any hydrogen. Later developments are quite complicated, but one can see that in due course such stars will be unable to maintain their heat balance. They will begin to cool and to shrink. It turns out that as long as the star remains a pure gas, there is no limit to the shrinkage. However, the material eventually becomes so dense that the constituent particles become tightly packed. It then becomes very hard to compress them any more, and so the material has ceased to behave like a gas. It is at this stage that the star presents the appearance of a White Dwarf. The material has been compacted as far as it will go. It has attained the required strength by being so terribly dense.
>
> Hermann Bondi, *The Universe at Large*

This paragraph packs in a good deal of information with its "and then . . . and then" structure. Bondi realizes that as he explains the process he also has to explain the concepts. He does this easily and without talking down to his audience.

☐ CAUSE AND EFFECT

This pattern is widely used in structuring paragraphs. Usually such paragraphs begin by stressing a cause, then discussing its possible effects, but the opposite order—defining an effect, or effects, then exploring a number of causes—is also possible. The following paragraph begins by stating a cause and an effect and then demonstrates the relationship by example. Notice how the author uses research data to establish the validity of the effects he presents.

> Much of the research . . . has led to the conclusion that TV and movie violence could cause aggressive behavior in some children. . . . Research by Stanford psychologist Albert Bandura has shown that even brief exposure to novel aggressive behavior *on a one-time basis* can be repeated in free play by as high as 88 percent of the young children seeing it on TV. Dr. Bandura also demonstrated that even a single viewing of a novel aggressive act could be recalled and produced by children six months later, without any intervening exposure. Earlier studies have estimated that the average child between the ages of 5 and 15 will witness, during this 10-year period, the violent destruction of more than 13,400 fellow humans. This means that through several hours of TV watching, a child may see more violence than the average adult experiences in a lifetime. Killing is as common as taking a walk, a gun

more natural than an umbrella. Children are taught to take pride in force and violence and to feel ashamed of ordinary sympathy.

Victor B. Cline, "How TV Violence Damages Your Children," Ladies' Home Journal

The cause-and-effect relationships that the author examines are not simple. He first states the finding that even brief exposure to violence on TV can result in violent play in children. He then reports on behavior produced in children six months later. He ends with a more general conclusion, that children are taught to take pride in force and violence and feel ashamed of sympathy.

☐ COMPARISON AND CONTRAST

Comparison usually emphasizes similarities, while contrast always deals with differences. Be careful to tell your readers which you will emphasize—similarities, differences, or both. One way to organize such a paragraph is to present one subject in the first half, and the other in the second. The following student paragraph begins with a topic sentence that speaks of the differences between baseball and football fans and continues by considering first one subject, then the other.

> As anyone who regularly attends professional baseball and football games knows, the fans for each sport are decidedly different. Go to a baseball game any warm summer afternoon and what do you see? People dressed casually, some without shirts, beer in hand, watching the game. Conversation flows freely and barriers of class and race seem to dissolve in the warm sunshine. Certainly the game is important, but what baseball fans care about most is being there and sharing their enthusiasm for the game. Now go to a football game in the middle of winter with temperatures hovering around ten degrees. People are bundled in layers of coats, scarves, and blankets. The atmosphere is tense, reminiscent of troops waiting to go into battle. The silences between plays are punctuated by isolated cheers or occasional arguments about a player's performance or the coach's strategy.
>
> Melissa Donner

Melissa carefully discusses the same points in both parts of her paragraph. She examines the way people dress, the atmosphere in the stands, and the interaction of the fans for both sports, and by so doing, she sheds light on the differences between them. When Melissa shifts from baseball to football, she signals her audience by using the phrase, "Now go to a football game . . . ." The smooth transition eliminates any chances of confusion.

☐ CLASSIFICATION

In a classification paragraph, you take a general group of things and place them into classes or subtypes. At the heart of any classification paragraph is the principle by which you group information. You could group colleges according to size, location, or the types of degrees they offer. Or you could classify them according to tuition cost or even what basketball conference they belong to. The following paragraph focuses on book owners and puts them into three classes.

> There are three kinds of book owners. The first has all the standard sets and best-sellers—unread, untouched. (This deluded individual owns woodpulp and ink, not books.) The second has a great many books—a few of them read through, most of them dipped into, but all of them as clean and shiny as the day they were bought. (This person would probably like to make books his own, but is restrained by a false respect for their physical appearance.) The third has a few books or many—every one of them dog-eared and dilapidated, shaken and loosened by continual use, marked and scribbled in from front to back. (This man owns books.)
>
> Mortimer Adler, "How to Mark a Book," *Saturday Review*

Adler begins by talking about three kinds of book owners. He itemizes the basis of classification using the pattern, "the first," "the second," and "the third." The parallel structure of the sentences, and the parenthetical insertions, make this paragraph coherent and easy to understand.

EXERCISES

1. Read each of the following paragraphs and determine whether the underlying structure is coordinate, subordinate, or mixed. Next, identify the pattern of development.

a. Things change fast in the space age. "I got bored with Space Invaders, so I switched to Galaxian," says Chad Boyd, Michael Boyd's fifteen-year-old son. "It's harder because it moves in different patterns. Its laser comes at you much faster. It has all kinds of colors, it's three dimensional, and it has better noises. It's harder to play and fun to see. It's more exciting." Within two years, Space Invaders itself had become obsolete, losing out to such direct descendants as Deluxe Space Invaders, Galaxian, Defender, and to new concepts—Donkey Kong and Pac-Man. Space Invaders brought in new customers, forced out old machines, and disappeared. Today one must search the far corners of arcades to find even one Space Invaders. And Chad is right: by today's standards, this 1979 machine is boring. (David Surrey, "It's, Like, Good Training for Life," *Natural History*)

b. We have . . . recorded and analyzed four years of humpback [whale] songs from Hawaii, a major wintering area for humpbacks. Although the songs of the same year in Hawaii and Bermuda are different, it is intriguing that they obey the same laws of change, and have the same structure. Each song, for example, is composed of about six themes—passages with several identical or slowly changing phrases in them. Each phrase contains from two to five sounds. In any one song the themes always follow the same order, though one or more themes may be absent. The remaining ones are always given in predictable sequence. (Roger Payne "Humpbacks: Their Mysterious Songs," *National Geographic*)

c. Elvis—"Elvis the Pelvis"—was more than a pop superstar. With his sleepy, sensual looks, his sexy bumps and grinds and his black-sounding voice, he not only changed the course of pop music forever, he may have created the generation gap. Rarely does an entertainer so galvanize the unstated yearnings of an age and serve as a harbinger for the decade to come as Elvis did in the mid-1950s with the first of his long parade of hits, which included "Heartbreak Hotel," "Hound Dog" and "All Shook Up." After his famous first appearance on "The Ed Sullivan Show" in 1956, my aunt told me how foolish I was to sit screaming with joy at the spectacle of that vulgar singer on TV. It was then I knew that she and I lived in different worlds, and it was then that kids' bedroom doors slammed all over America. Boys wore greasy ducktail haircuts and tried to imitate Elvis's moves in front of the mirror. Girls gave up collecting charms for their bracelets for the forbidden charms of his 45-rpm records. Our parents hated Elvis and that was all right with us. From Elvis on, rock was rebellious. (Maureen Orth, "All Shook Up," *Newsweek*)

d.   Although fear of math is not a purely female phenomenon, girls tend to drop out of math sooner than boys, and adult women experience an aversion to math and math-related activities that is akin to anxiety. A 1972 survey of the amount of high school mathematics taken by incoming freshmen at Berkeley revealed that while 57 percent of the boys had taken four years of high school math, only 8 percent of the girls had had the same amount of preparation. Without four years of high school math, students at Berkeley, and at most other colleges and universities, are ineligible for the calculus sequence, unlikely to attempt chemistry or physics, and inadequately prepared for statistics and economics. (Sheila Tobias, *Overcoming Math Anxiety*)

2.   Write paragraphs based on two of the following topic sentences. Identify the pattern of development you use.

- High school differed from college in two ways.
- One event had a great influence on my life.
- I will never forget what (he/she) looked like.
- Certain things that people do bother me.
- Here is my definition of happiness.
- There is a certain dish I like to prepare.

INTRODUCTORY PARAGRAPHS

The body paragraphs of your essay carry the weight of your discussion. But other paragraphs, ones with very special jobs to do, have at least as much influence, if not more, on how well your readers will react to and understand your ideas.

Your *introduction* is probably the most important part of your essay. Done well, it establishes the context of your discussion and enables your audience to follow your discussion easily. Done awkwardly, your introduction confuses your readers and undercuts your entire paper. Your introduction draws your readers in, creates interest, and establishes your thesis or unifying idea. Usually a full paragraph and almost never a single sentence, it should make clear to your audience what follows in your essay.

Your introduction should agree in tone and style with the rest of your essay. It should be a natural part of it, not a different construction grafted on the top. (A humorous or conversational introduction is not appropriate for a research paper or a laboratory report.) Nor should your introduction make any false promises. It must present what you have to say accurately and not mislead an audience. (An introduction about your summer job may not lead your reader directly into a critical review of Studs Terkel's book *Working*).

You can introduce your essays in a number of ways. Think first about what your readers need. What information must you provide so that they can understand your discussion? You may have to begin your essay with a definition or an overview. You may have to think of ways to create interest. You can, for example, begin with an anecdote, a quotation, or a series of questions. At times you can combine approaches to capture your audience's attention as well as to state your thesis.

The kind of introduction you use depends on your audience, your purpose, and your occasion. You would not want to open a discussion of lasers with a barrage of highly technical information if your essay were intended for a general audience. In a final examination, you would not begin a discussion of the Battle of Verdun with a poetic description of a World War I battlefield. Each writing situation calls for its own approach, but here are seven general introductory techniques that experienced writers frequently use.

☐ DIRECT ANNOUNCEMENT

You may want to announce your thesis immediately and go right into your essay. Essay exams, reports, and short papers call for this direct approach. This introduction from an essay on horror movies uses a direct announcement.

> Although horror movies have recently been enjoying a vogue, they have always been perennial supporting features among Grade B and C fare. The popularity of the form is no doubt partly explained by its ability to engage the spectator's feelings without making any serious demands on his mind. In addition, however, horror movies covertly embody certain underground assumptions about science which reflect popular opinions.
>
> Robert Brustein, "Reflections on Horror Movies," *The Third Theater*

This opening of a report written for a technical writing course also announces its thesis directly. After reading this paragraph, an instructor, or a company executive, would have little doubt about what is to follow.

> This report will demonstrate that it would be to the advantage of Philadelphia Electric Company to expand their water-distribution facilities to rapidly developing areas. This approach would involve expenditures in establishing a distribution main along Pine Road and a pumping station at Leola Plaza. By taking these steps, the company could influence developers to tie into its water facilities.
>
> Sally Winn

☐ QUOTATION OR DIALOGUE

You can begin your essay by using a relevant quotation or bit of dialogue. The words of an expert or famous person can lend credibility and interest to your discussion and may help your readers to see your topic in concrete terms. Quotations can come from almost any reputable source: newspapers, magazines, books, encyclopedias, conversations, or interviews. Just be sure that the quotation you include agrees in tone and style with your essay, and, of course, that it supports your point.

An introduction from a student paper on the space shuttle uses a quotation to create interest and then proceeds to a thesis statement.

> "Are you animal—or vegetable—or mineral?" said a lion to Alice in *Through the Looking Glass.* Many scientists find themselves in the position of the lion as they view the latest discoveries in particle physics. New subatomic particles face physicists with the dilemma of deciding whether the basic building blocks of the universe are made of matter, energy, or a third, as yet undefined, substance.
>
> Gail Meyers

James Baldwin, the author of the following paragraph, uses a quotation to introduce his discussion of what it means to him to be an American.

> "It is a complex fate to be an American," Henry James observed, and the principal discovery an American writer makes in Europe is just how complex this fate is. America's history, her aspirations, her peculiar triumphs, her even more peculiar defeats, and her position in the world—yesterday and today—are all so profoundly and stubbornly unique that the very word "America" remains a new, almost completely undefined and extremely controversial proper noun. No one in the world seems to know exactly what it describes, not even we motley millions who call ourselves Americans.
>
> James Baldwin, *Nobody Knows My Name*

☐ DEFINITION

Often you need to begin an essay with a definition of an important term or concept. This technique is especially useful in examinations and research papers. Here is a first paragraph from a final examination in history that asked the student to discuss how the military philosophy of either France or Germany influenced tactics during the first months of World War I. The writer of this paragraph defines the French term *cran* to introduce his discussion of military tactics and to set up the framework for his entire answer.

> To the French "le cran" means nerve or guts. In 1914 this concept was epitomized in the French commitment to the "offensive without hesitation." For to them it was only by demonstrating "le cran" that they could hope to defeat Germany.

Unfortunately, by fixing upon attack, France ignored her defensive needs, and as a result, almost lost World War I a month after it began.

Dexter Frye

The author of the following paragraph begins by defining the term "topiary." Here the writer defines an unfamiliar term and stimulates the reader's curiosity at the same time.

The rare and ancient art of topiary is, simply, the art of training hedges or other plants—by years of continual clipping, trimming, twisting, and coaxing—to take shapes they do not ordinarily take. The results can be green spheres, spirals, pyramids and, with a bit more effort and imagination, dogs, peacocks, and sailing ships. Living sculpture, it is—a delightful example of how gardeners can indeed fool Mother Nature.

Dan Carlinsky, "Cultivating Living Statues in a Garden," New York Times

□ REFUTATION

You can begin an essay by disagreeing with a commonly held belief or idea. Refuting the most important argument against your stand right at the beginning may strengthen your position. This also creates a context for your discussion. Just make sure that the issue you knock down is a real one. If your audience thinks that you have contrived your opposition, they may reject your entire argument.

In this introduction from a short paper for a course in early childhood development, the author, by contradicting the widely held belief that common sense is all you need to raise children, sets the tone of his essay and smoothly introduces his thesis. By attacking a cherished belief, he also creates audience interest.

Many people feel that common sense and intuition are all that is necessary to raise a child. But, as much research has shown, childhood development is complicated and often presents problems that parents fail to appreciate. The issue of toilet training is one such issue that gives even the most well-intentioned parents an opportunity to damage their offspring psychologically.

Mark Williams

The following paragraph uses refutation successfully to introduce a discussion of reading tastes and habits.

Everywhere one meets the idea that reading is an activity desirable in itself. It is understandable that publishers and librarians—and even writers—should promote this assumption, but it is strange that the idea should have general currency. People surround the idea of reading with piety, and do not take into account the purpose of reading or what is being read. Teachers and parents praise the child who reads, and praise themselves, whether the text be The Reader's Digest or Moby Dick. The advent of T.V. has increased the false values ascribed to reading, since T.V. provides a vulgar alternative. But this piety is silly; and most reading is no more cultural nor intellectual nor imaginative than shooting pool or watching What's My Line.

Donald Hall, "Four Kinds of Reading," New York Times

☐ OVERVIEW OF THE SITUATION

Many times you need to begin an essay with background material or an overview of a subject. Bringing your readers up to date gives them enough information to understand the rest of your discussion. The following introductory paragraph presents a short historical overview of the author's subject, violent gangs in the United States.

> It is a truism that criminal organizations and criminal activity tend to reflect social conditions. Just as surely as the Bowery gang mirrored aspects of the 1900's, the Capone mob aspects of the twenties, and the youth gangs of the depression elements of the thirties, so do the delinquent gangs that have developed since the 1940's in the United States reflect certain patterns of our own society.
>
> Lewis Yoblonsky, "The Violent Gang," *Commentary*

Here is an overview from a history of science paper. The background statement recounts some of the ways people have tried to cure malaria, information which puts the rest of the paper into perspective.

> Malaria, the major infectious disease problem in the world, has plagued man and intrigued physicians since the beginning of history. Hippocrates considered the disease of primary importance; Alexander the Great died of malaria at the age of thirty-two; the Egyptian physician Erasistratus recommended tourniquets to prevent the passage of noxious blood and thus cure malaria; Pliny the Younger advocated the use of crab and wolf eyes; and Galen suggested that unlimited bleeding and purging was the treatment of choice. Not until the end of the Renaissance was the first effective treatment—quinine—discovered, and the history of the development of this treatment and of quinine's acquisition and extraction is a complex and exciting one. From the powdered bark of the Cinchona tree used in the seventeenth century to the capsules of quinine sulfate used today winds a fascinating trail of information.
>
> Tom Connelly

☐ QUESTIONS

You can also begin a paper with a question. This technique engages attention and creates interest by expressing some concern that the reader already feels. You can answer the question in your opening paragraph or take it up in the body of your essay. The following introduction comes from a short paper written for a class in mathematics. It begins with a catchy question and goes on to answer it with a thesis statement.

> How much of a gamble is gambling? Certainly most games of chance are skewed in favor of the house. But as some application of algebra and game theory will show, two games, dice and blackjack, present some situations where the odds almost favor the participant.
>
> Harry Higgins

This opening paragraph from a pamphlet distributed to campus student organizations also begins with a question and asks readers to read on for the answer.

> Can I really break the law just by using a Xerox machine? Unfortunately, the answer to this question is yes. New copyright laws make it a crime to duplicate reading materials for certain situations. As an examination of the regulation shows, all of us have probably broken the law at one time or another.
>
> Betty Roberson

☐ ANECDOTE

A short anecdote or story gives focus to your discussion and involves the reader at once. Your anecdote can come from personal experience or from history. In the following essay, the writer uses a story with a surprise ending to establish the situation and to interest the audience.

> Night falls over the Arctic tundra. A tracked personnel carrier churns through the snow, delivering a squad of hungry G.I.'s. One fills a bucket with moss, pours diesel fuel over it, lights a fire, and melts some snow. When the water boils, he throws in several plastic packets. The squad leader lifts the carrier's hood and lines more pouches along the hot manifold. Within ten minutes the entire arctic patrol is dining on turkey with gravy and beef stew accompanied by green beans with mushrooms, peas, and carrots, and crisp garden salad of celery and cucumbers in a lightly garlicked dressing. For those who prefer it, there is also a disk the size of a hockey puck that when soaked fluffs into a pot full of shredded cabbage. . . . This instant Arctic banquet is just one of the ways the U.S. Army Natick Research Laboratories at Natick, Massachusetts, makes life better for the military—and indeed for all of us.
>
> Bern Keating, "Uncle Sam's Workshop," *Science 81*

Using the same device, the writer of this short paper for a sociology course involves his audience and moves them toward his thesis in the last line.

> An ethnologist, John Calhoun, put Norway rats in a pen and allowed them to reproduce as much as they wanted to. He supplied them with all the food, water, and nesting materials they would need. As the rat population increased, the reproduction and social organization of the rat pen broke down. Males lost interest in reproduction and began attacking one another. Females stopped tending to the young and eventually began devouring them. Ultimately there was a massive die-off. Although limited to an animal population, the results of Calhoun's experiment raise serious questions concerning the effects of overcrowding in many of the world's underdeveloped countries.
>
> Alan Schindler

CONCLUDING PARAGRAPHS

Conclusions also have a special job to do. Readers base their final impression of your writing on your concluding paragraphs. A weak, irrelevant, or uninteresting ending deflates an otherwise strong essay. Not every essay demands a formal concluding paragraph. In personal experience essays, for example, such a conclusion might seem forced, as if you were trying to teach a lesson or impose a moral. For most essays, however, a strong concluding paragraph is essential.

What then should your conclusion do? Principally, it should provide a satisfying and appropriate close to your essay. Usually, however, you must do more than restate your thesis or your major points. Mere restatement bores your readers and does nothing extra to help them remember what you said. Far better is an expanded conclusion that emerges or follows from your essay. You can, for example, echo a powerful image or quote an authority mentioned earlier in your essay. Or, you can refer back to material from your introduction. By tying your conclusion to your introduction, you frame your essay and bring it full cycle. Finally, you can use your conclusion to predict the future or to recommend a course of action.

As with introductions, the length and strategy of your conclusion depend on your purpose, audience, and occasion. For most midterm and final examinations, a straightforward one- or two-line conclusion is all you need. A research paper or long technical report might need a conclusion of several paragraphs. Whatever the case, your conclusion must contribute something to your essay.

□ RESTATEMENT OR SUMMARY

You can use restatement or summary in limited cases. A straightforward essay, an examination answer, or a technical paper can end this way. Restatement gives you the chance to make sure your audience hears your major points one final time, and it is a good strategy to use when your major concern is conveying specific information.

In the sample below, the author uses a straightforward restatement as a conclusion for just this reason.

> This chapter has sought to show that research into childhood patterns of the late Roman and early Medieval periods is possible, and will yield more than minor and insignificant results. It has illustrated some of the kinds of evidence and results which may be expected, and pointed the way toward further areas of study.
>
> Richard B. Lymar, Jr., "Barbarism and Religion:
> Late Roman and Early Medieval Childhood," *The History of Childhood*

Using this same technique, a student ends her letter to the school paper with a summary of her reasons for reevaluating security provisions for campus housing.

> It is clear, then, that there are three reasons to reevaluate current security provisions for campus housing. First, there have been a number of crimes against property in recent months. Second, students are beginning to seek residence off campus, resulting in a loss of funds both for the university and for area businesses. Finally, the university has an obligation to both students and their parents to ensure that campus housing is safe.
>
> Chris Williams

☐ RECOMMENDATION OF A COURSE OF ACTION

Most of your writing assignments call for more than a summary. When your purpose is to persuade your readers of something, you may want to conclude by calling them to action. Writers of ads and TV commercials rely on this strategy constantly. "Don't forget to call" and "Act now!" are all too familiar. Isaac Asimov, the well-known science fiction and science writer, recommends a course of action in the conclusion to his essay "The Case Against Man." Following an objective analysis of the dangers of overpopulation, this rather emotional appeal emphasizes the seriousness of the situation and stays with the reader.

> So if birth control *must* come by A.D. 2430 at the very latest, even in an ideal world of advancing science, let it come *now,* in heaven's name, while there are still oak trees in the world and daisies and tigers and butterflies, and while there is still open land and space, and before the cancer called man proves fatal to life and the planet.
>
> Isaac Asimov, "The Case Against Man"

A student in a public health course also ends her short research paper with a recommendation. By doing so, she draws her paper's lines of thought together in an effective close.

> Homeopaths and allopaths disagree as to whether homeopathy really works or not, and unless studies are performed to determine homeopathy's effectiveness, the question may never be resolved. Still, the simultaneous existence of the two systems of medicine indicates that neither allopathy nor homeopathy is able to satisfy all consumers seeking health care. The conscientious physician may, therefore, do well to combine the scientific technology of allopathy with the holistic approach offered by homeopathy.
>
> Jean Paul

☐ PREDICTION

You might want to end an essay with a prediction. Not only do you sum up your major points; you make a projection based on those points. In his conclusion to an article entitled "Growth," Dennis Gabor, winner of the 1971 Nobel Prize in physics, uses this strategy to leave his readers with a guarded but optimistic message.

> Such lofty ideals, like happiness, cannot be approached in a straight line. Almost all the present trends of our world are against us: overpopulation, nationalism, economic group inertia and general aimlessness. Our best potential ally, youth, is deeply confused. All this must not discourage the truly creative intellects among us. If they rise to the real, great challenge of our times, mankind may be able to step on a higher plateau without, as usual, first falling into an abyss.
>
> Dennis Gabor, "Growth," *Intellectual Digest*

This conclusion from a paper written for a marketing course also uses prediction. After restating her thesis, the writer predicts that fast-food restaurants will eventually become a thing of the past.

The fast-food industry has been built on two assumptions: the availability of inexpensive gas and the desire of Americans for quick service and simple food. Both these conditions will probably disappear in the near future. With the rapid escalation of gasoline prices, people will, by all predictions, be driving less. Even now the effect of this can be seen. There has been a significant increase in bankrupt franchises, a situation that would have been thought impossible just a few years ago. With the high cost of both transportation and food, Americans will most likely begin to eat at home again. Thus fast-food restaurants will eventually be a thing of the past, a phenomenon that we will tell our grandchildren about.

Sharon Sewer

☐ QUOTATION OR DIALOGUE

Quotations can add authority and interest to your conclusions. Carefully chosen, the words of an expert strengthen your concluding remarks. The distinctive writing styles of professional writers also provide variety. Quoting literary critic Edmund Wilson, the writer of this conclusion adds force to his argument.

What is fatal for a writer, Edmund Wilson told us some years ago, is to be brilliant at a disgraceful job. Never has brilliance come so cheap as it does today. Never have the fatally stricken—writers, painters, mere T.V. directors—thrived so. Never have they had so many fascinating toys to play with, such an audience so eager to be entertained, so much time and space at their disposal. Never has it been easier for them to interpret an hour's exhilaration as the proof of creativity. Never has the marketplace of the arts depended so much on noise and common posturing, and never has it been so deficient in the discipline that precedes art.

Walter Goodman, "On Doing-One's-Thing," The American Scholar

A student uses a quotation by Jean Jaurès, a French historian, to end her essay for a take-home final exam. The quotation not only adds flair, it also gives meaning to the actions of the Spartans who died defending the pass at Thermopylae.

Jean Jaurès, the French historian, once wrote, "What matter the errors of fate and false directions in life? A few luminous and fervent hours are enough to give meaning to a lifetime." The same can be said of those Spartans commanded by Leonidas who defended the pass at Thermopylae from invading Persians led by Xerxes. Even though the Spartans lost the battle and were killed, they still serve as an example of heroism to free people everywhere. In this respect they epitomize the Greek spirit and the sense of nationalism that was to emerge in the West during the Renaissance.

Mary DiMarco

☐ CHRONOLOGICAL WIND-UP

When your essay tells a story or recounts a series of events, it is natural to end it by bringing your readers up to date. The final paragraph of an essay on the history of medicine shows uses this strategy.

The big medicine shows prospered well into the 1900's. Then under the eyes of the awakening medical associations and the new Food and Drug Administration, itinerant quacks could no longer make the wild claims of the past. The picturesque practitioners of medicine show days have gone to their Valhalla. Today we have T.V. hucksters to warn us of "Tired Blood."

Sisley Barnes, "Medicine Shows Duped, Delighted," Smithsonian

This personal experience essay written for a freshman composition course also closes with a chronological wind-up.

You might be wondering what I gained from my rebellion. My former friends are still living exclusively for today and thinking very little of what will come tomorrow. My parents, of course, are overjoyed that I have finally "gotten down to business." My former teachers seemed genuinely surprised when I told them one day last year that I had been on the Dean's List. I certainly am not having as much fun as I used to, but I have finally learned that if I am ever to achieve the goals I have set, I will have to postpone satisfaction for a while.

Arthur Valesquez

Remember that the conclusion is an integral part of your essay: it should not seem weak or tacked on. Work especially hard to develop an interesting and appropriate conclusion, one that fulfills the promises that you made in your introduction.

EXERCISES

1. Read the following essay and analyze its introduction and conclusion, paying special attention to how each functions in the essay and how effective each is. Also identify what pattern or patterns they conform to. What other strategies might the author have used?

Hi, House, Goodbye Ideals
Norman Provizer

Anyone who has looked to buy a house on today's market knows all too well what a traumatic experience that search can be. The cost of a home has soared to incredible heights. But after spending some weeks with my wife wandering through assorted bedrooms, bathrooms and closets, it finally dawned on me that beyond the price, the buying of a house required the making of difficult political decisions.

Yes, I realize it sounds rather strange, but the seemingly individual act of purchasing a home is connected to the gravest problems that affect the entire social fabric of this country.

Let me give a few examples. Before looking for a house, I never gave serious consideration to school-district lines. That naïveté did not last very long once the search began. It was made quite clear that certain areas were "better" than others and that I would be foolish not to take school lines into account.

So, before too long and despite the fact that my wife and I have no children, I found myself going from door to door asking what schools served the neighborhood. Whatever rationalizations I came up with, the ugly truth remained: I had become part of the web of institutional racism, pushed on by the gods of appreciation and resale value. I was too vulnerable to resist.

Beyond race, I also found that class distinctions entered into the equation of house buying. As with the question of race, the omnipresent figure of real estate value lurked constantly around the corner. For a country that prides itself on its classless nature, America, I soon discovered, grants quite a bit of significance to the class labels of one's neighbors.

Class and race, race and class, these ideas swirled in my mind even as I examined energy-efficient doors and measured wood-paneled family rooms. They seemed to be the constants in the fluid world of floor plans and square footage. They were enthroned and seemed unchallengable. Yet they existed not because of cabals and conspiracies but because of the scripts by which we live our lives.

There were no villains, no seedy operators manipulating my emotions. The advice offered to me was honest, forthright and friendly. It made sense, like the suggestion to take aspirin for a cold. Everyone was concerned with my best interests and I appreciated that fact. But it was my best interests which rested at the heart of the problem. Unlike Adam Smith's dictum, there is no "invisible hand" to insure that the pursuit of private self-interest leads to the furtherance of the public interest of all of society. In gaining the benefits of property ownership for myself, I realized that I was willing to sacrifice certain abstract social goals.

That realization has caused me anguish, for it has placed me on the horns of a true dilemma. I am certain that like so many others, I will soon rest my tired and guilty body into a "proper" home. And I will be happy, because my wife and I have certain material aspirations. Yet I cannot engage in self-delusion or convenient lapses in memory, and thus I know that I have become part of the problem, rather than part of the solution.

I will make my political decisions in house buying and they will be the wrong decisions made for all of the "right" reasons. *(Shreveport Journal)*

2.   Choose any pattern other than the ones used and write your own introduction and conclusion to the above essay. Make sure your paragraphs blend in with the body of the essay and be prepared to discuss why you designed your introduction and conclusion as you did.

3.   Look at an essay that you have written. Judge its introduction and conclusion. If you feel they can be improved, rewrite them. If not, write several paragraphs telling in what ways they are effective.

CHAPTER

6

Writing
Sentences

Different kinds of sentences provide you with ways to express your ideas precisely and to communicate subtle differences in meaning. Experimenting with different sentence patterns can help to make your writing clear and more interesting—in other words, more readable—to an audience. Before you start to explore the many options for sentence construction, you must first master the basic English sentence pattern and some methods of expanding it to build *simple, compound,* and *complex* sentences.

THE BASIC SENTENCE PATTERN

At the core of all sentences is a *subject* and a *predicate*. The subject is a noun, or a substitute for a noun, about which the predicate tells or asks something.

    ^s   ^p
Speed kills.

        ^s   ^p
The elections proceeded.

    ^s   ^p
Crime does not pay.

The simple predicate is the verb that tells something about the subject (kills, proceeded, does . . . pay). The complete predicate consists of the verb and any complements or modifiers:

         ^{cp}
Vengeance is mine.

        ^{cp}
Zaire is independent.

Although the basic sentence core—subject and predicate—does carry the general idea of the sentence, additional words, phrases, and clauses are usually needed to expand that idea. The basic sentence pattern is expanded through *modification, coordination,* or *subordination.*

MODIFICATION: BUILDING SIMPLE SENTENCES

To modify—or change—the elements in a sentence, you describe, add to, limit, or qualify them. Thus you enrich your meaning and make your ideas more precise and vivid. You may modify the nouns of a simple sentence with adjectives:

    Shinto is a *Japanese* religion.
    Cooley's anemia is a *genetic* disease.

or the verbs with adverbs:

    The situation deteriorated *rapidly.*
    Real estate prices rose *dramatically.*

and both nouns and verbs with adjective or adverb phrases:

    Buddhism is a religion *with over 50,000 worshippers in the United States.*
    Jesse Owens triumphed *at the 1936 Olympic Games.*

You can make your modifications at the beginning, in the middle, or at the end of a sentence. In many cases, you use different kinds of modification in different locations in one sentence, creating sentences that are rich and complex. In each of the following sentences, the modifiers that expand the basic sentence elements are bracketed. Notice that modifiers answer the readers' questions—Who? What? When? Where? What kind? Without these modifiers, the sentences wouldn't be full or accurate—in fact, they wouldn't communicate much at all.

> Flemish is spoken [in some parts of Belgium].
> [For the rest of his life] Reverend Hooper wore a [black] veil [to hide his secret sin].
> Give me [your tired, your poor, your huddled] masses, [yearning to breathe free]. (Emma Lazarus)

> Key figures [like Clarence Darrow and William Jennings Bryan] helped publicize [the Scopes "Monkey"] trial.
> The train went [on up the track] [out of sight,] [around one] [of the hills of burnt timber]. (Ernest Hemingway)

Without modifiers, these sentences would raise many questions. Where is Flemish spoken? Why did Hooper wear a veil? What kind of masses? Which key figures? Where did the train go? In simple sentences without modifiers, the options for description, clarification, and explanation are extremely limited.

EXERCISES

1. In the following sentences, mark the basic sentence pattern—underline the subject once and the verb twice—and bracket the modifiers. Then consider what information the modifiers add to the basic sentence. What questions does each modifier answer? Is each modifier necessary to convey the author's meaning? Why or why not?

a. He got up and stepped slowly toward the charming creature, throwing away his cigarette. (Henry James, *Daisy Miller*)

b. And then she began to dance, a slow sensuous movement; the smoke of a hundred cigars clinging to her like the thinnest of veils. (Ralph Ellison, *Invisible Man*)

c. She walks along the broad street, scanning the windows for the dress she needs, the necessary dress. (Muriel Spark, *The Driver's Seat*)

d. Kissler, formerly an egg candler, lived alone on social security. (Bernard Malamud, "The Mourners")

2. To understand the range and power of sentences, it helps to imitate different patterns of arrangement when you write your own sentences. This also allows you to practice different options. In an imitation exercise, you keep the *function words* (articles, prepositions, conjunctions, etc.) of the original, but you substitute different words for the other words in the sentence, making sure to use the same parts of speech in your substitutions.

Original

noun   verb   adverb
Opposites attract—but briefly.

Imitation

noun   verb   adverb
Friends remain—but reluctantly.

Now, reread the four sentences in exercise 1 carefully and write four sentences of your own which imitate them.

3.   Reduce the following paragraph to a series of basic sentences by eliminating all of the modifying words and phrases. What specific information is lost in the revision?

Houdini was a headliner in the top vaudeville circuits. His audiences were poor people—carriers, peddlers, policemen, children. His life was absurd. He went all over the world accepting all kinds of bondage and escaping. He was roped to a chair. He escaped. He was chained to a ladder. He escaped. He was handcuffed, his legs were put in irons, he was tied up in a strait jacket and put in a locked cabinet. He escaped. (E. L. Doctorow, *Ragtime*)

4.   Expand the following simple sentences by adding appropriate words and/or phrases at the beginning, in the middle, or at the end of the sentence.
   a.   Fairy tales can frighten children.
   b.   The sky grew dark.
   c.   Andrew Johnson was president.
   d.   The students prepared for the test.
   e.   Labor unions are growing stronger.
   f.   Baseball is addictive.
   g.   The computer seemed almost human.
   h.   The teller counted out the bills.
   i.   Skiing can be exhilarating.
   j.   Love is blind.

COORDINATION: BUILDING COMPOUND SENTENCES

Coordination is the pairing of similar elements—words, phrases, or clauses—giving each equal weight. One way of expanding a simple sentence through coordination is to pair it with another independent clause and link the two with a coordinating conjunction, usually *and, but,* or *or* (but sometimes *nor, for, so* or *yet*). Compound sentences suggest that the paired ideas are of equal weight, that neither is less important than or dependent upon the other. For example:

The world is very old, and human beings are very young.

Carl Sagan, *The Dragons of Eden*

Compound sentences appear frequently in writing that tells a story, where they convey a sense of sequence or continuity.

> It was now lunchtime and they were all sitting under the double green fly of the dining tent pretending that nothing had happened.
>
> Ernest Hemingway, "The Short Happy Life of Francis Macomber"

Sometimes coordination is used to suggest contrast.

> For a long time the issue of the scientist's social responsibility was discussed only in occasional seminars, but now it has become an important, frequently discussed issue for many scientists.
>
> Barry Commoner, "The Ecological Crisis," *The Example of Science*

Coordination isn't always used to link two independent clauses into a compound sentence. You can also use coordination *within* a simple sentence, linking similar elements to form a *compound subject* or a *compound predicate*, for instance:

compound subject
Homeopathy and allopathy are two different systems of medicine.

compound predicate
The fire *flickered and died.*

In these cases, coordination not only connects similar elements, but also produces clear, economical, and emphatic sentences.

EXERCISES

---

1. In the opening lines of his short story "The Rocking Horse Winner," D. H. Lawrence uses a series of sentences that have been expanded by coordination. Why do you think coordination has been used in each of these cases instead of separate sentences?

There was a woman who was beautiful, who started with all the advantages, yet she had no luck. She married for love, and the love turned to dust. She had bonny children, yet she felt they had been thrust upon her, and she could not love them.

2. Read the following paragraph, which is composed of fourteen simple sentences. Use coordination to expand as many sentences as necessary to help a reader understand the relationships between ideas.

Superman and Batman are both comic-book heroes. They have some superficial similarities. They have many important basic differences. Superman was a product of the 1930s. Batman came during the 1940s. In the 30s there was a depression. People were looking for a symbol of power. The result was Superman. He could do anything. During the 40s we were at war. People felt powerless. Batman was a clever hero. He was limited. Both Superman and Batman, however, answer a need in all of us.

3.   Write *three* different sentences in imitation of this compound sentence.

Shaking hands, nodding hello, saying my name, each man was a complex flash—eyes, hand, name—but one had definition. (Leonard Michaels, *The Men's Club*)

SUBORDINATION: BUILDING COMPLEX SENTENCES

When you want to subordinate one idea to another, you can place the less important idea in a modifying phrase. Or, you can place the main idea in an *independent clause* and the supporting information in a *dependent clause*. Such a sentence, composed of an independent clause and one or more dependent clauses, is called a *complex sentence*. For example:

independent clause   dependent clause
[The surgeon general has determined] [that smoking may be harmful to your health.]

independent clause   dependent clause
[She had gone to pieces in the strangest way,] [though not many people knew her well enough to notice.]

Margaret Drabble, *The Middle Ground*

independent clause . . .   dependent clause
[R. J. Bowman,] [who for fourteen years had travelled for a shoe company through
. . . independent clause
Mississippi,] [drove his Ford along a rutted dirt path.]

Eudora Welty, "Death of a Travelling Salesman"

Subordination lessens the emphasis on lesser facts and ideas in your sentence and focuses your reader's attention on your main idea. Thus it clarifies your emphasis, making the relative importance of your ideas clear to your readers.

Consider the following two sentences:

Louis L'Amour's novels continue to be very popular. The public remains interested in romantic westerns.

Your readers might wonder about the cause-and-effect relationship, if any, between these two ideas. Are L'Amour's books responsible for the western's popularity, or is it the other way around? If you revised using subordination, you could make the relationship between the two ideas clear.

[Louis L'Amour's novels continue to be very popular] [because the public remains interested in romantic westerns.]

The first version of the following statements will probably confuse most readers. Notice how the revision combines two simple sentences into a complex sentence in which one idea is subordinate to the other.

Original	Revised
Prohibition was enacted. Bootleg liquor sales boomed. (Which event came first? Which caused the other?)	After prohibition was enacted, bootleg liquor sales boomed. (*Or:* Bootleg liquor sales boomed after prohibition was enacted.)
Money market funds provide high interest. Deposits are not insured by the federal government. (Does the writer want to stress the high interest or the potential risk?)	While money market funds provide high interest, deposits are not insured by the federal government.

With subordination, you can also fit more information into a single sentence, making it tighter and more efficient. Look at these sentences.

Many Frenchmen fought in the American Revolution.
These men returned to France ready to fight for liberty and republican ideas.
Lafayette was one of them.

With subordination, these sentences can be combined into one complex sentence.

Because many Frenchmen, like Lafayette, fought in the American Revolution, they returned to France ready to fight for liberty and republican ideas.

This revision not only eliminates the choppiness of three separate short sentences, but also conveys ideas clearly and concisely.

EXERCISES: SENTENCE COMBINING

1. Read the following pairs of sentences carefully and decide what the relationship between each pair is. Then link the pairs, using a subordinating conjunction (*after, if, since, until, because, when, although, before,* etc.) to clarify that relationship and distinguish between the dependent and independent clauses.

a. World War II ended in 1945.
  The U.S. and the U.S.S.R. began a cold war.

b. I never realized that I had an interest in writing.
  I had to keep a journal for a creative writing class.

c. Some feminist groups criticized *Baby and Child Care.*
  Benjamin Spock made significant revisions.

d. Ptolemy believed the earth was the center of the universe.
  Copernicus believed the earth and other planets revolved around the sun.

e. Production had dropped 26 percent.
  A team of management consultants was called in.

f. Boris Pasternak's *Doctor Zhivago* was critical of communism.
  Khrushchev forced him to decline the Nobel Prize.

g. Jane Addams was shocked by the conditions of the Chicago slums.
  She founded a settlement house called Hull House.

  h.   Jane Eyre was treated harshly at Lowood Institution.
        She left as soon as she was old enough, determined to become a governess.

  i.   Helium is lighter than lithium.
        Hydrogen is lighter than helium.

  j.   Daniel D. Tomkins is not very well known.
        He was James Monroe's vice president from 1817 to 1825.

2.   In the following complex sentences, bracket the independent and dependent clauses. Then, using each sentence as a model for imitation, write five new sentences.

  a.   It was summer, when twilight in Warsaw lasts for a long time. (Isaac Bashevis Singer, "The Bond")

  b.   Near them were the untidy knots of sailors who had just fought the flagpole into the stormy soil. (James Clavell, *Tai-Pan*)

  c.   Abused and scorned as we may be, our destiny is tied up with America's destiny. (Martin Luther King, Jr., "Letter from Birmingham Jail")

  d.   After the visitors left, Mother washed the fragile shells herself and put them back in the glassed-in cupboard. (M. F. K. Fisher, "The Total Abstainer," *New Yorker*)

  e.   He was in fact a hairdresser, who came to this lonely part of the Atlantic coast to slough off his given name of Lionel, by which he was called at the rather expensive Salon de Coiffure in London, where he was eagerly sought after. (V. S. Pritchett, "Neighbors," *New Yorker*)

3.   The following sentences are taken, in somewhat altered form, from the article on Arkansas in the 1980 Hammond Almanac. Using subordination or coordination, combine these simple sentences into four or five more informative sentences that clarify the relationships among the various ideas. Eliminate unnecessary words and add words when necessary.

Arkansas is characterized by rugged hills.
The state has many scenic valleys and streams.
The land is generally flat in the south and east.
In the northwest, there are mountains.
Magazine Mountain is the state's highest point.
About four-fifths of the land is wooded.
Arkansas produces cotton, rice, soybeans, and livestock.
Arkansas boasts a famous spa called Hot Springs.
The state has a diamond mine which is now a state park.
Hunting and fishing are abundant.
Many tourists enjoy Arkansas' resources and attractions.

4.   Following is a block of information that has been broken into groups of sentences. Combine each group of short, choppy sentences into a single smooth sentence. Be sure your revisions clarify the relationships between ideas and produce richer, more efficient sentences. Consider several possible combinations before you decide, and be prepared to discuss why you made the choices you did.

The First Ten Men in Space
Manned space travel began in 1961.
The first man in space was Yuri Gagarin.

Gagarin was Russian.
His space voyage took place in April 1961.

Alan Shepard was the first U.S. astronaut.
Shepard's voyage took place one month after Gagarin's.
Virgil Grissom was the next American to travel in space.
His ship was called the Liberty Bell 7.

Gherman Titov was a Russian.
He was the next man to travel in space.
He traveled in space in August 1961.
He carried out a study.
The study was on the effects of prolonged weightlessness.

John Glenn was an American.
His spaceship was the Friendship 7.
He orbited the earth.
The orbiting was in February 1962.

Malcolm Carpenter re-enacted Glenn's flight.
The re-enactment was in May 1962.
His ship was the Aurora 7.

A Russian astronaut was the next man in space.
The Russian astronaut was Andrian Nikolayev.
Nikolayev began his voyage August 11.
Nikolayev flew 1.64 million miles.
Nikolayev operated a television.
The television was in space.
Nikolayev's ship was called Vostok 3.

Another Russian followed.
He followed the next day.
The Russian was Pavel Popovich.
His ship was Vostok 4.
Popovich set out to obtain data.
The data were on establishing contact.
The contact was with Vostok 3.

The next astronaut was American.
The astronaut was Walter Schirra.
Schirra's ship was the Sigma 7.
Schirra faced near disaster.
The disaster was due to a malfunctioning space suit.

Leroy Cooper was the next astronaut.
Cooper was American.
Cooper's ship was the Faith 7.
Cooper's space voyage began May 15, 1963.
Cooper also faced a problem.

His problem was the automatic control system.
The automatic control system failed.
Cooper's splashdown was manually controlled.
The splashdown was successful.

(Adapted from *The Book of Lists*)

5.   Carry out the directions in exercise 4 for these sentences.

Ten Medical Breakthroughs by Non-Doctors

Acupuncture was developed about 2700 B.C.
It is thought to have been discovered by the Emperor Shen Nung.
The Emperor was Chinese.

Leonardo da Vinci was an artist.
Leonardo was also an inventor.
He made accurate drawings.
The drawings were detailed.
The drawings were anatomical.
The drawings were the first.
He showed how the valves functioned.
The valves were of the heart.
He showed what the cavities looked like.
The cavities were of the brain.
His drawings were done about 1500.

Anton van Leeuvenhoek was Dutch.
He was a merchant.
He made his own microscope.
He discovered bacteria.
He discovered protozoa.
He discovered spermatozoa.
The discovery was through his microscope.
The discovery was in 1683.

Joseph Priestley was an Englishman.
He discovered oxygen.
The discovery was in 1771.
He isolated other gases.
Some of the other gases were nitrous oxide, carbon monoxide, and ammonia.
The discovery of oxygen had a medical application.
The application was oxygen therapy.

Anesthesia was first used in 1842.
Ether was the anesthesia.
Its use was suggested by an American.
The American was a chemistry student.
The student was William E. Clarke.
Ether was used during an operation.
The operation was a tooth extraction.

Louis Pasteur was French.
He was a chemist.
He was a bacteriologist.
He proved the existence of bacteria.
The bacteria were airborne.
His discovery was in 1861.
His discovery had a result.
The result was pasteurization of milk.
The pasteurization was to remove harmful bacteria.

X-rays were discovered in 1895.
They were discovered by Wilhelm Roentgen.
Roentgen was a professor.
He was a professor of mathematics.
He was a professor of physics.
He won many awards.
One award was the Nobel Prize.
The prize was for physics.

Fritz Schaudinn was German.
He was a protozoologist.
He discovered organisms.
The organisms were tiny.
The organisms were shaped like corkscrews.
The organisms carry syphylis.
The discovery was in 1905.

Heike Kamerlingh Onnes was Dutch.
Onnes was a physicist.
Onnes produced liquid helium.
Liquid helium led to developments.
One development was cryosurgery.
Another development was quick-freezing.
The quick-freezing was of blood plasma.
Onnes's discovery began a field.
The field was cryogenics.
The discovery was in 1908.

Marie Curie was a chemist.
She was also a physicist.
Pierre Curie was her husband.
He was a physicist.
They discovered polonium.
They discovered radium.
Their discovery was in 1910.
Their discovery led to a new development.
The development was of radiotherapy.

(Adapted from *The Book of Lists*)

STYLISTIC OPTIONS: VARYING THE BASIC SENTENCE PATTERN

Once you can expand the basic subject/predicate pattern using modification, coordination, or subordination, many other stylistic options also become available.

THE CUMULATIVE SENTENCE

The most common kind of sentence used in English is the cumulative, or "loose," sentence. It begins with a main clause that may then be followed by words, phrases, or additional clauses that expand or develop the main clause. Here, for example, is a basic sentence:

It was an immense crowd.

It can be expanded, or "accumulated onto," by any number of phrases or clauses:

It was an immense crowd, two thousand at the least.
It was an immense crowd, though it was not an unruly one.
It was an immense crowd, two thousand at the least and growing every minute.

George Orwell, "Shooting an Elephant"

These sentences are cumulative because the main clause, "It was an immense crowd," appears at the beginning of the sentence and the modifiers follow it.

Writers striving for an informal effect often like cumulative sentences because they can pile on modifiers in seemingly random order. Using several successive cumulative sentences or one long one can give the impression of thinking out loud, letting ideas tumble out. This excerpt from Mark Twain's *Autobiography* illustrates such an effect.

I can see the farm yet, with perfect clearness. I can see all its belongings, all its details; the family room of the house, with a "trundle" bed in one corner and a spinning-wheel in another—a wheel whose rising and falling wail, heard from a distance, was the mournfulest of all sounds to me and made me homesick and low-spirited and filled my atmosphere with the wandering spirit of the dead; the vast fireplace, piled high on winter nights with flaming hickory logs from whose ends a sugary sap bubbled out but did not go to waste, for we scraped it off and ate it; the lazy cat spread out on the rough hearthstones; the drowsy dogs braced against the jambs and blinking; my aunt in one chimney corner, knitting; my uncle in the other, smoking his corn-cob pipe. . . .

You may also choose to use cumulative sentences when you explain ideas to an audience. The student who wrote the following paragraph uses only cumulative sentences.

Horatio Alger was a writer who wrote serial stories about young men who rose from poverty and obscurity to become successful. His first serial story was *Ragged Dick* (1867), which was a best seller. Alger also wrote biographies of self-made Americans like Presidents Abraham Lincoln and James Garfield. Many of his books were set in exotic places like New York and the South Seas. All were adventure stories based on the "rags to riches" theme so appealing to naive small-town boys in the nineteenth century.

The cumulative structure of each sentence helps the student spell out each main idea before expanding or embellishing it.

EXERCISES

1. Identify the cumulative sentences in the following paragraph.

James Agee was a writer of strong talent and many interests, but when he died at forty-five he was by no means the master of his discerning, anguished intellect, not to mention his tempestuous emotions. Even at Harvard he had called attention to himself by the way he lived as well as by his abilities. Until heart disease slowed him down (and eventually killed him) he was much talked about as an insomniac, hard-drinking poet, novelist, and critic, and he was also well known as a film script-writer and essayist. An iconoclast, a rule-breaker, a performer, he was a visionary barely able to keep ahead of his own demons. Many of those who admired his prose viewed his life with pity or outright disapproval, thinking of the waste, the promise only partially fulfilled. (Robert Coles, *New York Review of Books*)

2. Edit the sentences in the paragraph above so that in each sentence the main clause appears at the beginning and the modifiers follow the main clause.

3. Add two or three details to each of these basic sentences to produce a longer cumulative sentence.
   a. Reading offers escape. . . .
   b. We ran to catch the train. . . .
   c. At last he gave in. . . .
   d. Slowly I turned. . . .
   e. The stars were bright. . . .

THE PERIODIC SENTENCE

A periodic sentence presents modifiers first, followed by the main clause. The effect is a gradual building up of intensity, sometimes of suspense, until the climax in the main clause is reached.

In the following sentence, the writer keeps his readers waiting with heightened interest. Finally the main clause at the end of the sentence ties all the modifying clauses together and reveals his meaning.

The wretched prisoners huddling in the stinking cages of the lock-ups, the grey, cowed faces of the long-term convicts, the scarred buttocks of the men who had been flogged with bamboos—all these oppressed me with an intolerable sense of guilt.

George Orwell, "Shooting an Elephant"

By the time readers have finished the sentence, they are prepared to understand the writer's guilt. Similarly, this next sentence builds in intensity to hold readers' attention until its climax.

> If you have ever left a meeting with the feeling that you failed to get your point across, or made no impact, if you think other people have a wrong impression of the kind of person you really are, if you know exactly what you want to say but it comes out in a way that doesn't satisfy you and leaves others uninterested—you have a communications problem.
>
> Michael Korda, *Success!*

In both of these sentences, the periodic structure places added emphasis on the main clause. Notice, too, that in both of these sentences parallelism in the modifying elements helps to heighten interest. (See pages 153–156 for a discussion of parallelism.)

A long periodic sentence that uses a series of parallel modifiers can have significant dramatic and emotional impact. In the following sentence from his 1963 "Letter from Birmingham Jail," Martin Luther King, Jr., builds on a series of parallel clauses to reach his climactic statement—that American blacks can no longer patiently wait for an end to segregation.

> But when you have seen vicious mobs lynch your mothers and fathers at will and drown your sisters and brothers at whim; when you have seen hate-filled policemen curse, kick, and even kill your black brothers and sisters; when you see the vast majority of your twenty million Negro brothers smothering in an airtight cage of poverty in the midst of an affluent society; when you suddenly find your tongue twisted and your speech stammering as you seek to explain to your six-year-old daughter why she can't go to the public amusement park that has just been advertised on television, and see tears welling up in her eyes when she is told that Funtown is closed to colored children, and see ominous clouds of inferiority beginning to distort her personality by developing an unconscious bitterness toward white people; when you have to concoct an answer for a five-year-old son who is asking, "Daddy, why do white people treat colored people so mean?"; when you take a cross-country drive and find it necessary to sleep night after night in the uncomfortable corners of your automobile because no motel will accept you; when you are humiliated day in and day out by nagging signs reading "White" and "Colored"; when your first name becomes "Nigger," your middle name becomes "boy" (however old you are) and your last name becomes "John," and your wife and mother are never given the respected title "Mrs."; when you are harried by day and haunted by night by the fact that you are a Negro, living constantly at tiptoe stance, never quite knowing what to expect next, and are plagued with inner fears and outer resentments; when you are forever fighting a degenerating sense of "nobodiness"—then you will understand why we find it difficult to wait.

Constructing an elaborate sentence like this one requires skills well beyond those of most beginning writers. King keeps his readers in mind at all times as he calculates the impact of his list of injuries. He hopes that by the time his audience finally reaches the sentence's main clause, they too will feel all the frustration that he feels.

EXERCISES

1. Identify each of these sentences as cumulative or periodic.

a. Everything was upside down—the automobiles, the people, the sidewalks, the police on horseback, the buildings. (E. L. Doctorow, *Ragtime*)

b. The correspondent, pulling at the other oar, watched the waves and wondered why he was there. (Stephen Crane, "The Open Boat")

c. The most innocent things disturbed Louise: water gushing from a fire hydrant, a woman leaning out a window who was obviously only going to water her plants. (Ann Beattie, *Falling in Place*)

d. In another moment down went Alice after it, never once considering how in the world she was to get out again. (Lewis Carroll, *Alice's Adventures in Wonderland*)

e. He followed her minutely as she moved, direct and intent, like something transmitted rather than stirring in voluntary activity, straight down the field towards the pond. (D. H. Lawrence, "The Horse Dealer's Daughter")

f. Yesterday, December 7, 1941—a date which will live in infamy—the United States of America was suddenly and deliberately attacked by naval and air forces of the Empire of Japan. (Franklin Delano Roosevelt)

g. She drew him into the salon (where the family waited, a boy and girl his daughter's age, his sister-in-law and her husband). (F. Scott Fitzgerald, "Babylon Revisited")

h. King Farouk of Egypt, before he was toppled from his own throne, forecast that there would soon be only five monarchies left in the world: the king and queen of clubs, diamonds, spades, hearts and England. (Jan Morris, *Redbook*)

i. It was the red of ripe tomatoes: tomatoes ready to be canned, pickled, mashed into sauce, diced into relish, sliced along all three axes or carved into a paraboloid to enclose a ball of tuna salad. (*Newsweek*)

j. Edith turned back to the window, staring intently down into the street. (Susan Fromberg Schaeffer, *Time in Its Flight*)

2. Review the sentences in exercise 1. Rewrite the cumulative sentences so that their structure is periodic and the periodic sentences so that their structure is cumulative.

PARALLEL AND BALANCED SENTENCES

Parallel elements are words, phrases, or clauses with the same grammatical function and form; they can be paired (Jack Spratt could eat no fat; his wife could eat no lean) or presented in a series (I came, I saw, I conquered). When you repeat parallel elements, you give force, unity, and consistency to your writing. Notice, for instance, how much more comprehensible and emphatic the second version of the following sentence is than the first.

Bones and flesh are made up of atoms, as are magazines, and plants and stars are too. *Bones, flesh, magazines, plants,* and *stars* are all made of atoms.

Parallelism is commonly used in newspaper classified ads:

We offer: base *salary,* lucrative *bonus plans,* car *allowance,* full benefit *program,* and *opportunity* for advancement.

in instructions:

Turn all letters face down at the side of the board or *pour* them into a bag or other container, and *shuffle. Draw* for first play.

in examination questions:

Discuss the influence of *Lady Gregory, George Moore, Sean O'Casey,* and *John M. Synge* on the Irish theater, considering each one's distinctive *style, characters,* and *themes.*

and examination answers:

The visible structures were the *cell wall,* the *nucleus,* the *vacuole,* the *cilia,* and the *mitochondria.*
Change can be *evolutionary, revolutionary,* or *cyclical.*
The causes were threefold: *economic, political,* and *ideological.*

Because certain words are usually paired, readers expect to see parallel phrasing used with them. Some of these word pairs are:

first—second	not only—but (also)
either—or	whether—or
neither—nor	both—and

You can use these word pairs to link nouns.

Neither *rain,* nor *snow,* nor *sleet,* nor *dark* of night can keep them from the swift completion of their appointed rounds.

You can use them with verbs.

They not only *tended* an entire family for twenty-five dollars a year but *furnished* the medicines themselves.

Mark Twain, *Autobiography*

Or they can introduce parallel independent clauses.

Not only [did we lack the purine and pyrimidine components,] but [we had never had the shop put together any phosphorous atoms. . . .]

James D. Watson, *The Double Helix*

Because parallel treatment makes it easier to write with precision, your readers can follow your thinking and retrieve information more readily.

Parallel structure also helps you combine a series of short, choppy sentences into one longer, more efficient one. Consider these three sentences.

When choosing a floor you should be interested in durability.
You should also be interested in texture.
Finally, you should consider color.

Combining these sentences, you get:

When choosing a floor you should consider *durability, texture,* and *color.*

Again, all three parallel elements in the series have the same form and function.

Finally, parallel structure can help you vary your sentence patterns and present ideas in interesting and sometimes memorable ways.

I wondered how time would have marred this unique holy spot—*the coves and streams, the hills* that the sun set behind, *the camps and paths* behind the camps.
E. B. White, "Once More to the Lake"

High up on the balconies of each cottage the children stand, *the girls in their red bows and white dresses, the boys in white suits and giant red ties.*
Tillie Olsen, "I Stand Here Ironing"

When a sentence neatly divides into two parallel structures, it is said to be *balanced.* For instance, Ogden Nash's

Candy is dandy, but liquor is quicker.

has balance. The parallel structures here are two independent clauses, each composed of a noun, the verb "is," and an adjective. As is often the case in a balanced sentence, the clauses are connected with a coordinating conjunction. The following sentences also illustrate this structure.

Life got tougher, so *we got stronger.*
We will win this battle, or *we will die* in the attempt!
Reading builds minds, and *minds build nations.*

Often, you can use a balanced sentence to suggest contrast, to weigh two alternatives. Everybody remembers Patrick Henry's famous statement:

Give me liberty, or *give me death.*

Here the balanced sentence consists of two independent clauses linked by a coordinating conjunction. In the following sentence, a comma substitutes for the conjunction.

His experience is wide, *his character* is well known.

Many experienced writers rely on balanced sentences to add emphasis by setting their key points in opposition. In particular, speakers—politicians and clergymen, for instance—find that balanced sentences make their statements more forceful and memorable.

And so, my fellow Americans, ask not what your country can do for you; ask what you can do for your country.

John F. Kennedy

In those days, the church was not merely a thermometer that recorded the ideas and principles of popular opinion; it was a thermostat that transformed the mores of society.

Martin Luther King, Jr., "Letter from Birmingham Jail"

You may also notice balanced sentences in advertising slogans and song lyrics. Balanced constructions are easy to remember and to repeat, so they suit these purposes well.

EXERCISES

1. Read the following paragraph from "School Is Bad for Children," by John Holt (*Saturday Evening Post*). Underline the parallel elements—words, phrases, clauses—in each sentence.

Almost every child, on the first day he sets foot in a school building, is smarter, more curious, less afraid of what he doesn't know, better at finding and figuring things out, more confident, resourceful, persistent and independent than he will ever be again in his schooling—or, unless he is very unusual and very lucky, for the rest of his life. Already, by paying close attention to and interacting with the world and people around him, and without any school-type formal instruction, he has done a task far more difficult, complicated and abstract than anything he will be asked to do in school, or than any of his teachers has done for years. He has solved the mystery of language. He has discovered it—babies don't even know that language exists—and he has found out how it works and learned to use it. He has done it by exploring, by experimenting, by developing his own model of the grammar of language, by trying it out and seeing whether it works, by gradually changing it and refining it until it does work. And while he has been doing this, he has been learning other things as well, including many of the "concepts" that the schools think only they can teach him, and many that are more complicated than the ones they do try to teach him.

2. Use each of the following five sets of notes to construct one *balanced* sentence. Edit the notes to create parallel words and sentence structure.

    a. Baby boom results: competition keener for admission to colleges; increased competition for jobs.

    b. Gasohol—one response to energy crisis.
        Solar heat—better response.

    c. Campaign slogans: 1964—Goldwater—"In your heart you know he's right"; Johnson (also 1964)—"All the way with LBJ."

    d. Emily Dickinson—poet, American, 19c, near-recluse who lived alone with father; Virginia Woolf—English novelist (20c), prominent member of Bloomsbury circle of artists and writers.

e. New scientific advances—organ transplants, word processors, space shuttle, CAT scanner—have been occurring in medicine and engineering.

3. Use parallelism and balance to generate three original sentences in imitation of this one:

Eugene wanted the two things all men want: he wanted to be loved, and he wanted to be famous. (Thomas Wolfe, *Look Homeward, Angel*)

WRITING EFFECTIVE SENTENCES

Nothing makes readers lose interest so quickly as a group of sentences that are all alike. Your writing should be varied enough to keep your readers engaged and smooth enough to keep them moving. If it is not, your essays will seem like a stretch of turnpike—boring, unchanging, and guaranteed to put your audience to sleep. You know that your sentences must satisfy your readers' expectations and communicate your ideas effectively. You also want them to create interest. To achieve these goals, you should pay special attention to making your sentences *emphatic, clear, economical,* and *varied.*

WRITING EMPHATIC SENTENCES

When you talk, you emphasize ideas with facial expressions, gestures, and vocal cues such as raising or lowering your voice. In writing, other techniques allow you to highlight important points. You can, with practice, create emphasis where you want it by careful sentence construction. Skillful repetition of words, phrases, and sentence patterns, as well as the choice of emphatic word order and voice, helps you to stress certain points and qualify others.

☐ USING REPETITION

Unintentional repetition makes sentences dull and monotonous.

The reformers *got* results when the newspapers *got* letters of protest.
The Mayor's investigators *also* found saloons open on Sunday, which was *also* against the law.

Intentional repetition, however, does a lot to place stress where you want it. In the following sentence, the student writer makes it clear that she wishes to emphasize the contrast between the common people's view of Caesar and the true picture of the man.

The common people were apt to pay *more attention* to what Caesar said he would do for them than what he actually did, *more attention* to Caesar the hero than to Caesar the man, *more attention* to Caesar the benefactor than to Caesar the tyrant.

Repetition for emphasis need not take the form of a series. The writers of these sentences achieve emphasis by repeating a key word or phrase just once:

At the age of 19 he was in college; *at the age of* 20 he was in Korea.

There is a night world that few men have entered and from whose greatest *depths* none have returned alive—the abysmal *depths* of the sea.

Loren Eiseley, The Immense Journey

As with all great art, the fairy tale's deepest meaning will be *different* for each *person,* and *different* for the same *person* at various moments in his life.

Bruno Bettelheim, The Uses of Enchantment

You may have noticed that some of these sentences achieve emphasis through balance and parallelism. Repetition is an integral part of both techniques. Notice how parallelism and balance, created by repeating structural patterns, strengthen the following sentences.

In *The Secret Agent* Conrad communicates Stevie's helplessness, Winnie's fear, and Ossipon's acute sense of frustration.

Bonny Strauss, student

And God made the two great lights: the greater light to rule the day, and the lesser light to rule the night. . . .

The Bible

Leonardo [da Vinci] looked at nature directly, not through the mind but through the eye.

J. Bronowski, "Leonardo da Vinci," Renaissance Profiles

The result, all over the country, is a spate of sudden population boomlets in hundreds of smaller communities—complete with soaring real-estate prices, rising demands for government services, and acrid controversies over continued growth.

Newsweek

In *The Great Gatsby*, by F. Scott Fitzgerald, the west is stable and romantic, an irrecoverable dream; the east is dynamic and sterile, a vulgar reality.

Richard Weaver, student

EXERCISES

1.   In the following passage from Charles Dickens's novel *Hard Times,* words, phrases, and sentence patterns are repeated frequently. Identify the repeated elements, noting how repetition creates emphasis in the passage.

It was a town of red brick, or of brick that would have been red if the smoke and ashes had allowed it; but as matters stood it was a town of machinery and tall chimneys, out of which interminable serpents of smoke trailed themselves forever and ever, and never got uncoiled. It had a black canal in it, and a river that ran purple with ill-smelling dye, and vast piles of buildings full of windows where there was a rattling and a trembling all day long, and where the piston of the steam engine worked monotonously up and down like the head of an elephant in a state of melancholy madness. It contained several large streets all very like one another, inhabited by people equally like one another, who all went in and out at the same hours, with the same sound upon the same pavements, to do the same work, and to whom every day was the same as yesterday and tomorrow, and every year was the counterpart of the last and the next.

2. Classified ads, especially those in the employment section, are frequently written in parallel terms. Using the information below, write a want ad for an editorial position. Be sure to use parallel sentence structure to make your ad emphatic enough to attract potential applicants.

The company designs electronic systems and equipment and manufactures electronic systems and equipment. They are looking for someone to set up a new corporate newspaper and plan and edit it as well as supervise its publication. This person should be a good writer who also has superior editorial judgment. The applicant also needs excellent interviewing skills and should have a general knowledge of graphics. In addition, the person they seek should have a general knowledge of photography and printing. The applicant should be able to organize and have an ability to meet deadlines. Other responsibilities may include preparing employee handbooks and the preparation of bulletins.

☐ USING WORD ORDER

Where you put the words in your sentences also emphasizes or deemphasizes certain ideas. Placing words or phrases either at the *beginning* or at the *end* of a sentence focuses attention on them. Readers expect the most important information to appear in these positions, and you should take care to fulfill their expectations.

Look at the following sentence:

> *To clone mice,* biologists Karl Illmensee, of the University of Geneva, and Peter Hoppe, of the Jackson Laboratory in Bar Harbor, Maine, used a procedure called nuclear transplantation.
>
> Carol Johmann, "A Tale of Three Mice," *Discover*

This sentence rightly places greatest emphasis on the controversial cloning procedure itself. The information about those who performed it and where they were located is subordinated. Phrasing the sentence another way changes the emphasis, focusing attention on the biologists instead of on cloning:

> *Biologists Karl Illmensee,* of the University of Geneva, *and Peter Hoppe,* of the Jackson Laboratory in Bar Harbor, Maine, cloned mice by using a procedure called nuclear transplantation.

When you need a straightforward, no-nonsense presentation—as you do in laboratory reports, memos, technical reports, and business letters—your sentences must present vital information first and qualifiers later.

Cadmium and lead will melt at this temperature except when pressurized above two atmospheres.

Lab report

New accounting positions will depend on the availability of recent graduates and the number of new accounts we have obtained.

Business letter

The writer of the first sentence wants to emphasize the melting point of cadmium and lead, not pressurization; the writer of the second sentence wants to stress new accounting positions, not the conditions that would create them. Both writers understand that their readers do not want to wade through a series of qualifiers to get to the point.

A dash or colon can be used to add emphasis when it isolates important words or phrases at the end of a sentence:

After the appetizer, after the soup, after the salad, entree, and cheese course came the chef's specialty—cherries jubilee.

The economic outlook was so bleak that advisors decided they could make only one recommendation: wait and see.

A special kind of emphatic word order, called *climactic order*, presents the information in a sentence so that it leads up to the most important idea. This structure gives strong emphasis to the main idea. In both of the following sentences the key idea is at the end, where momentum built up in the sentence gives it added force.

He feared that he would mumble indistinctly, forget his lines, and make a complete fool of himself.

If the grass in the back yard didn't grow soon, they vowed to plant a hardier variety, hire a lawn specialist, or put down Astroturf.

You can use climactic word order in journalistic, literary, or academic writing—anywhere you wish to build suspense or heighten interest.

Occasionally a writer may indicate a special emphasis by *inverting sentence order,* taking a word or phrase or clause out of the sequence in which readers expect to find it and focusing attention on the misplaced element or on the whole unusual sentence.

For instance, Mark Twain's statement

It was a heavenly place for a boy, that farm of my Uncle John's,

gives added emphasis to "that farm of my Uncle John's" by moving it from its expected position at the beginning. But Twain inverts the sentence order to stress his reaction. Similarly, by writing

Leaping ferociously through the forest came the fire

instead of

The fire came leaping ferociously through the forest,

the writer adds drama to the sentence by almost imitating the forward thrust of the fire. Compare the following pairs of sentences:

Expected order	Inverted order
The attraction was exciting baseball, and the excitement of their play was a wonder of the sociological Dodgers.	Exciting baseball was the attraction, and a wonder of the sociological Dodgers was the excitement of their play.
	Roger Kahn, *The Boys of Summer*
A series of what E. M. Forster would call flat characters highlights the complex characters of Jane Austen's Emma Woodhouse and Elizabeth Bennet.	Highlighting the complex characters of Jane Austen's Emma Woodhouse and Elizabeth Bennet are a series of what E. M. Forster would call flat characters.
	Debbie Feldman, student

In both cases, the inverted word order ensures that the reader catches each writer's emphasis—in the first sentence, on "exciting baseball," and in the second, on the two complex Austen characters.

EXERCISE

Read the following paragraph and underline the key ideas in each sentence. In each case, explain how the writer has structured the sentence to place emphasis on that key idea. For example, are the most important ideas placed at the beginning of most sentences? Does the writer use climactic order? Inverted order?

Trapped, like Ibsen's Nora, in a smothering society which allows women no individuality, is Doris Lessing's Martha Quest. Her mother is not disturbed at all by the fact that Martha, in a desperate attempt to find the propriety she has not been able to attain, is marrying a man she hardly knows. (Mrs. Quest's only concern is that Martha has no engagement ring.) In fact, Mrs. Quest's principal emotion at Martha's marriage is relief. But in Martha's age marriage is not indissoluble; there is a sequel to *Martha Quest* as there could not have been to Ibsen's *A Doll's House.* The "proper marriage" of the sequel's title shows the basic irreconcilability of the conflict between the complex individual and the institutions of the society in which she must live: the "proper marriage" ends in divorce.

☐ USING ACTIVE VOICE

The passive voice—"It was done by me" instead of "I did it"— focuses a reader's attention on the action itself or on its recipient rather than on the performer of the action. Sometimes, especially in scientific and technical writing, you want this focus because you want to emphasize the action or results. The passive construction "Penicillin was discovered in 1929" stresses the achievement, while "Fleming discovered penicillin in 1929" stresses the scientist who did the achieving. Remember, neither version of these two sentences is superior. Your purpose, your audience, and your occasion make one choice more appropriate than another. Consider the use of the passive voice in this introductory paragraph from an article in the *New England Journal of Medicine*.

> It is well established that women have an increased risk of venous thromboembolism, stroke, and myocardial infarction while taking oral contraceptives. The risk is also known to diminish soon after the cessation of use but it is not known whether there is long-lasting residual effect if oral contraceptives are taken for many years. With regard to myocardial infarction, there are particular grounds for concern about a residual effect, since oral contraceptives bring about changes in lipoprotein metabolism, blood pressure, and glucose tolerance that may increase the risk.

The writers of this paragraph want to stress the *effects* of oral contraceptives, not who was doing the study or who was being studied, and they do. In each sentence, the passive voice emphasizes "risks" and "grounds for concern." Where they emphasize causes, they use the active voice—"women have increased risk . . ." and "oral contraceptives bring about changes."

   Often, however, the passive voice dulls your emphasis and takes the life out of your presentation because it obscures your subject. The student writer of the following sentence only confuses his readers.

> The society which is struggled through in Bernard Malamud's novel *A New Life* is discouraging, for both comprehension of and control over life have been lost.

Who is struggling? Who finds the society discouraging? Who has lost comprehension and control? Compare that sentence with this revision.

> The society that Levin struggles through in Bernard Malamud's novel *A New Life* is discouraging, for his peers have lost comprehension of and control over their own lives.

Notice how this student destroys the immediacy of her story by overusing the passive voice.

> The onset of blindness occurred fifteen years ago. The diagnosis was made by an experienced ophthalmologist in a small city. It was subsequently confirmed by another ophthalmologist in New York City. The disease was the subject of research by the National Eye Institute. A partial cure was accomplished by their skilled physicians in 1965.

By writing these sentences in the active voice, the student achieves this more immediate version of her narrative.

> Fifteen years ago I began going blind. An experienced ophthalmologist in the small city where I lived at the time made the diagnosis. Another ophthalmologist in New York City subsequently confirmed his diagnosis. He told me, however, that the disease was being studied by researchers at the National Eye Institute. A year later, in 1965, their skilled physicians accomplished a partial cure.

As these sentences show, the active voice is more direct, more natural, and more emphatic than the passive voice.

EXERCISE

Revise this paragraph to eliminate excessive use of passive constructions and make the writing more emphatic.

If something is not done by the government soon, full benefits may not be able to be paid by the Social Security system to 35 million retirees or their survivors. To keep benefits coming, taxes may have to be raised by the federal government, or benefits may have to be cut by them. This was stated by trustees of the Social Security program in their annual report. It was also stated that all of the three Social Security programs funded by payroll tax will soon run out of money. To keep the system functioning, it was concluded by the trustees, the level of benefits or the number of recipients must be reduced by the government.

□   A NOTE ON SUBORDINATION

You can clarify your emphasis in a sentence through careful use of subordination. We have already examined subordination as a technique for creating complex sentences. Because it shows readers the relative importance of your ideas, you should use it not only to vary your sentence structure, but also to emphasize certain ideas. Turn back to our discussion of subordination (pages 144–145) and reread it in this context.

WRITING CLEAR SENTENCES

All experienced writers know that effective sentences don't just happen; they are the result of careful planning and revision. An effective sentence—one that communicates—is clear and coherent. It demonstrates your control of your writing.

□   KEEPING SENTENCES FOCUSED

When a sentence is out of control, it rambles along, overloaded with words that contribute nothing to a reader's understanding. A student in a social welfare class wrote this sentence in a paper on the treatment of the mentally ill in the United States.

In the period following the Revolution, a new solution for the problem of the mentally ill was being sought, and this was sparked, in part, by the humanistic values of the Enlightenment, such as the concept of freedom and the recognition that people could have some control over the events in their lives, and this had a profound effect on the way individuals viewed the mentally ill because people no longer felt helpless in the face of this problem, so now finding the cause of mental disorders soon became the goal.

In this almost incoherent sentence, the writer packed in all the information she could think of. Instead of establishing relationships among her ideas, she strung them together with coordinating conjunctions. She overloaded a single sentence with more information than her readers could possibly process. When she reviewed her work, she broke her single long sentence into units that readers could easily understand. And with fewer ideas in each sentence, her message became more accessible. Compare the sentence above with this paragraph.

> In the period following the Revolution, a new solution to the problem of the mentally ill was being sought, sparked, in part, by the humanistic values of the Enlightenment. These values, such as the concept of freedom and the recognition that people could have some control over the events in their lives, had a profound effect on the way individuals viewed the mentally ill. Now people no longer felt helpless in the face of this problem, and finding the cause of mental disorders soon became the goal.

The revision divides the original overstuffed sentence into three clear, well-controlled sentences. With excessive coordination gone, the reader can now find the ideas. The revised version is only three words shorter, but the distribution of information among the three sentences makes that information much easier to assimilate.

EXERCISE

These sentences, from a social welfare paper, are unclear because they are too long and lack focus and control. Revise these rambling sentences by breaking them into manageable units.

a. The community, especially in poor urban areas, is ill-equipped to handle the needs of the mentally ill, and these problems are typified by the long-term chronic client, who—after many hospitalizations and little treatment—is often not able to participate in our society so usually lives on welfare or Social Security payments and is hidden in shabby boarding homes that have become the new "back wards."

b. The psychiatrist, in this setting, becomes a pseudodruggist for the client, provides little therapeutic help for the client, and has little knowledge of (and, in some cases, interest in) the problems facing the client in his or her everyday life, which would probably be best left to the other staff or the aftercare service, but the difficulty with this setup is the typical understaffing of these workers, and in addition their time is often consumed by paper work.

☐ KEEPING YOUR PERSPECTIVE CONSISTENT

Unwarranted shifts in tense, voice, or number also interrupt the train of thought and confuse your audience. Although movement from past to present tense and first to third person often occurs in casual speech, make sure that haphazard shifts don't occur when you write. Look at the following pairs of sentences. Confusing shifts occur in the sentences at the left. Notice how much clearer the revised version to the right is.

Unclear	Clear

Shift in tense (past to present)

| The self-reliance Thoreau *was* seeking at Walden Pond *is* also a self-awareness. | The self-reliance Thoreau *was* seeking at Walden Pond *was* also a self-awareness. |

Shift in voice (active to passive)

| Citizens in Thomas More's Utopia *favor* fair trials, and war *is abhorred by them.* | Citizens in Thomas More's Utopia *favor* fair trials and *abhor* war. |

Shift in number (singular to plural)

| A *person* might be tempted to generalize about political corruption on the basis of Watergate, but *they* should not necessarily jump to conclusions. | *People* might be tempted to generalize about political corruption on the basis of Watergate, but *they* should not necessarily jump to conclusions. |

To avoid such shifts, look hard at your verbs and nouns to see if you have, without knowing it, moved from past to present tense, from active to passive voice, or from singular to plural. These errors seem to occur most often in narrative writing—in telling about yourself, in giving a plot summary of a book, or in describing an event. Narratives depend on a consistent presentation of related events, so you should avoid abrupt shifts in perspective. Usually you can find and correct these slips when you revise your first draft.

EXERCISE

Rewrite these sentences to correct inconsistencies in tense, voice, and number.

a.　In Shakespeare's Sonnet 18, the speaker compares the one he loves to a summer's day, but the suggestion is made that his love can live forever while the day must end.

b.　The reader may believe Shakespeare is being totally serious, but perhaps they should see the sonnet's playful side as well.

c.　In Shakespeare's play *Julius Caesar,* when both Brutus and Cassius vied for the same position, each is made to think he will be honored with it.

d.　We tend to think of Julius Caesar only as a Shakespearean hero, but one should remember him also as a central figure in George Bernard Shaw's *Caesar and Cleopatra.*

e.　In Shakespeare's *Julius Caesar* we are made more aware of Caesar as a public figure, while in *Caesar and Cleopatra* we saw more of the character's private life.

WRITING ECONOMICAL SENTENCES

An economical sentence uses as few words as possible to convey information. Wordy sentences—those that take an unnecessarily long time to make their point—try your readers' patience and make them lose interest. To make your sentences readable, then, you must take out extra words and empty phrases.

Many writers get into the habit of automatically using meaningless phrases, often introductory phrases, that take up space and add nothing to meaning. Such phrases are commonly called *deadwood*. Compare these sentences:

Wordy	Economical
With reference to your plan, it seems like a workable one.	Your plan seems workable.
In my opinion equal work should demand equal pay.	Equal work should demand equal pay.

These and other expressions like "obviously," "as the case may be," "I feel," "it seems to me," "in conclusion," or "by way of explanation" are nothing but space fillers. You may think they make a sentence sound balanced or filled out, but too often they only sound like empty apologies or self-conscious attempts to justify your position. Because deadwood gets in the way of what you want to say, you should delete it.

Another notorious source of wordiness is taking a roundabout way to say something, using ten words when five will do. This is sometimes called *circumlocution*, but whatever you call it, avoid it. Compare these sentences:

Wordy	Economical
The results were of a unique nature.	The results were unique.
It is not unlikely that he will run for reelection.	He will probably run for reelection.
She was not given the position due to the fact that she didn't meet the qualifications.	She was not hired because she wasn't qualified.
There were several factors contributing to her decision.	Several factors contributed to her decision.

A sentence is not economical simply because it is short. The important thing is how much information it conveys. If you can eliminate words without reducing the amount of information you present, then you should do so. Extra words, like excess baggage, weigh you down.

Sometimes wordy sentences are heavy with redundant words or phrases. Intentional repetition can add emphasis and clarity, but unnecessary repetition—unintentionally saying the same thing more than once—annoys your readers and obscures your meaning. Consider how redundancy weakens the following sentences.

In this *modern* world of *today*, people never walk when they can ride.
Without a doubt, this month has *certainly* been the coldest January on record.
We found an *old antique* clock in the attic.
At *first* his *preliminary* diagnosis was tuberculosis.

Unnecessary repetition also occurs when you say the same thing, in essentially the same words, in subsequent clauses. In this case, creating a compound subject or a compound predicate may solve the problem. The following sentences illustrate this type of redundancy.

The lab technician found the experiment difficult. The research chemist also found it hard.

"Found the experiment difficult" and "found it hard" say the same thing. A compound subject eliminates this.

Both the lab technician and the research chemist found the experiment difficult.

The revised sentence is far more economical than the original two sentences. A compound predicate can also eliminate unnecessary repetition. Thus

The father in Sherwood Anderson's story "The Egg" bought a diner. This character decided to become an entertainer. He began doing tricks for his customers.

can be revised to read

The father in Sherwood Anderson's story "The Egg" bought a diner, decided to become an entertainer, and began doing tricks for his customers.

This type of redundancy can also be eliminated by combining clauses and substituting the pronoun "who" for a repeated noun. Consider the following sentences.

Lt. Henry ran from the soldiers. The soldiers looked after him and fired.

Thomas Pynchon received the National Book Award for *Gravity's Rainbow*. Pynchon did not come to the ceremony to accept the prize.

The unnecessary repetition can be eliminated like this:

Lt. Henry ran from the soldiers, who looked after him and fired.

Thomas Pynchon, who received the National Book Award for *Gravity's Rainbow*, did not come to the ceremony to accept the prize.

EXERCISE

This paragraph summarizes part of a short story. (As it stands now, it shows signs of becoming as long as the original!) By removing as much deadwood and circumlocution and as many redundancies as you can, reduce the passage to its most economical, readable version.

In the short story called "Where Are You Going, Where Have You Been?" which we read during the course of this semester, the two main characters are the protagonist who is a young teenaged girl named Connie and her enemy or antagonist who is an older man called Arnold Friend. Joyce Carol Oates is the author of this short story. When the short story begins, it opens with Connie sort of dreaming, constantly thinking thoughts of boys all the time and trying to look older and more grown up. She and her girlfriend like to go on outings to the nearby local drive-in, where they can make attempts to pick up boys. One night Connie sees Arnold, who stares at her, looking at her for a long time. The next day, while her parents are out, Arnold drives by in his car to see her.

WRITING VARIED SENTENCES

There is no point in variety simply for its own sake. The form of each of your sentences, and the shape of your sentences in sequence, should be consistent with the ideas being expressed and with your audience and purpose.

But under the right circumstances, you have many options. You can alternate sentences of different lengths and structures, varying the way you begin your sentences and the number of words in each. You can use different stylistic patterns—cumulative, balanced, periodic—and juxtapose statements with questions or exclamations. You can also use parenthetical phrases or lists and catalogs to add interest. All of these techniques point to the same end: to convey your meaning most effectively and to make your writing more interesting to your readers.

The sentences of the following excerpt from E. L. Doctorow's novel *Ragtime* illustrate many of these different strategies.

(1) Tracks! (2) Tracks! (3) It seemed to the visionaries who wrote for the popular magazines that the future lay at the end of parallel rails. (4) There were long-distance locomotive railroads and interurban electric railroads and street railways and elevated railroads, all laying their steel stripes on the land, crisscrossing like the texture of an indefatigable civilization. (5) And in Boston and New York there were even railroads under the streets, new rapid-transit subway systems transporting thousands of people every day. (6) In New York, in fact, the success of the Manhattan subway had created a demand for a line to Brooklyn. (7) Accordingly, an engineering miracle was taking place, the construction of a tunnel under the East River from Brooklyn to the Battery.

These seven sentences differ widely in length and structure. The first two sentences are one-word exclamations; the others are declarative statements. Sentences 3 and 7 are periodic; 4, 5, and 6 are cumulative. Sentence openings are varied. Sentence 6, for instance, begins with a prepositional phrase. Sentence 7 opens with a transitional word. Sentence 4 includes a parallel series that adds interest. Sentence length is especially varied, ranging from one word to thirty-two.

Sentences of similar length and structure usually produce a very dull piece of writing. In the following excerpt, however, the skillful placement of long sentences with a final short one result in an engaging and emphatic paragraph.

(1) For one perfect evening last week the old mill town of Pawtucket, R.I., became the center of the baseball world. (2) Warmed by a bright orange sunset, nearly 6,000 fans packed the grandstand of venerable McCoy Stadium and more

than 100 journalists interviewed anything that talked. (3) It was only a minor-league game between the Rochester Red Wings and the Pawtucket Red Sox, but history was in the making: it was the longest game in the annals of professional baseball. (4) It had begun on the evening of April 18, had consumed 32 innings over 8 hours and 7 minutes, and had been suspended at 4:07 a.m.—to protect the glassy-eyed players from potential injury—as the Easter Sunday sun rose. (5) Before the game resumed last week, Pawtucket manager Joe Morgan, a seen-it-all veteran of fifteen seasons as a minor-league manager, explained quite simply why everyone was so excited. (6) Baseball, he said, "is God's game."

Newsweek

The *Newsweek* writer uses a variety of strategies to make this journalistic paragraph interesting. The author uses cumulative and periodic sentences and varies the sentence openings. Sentence 1, for instance, begins with a prepositional phrase, sentence 2 with a participial phrase, and sentence 5 with an adverbial clause. Imagine, however, what the effect of the paragraph would be if every sentence had the same pattern.

The first few sentences might read like this:

> It was a perfect evening last week. The old mill town of Pawtucket, R.I., became the center of the baseball world. Nearly 6,000 fans were warmed by a bright orange sunset. They packed the grandstand of venerable McCoy Stadium. More than 100 journalists interviewed anything that talked. It was only a minor-league game.

What makes this so dull? Despite the topic, the string of sentences sounds about as exciting as a shopping list, mainly because every sentence begins with the subject and has the same structure, but also because all are approximately the same length. If the whole paragraph read this way, the short last sentence of the original would have no impact at all.

EXERCISES

1.   Read the following paragraph and comment on the sentence variety. What techniques does the author use to vary his sentences?

In spite of it all, London remains for many the world's greatest city, the most livable, the most civilized. The parks are still thriving, superb even in winter. The transport system is still quite possibly the best in any metropolis. There is an air of authenticity about the place: A man seen wearing a fez is not a Shriner pretending to be a Turk; he is a Turk. An ad for a Tudor house does not mean a house built in Tudor style; it means a house actually dating to the 15th-Century Tudor era. An unremarkable and unremarked Islington pub, the Pied Bull, is the same inn (rebuilt, to be sure) where Sir Walter Raleigh once lived, and open-air Chapel Market next door, where he perhaps bought apples and cobnuts, still bustles daily. (Michael Kernan, *Washington Post*)

2.   In the following paragraph, dull, choppy sentences all begin with the subject. Revise the sentences to make them more varied and interesting, making sure they form a unified paragraph. Keep in mind that there is no one "right way" to combine the sentences. Experiment with the options we have discussed and see what works best for you.

Many well-known American writers also wrote screenplays. Maxwell Anderson was a U.S. playwright. He wrote the play *Winterset*. He also worked on screenplays. He worked on the screenplays "All Quiet on the Western Front" (1930) and "The Wrong Man" (1957). He worked on other films too. Raymond Chandler was a well-known writer of detective stories. He wrote the novel *The Big Sleep*. He wrote the scripts for the films "Double Indemnity" (1944) and "Strangers on a Train" (1951). Theodore Dreiser wrote the novels *Sister Carrie* and *An American Tragedy*. He wrote the screenplay for the film version of *An American Tragedy* in 1931. William Faulkner is the well-known author of the novels *The Sound and the Fury, Absalom, Absalom,* and many others about life in the South. He also worked in Hollywood. He wrote screenplays like "Road to Glory" (1936) and "To Have and Have Not" (1945) there. Finally, F. Scott Fitzgerald was a screenwriter too. He wrote novels like *The Great Gatsby* and *Tender Is the Night*. He also worked on screenplays like "Three Comrades" (1938) and "Gone with the Wind" (1939). (Adapted from *The Book of Lists*)

SENTENCE REVIEW EXERCISES

1.   Read each of the following paragraphs and evaluate each according to how successful the author is at achieving clarity, emphasis, economy, and variety in his or her sentences.

a.   America's ills are attributed to changes abroad and, variously, to lack of will, failure of nerve, moral decay, selfishness and sloth, the shattering of community feeling. One can find signs of all of these, but the key may be something else: the fact that Americans want just about everything, without considering or fully understanding the cost. We want freedom as well as order, individual liberty as well as equality, safety as well as the benefits of risk-taking, a wide-open society as well as less crime, material wealth as well as spiritual worth—without stopping to think that each of these values takes something away from the other. To use an ungainly but accurate word, we have forgotten the trade-offs. (*Discover*)

b.   Airfields blossomed everywhere. For the great air offensive 163 bases were constructed in addition to the scores already in existence, until at last there were so many that a standard gag among 8th and 9th Air Force crewmen was that they could taxi the length and breadth of the island without scratching a wing. Ports were jammed. A great supporting naval fleet of almost nine hundred ships, from battleships to PT boats, began to assemble. Convoys arrived in such great numbers that by spring they had delivered almost two million tons of goods and supplies—so much that 170 miles of new railroad lines had to be laid down to move it. (Cornelius Ryan, *The Longest Day*)

c.   Sharing emotions is healthy. Or to put it differently, keeping your feelings pent up can lead to psychosomatic illness. To see how this happens, remember the bodily changes that accompany strong emotions: digestion slows, heartbeat increases, adrenaline is secreted, and respiration grows quicker. Whereas these conditions are short-lived for people who can express their feelings, the failure to act on these impulses can lead to a constant state of physiological tension that damages the digestive tract, lungs, circulatory system, muscles, joints, and the body's ability to resist infections. One example of how the stress that accompanies the poor communication of emotions can damage health involves hypertension, or high blood pressure. Over a five-year period Flanders Dunbar studied a random sample of 1,600 cardiovascular patients at Columbia Presbyterian Medical Center in New York City. She found that four out of five patients shared common emotional characteristics, many of which are representative of either nonassertive or aggressive communicators. For instance, most of her patients were argumentative, had trouble expressing their feelings, and kept people at a distance. Difficulty in expressing feelings crops up in other characteristics of cardiovascular sufferers—easily upset but unable to handle upsetting situations, anxious to please but longing to rebel, alternately passive and irritable. (Ronald B. Adler and Neil Towne, *Looking Out/Looking In*)

2.   Study the following sentences and write two original sentences in imitation of each.

a.   The next great moment in history is ours. (Vivian Gornick)

b.   Happy families are all alike; every unhappy family is unhappy in its own way. (Leo Tolstoy, *Anna Karenina*)

c.   Such is the state of today's economy that every silver cloud on the horizon has a dark lining. (*Newsweek*)

d.   For my father's funeral I had nothing black to wear and this posed a nagging problem all day long. (James Baldwin, *Notes of a Native Son*)

e.   Being in love means never having to say you're sorry. (Erich Segal, *Love Story*)

f.   When the going gets tough, the tough get going.

g.   A woman without a man is like a fish without a bicycle.

h.   Beauty is the making one of opposites.

i.   Marry in haste, repent at leisure.

j.   We hold these truths to be self-evident, that all men are created equal, that they are endowed by their creator with certain inalienable rights, that among these are life, liberty, and the pursuit of happiness.

CHAPTER

7

Writing: Words

E very writer knows the frustration of trying to find the "right" word and the delight of finally succeeding. Whether you are describing your feelings at seeing a championship team in action or the components of a home computer, the problem remains the same: to choose words that convey your meaning precisely. This is difficult work for many reasons, one of which is that no single word in English has one correct meaning. But if you are aware of the subtlety and depth of language, you can express yourself in precise and sometimes original ways.

USING ACCURATE WORDS

Mark Twain once said that the difference between almost the right word and the right word was like the difference between the lightning bug and the lightning. As Twain knew well, words are the signals that communicate your message to your readers. If you send out the wrong signals—even the almost-right ones—your readers become confused or lost. When choosing words, you must know as much as possible about their shades of meaning.

DENOTATION

You can determine a word's *denotation*—its generally accepted meaning—by consulting a dictionary. Here you can always find a word's explicit meaning—what it signifies or stands for. Any good dictionary tells you that "rambunctious," for instance, means boisterous or disorderly, and that a "brouhaha" is an uproar. Most college dictionaries provide additional information about words. You can determine that "rambunctious," an adjective, is probably a form of an earlier word, "robustious," which in turn came from the Latin *robustus,* and that "brouhaha," a noun, is from the French and was probably imitative. Dictionary entries also supply information about spelling, syllabication, and pronunciation. Some entries supply additional historical or linguistic details: that "terminal," for instance, meaning a limit or end, refers to the stone figures of the god Terminus that the ancient Romans used as boundary markers. Some words may have complicated histories, or etymologies, as they are called, and others may be identified as "archaic" or "nonstandard."

Your dictionary may show you how a word is used as well as what its different meanings are. You can, for example, find out that you can't use "rambunctious" as a noun or "brouhaha" as an adjective, that "rambunctious" is probably not a word you would use to describe your family doctor, and that a "brouhaha" doesn't usually occur during a religious service. As usage changes, word meanings may become narrower or broader, more favorable or more negative. In addition, new inventions, discoveries, or applications create a need for new words or push old words to take on new meanings. (Consider the computer specialist's use of "batch," "program," and "bit.") Your own reading and writing supplement your use of the dictionary and increase your ability to know words and use them effectively. Understanding the denotations of the words you use—their explicit meanings—is just the first step toward effective diction.

EXERCISE

To refresh your memory about what the dictionary has to offer, use a good desk dictionary to help you answer these questions.

1. From what language can the words *skull, skeleton,* and *skirt* be traced?
2. What is the difference between *imply* and *infer*? Use each in a sentence.
3. What part of speech is the word *banyan*? *peristyle*? *tophus*?
4. What is a *catamaran*? A *catapult*? A *catafalque*? Are any of these words related to the word *cat*?

5. Which is correct, *hand gun* or *handgun*? *A lot* or *alot*?
6. Where is Grub Street?
7. What are the two meanings of the word *gudgeon*?
8. What is the origin of the word *jingo*?
9. What meaning did the word *enthusiasm* once have that it does not have now? Is the word *enthuse* acceptable?
10. When was Jesse James born?

CONNOTATION

The dictionary tells you the literal meanings of words, but most of the time it gives you only that, fixed meanings, or denotations. What a dictionary definition *doesn't* usually tell you is the *connotations* of a word, what a word suggests emotionally in a particular situation. Often only your own experience and your familiarity with language and its options give you this dimension of meaning.

Words may have similar denotative meanings but very different connotations. You choose a word with a positive connotation to convey approval and one with a negative connotation to convey disapproval. The word *crowd,* for instance, is fairly neutral; *gathering* suggests an orderly group with a common goal; *mob* brings to mind unruliness, even danger. You select words for their connotations, and as you write and revise, your purpose determines the words you choose.

EXERCISE

---

1. The following words have similar denotations, or accepted meanings, but different connotations—they suggest very different things to most people. Use each word in a sentence that illustrates its connotation and helps distinguish it from the others on the list. Consider whether each word suggests positive, neutral, or negative associations. Use a dictionary where necessary.
  a. temporary, fleeting, momentary, provisional, transient, transitory
  b. challenge, problem, undertaking, dilemma, project, task
  c. moving, affecting, pathetic, poignant, touching, stirring
  d. fat, chubby, corpulent, obese, plump, stout, overweight, husky
  e. deceive, betray, mislead, delude, double-cross

2. In the following paragraph, choose the word in each bracketed group that you think most accurately conveys the author's meaning. Use the context—and your dictionary if necessary—to help you decide.

My father was a Chrysler [salesman, dealer, distributor]. He started [pushing, selling, merchandising] Chryslers soon after he came to America with my mother in 1942. In those days he was called a "Desoto-Plymouth" [salesman, dealer, distributor] and it would have [embarrassed, shamed, mortified] him to think of himself as a "salesman." He was from Vilna, a city that was all but wiped out by the Nazis, but before the [war, hostilities, holocaust], he moved to

Paris and then Bucharest, and was "presenting" [vehicles, cars, automobiles] to a [fussy, discriminating, demanding] [public, populace, audience]. The [genuine, actual, true] sale, when it came, was almost [secondary, minor, incidental], a matter of shared appreciation between friends, which ended in a [discreet, secret] transfer of funds from one to the other, as a [token, symbol, talisman] of mutual [esteem, pride, respect]. The automobile itself was the treasure, which my father [offered, gave, donated] with grace. (Ingrid Bengis, "My Father Sold Chryslers," *New York Times*)

USING SPECIFIC AND CONCRETE WORDS

To make language work for you, you must use words that are precise enough to convey your exact meaning. The right words help your readers understand just what you mean.

SPECIFIC VS. GENERAL

Specific words signify particular persons, things, or events, while *general* words refer to classes or groups. "Charles I," for example, is more specific than "monarch"; "pleurisy" is more specific than "disease," and "Guam" is more specific than "island." Sometimes, of course, you need to use general words. A brief summary of a press conference, for instance, would not be as specific as a verbatim account, and, in the interest of simplicity and economy, a phrase like "major tax reforms" might be justifiable shorthand for many specific details.

Even so, if you want your readers to visualize a certain hexagonal building, it is not enough to say that it has "an unusual shape"; if you want your audience to see a painting, you must do more than note its "abstract shapes and vivid colors." What shapes? How big? How do they relate to one another? What colors? Careful selection of specific words conveys this information to your readers.

The novelist Joyce Carol Oates uses specific diction in the following fictional passage.

> The buildings were covered with ivy, very staunch and brittle. A bit ugly, like all these schools. The architecture was solid and masculine, squat, unimaginative, English and prison-like in an easy combination. Graveled walks for the boys to bicycle upon, and a series of waterfalls set up for visitors and parents and magazine photographers. (The water was *verboten* to us boys.) Rather narrow, cheerless dormitory rooms, but built solidly, with good solid imitation antique furniture. Country English. Down in the classrooms the floors were smooth and polished as if by a hundred years of feet, caressed by boys impatient for learning.
>
> Joyce Carol Oates, *Expensive People*

Here Oates wishes to convey an impression of a private boys' boarding school which is supposed to be conservative, traditional, and well-established. Thus she selects words like "staunch" and "masculine" and "prison-like" and "English." She also repeats the word "solid" twice and uses "solidly" as well. The words she chooses are specific enough to convey the impression of permanence, almost stolidity.

ABSTRACT VS. CONCRETE

Abstractions—beauty, truth, justice, and so on—denote intangible ideas, qualities, or classes of things that cannot be perceived by the senses. We need abstract terms to talk about concepts or qualities, but such terms are, by definition, short on tangible detail. Therefore, using abstract words to describe a particular object or event does not usually help your reader very much. Concrete diction, on the other hand, conveys a vivid picture by naming or describing things that readers can see, hear, smell, taste, and feel. Concrete words are specific: they get your points across. Abstract language is often too general to communicate much about real things. For example:

Abstract	Concrete
The seashell was beautiful.	The seashell was pink and pearly inside, with a rippled exterior.
The explosion was powerful.	The noise of the explosion shattered windows and caused an acrid cloud to settle over the town.
The sculpture was awesome.	The sculpture was a large, metallic triangle that reflected the sunlight for miles in all directions.
The cloth had an unusual texture.	The cloth had the texture of velvety fur, like nubby pony skin.

Of course, the terms "abstract" and "concrete" are relative—that is, a word's abstractness or concreteness is determined by its relationship to other words—just as "general" and "specific" are. The following word chains illustrate relative levels of generality. Notice how each moves from a very general concept to a very specific, concrete one.

○ science—life science—biology—zoology—Zoology 101

○ apparel—head covering—hat—beret

○ human being—man—pope—Pope John XXIII

○ reading matter—book—novel—*Pride and Prejudice*

○ machine—vehicle—automobile—Toyota

○ conflict—war—civil war—Civil War

○ work of art—painting—Van Gogh painting—"Starry Night"

○ structure—building—skyscraper—Empire State Building

○ entertainer—musician—rock musician—Mick Jagger

○ school—university—state university—Kansas State University

In each of these cases, the word at the left denotes a general category or class, and the one farthest to the right, a specific, tangible member of that class. The more specific and concrete your words and phrases, the more vivid the image you evoke in the reader.

In the following passage from the novel *Barren Ground,* notice how concrete diction helps the author, Ellen Glasgow, create a powerful impression of a part of the rural American South.

> Bare, starved, desolate, the country closed in about her. The last train of the day had gone by without stopping, and the station of Pedlar's Mill was as lonely as the abandoned fields by the track. From the bleak horizon, where the flatness created an illusion of immensity, the broomsedge was spreading in a smothered fire over the melancholy brown of the landscape. Under the falling snow, which melted as soon as it touched the earth, the color was veiled and dim; but when the sky changed the broomsedge changed with it. On clear mornings the waste places were cinnamon-red in the sunshine. Beneath scudding clouds the plumes of the bent grasses faded to ivory. During the long spring rains, a film of yellow-green stole over the burned ground. At autumn sunsets, when the red light searched the country, the broomsedge caught fire from the afterglow and blazed out in a splendour of colour. Then the meeting of earth and sky dissolved in the flaming mist of the horizon.

Glasgow wants to establish the local color of a particular region. To do this, she creates a visual overview by itemizing strong, sharp, sensory details. The resulting description has a startling clarity: reading this passage is almost like seeing a color photograph of the scene. Her concrete language illuminates the contrast between the "bare, starved, desolate" country and the flaming glow of the broomsedge as it "blazed out in a splendour of colour."

Few academic assignments call for such vivid writing. But the following student paragraph fails even to communicate much specific information:

> The Appalachian Mountains are a mountain chain in North America which spread for over 1000 miles from Canada to the United States. The Appalachians include many important ranges. The highest peak, in North Carolina, is almost 7000 feet high. The Appalachian Mountains, composed of two different kinds of rock, are divided by a valley.

This paragraph does very little to fix the exact location or size of the mountain chain. Indeed, it uses almost no concrete words. The following revision, which provides specific numbers instead of approximations and specific names instead of general categories or oblique references, is much more informative:

> The Appalachian Mountains are a mountain chain parallel to the east coast of North America. They stretch for 1600 miles from Canada's St. Lawrence River to

central Alabama. Principal ranges include the Blue Ridge, Catskill, Cumberland, and the Great Smoky Mountains. North Carolina's Mount Mitchell, at 6684 feet, is the highest peak. The Appalachians, composed of igneous rock and Paleozoic sediment, are divided by the Great Appalachian Valley.

One cause of vague, general diction is an overreliance on *utility words*, all-purpose words that seem to fit in just about anywhere. Because they are so familiar, they are often the first words that spring to mind when you start to write a rough draft. You have probably been told already not to use words like "nice," "great," "terrific" or "stuff." Most teachers see red when they encounter these words in a student paper because they know how empty they are. In the following sentences, precisely what do the italicized words mean?

> Napoleon's Italian campaign had *great* results.
> The results of the new tax cut were *nice* for consumers.
> Examination of the core samples revealed some *terrific* conclusions.
> The nine test animals did poorly because we did not have the proper *stuff* to feed them.

Even though you can use utility words in speech, or as placeholders in a rough draft, you should revise carefully to eliminate bland, colorless words from your writing. For example:

>   pockmarked
> The surface of Titan, one of the moons of Saturn, was ~~weird~~.
>   puzzling
> The effects of the new drug were ~~odd~~.
>   angry
> When General von Moltke heard news of the defeat, he looked ~~awful~~.
> blue satin designer
> The ~~pretty~~ dresses in the fall line sold well.

Of course you could substitute other words. The idea, however, is to select ones that accurately express your meaning.

EXERCISES

---

1.   Note how the use of specific words in the following paragraph strengthens the writer's message to his readers. What is the impression of the Mississippi River he wants his readers to share? What particular words and phrases help to create that impression?

I found the Mississippi in the family atlas. It was a great, ink-stained, Victorian book, almost as big as I was. "North Africa" and "Italy" had come loose from its binding, from my mother's attempts to keep up with my father's campaigns in the Eighth Army. North America, though, was virgin territory: No one in the family had ever thought the place worth a moment of their curiosity. I looked at the Mississippi, wriggling down the middle of the page, and liked the funny names of the places that it passed through. Just the sounds of Minneapolis . . . Dubuque . . .

Hannibal . . . St. Louis . . . Cairo . . . Memphis . . . Natchez . . . Baton Rouge . . . struck a legendary and heroic note to my ear. Our part of England was culpably short of Roman generals, Indians and Egyptian ruins, and these splendid names added even more luster to the marvelous river in my head. (Jonathan Raban, "River Log: Travels of a Modern Huck," *New York Times Magazine*)

2.   In the following passage, select from each set of words in brackets the one word which is most specific.

[Going, Walking] through the New Hampshire woods one [time, afternoon] in the spring of my last year of boarding school, I found a [young, baby] owl in a pile of [leaves, foliage] at the foot of a beech tree. [Tiny, Palm-size], covered with [grayish-white, light gray] fluff, he [looked, stared] up at me with dark, shiny eyes that projected more challenge than fear. [Overhead, Nearby] I could see the [hole, opening, place] from which he had [come, fallen]—a [drop, distance] of 30 feet that should have broken his neck. Instead, the little [thing, animal, bird, creature] was very much [okay, alive, intact], hissing and [moving, fluttering] his flipper-like wings. (Andrew Jones, "Land of the Owl," *Reader's Digest*)

3.   At the beginning of his book *The Armada*, Garrett Mattingly sets the scene for his analysis of the events surrounding the building and launching of the Spanish Armada. Mattingly's concrete diction helps his readers visualize the physical details of the spot where Mary, Queen of Scots, is to be beheaded. Read the passage carefully, and underline the concrete words that add vividness and interest.

The hall had been cleared of all its ordinary furniture. Halfway along its length a huge fire of logs blazing in the chimney battled against the creeping chill. Towards the upper end of the hall they had set up a small platform, like a miniature stage for traveling actors, jutting twelve feet into the hall, eight or nine feet wide, and less than three feet high. At one side a pair of stairs led up to it, and the fresh wood of the scaffolding had been everywhere decently covered in black velvet. On the platform, in line with the stairs, stood a single high-backed chair, also draped in black, and three or four feet in front of it a black cushion. Next to the cushion and rising above it something like a little low bench showed where the velvet imperfectly concealed an ordinary wooden chopping block.

4.   Revise this paragraph from a student's job application letter by substituting concrete, specific language for generalizations and utility words.

My *years* of experience in retailing make me well qualified for a job as a *worker* in your *store*. I have always gotten along well with the *people* in other *stores*. I feel I can do a *good* job because I have had experience in *many areas* of retailing and have worked in *quite a number of* different settings. I have sold *clothing* in a store with only a *few* employees and have also worked in a *big* store *nearby*. I find retailing a *nice* job, and I hope to make it my career *someday*.

ACCOMMODATING YOUR AUDIENCE

Part of being a careful, considerate writer is not just choosing the right word but also judging which words and phrases will baffle, annoy, or bore your audience. In your college writing, you will encounter problem areas in diction—jargon, clichés, euphemisms, and offensive words, for instance—as you write and as you revise your writing. Identifying these problem areas can sharpen your revision skills and help you achieve clear communication.

JARGON

The *American Heritage Dictionary* defines jargon as "nonsensical, incoherent, or meaningless utterance; gibberish," and also as "the specialized or technical language of a trade, profession, class, or fellowship." We shall focus here on the second meaning, but you can easily see that highly specialized language can be "incoherent" or "meaningless." Like slang, jargon is idiosyncratic, likely to have little meaning to readers who are unfamiliar with it. Nevertheless, many students deliberately use jargon for much the same reasons that politicians and bureaucrats use it—they want to impress people with obscure or learned words and complex constructions, usually to distract them from seeing that they don't have much to say. The effect, of course, is just the opposite. Nobody is impressed by what cannot be deciphered; when it comes to jargon, any intelligent reader is bound to see that the emperor has no clothes.

Jargon comes from the specialized vocabularies of government, the military, and all other professions. Medical doctors describe a patient's family history as being "unremarkable" or "noncontributory," while an examination might prove to be "essentially normal" or "unrevealing." Among police officers, every criminal is a "perpetrator" who, when "collared," must be "Mirandized"—read his or her rights as the Supreme Court decision in the Miranda case requires. In business, executives "prioritize" before they "finalize" their plans, "utilizing" care when considering how one goal "impacts on" another. Movie producers "take a meeting" to discuss which stars are "bankable." Mothers and fathers attend workshops in "parenting" while maintaining "meaningful relationships" of their own. In recent years the rise of computer technology has flooded our language with jargon. Now we "interface" with others and anxiously await "feedback." Committee members offer "input" instead of suggestions, and many businesses seek to "reprogram" instead of retrain employees.

Other characteristics of jargon, besides its origin in technical vocabularies, include its reliance on overly formal diction, overuse of the passive voice, and excessive wordiness. The empty phrases that clutter up prose, like "as regards" ("My position as regards the new budget remains flexible"), and the suffix "-wise" inevitably tacked on anywhere possible ("If we don't speed up production-wise we may be in trouble time-wise") also qualify as jargon.

What does the following passage say?

The No-Win Situation

At a given point in time there co-existed a hare and a tortoise. The aforementioned rabbit was overheard by the tortoise to be boasting about the degree of speed he could attain. The latter quadruped thereupon put forth a challenge to the former by advancing the suggestion that they interact in a running competition. The hare acquiesced, expressing inward amusement. The animals concurred in the decision to acquire the services of a certain fox to act in the capacity of judicial referee. This particular fox was in agreement, and consequently implementation of the plan was facilitated. In a relatively small amount of time the hare had considerably out-distanced the tortoise and, after ascertaining that he himself was in a more advantageous position distance-wise than the tortoise, he arrived at the unilateral decision to avail himself of a respite. He made the implicit assumption in so doing that he would anticipate no difficulty in overtaking the tortoise when his suspension of activity ceased. An unfortunate development occurred when the hare's somnolent state endured for a longer-than-anticipated time-frame, facilitating the tortoise's victory in the contest and affirming the concept of unhurriedness and firmness triumphing in competitive situations.

In its more familiar and accessible form, the fable says something like this:

A tortoise once overheard a hare boasting about how fast he could run and so challenged him to a race. The hare agreed, laughing to himself, and the animals asked a fox to act as judge. The fox consented, and the race began. The hare soon outdistanced the tortoise and, making sure he was far ahead, decided to take a nap, assuming he could easily overtake the tortoise when he awoke. Unfortunately, however, the hare overslept, allowing the tortoise to win and teaching the hare that "slow and steady wins the race."

What's the difference between the two versions? The first passage relies on jargon words: "aforementioned," "interact," "unilateral," "implicit," "time-frame," "facilitating" and "situations." It also uses clumsy, passive constructions: "the aforementioned rabbit was overheard by the tortoise" and "implementation of the plan was facilitated." Most noticeable are the wordy constructions. Compare:

Version 1	Version 2
at a given point in time	once
the degree of speed	how fast
put forth a challenge	challenged
advancing the suggestion	suggested
running competition	race
concurred in the decision	agreed
act in the capacity of	act as
was in agreement	consented
in a relatively small amount of time	soon
arrived at the unilateral decision	decided
made the implicit assumption	assuming
would anticipate no difficulty in overtaking	could easily overtake

As you see, jargon relies on complicated noun constructions instead of simple, clear verb forms. It also clutters up sentences with excess verbiage. If you want to write for your reader, you must rework jargon-filled sentences to make them smooth and easily understood.

CLICHÉS

A cliché is an expression that has been so overused that it now lacks interest or originality. Although these expressions may once have seemed fresh, overuse has left them flat and meaningless. Using clichés is a sign of laziness—a sign that you are more willing to think superficially than to search for accurate, original words.

Clichés are expressions that once had the power to call forth images. Sayings like "This isn't my cup of tea," "We're in the same boat," "That's the last straw," and "Let's get down to brass tacks" once did bring ideas into focus. But they have long since lost their concrete associations. Writers use clichés to paper over holes in their sentences without giving any thought to their original meanings. In doing so, they clutter sentences with useless phrases that dull meaning and hamper communication.

Overly familiar sayings are not the only clichés. In many pat phrases, words have become bound—"inextricably bound"—to other words. For example, political, social, or economic situations are often described as "rapidly deteriorating." The "generation gap" is frequently blamed for the nation's ills, unless "social unrest" is "deemed to be at fault." "Root causes" need to be uncovered, so "blue-ribbon panels" are frequently appointed. "Options are explored," "careful deliberation" takes place, "herculean efforts" are made, and sometimes "mutually agreeable solutions" are found. If not, "viable alternatives" may allow the two sides to "peacefully coexist." When they have been "unavoidably detained" for weeks, a "highly placed source" "categorically denies" any trouble "getting to the bottom of the problem." The panelists "dutifully note" that their discussions have made an "appreciable difference" and recommend "sweeping reforms." They report "great strides" toward a solution to "the nation's pressing problems," "snatching victory" from (you guessed it!) "the jaws of defeat."

It should be clear by now that clichés cripple any prose. Most readers have seen and heard them so often that they skip right over them. Imprecise and empty clichés are especially hazardous in academic writing.

EXERCISE

Revise these sentences, from a student paper on the vitamin C controversy, to eliminate jargon and clichés.

a. World-renowned scientist Linus Pauling has indicated that vitamin C may prevent untold suffering by significantly reducing the number of upper respiratory infections suffered by the average person.

b. Professor Pauling's megadose theory is based on the fact that the vast majority of animals, with the notable exception of primates, can synthesize ascorbic acid and thus do not possess a requirement for it as a nutrient.

c. Pauling has a vested interest in the results of clinical trials, which he believes warrant serious consideration.

d.   Pauling is of the opinion that a preponderance of studies employed insufficient quantities of the vitamin and therefore were unable to demonstrate the existence of substantial beneficial effects.

e.   An additional defect readily apparent to all who peruse the study is the researcher's failure to adequately describe the placebo.

f.   No conclusive evidence exists to warrant the utilization of vitamin C to effect symptomatic relief or achieve a cure for the common cold.

g.   The enormous popularity of vitamin C is due in part to the fact that the general public invariably finds miracle drugs appealing.

h.   Without the assurance provided by the double-blind study, a significant obstacle exists to the validity of the scientific study.

i.   All things considered, ascorbic acid seems destined to be the center of intense controversy for years to come.

j.   Only time will tell whether Pauling is correct in advocating vitamin C therapy across the board.

EUPHEMISMS

A euphemism is a special kind of cliché that tries to sanitize or "pretty up" subjects that are not appealing or that are not considered appropriate for polite conversation. In the Victorian era, legs—even piano legs—were delicately referred to as "limbs." An old saying notes that horses "sweat," men "perspire," and ladies "glow." Over the years, the Department of War has become the Department of Defense, used cars have become pre-owned automobiles, soap operas have become daytime dramas, and all corporate takeovers have become mergers. Graveyards became cemeteries, and cemeteries, memorial parks; old people, who became the aged, are now senior citizens, or "seniors"; and retarded children are "special" or "exceptional."

This trend toward euphemism has been particularly apparent in job titles. Thus, garbage collectors are sanitation workers; undertakers, morticians; prison guards, corrections officers; and welfare investigators, caseworkers or income-maintenance specialists. In each case, the original negative connotations (the associations with garbage, death, jail, and poverty) have been made neutral or positive.

In the following passages two professional writers comment on the trend to euphemize job titles. Notice the illustrations they use.

> The American Correctional Association—composed of wardens, jailers, and others in the business of locking people up, was formerly known as the American Prison Association. The name was changed in 1952 by the prison bureaucracy as part of a general move to package their product under a more agreeable name and incidentally upgrade their jobs: guards have become "correctional officers" or "correctional counsellors"; solitary confinement is "seclusion," "adjustment," or even "meditation"; the prison is a "correctional therapeutic community."
>
> Jessica Mitford, *New York Times Book Review*

I am an electrocutioner—I prefer this word to executioner; I think words make a difference. When I was a boy, people who buried the dead were undertakers, and then somewhere along the way they became morticians and better off for it.

Take the one who used to be the undertaker in my town. He was a decent, respectable man, very friendly if you'd let him be, but hardly anybody would let him be. Today, his son—who now runs the business—is not an undertaker but a mortician, and is welcome everywhere. As a matter of fact, he's an officer in my lodge and is one of the most popular members we have. And all it took to do that was changing one word to another. The job's the same but the word is different, and people somehow will always go by words rather than meanings.

Stanley Elkin, "The Question"

College writing is no place for coyness or delicacy. In the interests of accuracy, say what you mean—"pregnant," not "expecting"; "died," not "passed away"; and "strike," not "work stoppage."

EXERCISE

Which of the following expressions are euphemisms and which are not? Explain.

1.	broken home	7.	terminal illness
2.	single parent	8.	strategic withdrawal
3.	Special Olympics	9.	parental discretion
4.	love child	10.	investment counselor
5.	family planning	11.	open marriage
6.	hard of hearing	12.	bathroom tissue

OFFENSIVE LANGUAGE

At the other extreme is diction that takes no pains at all to avoid insult—the truly offensive language of racial and ethnic slurs, obscenities, sexist rhetoric, and any other kind of language that rightly offends a segment of your audience.

☐ RACIAL AND ETHNIC SLURS

One cannot always judge which epithets have truly offensive connotations, so it makes good sense to exercise considerable caution when referring in your writing to any minority group. A good rule of thumb is to use words with neutral connotations, or to refer to groups the way they refer to themselves in writing. You may have the judgment to avoid obviously insulting language like "chink," "nigger," and "kike," but what about seemingly less offensive terms like "Chinaman," "colored," or "Jewess"? Chances are that many people won't be much happier with these alternatives. Using the current acceptable term for members of minority groups is extremely important if you want to avoid embarrassing yourself and hurting others. Use "Asian" instead of "Chinaman," "black" instead of "colored," "Jewish woman" instead of "Jewess."

Often the connotation is as important as the word itself: "chicks" insults women, "cripples" insults handicapped people, "queers" insults homosexuals, "wetbacks" insults Mexican-Americans (Chicanos or Chicanas), and "rednecks" insults rural white Southerners. Of course these terms sound just as insulting to all fair-minded people, regardless of ethnic, geographic, physical, or sexual classification. Remember also that ethnic stereotypes are as damaging as racial slurs, and take care to avoid biased generalizations such as those that brand the Irish as drunks, Poles as stupid, Scots as tight with money, or Jews as pushy.

□ SEXISM

Stereotypes also extend to the sexes. Not all men are strong and brave; not all women are shy and retiring and "know their place." Any attempt to advance such ideas will be met with scorn or disbelief. Thus observing that it is "just like a woman" to be helpless when a tire needs changing (or "just like a man" to be helpless when a diaper needs changing) is as unconvincing as it is unrealistic.

Not all sexist writing is rife with sweeping statements about "broads" and "chicks" and "women drivers." Most often, sexism is much more subtle. For instance, assuming that all telephone operators and nurses are women, or that all welders and pilots are men, is sexist. So is the automatic use of job titles like "policeman" (instead of "police officer") and "fireman" (instead of "fire fighter"). Naturally, old habits are hard to break and usage in these areas changes slowly.

The title "Ms.," as the counterpart of "Mr.," is a good example of how difficult it is to change traditional terms. Some women—and even some publications, such as the *New York Times*—have resisted this change, continuing to use "Miss" or "Mrs." Most businesses, people, and publications, however, feel the term makes things simpler. "Ms." is certainly a more neutral term because it does not specify marital status for women (just as "Mr." doesn't for men). To decide whether to use Ms. or not, you need to know your audience. When in doubt, however, "Ms." is a good bet.

Sexism also shows when a writer fails to use the same terminology in referring to men and women. For instance, you should refer to two scientists with Ph.D.s as Dr. Sagan and Dr. Yallow, not Dr. Sagan and Mrs. Yallow; you should call two writers Thackeray and Austen, not Thackeray and Miss Austen.

Finally, try to avoid constant use of the pronouns "he" or "him" when your subject could be either male or female. You have several options in this situation. You can alternate "he" and "she" in a long passage, but this can become rather heavy—as in *Baby and Child Care*, where Dr. Benjamin Spock, in response to pressure from women's groups, uses phrases like "Your baby—let's assume it's a girl." You can use "he/she," but this construction looks clumsy and reads worse. As writer Cyra McFadden observes, spoken aloud "he slash she" sounds like "a replay of the Manson killings." Finally—probably best of all—you can use the plural "they" whenever possible. Be careful, however, not to create ungrammatical constructions like this one, from an advertisement, quoted by William Safire: "Someone close to you is hoping for a Longines. Don't disappoint them."

□   OBSCENITIES

Contrary to popular belief, the freedom to use obscene language is *not* one of the prerogatives that sets college writers apart from their younger, less experienced counterparts. Writing an X-rated paper does not impress your instructor with your sophistication. It does reveal immaturity, an eagerness to shock, and a lack of good taste, good judgment, and respect for your audience.

CHOOSING EFFECTIVE IMAGERY

In some of your writing assignments you may try to go beyond choosing words simply on the basis of accuracy, appropriateness, and specificity and look for words that convey meaning through imaginative comparisons. When we speak of diction, we can identify two kinds of imagery. First are *images*, or word pictures, such as those created by Ellen Glasgow (page 178) with phrases like "the abandoned fields," "grasses faded to ivory," "yellow-green over the burned ground," and the "mist of the horizon." Second are figures of speech, such as *similes* and *metaphors*.

All figures of speech are based on comparison—on finding a similarity between two basically dissimilar things. For instance, the fog and a cat's feet are not literally comparable. Still, when the poet Carl Sandburg writes "The fog came in on little cat feet," he encourages us to search for some basis of similarity and, in so doing, to see the fog more vividly and in a new way. And, if you have ever seen fog drift in over a city, you can see a basic similarity between the soundless approach of a cat and that of the fog.

There is no general rule that determines when you should use figures of speech. You should not overuse them, but you should not be afraid to try them. Figures of speech are not just for literary writing; they have their place in journalism, academic writing, and even in scientific and technical writing.

The five most frequently used figures of speech—and those that should be most useful to you in your writing—are *simile*, *metaphor*, *analogy*, *personification*, and *allusion*.

SIMILE

A simile makes a comparison between unlike things, suggesting an unexpected likeness, and it uses the words "like" or "as" to do so. In issues of *National Geographic* magazine, sharks at rest are described as reclining "as if drugged in an opium den," Saturn's atmosphere is seen to be "as bland as butterscotch," and the mountains of Molokai look "like thirsty giants." In the first simile, sharks are likened to addicts in artificially induced stupors; in the second, something foreign and mysterious is made ordinary and concrete; and in the third, a sense of power and majesty is imparted to the mountains. All of these similes deepen and enhance meaning. Consider these examples:

His hand was small and cold; it felt like wax.

Margaret Truman

A poem should be palpable and mute
As a globed fruit,

Dumb
As old medallions to the thumb

Archibald MacLeish, "Ars Poetica"

In the morning the dust hung like fog, and the sun was as red as ripe new blood.

John Steinbeck, The Grapes of Wrath

[H]er mind was to be his—attached to his own like a small garden-plot to a deer-park.

Henry James, Portrait of a Lady

Gatsby pursues Daisy like a knight seeking the grail.

Raymond Lim, student

Caddy with flowers in her hair and a long veil like shining wind.

William Faulkner, The Sound and the Fury

Perhaps the best reason for writing a letter is to get rid of it, to take the words that have been lolling about the brain like summertime teen-agers, and to put them to work.

Roger Rosenblatt, Time

Everyone was like the faces on a playing card, upside down either way.

Saul Bellow, Seize the Day

METAPHOR

Like a simile, a metaphor compares two essentially dissimilar things, but instead of saying one thing is like another, it equates them, saying that one *is* the other. Metaphor stretches language beyond its ordinary limits. Consider this stanza from Gwendolyn Brooks's poem "The Blackstone Rangers," about a Chicago street gang.

There they are
Thirty at the corner.
Black, raw, ready.
Sores in the city
That do not want to heal.

Here, with one image, Brooks sums up her contradictory feelings about the gang. To her they are dangerous, proud, and stubborn, but they are also sores "that do not want to heal."

For its impact, metaphor depends on the concreteness and meaning of the imagery it contains. When it works, this kind of comparison clarifies thought and brings it to a point, sometimes with direct and stark efficiency. Notice how the writers of the following metaphors present images in new and interesting ways.

Isabel Archer is afraid to open up, afraid to spread her emotional wares out to anyone who might be free to consider them.

Kira Nyysola, student

The humorous story may be spun out to great length, and may wander around as much as it pleases, and arrive nowhere in particular; but the comic and witty stories must be brief and end with a point. The humorous story bubbles gently along, the others burst.

Mark Twain, "How to Tell a Story"

Time is but a stream I go a-fishing in. I drink at it; but while I drink I see the sandy bottom and detect how shallow it is. Its thin current slides away, but eternity remains.

H. D. Thoreau, *Walden*

Suddenly the whole room broke into a sea of shouting, as they saw me rise. Waves of rejoicing swept the place.

Langston Hughes, *The Big Sea*

The two great armies were locked together on a five-thousand-yard front flanked by the Pacific Ocean to the east and the East China Sea to the west. Hills, ridges, and cliffs rose and fell along the front. It was a moonscape. There was nothing green left; shells had denuded and scarred every inch of ground.

William Manchester, *Life*

For a metaphor to work, it has to employ images that your audience knows. Metaphors fail, however, if they rely on subjects that are too common. Normally called "dead metaphors," overused comparisons do nothing to enhance your writing (see also "Ineffective Imagery," page 192).

ANALOGY

An analogy is an expanded metaphor or simile. Sometimes extended over several sentences or even several paragraphs, analogies help readers understand an unfamiliar, usually abstract, idea by comparing it to something concrete they already know. For example, in 1943, at the age of twenty-five, Leonard Bernstein appeared as guest conductor of the New York Philharmonic. A music critic at the time used an analogy to liken his highly successful debut to "a rookie making a shoestring catch," thus describing Bernstein's achievement clearly to readers in familiar terms. The writer Nikos Kazantzakis uses the following analogy in his book *Zorba the Greek.*

> To my mind, the Cretan countryside resembled good prose, carefully ordered, sober, free from superfluous ornament, powerful and restrained. It expressed all that was necessary with the greatest economy. It had no flippancy nor artifice about it. It said what it had to say. . . . But between the severe lines one could discern an unexpected sensitiveness and tenderness; in the sheltered hollows the lemon and orange trees perfumed the air, and from the vastness of the sea emanated an inexhaustible poetry.

Here Kazantzakis draws an analogy between the Cretan landscape and language, comparing something we are not familiar with (the landscape) with something we do know (good prose).

The pattern of extended analogy resembles that of comparison and contrast that we discussed earlier, with one important difference. In a comparison-and-contrast essay you give equal weight and value to both things you are comparing or contrasting—the point *is* the comparison. In extended analogy you use one part of the comparison for the *sole* purpose of shedding light on another. Notice how Lewis Thomas uses the behavior of social insects to explain the behavior of people in the first paragraph of his essay "On Societies as Organisms."

> Viewed from a suitable height, the aggregating clusters of medical scientists in the bright sunlight of the boardwalk at Atlantic City, swarmed there from everywhere for the annual meetings, have the look of assemblages of social insects. There is the same vibrating, ionic movement, interrupted by the darting back and forth of jerky individuals to touch antennae and exchange small bits of information; periodically, the mass casts out, like a trout-line, a long single file unerringly towards Child's [a restaurant]. If the boards were not fastened down, it would not be a surprise to see them put together a nest of sorts.

One word of caution: analogies only work when the subjects you are comparing have some similarities. If the things you compare are dissimilar, your analogy doesn't hold up. Trying to draw an analogy, for instance, between a building and a rubber band would be a problem. But to explain the configuration of a space vehicle by comparing it to a giant insect (both can be seen to have ears, arms, and eyes) would work.

PERSONIFICATION

In personification, an inanimate thing—even a concept or an idea—is given the attributes or qualities of an animal or human. In speech and in writing, we all use phrases like "love is blind" and "the wind howled." With these phrases we give characteristics usually associated with people or animals to the abstract concept "love" and the inanimate "wind." Such figures of speech are useful because they can make an abstract concept or hard-to-describe thing more concrete, more familiar, and perhaps more interesting. Still, you should use personification cautiously in college writing. Overusing figures of speech makes your writing sound "flowery" or overdone.

Consider these successful examples of personification:

> Family likeness has often a deep sadness in it. Nature, that great tragic dramatist, knits us together by bone and muscle, and divides us by the subtler web of our brains; blends yearning and repulsion, and ties us by our heart-strings to the beings that jar us at every moment.
>
> George Eliot, Adam Bede

> There stood, facing the open window, a comfortable, roomy armchair. Into this she sank, pressed down by a physical exhaustion that haunted her body and seemed to reach into her soul.
>
> Kate Chopin, "The Dream of an Hour"

> When primal Dawn spread on the eastern sky her fingers of pink light, Odysseus' true son stood up, drew on his tunic and his mantle . . . .
>
> Homer, The Odyssey

> The creek bed is choked with soil, and toppled trees are beginning to dam the stream's flow.
>
> James Risser, Smithsonian

> September 27 last year was a beautiful, clear football Saturday in Connecticut, kissed by the first crispness of early autumn.
>
> Frank Defird, Sports Illustrated

> The wind took the house in its teeth and shook it as a dog shakes a rat.
>
> McKnight Malmar, "The Storm"

ALLUSION

An allusion makes a reference to a familiar person, place, or event in literature or history. Writers use allusions to enrich their readers' understanding of a subject by bringing to it the context of another subject which in some way resembles it. Allusion puts the writer's work in a larger setting. If successful, it provides a favorable emotional, moral, aesthetic, or historical aura for the plain word on the page.

Of course allusion depends for its effectiveness on the reader's knowing about what is being alluded to. Obscure or unnecessarily difficult references alienate readers. So you should carefully consider your audience and purpose before using this device. For instance, an observation that your boss is "a twentieth-century Simon Legree" means nothing to someone who doesn't recognize Legree as the ruthless slave trader in the novel *Uncle Tom's Cabin*. But if your reader does know the name, your allusion quickly communicates your negative attitude.

Some works are so rich and so well known that many writers allude to them. A famous passage in Shakespeare's *Macbeth*, for example, reads,

Out, out brief candle!
Life's but a walking shadow, a poor player
That struts and frets his hour upon the stage
And then is heard no more.

It is a tale
Told by an idiot, full of sound and fury,
Signifying nothing.

A Robert Frost poem about the accidental death of a young boy is called "'Out, out—,'" and William Faulkner entitled his novel about the decline of a southern family *The Sound and the Fury*. Both writers assumed that their readers would recognize the allusion to *Macbeth* and that the content of the whole passage would enhance their understanding.

INEFFECTIVE IMAGERY

We have seen that effective imagery does a lot to enrich your diction. But ineffective imagery—*dead metaphors, mixed metaphors*, and *overblown imagery*, for instance—seriously damages it.

Imagery just doesn't work—or backfires with humorous or embarrassing results—when you don't know the meaning or origin of the figure of speech you have used. More often, problems result from a failure to think an image through, to see how it reads or sounds. The television commentator who noted that all applicants for jobs as air traffic controllers would have to take a crash course in order to qualify used language without fully considering its implications.

☐ DEAD METAPHORS

A *dead metaphor*, like "Achilles' heel," is one that has been used so often that it no longer calls up an image, vivid or otherwise. Instead, it has become a cliché, a pat, meaningless phrase used by people too lazy to invent fresh figures of speech. Here are some common dead metaphors.

old as the hills	off the track
ugly as sin	pave the way
cool as a cucumber	tackle a problem
toe the line	smooth sailing
play into the hands of	dead as a doornail
swan song	blind as a bat
hotbed	slow as molasses
axe to grind	

In most of these cases, the exact meaning of the metaphor isn't even clear. How old *are* the hills? Are bats really blind? When such expressions lose their impact, using them costs you any chance of making your own impact.

☐ MIXED METAPHORS

A mixed metaphor results when you combine more than one image in a single figure of speech. Mixed images confuse readers, leaving them wondering what you are trying to say, or amuse them by what you have said unintentionally.

Mixed

When the *ravenous* German army advanced into Russia, it *swept* everything out of its way.

Mixed

We should *wash out* corruption before it *multiplies* to all departments of city government.

When you revise mixed metaphors, straighten out your imagery and make it consistent. Notice that the revised versions of these sentences contain no odd or hidden meanings to undermine the message.

Revised

When the *ravenous* German army advanced into Russia, it *devoured* everything in sight.

Revised

We should *wash out* corruption before *its stain* spreads to every department of city government.

☐ OVERBLOWN IMAGERY

Overdone, flowery diction is always out of place in college writing, where your purpose is to present information clearly and logically. Overblown imagery only distracts your readers as they search for your point. The following passage, part of a research paper, illustrates the dangers of exaggerating figures of speech.

> The Tammany Society [a political association] was an all-engulfing weed that rapidly overran and choked New York City's political gardens. Times were filled with danger for those who dared protest this corruption. Even the champion of the people—the *Sun*—refused to encourage the few flowers that dared to rear their heads in that field of briars. Although the situation improved somewhat in the hands of skillful gardeners, much corruption existed for years to come.

This paragraph has many problems. The overblown imagery defies anyone who tries to get through it. One cannot even decipher the writer's meaning, much less tell whether the extended analogy is consistent or not. Comparing Tammany to a weed is valid, but this imagery is out of control. Compare the paragraph above with this one, revised for clarity and consistency:

The Tammany Society was a weed that quickly overran New York City. Times were hard for those who dared to speak against its spread; even the *Sun* did not encourage reformers. Although the situation improved somewhat in the hands of reform-minded politicians, much corruption existed for years to come.

EXERCISES

1.   Identify the figures of speech used in the following passages, noting in each case the two things being compared and why the comparison is appropriate.

    a.   Their life seemed to be like a snake biting its tail. (Doris Lessing, "To Room Nineteen")

    b.   I wandered lonely as a cloud
        That floats on high o'er vales and hills.
                (William Wordsworth)

    c.   . . . tall Rostov, his scarf like a striped bandage, taking long strides, his too-short trousers flapping like flags . . . . (Ken Follett, *Triple*)

    d.   I wanted to live deep and suck out all the marrow of life . . . . (H. D. Thoreau)

    e.   There grows all over what was once the child a sort of prickly protection like hair; a callousness, a carelessness . . . with a readiness to accept conventions. (G. K. Chesterton)

    f.   It was December—a bright frozen day in the early morning. (Eudora Welty, "A Worn Path")

    g.   The sky was rarely more than pale blue or violet, with a profusion of mighty, weightless, ever-changing clouds towering up and sailing on it . . . . (Isak Dinesen, *Out of Africa*)

    h.   Nature conceals her mystery by means of her essential grandeur, not her cunning. (Albert Einstein)

2.   Read the following paragraphs carefully and underline the examples of effective imagery. Specify in each case the figure of speech being used.

    a.   It is as big and depthless as the sky itself. You can see the curve of the earth on its surface as it stretches away for miles to the far shore. Sunset has turned the water to the color of unripe peaches. There's no wind. Sand bars and wooded islands stand on their exact reflections. The only signs of movement on the water are the lightly scratched lines which run in parallels across it like the scores of a diamond on a windowpane. In the middle distance, the river smokes with toppling pillars of mist which soften the light so that one can almost reach out and take in handfuls of that thickened air.

    It is called the Mississippi, but it is more an imaginary river than a real one. (Jonathan Raban, "River Log: Tales of a Modern Huck," *New York Times Magazine*)

    b.   "I have traveled a good deal in Concord" said the stationary pilgrim Henry Thoreau. Today his descendants move from country to country instead, some seeking wisdom, some seeking academic credit, some only fun. Indeed, a latter-day Children's Crusade is upon us. No crusaders are sold into slavery, but nobody can say whether any will reach Jerusalem. (Hans Rosenhaupt, "The New Children's Crusade, or Going to Jerusalem on a Grant")

    c.   Every winter beach has its special seaweed tapestries into which are woven shells, fish bones, feathers, egg cases, larvae, sponge bits—tailings from every phylum of the sea. And under every patch of seaweed is a whole city of organisms—ghost shrimp, crabs and ribbon worms scooting about in chimneys and passageways below the beach face. Sand hoppers, tiny flea-like creatures with 14 pairs of legs, scavenge in the weed. If disturbed, they start digging furiously, passing grains of sand back through their legs in bucket-brigade fashion. (Jean George, "Lure of the Winter Beach," *Reader's Digest*)

d.   North Richmond Street, being blind, was a quiet street except at the hour when the Christian Brothers' School set the boys free. An uninhabited house of two storeys stood at the blind end, detached from its neighbors in a square ground. The other houses of the street, conscious of decent lives within them, gazed at one another with brown imperturbable faces. (James Joyce, "Araby")

e.   And the mall is clean, like Switzerland, a clean, well-lighted place that has been carefully designed and maintained as a venue for the easy exchange of money between strangers. (Ron Javers, *Philadelphia Magazine*)

USING AN APPROPRIATE LEVEL OF DICTION

Even if you choose the words that accurately convey your meaning, your diction still may not meet your reader's expectations. Different situations and audiences call for different *levels* of diction. Although "man" and "guy" mean much the same thing, the latter is inappropriate in many situations. What would you think at a wedding, for instance, if you heard, "Do you take this *guy* to be your lawfully wedded husband"?

When you have a firm sense of audience and purpose, selecting an appropriate level of diction—and maintaining it throughout your writing—is much easier. When you know who your readers are and how you want to reach them, you are ready to choose an appropriate level of diction. *Formal* and *informal* diction fall at either end of the scale. Most college writing situations, however, call for *popular* diction, which falls somewhere in between.

FORMAL DICTION

When reserve and decorum are in order—in presidential addresses, eulogies, articles for scholarly journals, and legal documents, for example—readers expect formal or learned language. Anything else simply confuses or annoys an audience. A formal essay or speech addresses "gentlemen" rather than "men" or "guys" and, in general, uses words likely to be familiar to educated rather than uneducated people: "impoverished" instead of "poor," "wealthy" instead of "rich," "intelligent" instead of "smart," "automobile" instead of "car," "television" instead of "TV," "penultimate" instead of "next-to-last," "perhaps" instead of "maybe." Contractions, shortened word forms, and all-purpose utility words like "nice" do not appear in formal diction.

In this passage the nineteenth-century essayist John Stuart Mill uses formal diction for a learned audience:

It is true that similar confusion and uncertainty, and in some cases similar discordance, exist respecting the first principles of all the sciences, not excepting that which is deemed the most certain of them, mathematics, without much impairing, generally indeed without impairing at all, the trustworthiness of the conclusions of those sciences. An apparent anomaly, the explanation of which is that the detailed doctrines of a science are not usually deduced from, nor depend for their evidence upon, what are called its first principles. Were it not so, there would be no science more precarious, or whose conclusions were more insufficiently made out, than algebra; which derives none of its certainty from what are commonly taught to learners as its elements, since these, as laid down by some of its most eminent teachers, are as full of fictions as English law, and of mysteries as theology.

John Stuart Mill, *Utilitarianism*

Mill's diction is precise—almost stilted—with no shortened word forms or contractions. Notice how far removed from everyday speech are the phrases "deemed the most certain" and "were it not so." Mill's vocabulary is aimed at a highly literate audience, readers who will be familiar with words like "discordance" and "anomaly."

You will not have occasion to use formal diction in your college writing. Your audience does not expect you to be reserved or distant, and you shouldn't be. You may, however, read works or hear speeches which rely on formal diction, so it makes sense for you to be familiar with its requirements.

INFORMAL DICTION

At the opposite extreme, informal diction uses familiar words, along with *colloquialisms* and *slang,* neither of which is appropriate for most college writing assignments.

☐ COLLOQUIALISMS

Colloquial diction occurs in casual speech, and it is perfectly acceptable when you are speaking on any but the most formal occasions. Contractions—"isn't," "won't," "I'm," "he'd"—are typical colloquialisms, as are the shortened forms of words—"phone" instead of "telephone" or "exam" instead of "examination," for instance. Other colloquial phrases are the ubiquitous placeholders "you know," "sort of," "kind of," and "I mean." In the following passage from J. D. Salinger's novel *The Catcher in the Rye,* the narrator, Holden Caufield, uses colloquial diction.

We always had the same meal on Saturday nights at Pencey. It was supposed to be a big deal, because they gave you steak. I'll bet a thousand bucks the reason they did that was because a lot of guys' parents came up to school on Sunday, and old Thurmer probably figured everybody's mother would ask their darling boy what he had for dinner last night and he'd say, "Steak." What a racket.

The narrator's use of contractions ("I'll," "he'd") and words like "bucks," "figured," and "guys" immediately identifies the diction as colloquial. This paragraph, and in fact the entire novel, is told in the voice of a sixteen-year-old boy, so it is not surprising to see slang expressions such as "big deal" and "what a racket." The use of "old" and "darling" gives the passage a tone of casual familiarity.

□ SLANG

Whether invented or borrowed, slang words take on their meanings as a need emerges. Words like "high," "spaced out," "turn on," "dove," "hawk," "hippie," "trip," "teeny bopper," "speed," "uptight," "kinky," "swinger," "groovy," "foxy," "freaked out," "rap," "heavy," "be-in," "happening," "acid," "grass," "rip off," "trash" (v.), and "bummer" emerged in the 1960s as part of the counterculture that arose around rock music, drug use, and opposition to the Vietnam war. During the 1970s, computer technology, music, politics, and feminism influenced our slang vocabulary, giving us words like "disco," "input," "output," "stonewalling," "Watergate," "nukes," "burn-out," "live on tape," "macho," "sexist," and "male chauvinism." Some of these words of the 60s and 70s have become valuable parts of our vocabulary; others have quickly faded into disuse and now appear as dated as the 1950s "beatnik," "daddy-O," "cool," "hep," "cat," and "square."

Because slang is highly idiosyncratic, and because it varies so much according to geographical location, age, interests, and background, it can obscure meaning and sidetrack the reader. It becomes dated very quickly. Avoid using slang in your college writing—except when you are purposely imitating speech or dialect.

POPULAR DICTION

Between formal and informal diction falls *popular diction,* and you will use it for most of your college writing. It is the level of diction we use in this book. Like informal diction, popular diction sounds natural and uses some familiar words and, occasionally, contractions. Like formal diction, however, popular diction is grammatically correct and employs learned words when the audience and the occasion warrant it. Mass-audience magazines, newspapers, textbooks, and non-fiction best-sellers use popular diction because that is what their audiences expect and feel comfortable with.

This paragraph, written by a student for a composition class, uses popular diction.

> Located in Chicago, the Sears Tower is a solitary structure that seems to dominate the entire city. The awesome one-hundred-and-ten-story tower was built to serve as an office building. Seemingly reaching for the heavens, the Sears Tower is encased in black duranodic aluminum. The exterior of the tower is covered with thousands of bronze-tinted windows that seem to blend to form a black shadow against Chicago's skyline. Composed of nine squares, the tower engulfs an entire

acre of land in the heart of the city. Two of these squares climb 1,454 feet above the city, while two recede at both the fiftieth and sixty-sixth floors, and three squares reach to the ninetieth floor. The tower, which took four years to build, is supported by 114 rock caissons, each embedded 150 feet into the ground. The skeleton of the tower is constructed of 76,000 tons of steel. Although the tower seems rigid, the top has been known to sway several inches from side to side in the strong winds that blow off Lake Michigan.

Eric Milus, the student who wrote this passage, uses no contractions or technical terminology, except in one case—"duranodic aluminum." He aims his passage at a general educated audience. His word choice shows how he assesses his audience—"structure," not "building," "awesome," not "scary," and "composed of," not "made of." In spite of Eric's occasional use of learned diction, his paragraph moves easily and conversationally (although he avoids slang and colloquial diction).

In your college writing, avoid words that are overly formal, and limit your use of colloquialisms and slang to dialogue in personal experience and narrative essays. Above all, use a level of diction that is appropriate for the occasion.

EXERCISES

1. Complete the following chart by filling in a popular equivalent for the formal and informal words supplied.

	Informal	Popular	Formal
Example:	flick	movie	film
	gig		position
	tube		television
	guts		courage
	take off		depart
	bombed		inebriated
	wiped out		decimated
	croaked		expired
	wheels		automobile
	rip off		expropriate
	rub out		eliminate
	loaded		affluent

2. This paragraph, from Mark Twain's *Adventures of Huckleberry Finn* (1884), is an example of informal, colloquial diction. As the speech of a fourteen-year-old boy, it is laced with slang and grammatical inaccuracies. Underline the words that identify this paragraph's diction as informal.

Well, I got a good going-over in the morning from old Miss Watson, on account of my clothes; but the widow she didn't scold, but only cleaned off the grease and clay and looked so sorry that I thought I would behave a while if I could. Then Miss Watson she took me in the closet and prayed, but nothing come of it. She told me to pray every day, and whatever I asked for I would get it. But it warn't so. I tried it. Once I got a fish-line, but no hooks. It warn't any good to me without hooks. I tried for the hooks three or four times, but somehow I couldn't make it work. By-and-by, one day, I asked Miss Watson to try for me, but she said I was a fool. She never told me why, and I couldn't make it out no way.

The next passage uses formal diction. Underline the words that identify it as learned or formal. What characteristics of informal diction are absent?

Although it is a commonplace that in American literature there are few writers of really major rank, it is perilous to offer an opinion as to just who these writers are. Whatever the list, the objection will be made that the prizes were not fairly awarded. But it seems fairly certain that if the list is a brief one Poe's claims for inclusion in it are by no means considered self-evident in this country, and have seldom been convincingly sponsored. The general reading public, which might be expected to show a warm interest in Poe, or at least a dutiful respect for him, has shown neither. (Patrick F. Quinn, "The French Response to Poe")

3. This paragraph, written by a student in an education class, does not maintain a consistent level of diction. Although popular diction would have been appropriate for his audience and writing occasion, he sprinkles his paragraph with words too formal or too informal for his writing task. Identify the inconsistencies of diction in the paragraph, and substitute appropriate equivalent words where necessary.

Of the four studies of educational innovation perused for this assignment only one—the N.Y.U. case—can be picked as a sure winner. The other ones—Cambire, Columbia, and the Alternative Schools—are examinations of real disasters. Each of these three studies contains some explanation for its respective failure. In the case of the Cambire experiment, they couldn't implement the innovation. In the Columbia case, the innovation was inextricably bound to a string of other tries so that the failure of one made the entire bunch crumble like a house of cards. Finally, in the case of the Alternative Schools, a hostile environment brought about the experiment's demise.

CHAPTER

8

Tone
and
Style

When you write, you must adopt an attitude toward your material and toward your audience. Your point of view and your voice vary widely, depending on what you want to do, when you write, and the way you present yourself to your reader. Your mood may be serious or lighthearted, respectful or condescending, intimate or detached—or just about anything in between. Your *tone* is what reveals this attitude—which includes point of view, voice, and mood—to your reader. When we speak of a writer's *style*, we usually mean the way he or she uses language to express ideas. In other words, style is the manner in which a writer chooses and arranges words to convey meaning to an audience. In the pages that follow, we will deal with both *tone* and *style* in more detail.

TONE

Your tone gives your readers the clues they need to discover your attitude toward them and toward your material, and this, in turn, helps them to understand what you say. Written prose lacks the helpful signals of speech—gestures, facial expression, tone of voice—but writers can make choices in sentence structure and diction that serve the same function.

How do you, as a writer, decide on the appropriate tone for a piece of writing, the attitude that accurately communicates your feelings about your material and your readers? This decision is usually made during the prewriting stage. As you consider your purpose and define your audience, an attitude toward your material emerges, and this determines your tone. As you revise, make sure that this tone stays consistent with what you want to do.

PURPOSE AND TONE

Your *purpose*—that is, whether you are writing primarily *to inform* or *to influence* your reader—helps to determine your tone. If your general purpose is to present information, you will choose words and construct sentences that make your writing objective and informative. A factual, straightforward, reasonable—even impersonal—tone conveys a no-nonsense attitude. As you write, you step back and consider your material at a distance. On an examination, for example, your purpose is to convey information, thereby demonstrating your command of it. A direct, serious, "no-frills" style best serves this purpose and fulfills your audience's expectations. A sarcastic tone or a playful one would be inappropriate. Your words and sentence patterns must match your intent.

If, however, your general purpose is to influence your readers, to sway their opinions or appeal to their emotions, to make them angry or sympathetic, you must select words and shape sentences that serve this end. You will become involved in what you are writing instead of trying to maintain distance. Your tone will not be straightforward and factual, but ironic or harsh or sentimental or cold or bitter or compassionate—whatever best reflects your attitude and serves your purpose.

☐ WRITING TO INFORM

When your purpose is to convey information—on an exam, in a research paper, in a technical report—your tone reflects your objectivity. Your account will be unbiased and your judgments based on demonstrated facts, not emotional reactions. Your voice must be relatively impersonal and detached. Of course it is difficult—and sometimes inappropriate—to maintain complete objectivity throughout a piece of writing. The decision to include some details and exclude others is itself subjective, and the way you arrange your material also influences your reader in subjective ways.

Relatively objective writing can still be persuasive. A technical report, for instance, may present information in a direct, analytical manner and also convince a reader that additional research is necessary or that new staff should be hired. In fact, most academic writing presents information to make a point: it is written both to inform and to influence readers.

Notice how the language of this passage from a botany research paper reflects its informational purpose and contributes to its objective tone.

> Also found in the Datura plant is atropine, which has two types of actions. It can act on the central nervous system, causing respiratory stimulation and sedation (in selected diseases), and it can also act by depressing smooth muscles and secretory glands innervated by parasympathetic (cholinergic) nerves. Although atropine has many uses, it has almost no selectivity of action. For instance, if atropine is given prior to anesthesia to inhibit excess salivation, the patient must also tolerate the blurred vision, dry mouth, and constipation that go along with it. Atropine is used mainly to stimulate respiration, to temporarily relieve paralysis agitans and postencephalic Parkinsonism, and to relieve spasticity and rigidity.
>
> Tina Bubri

Tina's purpose is to present factual information about the plant *Datura stramonium*, or jimson weed, and its medicinal uses. Her paragraph is dense with information but free of her own opinions. She reports factually on the actions and uses of atropine and supports her reservation about its application with a concrete, convincing example. Her tone is straightforward and direct; her voice, appropriately anonymous.

□ WRITING TO INFLUENCE

Writers often aim to sway their audiences—in newspaper editorials, in book and film reviews, in letters to the editor or to government officials, in leaflets or position papers, and so on. You may need to write a persuasive essay in composition class, or a letter or editorial for your school newspaper, or a recommendation report for your job. Your task is to make your audience feel the way you do by conveying opinion as well as fact. Your tone, then, will be subjective and judgmental, and you will immerse yourself in your material rather than keeping some distance from it.

Notice how the writer of this paragraph from a student book report uses highly positive language to convey her enthusiasm and influence her audience.

> *Prescription Drugs*, by Thomas A. Gossel and Donald W. Stansloski, is designed to educate the average consumer about prescription drugs and other aspects of health care. The authors appeal to consumers by suggesting that it is their duty to be informed about medical treatment; they claim their book is the answer, and they are

certainly correct. The drug listings are extremely comprehensive, and the authors' tone is excellent—patient without being condescending. The authors are obviously well qualified, and they present their material clearly and accurately, revealing their astute professional judgment throughout. In short, the book is highly recommended.

Becky Nagle

While this paragraph includes a fair amount of information, Becky uses language to sway the reader to her point of view. She does not disguise her favorable opinion of the book, and judgmental adjectives like "excellent" and "astute" and emphatic adverbs like "certainly," "extremely," and "highly" reveal her attitude. Her self-assured stance suggests her confidence that she knows more than her readers do about her subject. Her attitude toward her subject is very positive, and the tone of her writing is openly enthusiastic.

EXERCISES

1. Each of the following paragraphs was written either to *inform* or to *influence* its readers. In each case, decide what the writer's primary purpose was; then show how the paragraph's tone is consistent with this purpose.

a. History is the study of change over time and historians have seen many changes in their own discipline in recent years . . . . Yet while new historical interest and knowledge have grown, the broad public has paradoxically appeared to become less interested in history in general and in more distant European history in particular. Appreciation for the study of the past often seems quite limited among the intelligentsia as well . . . . It has been our conviction, based on the experience of a dozen years of introducing large numbers of students to the broad sweep of Western civilization, that the books currently available for this purpose, some of which are fine works, do not adequately incorporate the new areas of interest and discovery within the profession. We feel that a book which reflects these current trends can be exciting and can inspire a new interest in history and a new curiosity about our Western heritage. (McKay, Hill, Buckler, *A History of Western Society,* Vol. I)

b. Geography further encouraged isolation by closing Egypt off from the outside world. To the east and west of the Nile valley stretched grim deserts. The Nubian Desert and the cataracts of the Nile discouraged penetration from the south. Only in the north did the Mediterranean Sea leave Egypt exposed. Thus geography shielded Egypt from invasion and from extensive immigration. Unlike the Mesopotamians, the Egyptians enjoyed centuries of peace and tranquility, and during these years they developed their own unique and distinctive civilization. (McKay, Hill, Buckler, *A History of Western Society,* Vol. I)

c. Years ago, guns were essential for obtaining food to feed many families. However, since we started domesticating animals, guns have become less important for obtaining food. Instead they have been widely used for crimes and have caused many accidents. When respected and used properly, however, guns can improve, protect, and even save many people's lives. (Kevin Gale, student)

d. As for the Desdemona of Shannon John, it is rather less effective than if the pinch-hitting stage manager, script in hand, were to walk through the part. Looking like a vapid starlet on the beach at Malibu, cursed with a voice as infantile as a moppet's whose only modes are utter flatness or singsong, Miss John must have been a huge success the last time she acted for Peter Coe, when she portrayed Anne Baxter's autistic daughter, though that seems insufficient reason to repeat the characterization here. Miss John, the program says, has studied acting with Herbert Berghof, and it is more than likely that she is entitled to have her entire tuition refunded. (John Simon, *New York*)

e.   In the 79-year history of the Yankees, only six pitchers have thrown no-hitters against them. Bob Ojeda, a 23-year-old rookie, came within one inning of becoming the seventh yesterday.

Ojeda held the Yankees hitless until Rick Cerone led off the ninth inning with a pinch-hit line drive that soared just out of the reach of a lunging Dwight Evans in right-center field. The hit went for a double, and when Dave Winfield followed with another pinch-double, Mark Clear relieved Ojeda and preserved a 2-1 victory for the Red Sox. Clear struck out Willie Randolph and Jerry Mumphrey, then walked Oscar Gamble, batting for Lou Piniella. Clear ended the game by getting Reggie Jackson on a first-pitch fly to left. (Murray Chass, ''Rookie Misses No-Hitter in Ninth,'' *New York Times*)

2.   Use the list that follows to write two paragraphs: one in which your purpose is to inform your readers of the nature of the Media Alcoholism Center's services and clientele, and one in which your intent is to convince your audience that the center deserves continued funding. You may add brief remarks that serve your purpose in each paragraph, but be sure that each paragraph uses *all* the information provided below—and *only* this information. In this exercise your choice of language—not your choice of content—should help you achieve the desired effect.

The Media Alcoholism Center

○ Clientele 75 percent male

○ Clientele mostly between 18 and 25, although Clinic serves those between 14 and 70

○ Outpatient clinic

○ Center holds Alcoholics Anonymous meetings

○ Couple and family therapy available

○ Agency serves 150 to 200 clients

○ Cuts in government funding led to staff cutbacks; now only two full-time and eight part-time employees

○ Only one-third of funds come from government; clients pay $10 per session

○ Director would like to add more seminars on topics like self-awareness, how to meet people, self-assertiveness, and stress management

○ Darby Center, a similar (but larger) facility, is nearby

AUDIENCE AND TONE

Just as your involvement with—or detachment from—your material affects your tone, so does your degree of involvement with your reader. Whether you identify with or separate yourself from your reader plays a critical part in shaping and maintaining an appropriate and consistent tone. In a person-to-person situation when you speak directly to a reader (as in a personal letter) or pretend to (as in a self-help article), you use a more personal and conversational tone than when you address a general audience indirectly in an anonymous voice. In the latter case, you are more reserved, more remote, and somewhat more formal.

Your attitude toward your audience also affects the tone that emerges as you write. Your attitude toward your readers can be positive or negative, sympathetic or superior, concerned or condescending, friendly or critical. If you are friendly or sympathetic to your readers, you feel close to them; if you are critical or superior—or neutral—you feel distant from them.

Notice how the writers of these two paragraphs treat their audiences:

> Those of you who have lived many years suffering from headaches should take some comfort in knowing that you are among an exclusive group of fellow headache sufferers. The list of famous headache sufferers is quite impressive and includes such notable individuals as Cervantes, Thomas Jefferson, Sigmund Freud, Ulysses S. Grant, Karl Marx, Julius Caesar, Leo Tolstoy, Virginia Woolf, Edgar Allan Poe, Lewis Carroll, Tchaikovsky, Chopin, Charles Darwin, and George Bernard Shaw. These notables, like you, experienced the agony and limitations imposed by this disabling affliction. And, like many of you, they persevered day by day to overcome the disability.
>
> Joel R. Saper, M.D., and Kenneth R. Magee, M.D., *Freedom from Headaches*

Instead of speaking to a general audience, these doctors characterize their readers as headache sufferers and speak to them as such. They identify very strongly with their readers and the medical problems they have. Their sympathetic language reassures their readers; they use "you" to address their audience directly, almost as if they were speaking to them in person. Their tone is conversational and encouraging.

> Children's traditional games offer an ideal topic for folklore research. They are passed from child to child in almost pure oral tradition with no reference whatever to print, and probably with negligible influence from teachers, parents, or recreation leaders. The players are naturally conservative about their texts and will strive to maintain the "right way" of playing against all variations. Thus old games may survive, little altered, through many generations of children. Children's games also develop clear regional subtypes. When families change neighborhoods or move to other communities, the children will soon discover whether their old versions are played in the new home or whether they must adopt new ones, for seldom do newcomers succeed in converting their playmates to outside games. Finally, children are usually excellent informants—easy to locate, eager to perform, and uninhibited with their responses.
>
> Jan Harold Brunvand, *The Study of American Folklore*

Unlike the previous passage, this paragraph takes a fairly distant tone. The author does not use "you," nor does he characterize his audience in any particular way. In fact, he focuses on information, not on his readers' reaction. While the tone is not stiff or formal, it is not conversational, and the author remains somewhat aloof from his readers.

EXERCISES

---

1.   The author of the first of the following two passages adopts a tone that keeps him rather distant from his audience; the authors of the second passage get relatively close to their audience. Read the two passages and list, in note form, the ways the authors reveal their attitude toward their respective audiences.

  a.   To return to our original definition, news is an honest, unbiased, and complete account of events of interest or concern to the public. Professor George H. Morris of Florida Southern University, who was a newspaperman for many years before he became a teacher, character-izes news as "history in a hurry." He says "Read several papers, day after day, and eventually the truth will emerge."

  No newspaper, because of the limitations of time and space, can print all of the facts that make the news in any one issue. No reader can understand what is happening by scanning any one issue of any one paper.

  It is difficult for even the best newspapers to do a good job of gathering and writing the news. The good reader will evaluate it by reading carefully day after day and comparing the way identical stories are covered in papers with different viewpoints. (Duane Bradley, "What Is News?" *The Newspaper: Its Place in a Democracy*)

  b.   You've read your local newspaper. You've tuned in the hourly news on radio and watched the evening news on television. You've read *Time* or *Newsweek*. In other words, you have read, seen and heard the "news." All of it was intended to provide you with information you need and want to know.

  But it wasn't all the same, was it? Your newspaper told you about people and events that didn't rate a mention on television's "6 O'Clock News." The radio reports stressed fresh occurrences within the hour, while the magazine you read presented detail and analysis available nowhere else.

  In short, there is no single, universally accepted definition of "news." The city council meeting that is the day's big story in Danville, Illinois, is of no interest or importance to a television network's nationwide audience, and of little interest to readers in Urbana, Illinois, less than 50 miles away. (Brian S. Brooks, et al., *News Reporting & Writing*)

2.   The following paragraph was written by a freshman composition student on the topic "The Drinking Age Controversy." Revise it so that its tone is appropriately distant from the audience, in this case, the student's English instructor.

  Eighteen-year-olds have many responsibilities, but the law does not allow them to drink in this state. When you turn sixteen and a half, you are given the right to drive on the nation's highways with an adult in the car. When you turn seventeen, you are free to drive alone. When you turn eighteen, you're considered an adult in the eyes of the law: you can vote, be drafted, get married, or quit school without your parents' consent. You can see how unfair this is. In the eyes of the law, eighteen-year-olds are adults with all the responsibilities that go along with adulthood. Shouldn't drinking and the control of your body be among those responsibilities?

STYLE

Although most of us use the word "style" to mean "how we write," writers use "style" in two other senses. In one sense, "style" conveys a standard of excellence, a measurement of how close a writer comes to achieving his or her rhetorical goals through the use of language. "Good" style, then, is the pattern of language that most effectively conveys a writer's meaning.

In another sense, "style" is a means not of judging writing but of classifying it. In this sense, style can be defined according to its use ("journalistic style"), its association with a particular writer ("Shakespearean style") or literary period ("romantic style"), its degree of elaborateness ("plain style," "ornate style"), or its level of formality. This last notion of "formal," "informal," and "intermediate" or "popular" style is probably the most applicable to student writing.

The level of formality you choose should always be appropriate for your audience, purpose, and writing occasion. It should also be consistent—that is, readers will expect you to stay with one level of formality throughout a piece of writing. In college writing, where you aim to convince your audience that you have command of a body of information, showing that you have control over your style is particularly important.

FORMAL STYLE

Formal style uses relatively long and complex sentences, a learned vocabulary, and a serious tone. This level of style is appropriate to serious occasions—scholarly research, political treatises, and the like. Rarely, if ever, do you use it in college writing, which has a more general audience.

Sentences in formal writing tend to be long and varied, with fairly frequent use of balanced sentences. Sentence structure is always complete, with no fragments. Sentence patterns include simple and compound sentences, but complex sentences predominate.

Words in formal writing are often learned, with allusions and figurative language enriching the vocabulary. As we have seen (see pages 195–196), formal diction avoids contractions, slang, and utility words.

Tone is likely to be distant. The writer remains relatively anonymous, making no attempt to speak directly to anyone. The personal "you" never appears, and only occasionally does "you" refer to the audience in general terms. If used at all, "I" represents a neutral observer, a representative spokesperson or authority, or an anonymous guide leading the reader through an argument. "We" stands for a collective "editorial we," for representatives of a particular position, or as short-hand for human beings in general. Finally, the formal style often substitutes the anonymous "one" for "I" or "we."

This example of formal style contains many of these characteristics.

> To be "outside American Society" is of course to be in the great American literary tradition. It is a tradition, transcendentalism and romanticism being only two aspects of it, in which individuals are characterized less by their relation to one another than by their relation to the conglomerations of power that fill space and that determine the apportionments of time. The conglomerations go under different names: Nature, The City, Society, The Dynamo, The Bomb, The Presidency, and aspects of any one of these may be ascribed to any other. The force that joins people together in Dreiser's world does not manifest itself in marriage, any more than it does in most other American writers. People are instead merged in a common bondage to the humming, soaring vistas of the city with their evocations of mysterious promise. Personal attachments, sporadic and "chemic," can take place within such an environment, but they do not compel the interest of Dreiser or his characters. These characters are compelled instead by the nonpersonal forces that fill the yearning eye with steel and concrete, that manipulate time by the pulsations of manufacture and of money-making.
>
> Richard Poirier, "Panoramic Environment and the Anonymity of Self"

The writer here does not present himself as a distinctive personality; his individual voice is less important than his information. *Sentences* range from sixteen to forty-four words, with almost all over twenty-five words long. The opening sentence is balanced, and the others vary in structure and complexity. The writer has selected his *words* with an educated audience in mind, using terms like "transcendental-ism," "conglomerations," "apportionments," "manifest," and "chemic" as a matter of course. He uses no contractions, slang, shortened word forms, or utility words. The *tone* is reserved, serious, and scholarly. Poirier does not address his readers, and nothing in the paragraph suggests everyday speech.

"ELEVATED" STYLE

Sometimes, in a conscious effort to impress their readers, student writers "elevate" their language, straining its natural order and distorting its purpose. The result is an overblown, tangled, silly piece of prose.

Read this excerpt from a student essay. The assignment was a brief essay, in class, on the topic, "How do you expect your life to be different from the lives of your parents?"

> Even though many of one's parents' traits are inherited, the expectations of their offspring may be appreciably different from theirs. The conclusions expressed in this essay are based in part on the fact that the structure of society has changed since the

time most of our parents commenced their professional careers. Also, recent social and economic developments have allowed further education to be both perceivable and achievable. Another point to consider is that the economic situation of most persons has been ameliorated, and sex roles are not as rigidly stereotyped as they once were. Finally, unlike their parents, many young adults today possess a sense of realism in dealing with the evolving modern world.

The assignment suggests a straightforward, informal style. This student, however, created an overly formal, stilted introductory paragraph for her essay. Her distance from her readers, given the wording of the question and her instructor's expectations, is inappropriate. The student goes to such extremes to avoid the pronoun "I" that she produces convoluted sentences full of abstractions. Impersonal pronouns and stiff, passive-voice constructions set her tone. Her diction also misses both her purpose and her audience. After revising her paper, she turned in the following paragraph.

> Even though I have inherited many of my parents' traits, I expect my life to be very different from theirs. I base my conclusions in part on the fact that the structure of society has changed since the time my parents began their professional careers. Also, recent social and economic developments have made further education something I know I can achieve. My family's financial situation now is better than that of their own families when they graduated from high school, and my parents' expectations for me are not as rigidly stereotyped according to sex as their parents' were for them. Finally, unlike my parents, I have a sense of realism as I approach the changing world I live in.

Now she speaks more directly to her audience, and her general style fits her purpose and her audience's expectations better.

INFORMAL STYLE

Informal style most closely resembles the style of everyday speech, that which you use when you are among friends and not carefully watching grammar or word use. It is marked by short sentences, colloquialisms and slang, and a conversational tone. You seldom use it in college writing, however, because it is not serious, precise, or correct enough for an academic audience.

Sentences tend to be cumulative rather than balanced or periodic, with occasional fragments. They are also likely to be short, and subject-verb-object order is common. *Words* are frequently popular and colloquial, including slang, utility words, contractions, and shortened forms. *Tone* is casual and conversational. The writer speaks directly to the reader in a voice that is subjective and individual rather than objective and anonymous. The first person "I" expresses personal experiences and feelings; "we" creates a sense of unity or identification between the reader and the writer. Rarely does the formal pronoun "one" substitute for "I" or "we." Here is an example of informal style:

Now you've made up your mind. You want to buy a bicycle. But what *kind* of bicycle should you get? New or secondhand? Coaster brakes or caliper brakes? A three-speed "racer" or one of those fancy jobs with turned-down handlebars and lots of gears and things hanging down from the rear wheel? Where should you buy your bicycle? Do you go to a discount house or a bike shop? How about a take-apart bicycle—handy to store in the trunk of the car, neat, too—very "camp." And how can you tell a topgrade bicycle from a piece of junk that will give you nothing but trouble and needless expense?

Eugene A. Sloane, *The Complete Book of Bicycling*

The writer's purpose is to offer friendly, helpful advice to an audience of novice bicyclists, so he speaks directly to his readers in a conversational, colloquial way. His sentences are relatively brief and uncomplicated; the longest is twenty-five words, but the average length is much shorter. The paragraph includes three sentence fragments in the form of questions. The writer's words include contractions ("you've"), shortened forms ("bike"), slang ("fancy jobs," "camp"), and utility words ("gears and *things* hanging from the rear wheel"). The tone is light and chatty, and the overall effect is extremely loose and informal.

Writers of fiction often use informal style to convey the speech of a character. This gives readers insight into the character and creates a sense of immediacy and realism. This excerpt from the short story "I'm a Fool," by Sherwood Anderson, was written in 1923. The words of the boy who tells the story recreate the rural slang of the period.

You know how it is. Gee, she was a peach! She had on a soft dress, kind of a blue stuff and it looked carelessly, but was well sewed and made and everything. I knew that much. I blushed when she looked right at me and so did she. She was the nicest girl I've ever seen in my life. She wasn't stuck on herself and she could talk proper grammar without being like a school teacher or something like that. What I mean is, she was O.K. I think maybe her father was well-to-do, but not rich to make her chesty because she was his daughter, as some are. Maybe he owned a drugstore or drygoods store in their home town, or something like that. She never told me and I never asked.

Passages like this one are carefully crafted, in spite of their informal style. Even though this prose sounds like actual speech, its rhythm and balance mark it as the product of an experienced writer.

POPULAR STYLE

Popular style is the one to use in your college writing assignments. Its sentence structure, diction, and tone fall midway between the formal and informal styles. With this intermediate style, you write *sentences* longer than those associated with informal style, yet generally shorter than those of formal style. Cumulative sentences are most common, but some balanced and periodic sentences appear as well. *Words* may be classified as popular, and occasionally you will use utility words, colloquialisms, and contractions. You may also use some learned words, the special vocabulary of the discipline you are writing in, in papers and tests. Your *tone* may be distant and objective or close and subjective; your voice, serious or casual. You may show some individuality, using the personal "I," using "you" to address your readers as people, and only rarely using the formal "one." Here is an example:

> Whatever the reason, there is little question that "General Hospital" gives viewers what they want. It has been particularly successful in attracting younger viewers, who have traditionally regarded soap addiction as a sure sign of senility. A. C. Nielsen estimates that nearly three quarters of the show's audience falls into the 18-to-34 group so prized by TV advertisers. College students seem particularly susceptible to its appeal. When several of the show's stars appeared at Harvard University for a "General Hospital Weekend" last May, the staid campus erupted with groupie hysteria reminiscent of a '60s Beatles concert. And as the nation's campuses spring back to life this month, overflow audiences of "GH" scholars are again surrounding giant-screen sets in student unions and dormitory lounges.
>
> "Television's Hottest Show," *Newsweek*

The writer of this journalistic passage hopes to convince a wide general audience that the daytime drama *General Hospital* is very popular. Sentences range from eight to thirty words in length, with most about twenty words long. The author does not use any elaborate balanced or parallel sentences, but the sentence structure is correct and varied. Words are both formal and informal. For instance, the author uses learned words like "susceptible" and "reminiscent" and avoids contractions. And, while shortened forms like "TV" and "'60s" are used, "dormitory" is not abbreviated as "dorm." On the other hand, we do see occasional slang like "soap" and "groupie" and the colloquial "sure sign." The tone is direct and straightforward without being either aloof from or intimate with the reader. Neither the writer nor the audience is personalized in any way.

You also see this intermediate style in academic writing. Consider this passage on water pollution from a student's research paper.

> New Orleans, like most cities, gets its water from a heavily polluted source—the Mississippi River. Even though the city residents are alarmed by the taste and color of the water, the Public Health Survey has declared the water "safe"—which means that it will not cause typhoid, cholera, or other bacterial diseases that standard water-treatment plants are designed to prevent. In 1969 the Federal Water Pollution Control Administration tested New Orleans' "safe" water for organic compounds, and thirty-six such chemicals were identified: three were cancer-causing substances, and three others were identified as having caused liver damage in animals. The effects of drinking this water are inconclusive, but according to the *Environmental Defense Fund Letter* (1975), New Orleans had the highest rate of kidney cancer and the sixth highest rate for cancer of the urinary tract of the 163 areas studied.
>
> Roman Midzak

This paragraph aims at a general academic audience. The sentences are relatively long and varied. The style properly reflects the occasion of the assignment, and the writer avoids overly technical terms—he uses "cancer-causing" as opposed to "carcinogenic" and does not list the specific cancer-causing substances he refers to. The tone of the passage is objective but not formal, in keeping with the seriousness of the subject matter.

How does a writer revise his or her work to achieve this intermediate style? Here is how one student, Dave Stola, went about it.

Dave's task was to write a paper about the isolation of Jerry, a character in Edward Albee's play *The Zoo Story*. A quick first draft of one paragraph looked like this:

> Jerry's loneliness was totally his own fault. It made him miserable and even made him want to kill himself. I think he really wanted a friend to talk to and confide in, but instead of meeting people he'd just hang around and think about other people's problems. This made his own life seem pretty good. He did take a shot at getting friendly with his landlady's dog, but it seems to me he did it the wrong way. When the dog didn't do what he wanted, he tried to kill it. I know he could've easily gotten in good with the landlady because she kind of liked him, but he would rather have killed himself. (Wise choice on his part, in my opinion.)

Dave saw that his remarks were much too informal for his audience, purpose, and writing occasion. Slang expressions like "hang around," "take a shot at," and "gotten in good with" were clearly inappropriate, as were his closing parenthetical fragment, his frequent contractions ("he'd," "didn't," "could've"), his use of "I" and "me," and his empty colloquialisms ("really," "kind of").

Dave's first revision aimed for an intermediate style; unfortunately, he went a little too far in the opposite direction.

> One can easily observe that the loneliness experienced by Jerry is due to his own devices. This condition of misery led him to consider taking his own life. Desperately desiring a friend to speak with and confide in, he could occupy his mind only with the difficulties of others rather than possible means of achieving meaningful personal contacts. This fixation caused his own existence to appear considerably less miserable. Although Jerry made a valiant effort to become friendly with a dog belonging to his landlady, he went about this activity counterproductively. When the dog failed to respond in the expected fashion, he attempted to exterminate the creature. While one can easily perceive that Jerry could have befriended his landlady, who seemed to possess genuine affection for him, he preferred not to.

This "translation" resulted in a pretentious paragraph in the "elevated" style, full of excess verbiage, roundabout constructions, and ten-dollar words. In his final version, Dave did his best to eliminate all traces of overly formal as well as overly informal style and to aim for a clear, natural style.

> Jerry's loneliness, which was entirely his own fault, caused him to be miserable and even to consider suicide. He desperately longed for a friend whom he could talk

to and confide in, but instead of meeting people he just occupied himself by thinking about other people's problems. These at least made his own life seem less miserable. He did make one attempt to befriend his landlady's dog, but he went about it in the wrong way. When the dog didn't do what he wanted it to, he tried to kill it. He could have become friendly with his landlady, because she was fond of him, but he chose not to.

As you can see, achieving an appropriate tone and style sometimes takes a bit of work. But this kind of revision is worth the effort because it ensures that you are conveying your exact attitude toward your material and your audience in the most appropriate manner.

EXERCISES

1. Read each of the following three paragraphs carefully to determine whether it is written in informal, popular, or formal style. Then write a paragraph about each in which you analyze its style. Be sure to consider sentence structure, diction, and tone as you decide how formal each paragraph is.

a. The other day I had fifty-five minutes to serve 101 coach passengers, a cocktail and full-meal service. You do it fast and terrible. You're very rude. You don't mean to be rude, you just don't have time to answer questions. You smile and you just ignore it. You get three drink orders in a hurry. There's been many times when you miss the glass, pouring, and you pour it in the man's lap. You just don't say I'm sorry. You give him a cloth and you keep going. That's the bad part of the job. (Terry Mason, "Airline Stewardess," in Studs Terkel, *Working*)

b. The thyroid gland is particularly susceptible to environmental influences and, therefore, is unique among the endocrine glands as far as direct environmental impact. The thyroid gland becomes hyperplastic and a goiter develops when there is severe nutritional iodine deficiency. This is the reverse of the usual meaning of toxic effects of a substance on an organ. In fact, the abnormality occurs when there is an insufficient amount rather than an excess of one of the important chemicals needed for that particular gland. (Edmund B. Flink, "Introductory Remarks: The Thyroid Gland," *Environmental Health Perspectives*)

c. Ask anyone the question "Is it more advantageous to live on campus or to commute?" and chances are most people will agree it is more beneficial to move away from home and be out on your own than to try to combine college life with home life. Going to college is a full-time commitment. You can't just "play college" during the day and then go home and be taken care of by your parents. College isn't just a continuation of high school; it's a totally new experience. Besides providing a greater opportunity to spend more time on your studies, living on campus is practical and convenient. And the only way to become a responsible, self-sufficient adult is to live on your own. (Stephen Knittweis, freshman composition essay)

2. Reread the three paragraphs in exercise 1. Rewrite paragraph a so that it is considerably *more* formal in sentence structure, diction, and tone. Then, rewrite paragraph b so that it is *less* formal (use a dictionary if necessary).

III

Revising

When you write your first draft, your goal is to get ideas on paper. At this stage you don't worry much about meeting the needs of a particular reader. You might find it helpful to realize that in your rough draft you are talking to yourself, giving yourself ideas that you will work with later. This shift—from writing for yourself to writing for others—is basic to revision.

Revision usually emerges as a central concern after you have completed your first draft. This is when you "re-see" what you have written and make changes based on what your reader needs to understand your information. Your most important task is to put yourself in the place of your reader. Sometimes you have to imagine the audience you are addressing. If you are writing to an academic audience, you picture your instructor as the representative of this group. Other times you have the opportunity to get responses from an audience. Your instructor may allow you to revise your work based on his or her comments. You may share your work with your classmates and get their responses. The advice you get is useful in seeing what changes to make on your rough draft.

Remember, however, that "revising" does not simply follow "prewriting" and "writing and arranging" as the third step in a sequence; rather, it is a process that involves you from the moment you begin to discover ideas. Throughout the prewriting and writing and arranging stages, and especially as you write out a number of drafts, you are constantly revising—rethinking your topic or thesis and reconsidering the order of your ideas or their relationship to each other. Your purpose is to "go public," to get your ideas across to your audience. This activity is different for everyone because revision, like writing itself, is a creative and idiosyncratic process. You will have to do a lot of experimenting before you find techniques that work for you.

CHAPTER

9

Revising

Your

Essay

When we see a good movie or play, we say we're "caught up in it. " We use words like "gripping" and "absorbing" to describe our response to the finished product. When we stop to think about it, we realize that the writer wrestled with ideas and words (and probably with directors and producers and financial backers as well) to produce a script; that the casting people held auditions; that contracts were negotiated; that actors and actresses rehearsed; that set designers, carpenters, and the prop department furnished the sets; that sound, light, and other technicians put the production together; that costume designers dressed the cast; and that hairdressers and make-up people applied the finishing touches. All this is perfectly obvious, but we don't stop to think of these things while the action "grips" us. Our awareness of the process is submerged in our enchantment with the product. Only after the piece is over do we analyze it.

A good piece of writing seems finished to the reader; it creates the illusion of having been created almost effortlessly. The reader has no sense of the work that went on behind the scenes: the writing process remains invisible to everyone but the writer who has struggled with it. But the struggle is real. Let's look at the work-in-progress of two writers—one a student, one a professional.

A student, Honora Galgay, was asked to write an English composition essay on the topic "Will there be a world for tomorrow?" Here is what the first paragraph of her rough draft looked like after she revised it and before she recopied it.

Notice the work that went into this section of her revised draft. Honora considered, reconsidered, and rejected a number of items. She also altered the structure of the paragraph, changed words, and sharpened her focus.

The page opposite comes from a manuscript by the contemporary Chinese-American writer Maxine Hong Kingston. Like Honora Galgay, Kingston worked hard to put her thoughts into words. Not only did she change words and add ideas, but, perhaps most painful, she deleted portions of text, moving just a few of the salvaged phrases to earlier or later pages. Only by such drastic action was she able to achieve the effects she wanted.

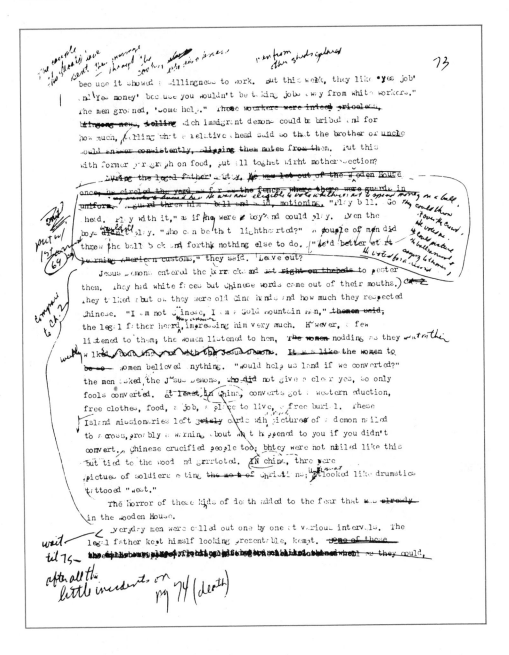

Any draft represents only one of many possible versions of your ideas. By trying out a number of ways to express your thoughts, as Honora Galgay and Maxine Hong Kingston did, you will find the version that seems best to you. It isn't easy for anyone to learn to revise. In fact, research shows that inexperienced and experienced writers see revision differently. Beginning writers see revision as admitting that something is wrong. They feel that if their papers are not perfect on the first try, they have somehow failed. More experienced writers, how-ever, *expect* to revise as a necessary part of the writing process. They have learned that there is no such thing as perfection, and they see themselves as revising from the beginning.

Experienced and inexperienced writers also differ in *how* they revise. When beginning writers revise, if they do it at all, they refine word choice, check spelling and grammar, proofread for mechanics and accuracy, and recopy to make a paper neater. In short, they work on the surface of the paper. Experienced writers, however, see revision as a series of deeper activities that involve internal upheaval: re-seeing ideas, rethinking a thesis, disassembling and reassembling an entire essay, and finding a voice and shaping a design for their writing.

Writing well involves major upheavals, and you must develop a system to deal with it. If you acknowledge from the start that you will probably be tearing apart much of what you write, you can prepare your first draft so that revisions are less painful. First, skip lines. This makes it easier for you to notice mechanical errors and gives you plenty of room to add new material or to rewrite sentences you're not happy with. Next, develop some system of asterisks, arrows, carets, brackets, num-bers, letters, and the like—a set of signals you can use regularly when you revise. For instance, you can get into the habit of circling words and using brackets or boxes for longer word groups (or even entire paragraphs) when you know you want to relocate them in your paper. Then, use an arrow to indicate the new location, or use asterisks or matching numbers or letters to remind you how you intend to rearrange ideas. To add a few words, use a caret, like this. Finally, be sure to write on only one side of the page. This enables you to study your pages side by side so logical and stylistic links will be most obvious. It also allows you to do some serious scissors-and-tape revising without destroying material on the reverse side of the page. Don't hesitate to cut a section out of a page and tape it where it seems to belong, and don't be afraid to keep rearranging the sections or paragraphs of your paper until you get the order right. This is revising at its most thorough and most useful.

REVISING FOR AN AUDIENCE

Revision makes your writing consistent with the original goals defined by your purpose, audience, occasion, length, and knowledge. Your own changing ideas, feedback from peers, teachers' comments, and new readings and experiences and observations also are sources of information for revision. In this sense, then, revi-sion reflects not just your critical reaction to your first draft, but your reaction to outside influences as well. You revise not just to satisfy yourself, but also to accom-modate your readers, so you must balance your own goals against what you think your reader needs and expects. The revising process, in fact, brings you closer and closer to your reader.

As you revise, your evaluation of your audience always influences your decisions. You want to be as readable as possible, and readers want to keep moving forward as they read. All of your changes should make what you say clearer and more interesting. Certain signals and strategies can help you make your ideas more accessible to your readers.

1. *Present one idea at a time and sum up regularly.* Don't overload your text with more information than a reader can understand or remember; don't force your audience to backtrack constantly in order to understand your logic.

2. *Fulfill your readers' expectations.* Readers expect the promise of your thesis to be fulfilled; they expect you to put your ideas in an understandable order, and they count on your paragraphs to expand the statements your topic sentences make. They also expect parallel elements to appear in parallel terms; subjects to agree with verbs and pronouns to agree with antecedents; and person, voice, tense, and mood to remain constant.

3. *Remind your readers frequently of the context for your ideas.* Repeating key points regularly, using clear topic sentences and transitions, and subordinating ideas accurately all help your reader.

4. *Accommodate your audience by paying close attention to editing and proofreading.* When you edit and proofread, you approach your work as a critical reader might, checking spelling and punctuation, mechanics, manuscript conventions, and the like. More important, however, is your need to shape and control your paper's content, form, language, and tone to make your writing readable.

You may reconsider audience, purpose, thesis, support, style, and tone at any point in revising. In general, though, when you focus on revision, you narrow your focus from concerns with relatively large elements—like purpose or audience—to more detailed concerns—like the structure and content of the paragraphs—finally concentrating on individual sentences, phrases, and words. Of course you don't move this way mechanically; rather, you move from one aspect to another over and over again.

REVISION STRATEGIES

Everyone revises differently, and every writing task demands a slightly different kind of revision. Three strategies, however, can help you as you reconsider the effectiveness of what you have written. You can use these revision techniques individually or in combination, in a classroom setting or on your own.

PEER CRITICISM

Instead of trying to picture a general audience, you can ask an actual person—a friend, a classmate, a work associate—to read your draft and comment on it (with your instructor's permission, of course). What you want is not an itemization of every spelling error or missing comma but a general sense of whether your essay has the effect you want it to have—and, if you're lucky, an analysis of why it succeeds or fails. Peer criticism is a kind of test marketing for your essay: you know what effect you want; now you have to find out whether a reader reacts that way.

Peer criticism can be relatively formal—your instructor may ask you to exchange papers with another student and may even require you to complete an evaluation form—or just a casual request of a friend. In either case, take the analysis of your paper's strengths and weaknesses seriously. After all, if your writing doesn't communicate your ideas, it doesn't matter how sharp your observations are.

Here is a look at how peer revision works. Ann Leon had to write an essay for freshman composition in which she made a prediction about the future. Here is her second draft.

Factory Workers vs. Robots

Modern robots are considered novelties whose potential has yet to be recognized. They are not widely used now, but future societies may become dependent upon their capabilities to eliminate many of the mundane aspects of work. Although widespread application of robots would probably improve general economic conditions, unskilled laborers could suffer severe psychological impairment.

Assignments on an assembly line are tedious and unfulfilling. Consultants have reported that worker productivity drops steadily until it finally reaches less than fifty percent at the end of a nine-hour shift. At the same time there is a decrease in efficiency due to fatigue. Robots not only would not suffer these counter-productive effects but also would probably be less expensive to maintain. Corporate savings could be passed on to consumers, benefiting the economy.

However, the impact this reorganization would have on blue-collar workers must be considered. These men and women would be forced into an already overcrowded job market with skills that are obsolete. Suited for no other type of employment, the prospects of finding another job would be bleak and they would find themselves reliant on government assistance.

Perhaps the greatest tragedy would be that many of these people would attempt to boost their self-esteem through artificial stimuli. The false euphoria created would be more appealing than the stark reality confronting them. A vicious, destructive cycle would be begun with very little chance for improvement without professional treatment. Already a greater percentage of factory workers than any other workers suffer from some type of mental illness. Most of these people will not seek treatment, thus denying themselves the opportunity to express their anxieties constructively. The extreme possibility is that with alcohol or drugs suppressing their inhibitions, factory workers might stage a rebellion that could become a bloodbath if not handled properly. At the very least, the little self-respect this group feels would be stripped away.

A restructuring of industry would be beneficial to a sagging economy that has ceased to be as productive and competitive as it once was. Yet the ramifications to a large segment of our population should be recognized, and preparations must be made to deal with the impact. For too long the average worker has been part of the unappreciated backbone of our society and his responsibility can not now be taken away without thought.

Before Ann handed her paper in, her instructor asked the class to do a peer revision exercise. He collected all the papers and gave each one to another student to read. Along with the paper, he gave each student a page of questions to answer (anonymously) and return to the original paper's author. His questions focused on specific concerns he intended to go over in class. (Formats for peer evaluation vary widely, however; a different set of questions appears in the exercise below and on page 227.) When Ann's essay came back to her, the sheet on page 226 was attached.

Her reviewer's comments forced Ann to do some thinking about what she needed to revise. Looking back at her paper, she thought its structure sound, so she focused on the comments about style and content. First Ann took her reader's advice about adding information to paragraph 3. She also wrote a new topic sentence for paragraph 2 ("Robots would clearly have some advantages over human workers") and changed paragraph 3's topic sentence to read "However, the negative impact. . . ." She looked at the words and phrases her reader had found troublesome, removed the clichés, and clarified other words. For instance, in paragraph 4 she added "such as drugs and alcohol" after "stimuli" and changed "professional treatment" to "psychiatric treatment," and in paragraph 5 she expanded "ramifications" to "potential ramifications of robot workers." When she looked at the sentence her critic felt "sounded funny," she realized that "Suited for no other type of employment" was a dangling modifier. She revised the sentence to open with "Because these workers would be suited for no other type of employment. . . ."

EXERCISE

Select a paper you have written this term and reread it carefully. Then:

○ Underline your thesis and topic sentences.
○ Circle the three most important details in each paragraph.
○ Star the words and phrases that you think do most to convey your meaning.
○ Cross out anything that does not contribute to your meaning or purpose.

Now answer these questions:

1. What exactly did you mean to tell your audience when you wrote this paper?
2. Analyze what you wrote, paying special attention to the elements you have highlighted. How effective were you at achieving your original goals?
3. How do you think your writing should be revised to meet your goals? When you have made some tentative decisions about the kind of work your paper needs, ex-

Exercise: Peer Revision

Reread the essay through carefully and answer each of the following
questions on this page. Do not put your name on this sheet.

1) Is the thesis clearly worded? If not, how could it be improved?
    (Don't rewrite it; just suggest changes.)
    *Yes, thesis is clearly worded. The word "use" might be
    better than "application."*

2) Does the opening paragraph attract your attention? Does it move
    from general to specific? What strategy might add interest or be
    more appropriate?
    Yes, it attracts the reader's attention

3) Do the body paragraphs support the thesis? Is any information in
    these paragraphs irrelevant? Is any needed information missing?
    *Yes, each ¶ has a specific purpose and supports the
    thesis. But ¶3 needs more details. What reorganization would
    occur? In what jobs could robots replace workers?*

4) Does each body paragraph have a topic sentence? Does this topic
    sentence clearly summarize the information in the paragraph? Are
    the topic sentences clearly related to the thesis? Identify
    any problems.
    *Yes - but ¶2 needs a topic sentence that shows the ¶ will
    talk about advantages of robots, and the first sentence
    of ¶3 needs to say the impact will be negative*

5) Are all needed transitions provided? Are any additional logical
    links needed between sentences or between paragraphs? If so,
    where?
    *Paper goes in a logical order, stating the advantages of
    robots and then the negative effects on workers
    (as stated in the thesis).*

6) Is the conclusion effective? Does it add interest to the essay
    and reinforce the essay's major points? Would another strategy
    be more effective?
    *Yes- it makes the reader realize the importance of the
    blue collar workers and reinforces what would happen
    if robots were used.*

7) Consider the smaller aspects of this paper - the sentences and the
    words. Does the essay have errors in sentence structure? spelling
    or punctuation? phrasing or word choice? If so, where? (Don't
    correct the errors; just identify them.)
    the last sentence in ¶3 sounds funny.

8) Is anything unclear or confusing?
    *What artifical stimuli (¶4)?
    What kind of "professional treatment" (¶4)?
    What do you mean by "ramifications" in ¶5?*

9) What is the essay's greatest strength?
    Its organization

10) What is the greatest weakness?
     *Some clichés - like "backbone of our society" (¶5),
     "bleak" (prospects) in ¶3, "vicious, destructive
     cycle" (¶4), etc.*

change papers with someone in your class. Read your classmate's paper and have him or her read yours. Both of you answer these questions (in writing):

   a.   What did the writer mean to communicate?

   b.   How does the paper affect you?

   c.   How effective was the writer at achieving his or her goals?

   d.   How might his or her writing be revised?

Now, using your own and your classmate's critiques, revise your essay.

OUTLINING

Another revision strategy is to write a formal outline based on the content of your rough draft. This won't tell you about audience reaction or stylistic or grammatical flaws, but it will certainly help you check the structure of your paper. An outline of your essay shows you at once what points are irrelevant or poorly placed, or if a critical point is missing. You can also see the hierarchy of your ideas—which points are dominant and which are subordinate. And you can make sure that you have supplied the cues your reader needs to follow your ideas—topic sentences, transitions, and so on.

When John Gibbons, a student in a journalism class, was asked for a short article on an issue of national concern, he narrowed his general subject to the topic "Large-Scale Evacuations." Then he brainstormed, isolated key concepts and grouped relevant points under them, and formulated a tentative thesis. After two drafts, his article looked like this:

Large-Scale Evacuations

Introduction   When the need for plans to evacuate residents from an area surrounding a nuclear power plant is discussed, some critics raise basic objections. They claim that massive traffic jams will clog all roads, making movement impossible. They point out the lack of existing facilities to house and feed the evacuees. They predict that residents will ignore orders to evacuate or will lack transportation. In short, many critics claim that evacuations on the required scale will be impossible to achieve. In fact, however, large-scale evacuations occur periodically in the U.S. and Canada, under conditions similar to or worse than what might be expected in a nuclear evac-

Thesis   uation. Some recent events requiring evacuations will illustrate how unfounded the fears of these critics are.

Hurricanes David and Frederic

Supporting examples 1 and 2   Within a few weeks of each other, two major hurricanes threatened the southern part of the United States. The first, Hurricane David, caused major destruction in the Caribbean, killing 600 in the Dominican Republic alone on August 31, 1979. It brushed the east coast of Florida on September 3, forcing 300,000 to flee inland. Fifteen thousand persons were evacuated from the Florida

Keys alone. Fortunately, the main force of the storm stayed at sea as the hurricane veered northward. When it finally went inland in Georgia, its strength had considerably diminished. Nevertheless, the death toll in the United States reached 16 before the storm blew itself out as it moved north through Virginia on September 6. Experts agree that the sensible actions of thousands of residents when they voluntarily left the area prevented an even higher mortality.

On September 12, Hurricane Frederic struck the Gulf Coast on a one-hundred-mile front from Mississippi to Florida. One of the hardest hit areas was Mobile, Alabama, where twenty-foot waves surged through downtown streets. Winds of 130 mph were recorded. Over 400,000 people were reported to have evacuated coastal regions. The success of the evacuations is believed to be the reason only nine deaths were reported. The significance of this figure becomes clear when you consider that in 1969 Hurricane Camille killed 256 people in the same area.

Mississauga, Ontario

Supporting example 3

Shortly before midnight on Saturday, November 10, 1979, a 106-car Canadian Pacific freight train derailed in Mississauga, Ontario. Mississauga, a suburb of Toronto, has a population of 276,000 and also contains the airport serving the Toronto area. Within minutes of the derailment, propane tank cars began exploding, hurling debris nearly half a mile. Other dangerous chemicals were scattered by the wreck, but quick action by the train crew enabled them to remove 26 cars from the wreck, preventing a more serious accident. However, they were unable to prevent chlorine from leaking from a 90-ton tank car which was also threatened by flames from the fire. When the situation threatened to get out of hand, authorities ordered an evacuation. By late Sunday, an estimated 250,000 people had been evacuated. By some estimates, as few as 5,000 of the evacuees stayed in public shelters; the rest were able to move in with friends and relatives, found space in hotels and motels, or were taken in by sympathetic strangers. Observers from emergency planning groups in the United States and other countries arrived on the scene even before the evacuation was complete. Generally, they were impressed by the smoothness of the operation. Particularly impressive was the evacuation of 448 patients from Mississauga Hospital, including 10 intensive-care cases and one child born during the emergency. Other tricky situations developed, including the need to deal with large numbers of people who could not speak English, but all were handled efficiently.

By Tuesday, November 13, about 100,000 people were permitted to return to their homes. The following day another 100,000 people were allowed to return, and by the end of the week, the

Conclusion

Restatement of
major points

50,000 people who lived closest to the wreck were also back in their homes.

 These evacuations at Mississauga, in Florida, and along the Gulf Coast were not the only ones in North America in recent years. For instance, in 1979 an additional 160,000 persons were involved in other evacuations in the United States as a result of floods, tropical storms, and threatened explosions. The relative ease with which hundreds of thousands of people moved themselves out of harm's way and managed to feed themselves without specific government aid puts into question the objections of critics to present contingency plans to evacuate people from areas surrounding nuclear power plants in the event of an accident. It appears that specific plans to transport, house, and feed people need to be considered for only a fraction of the population, notably those in hospitals, prisons, old age homes, and the like. Certainly any future regulations relating to planning for evacuations around nuclear power plants should be based on the information available from actual evacuations, and not on vague fears and uninformed assumptions.

John knew that his article should have an introductory paragraph, several body paragraphs, and a concluding paragraph. He used his opening paragraph to introduce his subject and present his thesis: that criticism of evacuation plans for areas around nuclear reactors is unfounded. In his body paragraphs, John presented three examples—hurricanes David and Frederic and the Mississauga derailment—to support his thesis. He evaluated the evacuation necessitated by each disaster and supplied facts and statistics to demonstrate its success. In his conclusion, John restated his major points and made recommendations for the future. Anticipating that some of his readers might have wanted more supporting examples, he began his conclusion by alluding to evacuations other than the three that he discussed in his article. In 1979, he says, over one hundred thousand people were evacuated due to storms, floods, and other catastrophes. John thought that his clear, concrete examples would convince his readers that he understood the problem and had explained it fairly and accurately. In general, then, he felt quite satisfied. Before turning the article in, however, he prepared this outline to make certain that its structure was balanced and logical.

Large-Scale Evacuations
 I. Introduction
  A. Critics fear large-scale evacuations won't work
   1. Roads will be blocked
   2. Facilities will be inadequate
   3. People won't cooperate
  B. Recent events prove critics are wrong

   II. Hurricane David
      A. Struck Caribbean
         1. Caused destruction and death
         2. Killed 600 in the Dominican Republic
      B. Evacuation was successful in Florida
         1. 300,000 fled Florida coast
         2. 15,000 were evacuated from Florida Keys
         3. Killed only 16 in U.S.
  III. Hurricane Frederic
      A. Struck Gulf Coast
         1. Spread from Mississippi to Florida
         2. Mobile, Alabama, was hardest hit
            a. 20-foot waves
            b. 130-mph winds
      B. Evacuation was successful
         1. 400,000 people were evacuated
         2. Only 9 deaths were reported
  IV. Train derailment in Mississauga, Ontario
      A. Danger threatened Toronto area
         1. Propane tank cars exploded
         2. Chlorine leaked from tank car
      B. Evacuation was successful
         1. 250,000 were evacuated
             a. hospital patients
            b. non-English-speaking residents
   V. Conclusion
      A. Additional evacuations were also successful
         1. Floods, tropical storms, threatened explosions
         2. Evacuations proceeded without government aid
      B. Future plans should be based on these experiences

When John constructed his outline, he was careful to follow the method he had learned in high school. He arranged major and minor points in the order in which he wanted to present them. At the same time he indicated his major categories with large Roman numerals (I, II, III, and so on), and his subordinate points, in descending order, with capital letters (A, B, C), Arabic numerals (1, 2, 3), and lower-case letters (a, b, c). He remembered that the indention of each item indicates its relative importance, so he placed the most important points at the left-hand margin and indented subordinate points under each category.

    This accurately constructed outline enabled John to see obvious structural problems in his article. First, he noticed an omission: he had not supplied any information about the kind of damage Hurricanes David and Frederic did. John realized that since he was drawing an analogy between these disasters and a possible nuclear accident, he had to add this material to convince readers of the severity of the hurricanes. Before he could consider his article complete, then, he had to do some more research to find out the nature and extent of the hurricane damage.

He also saw that he had not given parallel treatment to the three disasters. His outline showed that in discussing the train derailment, he had not said how many deaths occurred—information he *had* provided for the other successful evacuations. (IV B had only one subcategory, and, of course, any division must have *at least two* parts.) After checking his notes, John added that no deaths were reported, a point that strengthened his claim that large-scale evacuations could proceed smoothly.

EXERCISE

Using the form of John Gibbons's outline on pages 229–230 as a guide, construct a formal outline of the following paper by Kathy McCormack, a freshman composition student. When you have finished your outline, revise the essay's structure in any way you feel is necessary. Consider, for instance, these and other questions that occur to you:

○ Do the topic sentences accurately reflect the essay's divisions or main points? If not, rewrite them.

○ Are the points presented in logical order? If not, relocate any sentences or paragraphs you feel should be moved.

○ Do the points support the thesis? If not, make any necessary changes in the wording of the thesis or the presentation of the supporting information.

Irish Step Dancing (Championship)

There are many types of Irish Step Dancing, such as solo, figure, and championship. Of these three, championship is not only the most difficult competition but also the lengthiest. Solo and figure are less formal than competition and the judges are not as selective about who may enter the competitions and who will win them. A championship competition, on the other hand, is a long drawn-out process; however, once you get used to it, it all becomes part of the fun.

The first step is to enter the competition well in advance, because the closing dates are always a month or two before the competition. To enter, one must meet the requirements, including dancing for a licensed teacher, having won first place in a "prize winner" competition, and having competed in the "Oriechtas Rince." If the proper requirements are met, the teacher will sign the entry card and send it in with the entry fee.

About two hours before the competition, competitors are called to draw rotation numbers. These are to determine who will dance first, second, third, etc. The numbers are small pieces of paper drawn out of a large envelope. After each competitor has drawn a number, it is recorded by a stagehand. Now the dancer is free until his or her competition is called.

There are two musicians at every stage, usually one accordionist and one violin player. Just before the competitors dance, they will walk over to the musicians and tell them the name of the music they would like. The musicians begin to play and the dancer then chooses the speed. A hand waved upward means faster, downward means slower, and a nod of the head means the music is fine.

The actual dance, if a soft-shoe, is three steps: a lead around and two other steps. If a hard-shoe dance is being done, it consists of a step and set.

After everyone has danced, the judges will pick those they think are the top dancers in that particular competition. Then there is a recall. All dancers who are recalled must dance again, this time the opposite of what was danced the first time. If one is not recalled he or she has automatically lost.

After the recall the dancers are graded by each judge individually, and then all judges compare their scores. The top three or four (depending on how many prizes are being awarded) competitors are called up to the stage. A trophy is awarded to each dancer in ascending grade. The dancer must then sign a sheet of paper to say he or she has received the award. The competition is now officially over.

Although championship competitions are very lengthy, the thrills and sometimes rewards are much greater than those from solo or figure dancing. This is because even if one does not win, it is an honor to be allowed to compete in a championship competition. Most dancers are very satisfied if they know they have done their best and have made no mistakes. Every competitor knows in his or her own mind that there is always a next time.

USING CHECKLISTS

Airplane pilots preparing for takeoff use checklists to make sure they don't miss anything. You too can use checklists to help you revise your essay. Checklists give you a systematic, comprehensive look at what you have written. They help you focus on the four different levels of revision: revising the whole essay for content and form; revising your paragraphs; revising your sentences; and revising diction, tone, and style.

If you have a good deal of time, run through all the questions and get a comprehensive view of your essay. Some questions might not apply to all assignments, but the ones that do will do a lot to help you. If you don't have time to consider every item on the list, use those that apply to the larger elements of your essay or to those areas that usually cause you trouble.

CONTENT AND FORM

Structure

° Is your overall pattern of development appropriate for your topic, purpose, and audience? Consider other ways of arranging your ideas.

° Do all body paragraphs support your thesis? Revise paragraphs or thesis so they are consistent.

° Can your thesis and supporting points be easily identified and understood? Make sure they are correctly placed and worded.

Coherence

◦ Have you drawn explicit connections between your thesis and your supporting information? Make sure the relevance of support to thesis is clear.

◦ Did you present your ideas in a logical sequence and your paragraphs in a logical order? Reorder ideas so they make sense.

◦ Have you discussed everything you promised in your thesis? Develop additional points if necessary.

◦ Do clear transitions between paragraphs allow your readers to follow your paper's structure? Add needed transitions or modify existing ones.

◦ Have you stressed key points through judicious repetition? Underscore major concepts when necessary.

◦ Do you sum up regularly? Be sure to take stock of your ideas at regular intervals.

Completeness

◦ Did you present enough information—reasons, examples, arguments—to make your point? Add information if necessary.

◦ Have you raised any questions, explicitly or implicitly, that you have failed to answer? Complete all your thoughts, or delete passages which raise unanswered questions.

PARAGRAPHS

Unity

◦ Does each body paragraph contain only one main idea? Delete or relocate extraneous information, and make sure topic sentences identify each main idea.

◦ Are topic sentences clearly recognizable and linked to the thesis? Make a mini-outline to check.

Completeness

◦ Do your body paragraphs contain enough detail—reasons, facts, examples—to support your ideas? Add any necessary information.

Order

◦ Have you constructed paragraphs according to useful patterns? Be sure to use recognizable patterns which your readers will readily understand.

Coherence

◦ Have you used transitions to link sentences within paragraphs so that their relationships are clear? Add whatever words or phrases your audience will need to follow your ideas.

Special-purpose paragraphs

○ Do your introductory paragraphs arouse reader interest and prepare for what is to come? Consider several different possible introductory strategies.

.○ Do your concluding paragraphs sum up your main points? Be sure that they provide a sense of closure.

SENTENCES

Clarity

○ Are sentences overloaded with too many clauses? Break long, hard-to-follow sentences into shorter units that your reader can understand more easily.

○ Have you made sure that there are no potentially confusing shifts in tense, voice, or number? Edit to eliminate such shifts.

Emphasis

○ Have you used repetition, balance, and parallelism to strengthen sentences? Look for places where you might use these strategies.

○ Have you used emphatic word order? Try to revise sentences to place stress where you want it.

○ Have you overused the passive voice? Eliminate it wherever it might confuse or slow down your readers.

○ Have you used subordination to signal the relative importance of clauses in a sentence and their logical relationship to one another? Combine or otherwise revise sentences where necessary.

Economy

○ Have you eliminated deadwood, circumlocution, and redundancies? Delete any phrases or sentences which could obscure your meaning and distract or annoy your readers.

Variety

○ Have you varied your sentence structure? Experiment with different constructions to make your presentation more interesting.

○ Have you combined sentences where necessary? Link sentences to clarify relationships between ideas and to avoid monotony.

WORDS

○ Have you taken care to select accurate words? Consider both the denotations and connotations of your words.

○ Have you selected and maintained a level of diction appropriate for your audience and purpose? Revise to make sure diction is suitable and consistent.

○ Have you chosen words that are specific, concrete, and unambiguous? Replace any words which aren't precise.

○ Have you used imagery to enrich your writing? Add imagery where appropriate.

○ Have you eliminated jargon, clichés, euphemisms, ineffective imagery, and empty utility words from your writing? Make sure these expressions do not clutter up your writing.

TONE AND STYLE

○ Is your tone consistent with your purpose? If your purpose is to inform, use an objective tone. If you are writing to influence the emotions of your readers, consider the uses of a subjective tone.

○ Have you maintained the proper distance from your reader? Make sure your tone reflects your relative involvement with (or detachment from) your audience.

○ Is your style appropriate for your subject, purpose, and audience? For college writing, use a popular style.

EXERCISE

Choose an essay of your own that you feel needs revision and apply some or all of the guidelines on pages 232–235 to your work. Revise the essay according to what this exercise reveals.

All of the techniques discussed in this chapter will help you revise your paper. You can concentrate on one strategy or use several in combination. What methods you use depends upon your assignment, your personal preferences, and how much help you feel you need. The following case study illustrates how one student revised her paper.

CASE STUDY: A STUDENT REVISES

Toward the end of the semester Michele Misher, a student in a composition class, received the following assignment: "Write a 750-word personal experience essay that uses descriptive detail to put your readers in your place, so that they can share your experience and understand your emotions."

Michele had two weeks to prepare the assignment out of class. She did her prewriting, wrote the first draft fairly quickly, and then put it aside for a few days. When she looked back at what she had written, she realized she had a lot to do to shape her essay for her audience. Michele's instructor asked her to record her thoughts as she went through the several stages of the composition process. Here is her first draft, along with her comments on it.

First Draft: An Experience

1   We were in the bowels of Thomas Jefferson University Hospital, below ground, where the walls were cinder blocks and the floor tiled; except for a drop ceiling, the surroundings probably haven't changed much in at least twenty years. To the left was a large crypt refrigerated to store bodies temporarily. Along a wall was a cabinet holding Mason jars filled with specimens from past autopsies. Along another was a table with several rows of tools. For the job at hand, there was a tray with scalpels, scissors, a metallic hammer whose handle ended in a hook, a chisel, a set of fan-shaped blades for a powersaw, and the saw. The furniture was dominated by the two stainless-steel autopsy tables, which were tilted slightly and had several small holes to let streams of water run through and to help wash away any blood. There was a scale at the lower end. There was the obvious: a body on the table. It was pale with mauve blotches. The dark areas, Dr. Jay Barnhart, a resident in pathology, explained to the group, were miniature pools of blood under the skin. The body was supine and naked.

2   The first cut was the unkindest one of all. I blinked my eyes as Leonard Stephen, the technician, wielded his scalpel. Three students were observing; they stepped back smartly, bumping into one another. I wondered whether they had been expecting such unsettling moments when they entered the room. The students watched as Stephen leaned over the chest area and simulated the act of cutting, as if measuring his strokes. When he cut, the blade glided effortlessly, and the skin parted like pudding.

3   Beginning underneath the breasts, Stephen carved a two-sided Y down the center of the body. The skin below the surface was yellow. Stephen separated the muscle beneath the skin from the breast plate and placed the semi-triangle formed by the top of the incision over the face. Stephen sawed open the rib cage, and the observers found themselves twitching when they heard the noise of the saw. Still, the students didn't say much, and no one left.

4   Stephen uncovered the viscera, and the tension in the room relaxed. Somehow looking at parts of a body didn't upset us the way it did to look at a whole body. Stephen gently forced his hand between several organs and lifted out the heart to show us. Then he replaced it because he wanted to remove the viscera all at once. Then cuts were made from the lower pelvis to the Adam's apple until the viscera could be removed. When he lifted them out, he placed them together on a large wooden board at the foot of the table.

5   Dr. Barnhart and Dr. P. Reuter began a dissection. As they proceeded, I weighed the separate organs and recorded any comments on the findings that the doctors had. They talked back and forth to each other describing symptoms and explaining their own thinking about the process of the disease.

6   To them, the woman seemed to have died of a stroke. If it was a stroke, was it due to atherosclerosis or was it secondary to other things? What they decided would determine what they would seek during the autopsy. They had already studied the patient's medical reports and decided what procedures they would carry out. By the time the doctors had started the dissection they had already formulated several possibilities to check.

7   They examined each organ in turn, putting specimens of each into two Mason jars, a left and right side, filled with the fixative whose smell hovered over the room. The stomach and intestines were laid out. The stomach had a modestly ridged surface, except for a tumor in it, which was thick with pronounced lumps. Dr. Reuter took a sterile blade from a packet, and after sterilizing the area by singeing with a hot knife, he sliced into the tumor. He wiped a cotton culture applicator upon the tumor's exposed surfaces and dropped the swab into an air-tight tube. The dissection was much less interesting than the initial work of Stephen, and the students changed their positions and altered their attention by quietly talking to one another. At one point, after watching the doctors for so long, they looked up to see Stephen swing a hammer and drive a chisel into the skull. Their faces shared expressions of despair as if the standard technique for getting to the brain was a horrible crudeness. But Stephen worked cleanly and swiftly. He had been doing this sort of thing for seventeen years.

8   Eventually, he prepared to put the body away. I assisted him in sewing the skin back in place, folding the arms, cleaning the face with soap and water, rinsing the body free of blood, covering the body, and wheeled it into the freezer. The students decided that the autopsy wasn't as bad as they had expected it to be. Still, the three of them said that they wouldn't want autopsies done on them unless they died suspiciously.

9   I don't agree with them. My body will not be doing me any good once I die, and if an autopsy can help expand the realm of medical knowledge, I will definitely agree to one.

Comments

My first reaction was something like "This isn't as good as I remember it." For one thing, it didn't seem immediate enough. The autopsy situation can be very dramatic, and that's what I tried to bring out. But instead it seems routine and businesslike.

I wanted to help the readers to understand and see the process—this is what the assignment asked. I also wanted to demystify it, to make readers feel less squeamish and remove their fears. So, I thought the paper had to be pretty descriptive—and this was also part of the assignment—but matter-of-fact, honest but not sensational. I tried to be as precise as possible and use objective description. I figured my audience—my instructor, the other students—probably wouldn't know too much about the reasons autopsies are performed or about the procedure itself, and what they did know would be influenced by TV or movies and not too accurate. So I wanted everything to be factual and orderly. I think I was pretty successful at getting factual information across, and the paper seems to be pretty well organized, with one step in the procedure following the next.

The main thing that still bothers me is that while I do create the atmosphere I want, I don't seem to be getting my point across. I want to show (not tell!) that the procedure isn't as disgusting as they probably think it is, and I want to suggest how important autopsies are without being too moralistic or patronizing. I want people reading this to see the drama and excitement and tension I see, but I don't want them to think I'm just explaining what an autopsy is or talking in general about a time I saw one. I guess what I need is some kind of central unifying idea—probably pretty specific—to tie the whole thing together.

After thinking about these points, Michele completed a second draft and recorded her reactions to it, too.

Second Draft: The Need for Autopsy

1   The first cut was the unkindest one of all. I blinked my eyes as Leonard Stephen, the technician, wielded his scalpel. Three students were observing today; they stepped back smartly, bumping into one another.

2   One of the students, Diane, dropped into the only chair in the room. Bob held on to a table but didn't turn his face from the cutting. Susan put her hand over her mouth and let her fingers play on the rest of her face. Stephen, methodical and attentive, leaned over the chest area and simulated the act of cutting, as if measuring his strokes. When he cut, the blade glided effortlessly and the skin parted like pudding.

3   We were witnessing an autopsy, that mysterious and gruesome procedure talked about in whispers and euphemisms. But grim as the autopsy experience can be for the first-time observer, I have come to see it as necessary to medical science. An understanding of the need for autopsies and a familiarity with the procedure itself has done a lot to increase the public's acceptance of the autopsy's role in medicine.

4   We were in the bowels of Thomas Jefferson University Hospital, below ground, where the walls were cinder blocks and the floor tiled; except for a drop ceiling, the surroundings probably haven't changed much in at least twenty years. To the left was a large crypt refrigerated to store bodies temporarily. Along a wall was a cabinet holding Mason jars filled with specimens from past autopsies. Along another wall was a table with several rows of tools. For the job at hand, there was a tray with scalpels, scissors, a metallic hammer whose handle ended in a hook, a chisel, a set of fan-shaped blades for a powersaw, and the saw. The furniture was dominated by the two stainless-steel autopsy tables, which were tilted slightly and had several small holes to let streams of water run through and to help wash away any blood. There was a scale at the lower end.

5   And there was the obvious: a body on the table. It was pale with mauve blotches. The dark areas, Dr. Jay Barnhart, a resident in pathology, explained to the group, were miniature pools of blood under the skin. The body was supine and naked, and this is what seemed to shock the visitors. They stared with a mixture of curiosity and terror. The patient received empathetic attention from the visitors, but not what you might call sorrow.

6   Beginning underneath the breasts, Stephen carved a two-sided Y down the center of the body. The skin below the surface was yellow, tolerable to look at

because it reminds you of the yellow fat on chickens. Stephen separated the muscle beneath the skin from the breast plate and placed the semi-triangle formed by the top of the incision over the face. Stephen sawed open the rib cage, and the observers found themselves twitching when they heard the noise of the saw. Still, the students didn't say much, and no one left. Stephen uncovered the viscera (internal organs) and the tension in the room relaxed. Somehow looking at parts of a body didn't upset us the way it did to look at a whole body. Stephen gently forced his hand between several organs and lifted out the heart to show us. Then he replaced it because he wanted to remove the viscera all at once. (If all the organs are connected when removed, it is less likely that subtle evidence will be missed.) Then cuts were made from the lower pelvis to the Adam's apple until the viscera could be removed. When he lifted them out, he placed them together on a large wooden board at the foot of the table.

7   Here Dr. Barnhart and Dr. P. Reuter began a dissection. As they proceeded, I weighed the separate organs and recorded any comments on the findings that the doctors had. They talked back and forth to each other describing symptoms and explaining their own thinking about the process of the disease.

8   To them, the woman seemed to have died of a stroke. If it was a stroke, was it due to atherosclerosis or was it secondary to other things? What they decided would determine what they would seek during the autopsy. They had already studied the patient's medical reports and decided what procedures they would carry out. By the time the doctors had started the dissection they had already formulated several possibilities to check.

9   They examined each organ in turn, putting specimens of each into two Mason jars, a left and right side, filled with the fixative whose smell hovered over the room. The stomach and intestines were laid out. The stomach had a modestly ridged surface, except for a tumor in it, which was thick with pronounced lumps. Dr. Reuter took a sterile blade from a packet, and after sterilizing the area by singeing with a hot knife, he sliced into the tumor. He wiped a cotton culture applicator upon the tumor's exposed surfaces and dropped the swab into an air-tight tube.

10   The dissection was much less interesting than the initial work of Stephen, and the students changed their positions and altered their attention by quietly talking to one another. At one point, after watching the doctors for so long, they looked up to see Stephen swing a hammer and drive a chisel into the skull. Their faces shared expressions of despair as if the standard technique for getting to the brain was a horrible crudeness. But Stephen worked cleanly and swiftly. He had been doing this sort of thing for seventeen years.

11   Eventually, he prepared to put the body away. I assisted him in sewing the skin back in place, folding the arms, cleaning the face with soap and water, rinsing the body free of blood, covering the body, and wheeled it into the freezer. The students decided that the autopsy wasn't as bad as they had expected it to be. Still, the three of them said that they wouldn't want autopsies done on them unless they died suspiciously.

12   I don't agree with them. My body will not be doing me any good once I die, and if an autopsy can help expand the realm of medical knowledge, I will definitely agree to one.

Comments

   When I finished reading my first draft the first thing I decided I had to change was the way the essay started. I hated the introduction. It seemed too dull to plunge right into the procedure itself, with all its precise, objective technical detail. It would probably take people too long to figure out I was talking about an autopsy. I wanted to make that clear right away, and also talk a little about my feelings. So I changed my title, and I wrote a new paragraph to add to the paper. This paragraph wound up as paragraph 3 on the second draft and gave the essay a unifying idea, a focal point. At first I wanted to start my essay off with this new paragraph, but it sounded too preachy, and it just wasn't enough to draw readers in—especially those who weren't too comfortable with the idea of an autopsy, which was probably most people. So I hit on the idea of moving up "The first cut . . ." from paragraph 2 of my first draft. Not only did I really like that line for an opening, but I also thought that mentioning the students' uneasiness right away would draw my readers in, because they would identify with the students. This led me to take out the line "I wondered whether they had been expecting such unsettling moments when they entered the room" in my new opening paragraph—I figured it created too much of a distance between me and the students (and therefore, between me and the reader).

   As I made these changes I broke up what had originally been paragraph 2 and put some of it in my new paragraph 1. I put the rest in paragraph 2, also adding some stuff about Stephen and the students' reactions. Then I wrote a new paragraph 3.

   Knowing many people reading my essay might be turned off—or at least confused—by the subject, I tried to make things a little easier for them. I added the comparison with chicken fat and defined "viscera" in paragraph 6. I think the addition of the parenthetical explanation later in the paragraph really helped too.

   I decided to break up my first draft's long opening descriptive paragraph (now paragraphs 4 and 5) and begin a new paragraph with the dramatic introduction of the body on the table. I added "And" to the beginning of this new paragraph, and I also added other transitions between paragraphs to keep things moving along: "Here" at the start of paragraph 7 and "Eventually" at the beginning of paragraph 11.

   I think I'm making the points I want to make now, but I still don't feel this paper will really get readers involved. Other things still bother me too, especially the last paragraph, which seems kind of skimpy, and some clichés.

After further revisions, Michele completed her final draft.

Final Draft: The Autopsy Experience

1   The first cut is the unkindest one of all. I blink my eyes as Leonard Stephen, the technician, picks up his scalpel. Three students are observing today; they step back smartly, bumping into one another.

2   One of the students, Diane, drops into the only chair in the room. Bob holds on to a table but doesn't turn his face from the cutting. Susan puts her hand over her mouth and lets her fingers play on the rest of her face.

3   Stephen, methodical and attentive, leans over the chest area and simulates the

act of cutting, measuring his strokes. Then he cuts. The blade glides smoothly. The skin parts like pudding.

4 We are witnessing an autopsy, that mysterious and gruesome procedure talked about in whispers and euphemisms. But grim as the autopsy experience can be for the first-time observer, I have come to see it as vitally important to medical science. An understanding of the need for autopsies and a familiarity with the procedure itself has done a lot to help me to accept the autopsy's role in medicine.

5 We are in Thomas Jefferson University Hospital, below ground, where the walls are cinder blocks and the floor tiled; except for a drop ceiling, the surroundings probably haven't changed much in at least twenty years. To the left is a large crypt refrigerated to store bodies temporarily. Along a wall is a cabinet lined several rows deep with Mason jars filled with specimens from past autopsies. Along another wall is a table with several rows of tools. For the job at hand, there is a tray with scalpels, scissors, a metallic hammer whose handle ends in a hook, a chisel, a set of fan-shaped blades for a powersaw, and the saw. The furniture is dominated by the two stainless-steel autopsy tables, which are tilted slightly and have several small holes to let streams of water run through and to help wash away any blood. There is a scale at the lower end.

6 And there is the obvious: a body on the table. It is pale with mauve blotches. The dark areas, Dr. Jay Barnhart, a resident in pathology, explains to the group, are miniature pools of blood under the skin. The body is supine and naked, and this is what seems to shock them. They stare with a mixture of curiosity and terror. The patient receives empathetic attention from the visitors, but not what you might call sorrow.

7 Beginning underneath the breasts, Stephen carves a two-sided Y down the center of the body. The skin below the surface is yellow, tolerable to look at because it reminds you of the yellow fat on chickens. Stephen separates the muscle beneath the skin from the breast plate and places the semi-triangle formed by the top of the incision over the face. Stephen then saws open the rib cage, and the observers find themselves twitching when they hear the noise of the saw. Still, the students don't say much, and no one leaves.

8 Stephen uncovers the viscera (internal organs) and the tension in the room relaxes. Somehow looking at parts of a body doesn't upset us the way it does to look at a whole body. Stephen gently forces his hand between several organs and lifts out the heart to show us. Then he replaces it because he wants to remove the viscera all at once. (If all the organs are connected when removed, it is less likely that subtle evidence will be missed.) Then he makes cuts from the lower pelvis to the Adam's apple until the viscera can be removed. When he lifts them out, he places them together on a large wooden board at the foot of the table.

9 Here Dr. Barnhart and Dr. P. Reuter begin the dissection. As they proceed, I weigh the separate organs and record any comments on the findings that the doctors have. They talk back and forth to each other describing symptoms and explaining their own thinking about the process of the disease.

10 To them, the woman seems to have died of a stroke. If it was a stroke, was it due to atherosclerosis or was it secondary to other things? What they decide will determine what they will seek during the autopsy. They have already studied the patient's medical reports and decided what procedures they will carry out. By the time the doctors started the dissection they had already formulated several possibilities to check.

11   They examine each organ in turn, putting specimens of each into two Mason jars, a left and right side, filled with the fixative whose smell hovers over the room. Eventually, they lay out the stomach and intestines. The stomach has a modestly ridged surface, except for a tumor in it, which is thick with pronounced lumps. Dr. Reuter takes a sterile blade from a packet, and after sterilizing the area by singeing it with a hot knife, he slices into the tumor. He wipes a cotton culture applicator upon the tumor's exposed surfaces and drops the swab into an air-tight tube.

12   The dissection is much less spectacular than the initial work of Stephen, and the students change their positions and alter their attention by quietly talking to one another. At one point, after watching the doctors for so long, they look up to see Stephen swing a hammer and drive a chisel into the skull. Their faces share expressions of despair as if the standard technique for getting to the brain is a horrible crudeness. But Stephen works cleanly and swiftly. He has been doing this sort of thing for seventeen years.

13   Finally, he prepares to put the body away. I assist him in sewing the skin back in place, folding the arms, cleaning the face with soap and water, rinsing the body free of blood, covering the body, and wheeling it into the freezer. The students decide that the autopsy wasn't as bad as they expected it to be. Still, the three of them say that they wouldn't want autopsies done on them unless they die suspiciously. I don't agree with them. My body will not be doing me any good once I die, and if an autopsy can help expand the realm of medical knowledge, I will definitely agree to one.

Comments

The biggest breakthrough came when I realized why the essay wasn't going to hit readers with the impact it should—because my use of past tense kept the experience distant, not immediate enough. Once I changed the past-tense verbs to present tense, everything fell into place. Now people reading my essay would be with me as I saw and felt things. (It also solved my confusion about what tense to use where in my second draft's paragraph 5.)

I did a lot of fine-tuning between the second and final drafts, to make my language more precise so I'd be communicating exactly what I wanted to say. I checked to make sure that I hadn't used any difficult technical words and that I'd explained why certain procedures were done. I didn't notice any problems that still remained.

I fooled around with the wording of paragraph 4 (paragraph 3 in the second draft), changing "necessary" to "vitally important" and substituting the verb form "to accept" for the noun "acceptance" so the phrase would be stronger and more direct. While I was at it I took out "the public" and substituted "me" in the same phrase. My purpose, after all, was supposed to be to communicate my feelings, not get up on a soap box and make a speech.

After I divided the second draft's paragraph 2 into the final draft's paragraphs 2 and 3, I saw that paragraph 3 had some potential for drama, because it described the first cut into the body—but it sounded too businesslike. I finally decided to break the last sentence ("When he cuts . . .") into three separate sentences, to make the "suspense" a little more obvious.

I still didn't like the last paragraph, which seemed too short and abrupt, but I didn't want to expand it because I was trying to tone down the preachy tone. I finally decided just to combine it with the paragraph before it, where the process is completed, hoping the readers would see my conclusion as a kind of extension of the procedure itself.

I decided my second draft's paragraph 6 was too long; it contained more information than the average reader would be able to absorb at once. I think I solved this by breaking it into two paragraphs (7 and 8), with the break separating straight dissection from the students' reactions.

I also added a few transitions between sentences to make the process "flow." In paragraph 7 I added "then" ("Stephen then saws . . ."), and in paragraph 11 I added "Eventually." (When I did this I had to change paragraph 12's "Eventually" to "Finally," which sounded better anyway.)

I had to get rid of a couple of clumsy and confusing passive-voice constructions so readers would be able to tell who was doing what. (After all, there are three people working here.) In paragraph 8 I changed "Then cuts were made" to "Then he makes cuts," and in paragraph 11 I changed "the stomach and intestines were laid out" to "they lay out the stomach and intestines." (I don't know why any kind of scientific description makes me want to use passive voice.)

At the end of my revising, I checked over all my words and changed some to make them more precise. In paragraph 3 I changed the too-familiar "effortlessly" to "smoothly" and took out "as if" (because he *is* measuring his strokes). In paragraph 5 I took out the word "holding" and substituted "lined several rows deep with," which sounded more specific. In paragraph 12 I changed "interesting" to "spectacular" because the original version made it seem as if the dissection was a bore.

I took out "the bowels" in paragraph 5 for a lot of different reasons. First, I realized it's a cliché—people always seem to use it as a fancy way of saying basement. Second, I *say* "below ground," so "bowels" is redundant. Third (and this makes me glad I noticed it), the association of "bowels" with body parts would be really distracting in an essay on an autopsy! I decided "wields his scalpel" in paragraph 1 had to go for pretty much the same reason—not only is it a cliché, but it also gives my essay the ring of a grade B movie, which is just what I want to avoid.

In the last paragraph I caught an error in parallelism in the second sentence; I changed "wheeled" into "wheeling" to match the other verbs in the series.

I'm going to edit and proofread this now, checking spelling (especially names) and punctuation as carefully as I can.

You will certainly not find it necessary—or possible—to revise as extensively as Michele did every time you write. The number and kind of strategies you choose to apply will vary according to your own taste, the nature of your assignment, and the amount of time you have to revise. What is important, though, is that you become accustomed to thinking of revision as an integral part of the writing process.

IV

Special assignments

CHAPTER

10

Argumentation

When you engage in argumentation, you attempt to influence the opinions of others. You try to establish that something is or is not so, is or is not correct, or ought or ought not to be. Argumentation is central to our lives. All of us seem to spend a lot of time trying to convince others to agree with us. And often the stakes are high, whether the subject is the defense budget, the environment, or genetic engineering. There is, of course, a difference between an argument and an exchange of opinions. Arguments follow rules that are calculated to ensure that ideas are presented fairly and logically.

WHAT IS ARGUMENTATION?

All argument aims to persuade, but not all persuasion is argument. Argument, the appeal to reason, is *one* means of persuasion, but not the *only* means. Other means of persuasion include appeals to emotion, to morality, and to self-interest. In arguing for the passage of a bill to limit the dumping of hazardous wastes you could appeal to your audience's emotions by telling how such dumping at Love Canal destroyed that community. You could appeal to their moral sense by showing how such dumping is wrong and should not be condoned by the state. And you could appeal to their self-interest by pointing out that *their* homes could be endangered, or that they pay substantial sums in taxes each year to clean up dump sites.

While any one of these appeals can serve as your primary means of persuasion, most often you use them in combination. Aristotle recognized this when he said that effective arguments often appeal to the emotions. How you make your appeal ultimately depends on what strategy you feel will work for your audience. There is, however, an ethical problem: the end does not justify just any means of achieving it. Most people believe that appeals to prejudice, or threats, or lies are unacceptable means of persuasion—even though they are used by diplomats, labor negotiators, and others attempting to wield power.

In your college writing such unfair persuasion is unacceptable; and, while you may use appeals to emotion, morality, or self-interest in moderation, your primary means of persuasion must be argument—the appeal to reason. Used in this sense, "argument" is not heated debate but a form of persuasion in which verifiable statements are offered in support of conclusions drawn from them.

Most arguments on the big issues of our day (abortion, gun control, nuclear disarmament, capital punishment) do not revolve around disagreements over facts. They involve disputes about *interpretations* of facts. If you look at the facts one way, for example, you will agree that private citizens should not own handguns. If you look at them another way, you will agree that they should.

WRITING AN ARGUMENTATIVE ESSAY

So far you have been writing essays whose primary purpose is to convey information. Now you will try your hand at writing essays that aim to convince, to use information in a well-reasoned argument. Argumentation allows you to test your ideas in the marketplace, to see how your ideas hold up. Charles Darwin recognized the importance of argument when he said, "How odd it is that anyone should not see that all observation must be for or against some view if it is to be any service." Argumentation has an important function. It forces you to take a stand, to analyze evidence, to defend your position, and above all, to draw a conclusion; if your idea cannot stand the test, you must change your idea. It is the invaluable tool that enables you not only to express your own ideas, but to upgrade them—at school, on the job, in your social and political lives—as well as to evaluate the ideas of others.

When you construct a written argument, you go through the same process that you follow when you write any essay. With argumentative essays, however, you have some additional concerns: you must take a stand, you must look at both sides of an issue, and you must be logical in your presentation.

CHOOSING A TOPIC

You can construct an argument around any debatable topic. It does help if you care about the subject. If you feel strongly that smoking should be banned in public places or that insurance rates for people under twenty-five should be lowered, you may want to write a paper about it—but do so only if you can present your argument objectively. Your feelings about an issue must never stand in the way of good judgment, and your stand must be reasonable and your evidence adequate. You must also anticipate the arguments that will be advanced against your cause. If you cannot view your subject objectively, you should abandon it in favor of one you can keep in perspective.

You should also be well-informed about your topic. The more data you can provide—facts, figures, or examples—the more likely you are to convince your readers. Neither unfounded opinions nor empty generalizations will do. General knowledge is usually not enough to make a case, and you will probably have to do some research. And you must make sure that your sources represent a fair range of opinion and that they are reliable. You may find that your topic is too wide to treat within the boundaries of your assignment and that a narrower version of the same topic works better.

Original topic

The pros and cons of bilingual education

Narrower topic

The debate about bilingual education in Riverside, California

You must also know just what you want your argumentative essay to accomplish. If you cannot easily state your purpose, your topic is too general or too vague. Your goal is to change the way your readers see an issue: unclear, biased, idealistic, or far-fetched approaches to a topic work against that end.

Finally, your topic must be arguable: it must be open to debate. For this reason you cannot cast your topic so that it depends exclusively on a moral or ideological judgment. Many topics are not subject to proper argument:

Is capital punishment wrong?
Are today's teenagers immoral?
Is TV bad for children?

Loaded words—like "bad," "good," "right," "wrong," and "immoral"—mean different things to different people. They involve judgments which cannot be demonstrated, and such judgments are not suitable for argument. At best, all you can do is give your reasons for believing in them. Your beliefs alone are not likely to convince anyone. Sometimes, though, you can restate a topic without using loaded terms:

Original

Is the Supreme Court's stand against prayer in the schools wrong?

Revised

Should a Constitutional amendment be passed that would allow prayer in the schools?

The wording of the original question focuses on personal moral beliefs. The second question focuses on an issue that can be effectively argued. Regardless of religious belief, a person can debate the *constitutional* question of prayer and the public schools. Data are available—court decisions, testimony, authoritative opinion—that could make a good case for either side.

TAKING A STAND

After you have selected your topic, the next step is to take your stand—to state your position on your topic—in the form of your thesis. A thesis should assert something or deny something about a subject:

The government should continue to require eighteen-year-olds to register for a possible draft.

This thesis says what the writer believes about the subject: that draft registration should exist and that the government should continue its present policy. This statement lays the foundation for the essay on which an argument can be built citing evidence that is true, logical, and persuasive.

One way to test whether your thesis takes a stand is to see if it yields a good *antithesis*. You form an antithesis by recasting your thesis in negative terms. You *can* say, for example, that the government should *not* require eighteen-year-olds to register for a possible draft, and this shows that the topic we have just looked at does take a debatable stand.

Being able to state your thesis in a single sentence requires that you have a good grasp of your ideas. Sometimes you will arrive at your thesis before you have done any research or any writing. If your subject is one you care about—student loans or censorship, for example—you might have a firm grip on your thesis from the outset. In other cases, especially if your subject is assigned to you, you will probably have to read, and possibly do some free writing, before you discover what you want to say about your topic. Whatever the case, a clearly stated thesis is a necessity for all argumentative essays.

GATHERING EVIDENCE

Evidence is information that supports your thesis. A *fact* is a piece of information that can be verified; an *opinion* is a personal judgment or belief that may or may not be borne out. Your textbooks contain factual information about science, business, engineering, history, and so on. It is a *fact,* for example, that Houston Power and Light stock sells at $19 a share, and that the Byzantine Empire fell in 1455. Your *opinion* might be that Houston Power and Light is a good investment, or that the fall of the Byzantine Empire cleared the way for the vast expansion of the Ottoman Empire. On these or any issues, it is up to you to demonstrate that your opinions are reasonable and your facts relevant.

Of course opinions and facts are not always so easily distinguished. The linguist S. I. Hayakawa points out that many words simultaneously convey facts and opinions. For example, "said" means one thing and "grudgingly stated" means another. The first word reports an act of speaking, while the second reports that act and judges it. When weighing or presenting evidence, you should make certain that judgments can be traced back to verifiable data. You should recognize that, without support, statements like "The mayor lied," "The president was candid," and "The candidate equivocated" are empty generalizations. Useful evidence includes more than judgments; it also includes the facts that lead to them.

Facts are not the only kind of evidence you can use. You can also marshal expert testimony to support your case. Quotations from experts recognized in the field you are discussing can do a lot to move an audience. In the following paragraph the author uses authorities to back up her point.

> Most college administrators admit that they don't prepare their graduates for the job market. "I just wish I had the guts to tell parents that when you get out of this place you aren't prepared to do anything," the academic head of a famous liberal-arts college told us. Fortunately for him, most people believe that you don't have to defend a liberal-arts education on those grounds. A liberal-arts education is supposed to provide you with a value system, a standard, a set of ideas, not a job. "Like Christianity, the liberal arts are seldom practiced and would probably be hated by the majority of the populace if they were," said one defender.
>
> Caroline Bird, *The Case Against College*

Bird's two quotations add credibility to her argument. Her evidence would have been more convincing, however, had she identified the administrators she quoted.

Keep in mind that an authority's opinion is meaningful only in his or her field. In other areas his or her testimony has no more weight than anybody else's. Paul Newman's opinions about nuclear disarmament, for example, do not have the same weight as Henry Kissinger's.

After you have your topic, you should gather as much evidence as you can to support your argument. If you know something about your topic, you can begin this process by brainstorming. If you need more information, you will have to do library research. Consult the subject card catalog and the specific indexes that your librarian suggests. You might also want to ask a knowledgeable instructor what books or articles you should consult. Once you actually go to the library shelves you will find other sources of information. Footnotes and bibliographies in the books and articles you look at first will send you to many other sources. Don't take this step lightly, for your argument is only as persuasive as the material you use to support it. (For a complete discussion of research, see Chapter 14, "The Library Research Paper.")

As you gather material, keep several things in mind. First, be sure that you keep a careful record of your sources and identify them in your paper. If you don't, your audience will question the authenticity of your information. An anonymous source that passes in a newspaper article may not do in your argumentative essay. Second, acquaint yourself with a reasonable cross-section of opinion on your subject. Don't restrict yourself only to material that supports your stand. To present your argument effectively, you must know both sides of the question. Not addressing and confronting the major arguments against your position seriously limits your ability to be convincing. Third, don't trust your memory. Even slight errors in facts or figures undermine your credibility. Incorrect dates, inaccurate facts, and misspelled book titles and authors' names raise doubts about your whole paper. Finally, you should understand that argument never proves a thesis conclusively. The best you can do is to establish a high probability that your thesis is reasonable. Choose your evidence with this in mind.

EXERCISE

The following student essay relies on an emotional appeal to persuade readers. Read it and answer the questions that follow it.

Should the Law Allow a Terminally Ill Person to Take His or Her Own Life?

Mr. Leonetti was released from Frankford Hospital last May. There was nothing more medical science could do to combat the cancer that had invaded his sixty-eight-year-old body. On a sunny Sunday morning two months later, he returned to Frankford Hospital—while his family was at church. Apparently, he wanted to spare them the trauma of finding his body. Entering the hospital unnoticed, he made his way to the third-floor landing of the east stairwell. There, according to the investigating detective, Mr. Leonetti knelt on the concrete floor and with his right hand shot a .38 calibre bullet into his temple. The slug tunneled through his head and ricocheted off the wall before coming to rest on a step. Minutes later, when his body was found, a portion of his brain was oozing onto the floor. In his throat he was making an unpleasant gurgling sound, like oatmeal makes when it boils. While efficient, dispassionate strangers, licensed and bound by oath, used all their resources to save his life, Mr. Leonetti got his last, lonely wish. I think he had a right to a more dignified departure from this life.

I spent several years working in nursing homes where I talked to patients (nursing home administrators prefer that these patients be euphemistically referred to as residents) who, if allowed, would have gladly taken their own lives. These were rational individuals, in complete possession of their mental faculties, who felt that the quality of their lives had become such that living was odious. But, against their will, they were being kept alive by artificial means, and warehoused in depressingly cheerful rooms to rot away. These pitiful creatures were prisoners sentenced to live on, long after the desire to live, and the physical ability to perform without humiliation life's simplest functions, had died. They were prisoners whose only crime was that they had outlived their bodies.

Think how it must be: Life as you have known it is over. No longer can you perform those acts that gave your life meaning. You must suffer the mortification of requiring assistance in the performance of life's easiest tasks: bathing, eating, going to the toilet. Would you really want to go on living?

More tragic than the nursing-home patient, however, is the young person who is stricken with a terminal disease. Such a person was portrayed by Richard Dreyfuss in the thought-provoking film, "Whose Life Is It, Anyway?" The film's protagonist, a vibrant young artist, decides not to let medical science keep him alive by mechanical means. He argues that the life being offered him is not life at all, but just a means of staying alive. Here you have an intelligent, sane young man who decides that staying alive just to be alive is not a valid reason for living. I believe it is his right to make that decision.

The terminally ill person or the aged, mentally alert person, incapacitated by physical infirmities, should have the right to choose between life and death. The Constitution gives each of us the right to pursue happiness. When one of us becomes incapable of exercising that right, doesn't it make sense that we should then have the right to choose a dignified death? (M. Jones)

1. What is the thesis of this essay?

2. Would a logical appeal have been more effective? Why or why not?

3. Make a list of the points that the writer could have supported with facts and figures and expert testimony.

4. Are there additional points the writer could have made?

5. If you were asked to rewrite this essay as an argument, what sources would you consult to gather evidence? What parts of this essay would you discard? Why? (Remember, most arguments appeal to the emotions as well as to reason.)

CONSIDERING YOUR AUDIENCE

Before you write any essay, you always consider what your audience already knows. With argumentation, you have the additional job of assessing your audience's likes and dislikes, their opinions and attitudes about your subject. When you try to convince people to change their minds, you *must* know something about them in advance—what are their concerns, and what kind of evidence will affect them? You would have no trouble persuading city transit workers that they should get a raise or elderly riders that they should have discounted fares. You would assume that both groups are friendly and would favor these proposals. The challenge of argumentation increases as you address neutral, skeptical, or even hostile audiences. How, for example, could you convince transit workers that they should take a pay cut or elderly riders that they should pay increased fares?

Plan your strategy with a specific audience in mind. What evidence will you need? Who are your readers going to be? Are they disinterested observers or people involved in the thick of things? Transit workers, elderly riders, and city taxpayers would all respond differently to an appeal for a wage freeze and a fare increase. (Keep in mind that these groups aren't mutually exclusive: transit workers and elderly riders are also city taxpayers; most transit workers will grow elderly, as will most taxpayers.) Putting yourself in your readers' shoes helps you understand their point of view—especially if it differs from your own. You want to appear fair and reasonable to all of your readers. At the same time, you want to establish that your course of action will best serve their interests. You could point out to transit workers that a raise in salary will mean a 20 percent cutback in jobs next year. If job security is their major concern, they might want to keep their wage demands to a minimum. You could show elderly riders that further decreases in fares would involve reductions in the services that they depend on. Remember, your aim is to move your audience to a position that is more closely in accord with your own.

Of course you can't expect your readers to accept your word for things. Transit workers want to see the likelihood of next year's budget crunch demonstrated. Elderly riders need proof that decreased fares would cause the curtailment of serv-ices. Your evidence should reinforce your points, not undercut them. As you can see, the evidence you use depends on your audience and their views of your sub-ject.

BEING FAIR

There is a fine line between making your case and being unfair. Unfortunately, no set of rules exists to make this distinction easy. Often writers of acceptable and sometimes brilliant arguments are less than fair to their opponents. We could hardly call Jonathan Swift "fair" when he implies that the English are cannibals in "A Modest Proposal." A supporter of King George III could have argued (and many did) that Thomas Jefferson and the other writers of the Declaration of Independence slanted evidence when they condemned English policy in the colo-nies. And consider the following from an essay in which William F. Buckley, Jr., supports the death penalty.

> Capital punishment is cruel. That is a historical judgment. But the Constitution suggests that what must be proscribed as cruel is (a) a particularly painful way of inflicting death, or (b) a particularly undeserved death; and the death penalty, as such, offends neither of these criteria and cannot therefore be regarded as objectively "cruel."

Because nowhere in the Constitution is the death penalty mentioned, Buckley could be accused of distorting evidence.

Of course "A Modest Proposal" is satire, and you could say that Swift's over-statement is acceptable in this form of persuasion. The framers of the Declaration of Independence were justifying their break with England, not trying to be fair to the king. Buckley's discussion of the death penalty in respect to "cruel and unusual punishment" is justified by legal precedent. Because argument advocates one position over all others, it is rarely balanced and objective. Even so, these writers do not intentionally falsify evidence. They attack their opponents and counter opposing points with arguments of their own. They understand that if they appear unfair or unreasonable, many of their readers will stop responding to their appeal.

In college writing, especially, you should try to stay within the bounds of fairness. You should make certain that your evidence is not misleading or distorted. For this reason you should familiarize yourself with the most common techniques of unfair persuasion.

☐ DISTORTING EVIDENCE

Distortion is misrepresentation of facts or statements. Consider the ad offering prime real estate in "central Florida," with "running water," "just a short drive from Disney World in Orlando." Imagine the surprise of people who bought the land, sight unseen, and found their property 75 miles from Orlando, partially under water. That is distortion, to put it mildly.

Writers sometimes intentionally misrepresent their opponents' views by exaggerating them and then attacking this extreme position. State Senator Caruso delivers a speech, for instance, advocating sex education in the public schools. This program, he says, will do much to reduce the rising rate of pregnancy among teenage girls. His opponent, Ms. Wilks, attacks, saying that clearly sex education in the schools is just the beginning of government interference in the private lives of individuals. Where will Caruso stop? Will he impose his personal morality on the public? Will he endorse teen-age sex? Abortion? Murder? Gun control? Military service for women? Wilks ends by saying that anyone who could favor such programs must be booted out of office.

Senator Caruso probably did not want to impose his morality on others, nor did he say anything about gun control or drafting women. He only said that some form of sex education in the public schools was a good idea. Ms. Wilks expanded his position beyond recognition. She could have directly questioned the merit of sex-education programs. She could have gathered facts, figures, and other data to challenge her opponent's proposal. Instead, she distorted Caruso's position and attacked it unfairly.

☐ QUOTING EVIDENCE OUT OF CONTEXT

Quoting out of context occurs when a writer or speaker removes someone's words from their original setting and uses them in another. When you use only certain words from a passage, you can easily change the meaning of what a person has said or written. We often see this method of unfair persuasion in ads promoting movies. In a recent review a movie critic said that a film was "Marvelous—if you had the mind of a three-year-old. Of course, the special effects are dazzling, but the plot is dull, dull, dull." The next day the ad quoted the critic: "Vincent Canby calls this movie 'Marvelous . . . dazzling.'"

The same technique is used all too often in political debates—and in other situations where people feel strongly. During a debate about abortion, this exchange took place.

Mrs. S.

I don't know why you are saying the things you are. Just last month in a *Newsweek* article you said that you had no doubt that abortion is murder. You should try to keep track of your own statements.

Dr. G.

I think you should have read that article more carefully, Mrs. S. I have a copy of it here. What I said was [reading] "There is no doubt that *at a very late stage* of fetal development, abortion takes a human life." I also went on to say, "I don't think you can fairly hold this view through the early phases of fetal development." As usual, you have distorted my position to suit yourself.

By repeating only some of Dr. G.'s remarks, Mrs. S. alters his meaning to suit her purpose. Seen in context, Dr. G.'s words indicate that he makes a distinction between abortion at a late and at an early stage of fetal development. In either case Dr. G. does not, as Mrs. S. does, use the term "murder."

☐ SLANTING EVIDENCE

When you select information that supports your case and ignore information that doesn't, you are guilty of slanting your evidence. Several years ago a well-known newspaper was accused of slanting when it reported that a prominent union official had been indicted for jury tampering. The point here was that the man did not have the moral character to hold a position of trust. Such a conclusion, however, was unjustified—the paper neglected to add that the union official's case had been dismissed for lack of evidence.

Slanting can be subtle. When constructing an argument, writers often rely on their readers' lack of knowledge to pass off examples that seem to support an assertion when in reality they do not. Consider this paragraph from an article addressing the widespread distribution of pornography.

Beyond Philadelphia, in northeastern and central Pennsylvania, the pornography business has turned increasingly violent with bombings, arson and attempted murder characterizing a long-running pornography war. Atlantic City and south Jersey are also beginning to play a larger role in this battle. . . . Some law-enforcement insiders are even convinced that the struggle . . . has included among its casualties Larry Flynt, founder and publisher of *Hustler* magazine, the most notorious pornography purveyor of his generation and the victim of an assassination attempt in 1978 in Gwinnett County, Georgia.

Philadelphia Magazine

This writer uses the attempted assassination of Larry Flynt to support the contention that the struggle for local pornography markets is increasingly desperate. Law-enforcement insiders, the writer says, are convinced that Flynt was a casualty of this conflict. Later on in the same article, however, one reads that the evidence connecting Flynt to the Pennsylvania pornography business is circumstantial and that not one suspect has ever been officially linked to the Flynt shooting. By omitting these pertinent facts, the author unfairly slants the evidence to support his conclusion.

EXERCISE

Read the short editorial that follows and decide whether it reflects the criteria for proper argument that we have presented so far. Be prepared to discuss how carefully the author has considered his audience's reactions, how fair his appeal is, and what steps he has taken to appear reasonable.

For those of us who believe that learning can, will, and should take place in a noncompetitive situation, any competitiveness is excessive. The distinction between standard and nonstandard grading is phony. The only real alternative to grading is not to grade, to refuse to turn the classroom into an arena where students are pitted against each other. This is done in several colleges and universities by offering individualized, nongraded evaluations of each student for each course at the end of the term. Ideally, such evaluations describe at length the nature and quality of a student's work but do not rank him or her in competition with others.

Landing jobs and getting into professional graduate schools is becoming more competitive; as a result, colleges and universities are asked *by the students* to grade as if life itself depended on it. At the University of California at Santa Cruz, for example, all analyses of declining admission applications identify ungraded courses at Santa Cruz as a reason many students apply more readily to other University of California campuses. And the *San Francisco Chronicle* ("Inside Colleges Today," February 4, 1975) reports that at places like Berkeley, Yale, and Stanford, students are so preoccupied with grades that their undergraduate lives are clearly desperate. Campus psychologists are kept busy assuaging student anguish over grades, and a popular elective among premeds at one university is "The Fear of Failure Workshop."

The outside political and economic world establishes the priorities of the university. Economic blunders of successive administrations in Washington have set the stage for a massive conservative movement in this country. All of higher education is vulnerable, but the first casualties will be liberalizing educational experiments like those that attempt to replace grading with more humane and pedagogically sound methods of evaluating student work. It is hardly the students, faced with an economy not of their making, who are to blame.

Nor can universities fighting for sheer survival be faulted for responding to the economic needs of their students. But the universities must not give in wholly to that which is obviously antieducational; they must not be devoted to grade grubbing. The Santa Cruzes and Evergreens and Hampshires must be encouraged by legislators and alumni, by professional associations, by future employers of their graduates, above all by other colleges and universities, in their efforts to provide alternatives to an otherwise monolithic grading system. (David Swanger, *Change*)

DEALING WITH THE OPPOSITION

While you want to present evidence that supports your position, you should also consider opposing views. By addressing the obvious objections that readers might have to your thesis, you can dispose of them before you present your case. That is why many writers deal with the opposition as soon as possible. When planning your essay, try to picture a skeptical reader saying, "Well yes, but what about . . . ?" Even people who agree with you will object to some of your suggestions. You can refute opposing views by showing they are partially untrue, unfair, or irrelevant. And you can concede a point if it is well taken and then, if possible, go on to discuss its limitations.

In this passage from a student essay arguing against drug use, Maria Kuredjian refutes an argument against her position.

Drug use has become a controversial subject among people of all ages. Some people feel that drugs such as amphetamines, cocaine, heroin, alcohol, and morphine help them. They think that these drugs lessen tension and give them a feeling of well-being. Nothing could be further from the truth. Many users develop a tolerance to these drugs and over a long period of time increase their dosage. Eventually they become psychologically or physically "hooked." As a result they can lose sleep and become confused, suspicious, or even paranoid. They are not capable of meaningful activity, and their lives revolve around obtaining and taking the drugs.

After acknowledging her opposition, Maria goes on to demonstrate how drug use does *not* contribute to the well-being of the user. If her readers accept her dismissal of this argument for drug use, her argument against it is all the stronger.

When you acknowledge your opposition, do not distort it or present it as ridiculously weak. This tactic, called *creating a straw man*, does not fool careful readers. For example, for an essay against an early-release program for prisoners, you decide to interview a sociology professor who supports the program. Among other things, she says: "We have to do something about the present prison situation. We have had a rise in violent crime; prisons are overcrowded, and costs are up. Would you believe that even the cost of prison bed linen has gone up 50 percent this year?" If you open your essay with: "It is hard to believe that Dr. Walters said that an early release program is necessary because the price of prison bed linen has gone up 50 percent," you have created a straw man. You have distorted Dr. Walters's position, and if your readers figure that out, you have lost them.

During the prewriting stage of your work, you should list all of the arguments against your thesis. Then you can pick which of your opponents' arguments to refute. Most experienced writers feel that only after recognizing their opposition can they construct a persuasive argument.

EXERCISE

Read the following argumentative essay and outline the points that the author makes. Can you think of any additional points he could have made in support of his thesis? Then list the objections to his position that the author refutes. Can you think of any potential objections to his case which he does not adequately refute? If so, where might you place such additional material?

I Am Not a Crook
Joseph Nocera

I am writing this because I need the money. Without a quick dollar fix, I will soon become a newsworthy statistic: I will be one of those people who have defaulted on their student loans.

I don't deny that people like me are a problem for the Federal government. The facts won't let me: the default rate in the federally guaranteed student-loan program is up to 12.2 percent, far higher than ever before. By comparison, the usual consumer-loan default rate is around 3 percent.

For the government, this means that the Department of Health, Education and Welfare, which acts as the insurer of the loans, has had to reimburse lending banks more than $500 million for about 344,000 defaults. The number of defaults on state-insured loans is also on the rise—in New York, for example, it's around 11 percent. In addition, the number of bankruptcies involving student loans has jumped from 760 in the years 1968–1970 to 8,641 in 1976, costing the government another $33.1 million in unpaid loans.

Not surprisingly, the reaction from some members of Congress and others in the Federal government has been outrage at the defaulters. They have been "irresponsible" and are "taking the easy way out" by failing to pay back their loans. One New York judge recently described former students filing for bankruptcy as "little stinkers."

Government has promised to get tough with these ungrateful wretches, to collect the money owed it. The State of New York has already hired a credit bureau and put a computer to work keeping track of defaulters. HEW plans to go even farther, by hiring a collection agency and, ultimately, taking ex-students to court to recover defaulted loans.

HEW has done something else, too. In order to publicize its efforts at cracking down on defaults, it scoured the records of its own employees, and came up with 316 of them who defaulted on their student loans. "We have to set an example here," said an HEW spokesman.

But while that "example" made great newspaper headlines, I think it missed the point completely. For instead of taking a good, hard look to see if, perhaps, there isn't something seriously wrong with the student-loan program, both Congress and HEW have simply assumed that all of the defaulting former students have been acting in bad faith.

Look behind the headlines: about 40 of those HEW people "exposed" by their employer make $15,000 or more, but most of the rest earn an average salary of $8,300. Hardly what you would call fat cats. Yet these are the people the government has decided to go after.

I make a little less than $8,300, which is certainly not poverty level in Washington where I work, but it's not a lot of money either. After paying my rent, food and pressing bills like phone and utilities, there isn't too much left over to send to the bank. As a result I have been on the edge of default for about the last six months.

I pay only when I have to: when I get a call from the bank telling me I am within three days of default and warning that if I don't send some money quickly my credit rating will be ruined forever. But I won't be able to do that much longer: I just don't make enough money.

At age 25, I am at the absolute bottom of my earning power, and so are many of my colleagues in default—though I am doing the kind of work I could only dream about while in school. It's a start, a solid beginning for my career. At my age, you pay dues, and dues never made anyone rich. It is not, then, the best of times to be saddled with a hefty debt.

I owe close to $7,000 for the four years I borrowed from the Higher Education Loan Program (HELP)—one of the most popular Federal student-loan programs. By law, it has to be repaid within ten years. To make matters worse, I was forced to get a one-year "hardship" delay after graduation because I didn't have a job. This added interest to my already sizable bill, while condensing the amount of time for repayment.

These and other realities—the problems of unemployment, of low earning power, of career confusion that often confront graduates—were not taken into account by those who created the guaranteed-student-loan program. The repayment schedules are too rigid and the monthly amounts—often between $50 and $80—are too high at the current wage rates for the newly employed.

It's almost as if the program tells ex-students: "Despite our compassion—and low interest rates—when you were going to school, we don't care about your problems anymore. Pay up or else."

As you can probably tell by now, I think the problems lie not with the ex-students but with the student-loan program itself, and I would suggest that the Federal government spend some time looking for ways to reform it. A few modest proposals from this borrower:

○ Make the terms more flexible. Instead of a ten-year deadline, make it fifteen or twenty years. Instead of beginning repayment within a year of graduation, why not four or five years?

○ Peg the repayment schedule to the person's wage scale. Why couldn't people making $20,000 a year pay at a substantially higher monthly rate than those making $6,000? Why couldn't the rate of repayment rise as a person's salary rises?

○ Handle those cases of serious fraud—and no one denies that they exist—on an individual basis rather than taking the current sweeping "they're all crooks" approach. The fact is we are not all crooks.

This should be a time for compassion and common sense rather than crackdowns. Yes, it is time to worry about the default rate—and do something about it. But former students should not be made the victims of a program that was supposed to pave their way to a promising future. (*Newsweek*)

ARRANGING YOUR ARGUMENT

Effective and reasonable arguments do not follow automatically from evidence. In argument there are two basic ways to move from your detailed material to your conclusions. Arguments either proceed *deductively*—from a general statement accepted as true to a particular conclusion—or *inductively*—from particular facts or examples to a general conclusion. Understanding these arrangements can help you organize your essays.

DEDUCTION

Let us say that you are walking down a street in New York. The day is dark and the rain is pouring down. Just as you begin wondering if you will ever make it to your appointment, a yellow automobile turns the corner. Overjoyed, you wave your hand and the car pulls up next to you.

This simple activity of hailing a cab depends on deductive reasoning. From your past experience, you know that most New York cabs are yellow and that they cruise the streets looking for passengers. When you saw the yellow car, you concluded that it must be a cab. Of course you could have been wrong, but based on your past experience, you knew you were probably right. Deduction, then, is a form of reasoning which holds that you can predict specific instances from general laws, or premises.

☐ THE SYLLOGISM

The basic form of deduction is the *syllogism*, a three-part chain of reasoning that contains a *major premise*, a *minor premise*, and a *conclusion*.

Major premise
All yellow cars are cabs.

Minor premise
The car is yellow.

Conclusion
Therefore, it is a cab.

Notice that in this syllogism, the conclusion contains no terms that have not already been stated in the major and minor premises.

At this point you must consider the distinction between the terms "validity" and "truth." *Validity* has to do with the form, or integrity, of the syllogism itself. A syllogism is said to be valid when its conclusion derives from correctly set up major and minor premises. On the other hand, *truth* pertains to the material contained in the syllogism. In the syllogism above, for instance, the major premise "All yellow cars are cabs" is not true. Some yellow cars are not cabs. But the syllogism is valid. Properly drawn conclusions can be valid whether the premises of the syllogism are true or not.

When you refute an opponent's argument, you should know whether you are questioning truth or validity. It is often hard to find fault with the truth of an argument because you don't always have the facts to establish that a statement is false. Because one's knowledge of the world is necessarily limited, one cannot challenge the truth of many arguments successfully. Despite the difficulty of proving the truth of some statements, you *can* assess their validity, however.

☐ STRUCTURING A DEDUCTIVE ARGUMENT

The strength of a deductive argument is that if your readers accept your premises, your conclusion logically follows. The trick is to get your audience to accept your premises. Suppose you argue that the United States should actively explore space and that a permanent space station is needed to do this. Your argument could be expressed as a syllogism:

Major premise
Space exploration is desirable.

Minor premise
A space station is a necessary part of space exploration.

Conclusion
Therefore, a space station is desirable.

Your major premise is usually an idea that you feel your audience accepts. Few people would disagree that space research yields vital scientific knowledge or that it results in technology that benefits society. Your main task is to establish that your minor premise and your conclusion are reasonable. You could do this by presenting quotations from experts that establish the need for a permanent orbiting space station. If your readers accept both your major and minor premises, they should also be ready to grant your conclusion.

When you write a deductive argument, you generally begin by stating your conclusion, which is also the thesis you intend to prove. You usually refute opposing arguments near the beginning, and then go on to present the data that support your argument. Often you save your best reasons for last so you can end your argument dramatically and persuasively.

The following student essay, written by Andrea Groth, is an example of a deductive argument.

The Responsibilities of Chemical Companies
in Chemical Warfare

Introduction
sets up the
deductive pat-
tern

Major premise:
Corporations
should be held
responsible for
their mistakes

Minor premise:
Some corpora-
tions made
mistakes

Conclusion:
Therefore,
those corpora-
tions should be
held responsi-
ble for their
mistakes

All of us would agree that corporations, like private individuals, should be responsible for their mistakes. A case in point concerns the chemical companies that manufactured Agent Orange, a
chemical defoliant that America used in the Vietnam War. Its
purpose was to clear the jungle, but it also had another effect.
Agent Orange destroyed the lives of many of the soldiers who were
exposed to it. Fifteen years after the war, veterans and their families are still paying medical bills for treatment because they were
exposed to Agent Orange. Of course time was short and national
security was at stake, so the chemical companies had to work
quickly. As a result, in-depth studies could not be carried out.
Even so, the chemical companies that made Agent Orange and
certified it "safe" should be held responsible for their mistakes.

Acknowledg-
ment of oppos-
ing arguments

Thesis

One of the major producers of Agent Orange says that all the
companies did adequate testing and found no harmful side effects.
Shortly after the war, veterans exposed to Agent Orange began
complaining of unusual side effects. Independent laboratories did
extensive testing and found that dioxin, the major contaminant in
Agent Orange, is one of the most toxic products known. It seems
odd that researchers with companies that developed Agent Orange
did not get the same results that private researchers did.

Refutation of
opposing argu-
ments

The chemical companies also ignored eyewitness accounts of
what happened when Agent Orange was used. The chemical was
used by the Army to defoliate the jungle in suspected enemy areas.
Within a few hours after spraying, leaves fell off trees, making it
easier for our soldiers to spot the enemy. Not only did the foliage
die, but so did all the animals. Birds that were flying one minute
were dead on the ground the next. The men who flew the planes
that carried the chemical developed rashes over their bodies; they
reported a shortness of breath and a burning sensation in their
throat and lungs. In villages downwind of the spraying sites, dog
ran around foaming at the mouth and later died. Soldiers who were
accidentally sprayed developed rashes, skin problems, and head-
aches. Weeks later some lost their eyesight and still later others
developed cancer.

Evidence

For a long time no one made the connection between the
spraying and the soldiers' symptoms. But eventually scientists did
establish a link. The chemical companies, however, tried to block
publication of the results and denied responsibility for what had
happened. In addition, the companies continued to produce pesticides that contained trace amounts of dioxin and were using them
in the United States for crop control. Only recently have the
chemical companies stopped the production of pesticides that contained dioxin.

Evidence

After fifteen years, the nightmare hasn't ended. Veterans who **Evidence** were exposed to very small amounts of dioxin are developing the same symptoms; they just took longer to emerge. Besides lung and liver cancer, they now have to deal with a wide variety of birth defects in their children. Even now the chemical companies deny any responsibility to these victims.

Conclusion restates the general principles stated in the beginning

If these chemical companies made mistakes, they should pay for them. Despite the extenuating circumstances, the chemical companies said that Agent Orange was safe. As a result of this certification, thousands of our troops, to say nothing of Vietnamese peasants, were exposed to a deadly chemical. If the courts forced the chemical companies to compensate victims, it would set a precedent. In the future they would know that they will be held responsible for the products they develop.

Andrea's introduction gives the background of the issue and sets up the premises for her argument. She begins with a major premise that she considers self-evident, then states her thesis. Her evidence is compelling and reasonable although she does not provide statistics or detailed accounts of studies done on dioxin. Nonetheless she makes a strong case that chemical companies should be held responsible for their products. She does establish that the chemical companies made errors with regard to dioxin, even though her case would have been stronger had she discussed specific companies, specific victims, or specific lawsuits.

As you can see, the first requirement of arguing deductively is using premises that your audience will accept. If they can't agree with your premises—if those premises are controversial or not easily established—you should use inductive argument, which leads your audience to your conclusion.

INDUCTION

In the early seventeenth century, Galileo carried out a series of experiments using induction as his method of inquiry. By measuring the relative speed of falling objects dropped from the Leaning Tower of Pisa, he formulated laws that describe the motion of falling bodies. Induction uses specific observations to move from an initial hypothesis, or supposition, to a general conclusion. Induction goes beyond the information of its premises and determines the implications of the data gathered for other related events.

Unlike deduction, inductive reasoning never arrives at a certain conclusion, only a highly probable one. The method by which you move from evidence to conclusion is called an "inductive leap." The more observations you make and the more information you gather, the better your chances of drawing an accurate conclusion. When you look out the window and predict that it will rain, you make an inductive leap. You base your conclusions on your many observations of similar situations in the past.

When you construct an argument that relies on inductive reasoning, you cite a number of observations that lead to a general conclusion. In arriving at the conclusion that a certain newspaper is biased, for example, you may cite several articles to make your point. But when you leap from known facts to a general conclusion, problems can arise. For instance, you might not supply enough examples to prove that the newspaper's stories are usually slanted. Or your examples might not clearly support your conclusion. When the gap between observable facts and your conclusion is too wide, or when the connection between the facts and your conclusion is not apparent, you can be accused of faulty reasoning.

□ STRUCTURING AN INDUCTIVE ARGUMENT

Despite their variety, inductive arguments follow a certain pattern. First you ask a question. Next you investigate the question by gathering a broad sample of evidence. Finally you reach a conclusion based on your evidence. Here is an example:

Question

Does Steven Spielberg make innovative movies?

Evidence

Steven Spielberg's *Jaws* is an innovative movie. (List details)
Steven Spielberg's *Close Encounters* is an innovative movie. (List details)
Steven Spielberg's *Poltergeist* is an innovative movie. (List details)
Steven Spielberg's *E.T.* is an innovative movie. (List details)

Conclusion

Therefore, Steven Spielberg makes innovative movies.

To make this argument convincing, you must be sure that your audience accepts your evidence. You have to define the term "innovative" and discuss its application to movies. After considering your evidence, you may decide that your claim is too general. What if Spielberg has made a traditional movie? After all, he has made more than the four you mention. You might feel safer qualifying your conclusion: "Steven Spielberg has made *a number of* innovative movies." Remember that for your evidence to work, it cannot be debatable. If it is, you will confuse your readers by opening up a second argument.

Here is an inductive argument written by Tara Williams for her composition class.

Good Neighbors

Introduction establishes the background of the problem and implies the

"Why our neighborhood?" "But this is a very fussy area." "Are they . . . well, you know, safe?" These remarks are typical of the responses that the Association for Retarded Citizens (ARC) receives when it approaches a community for permission to locate a

question to be answered: Should retarded citizens be permitted to reside in group homes in a community?

group home. Are these questions valid? Do residents of a community where a group home is to be located have cause for concern?

Perhaps the most widespread fear that community members voice is for the safety of their children. Residents have the misconception that mentally handicapped people are violent and uncontrollable. On the contrary, the majority of retarded people exhibit characteristic cheerfulness and friendliness. Only a small percentage have violent episodes, and with medication, these outbursts can be virtually eliminated.

Refutation of the major opposing argument

Evidence: Selectivity of admissions

To be admitted to a group home, a patient's psychological and physical records must be reviewed. Patients with a history of destructive activities are not accepted. A minimal amount of self-sufficiency is also necessary because of the life style of a group home. Supervisors live at the home with the residents, but their purpose is to stimulate and counsel, not to control or wait on the residents.

Evidence: Benefits of group homes to residents and to community

Group homes were originally set up as an alternative to large institutions. In states where the program has received support, there have been benefits for both the retarded citizens and the community. Many mentally handicapped residents of group homes have been successfully placed in low-skill employment. Living in the community enables them to go to jobs independently and achieve self-respect that is stifled in an institution. Many residents recognize their progress and take pride in their achievements.

Evidence: Example of residents showing their gratitude to the community

There have been many instances where retarded citizens who moved into an area showed their gratitude. One striking example occurred this Halloween. Residents of a group home decided on their own to have a Halloween party for neighborhood children. They realized that because of a rash of poisonings, many children would not be allowed to go trick-or-treating. Hesitantly parents permitted their children to attend, and by the end of the evening many people had changed their minds about the group home. The innocence and openness of their children had helped them change their opinions.

Conclusion based on the evidence presented above

The success of a group home depends on the attitude of the community in which it is located. Where the community and the group home establish a dialogue, no serious problems develop. In fact, both groups have benefited. However, this effective program will be discontinued unless the necessary support is forthcoming.

Thesis

The group home is an innovative concept that deserves funding and community support. An ARC slogan sums up this idea nicely: "Being retarded never stopped anyone from being a Good Neighbor."

Tara's argument proceeds inductively. The evidence in the body of her essay should lead her audience to her conclusion that group homes deserve community support. Because she feels that her audience shares the prejudice of communities that oppose group housing, Tara saves her thesis statement until the end of her essay. Of course, her thesis is implied throughout the essay. By leading her readers through an inductive process, she hopes to overcome resistance and gain support for her position. Notice also that Tara saves her most compelling evidence—the example of the Halloween party—for last. She hopes that by presenting her evidence in this order she will prepare her readers for her conclusion. She could have offered more examples of successful group homes, and she could have acknowledged the validity of some of her opponents' claims. But even so, her argument is well-structured and convincing.

EXERCISE

Look over the following essays in this chapter and determine whether each is structured *inductively* or *deductively*.

1. "Should the Law Allow a Terminally Ill Person to Take His or Her Own Life?" M. Jones (page 252)

2. "I Am Not a Crook," Joseph Nocera (page 259)

OBSTRUCTIONS TO ARGUMENT: FALLACIES

Fallacies are flawed techniques or arguments that cannot be defended logically. Because they so closely resemble sound arguments, fallacious arguments can be very convincing. Unscrupulous people intentionally use these techniques to give bad arguments the appearance of validity. We see this when politicians present unsound premises as if they were true or attack a person instead of an issue. Often fallacies creep into our arguments without our realizing it. At one time or another, everyone uses ambiguous language or relies upon unproved assumptions to make a point. When detected, fallacies can backfire and turn your audience against you. You should not only avoid fallacies in your own writing, but also watch out for them in the speech and writing of others. Here are some common fallacies that you should be aware of.

EQUIVOCATION

Equivocation occurs when you shift the meaning of a key word within your argument. By changing the meaning of a key term, you can make it seem that your conclusion follows from your premise. Notice in the following example how the judgment seems more sound than it really is.

> As far as I am concerned, the artistically creative people in this society should focus their creativity on the problems of poverty and hunger.

In this statement, the terms "creative" and "creativity" seem equivalent. The first term, however, refers to artistic creativity, and the second to inventiveness.

Sometimes the fallacy of equivocation can be very subtle. Consider the following excerpts from a court case deciding if D. H. Lawrence's book *Lady Chatterley's Lover* was or was not obscene.

> *Mr. Mindel (prosecutor):* I am asking the witness whether he wishes to change his answer as to his opinion of whether Lawrence felt that the words that he used were obscene . . . .
>
> *Judge:* You may answer.
>
> *The Witness (Alfred Kazin):* Lawrence did not believe that his use of these words was obscene. He believed these words were generally regarded as obscene.
>
> *Mr. Rembar (defense):* I should like to object to this line of questioning on the ground that it confuses two concepts. One is the idea of "obscene words" as meaning words which are suffering from some sort of taboo or other. The other is the use of the word "obscene" as employed in this statute to make certain words nonmailable . . . .

This testimony goes on for pages, all of it centering on the definition of the word "obscene." Part of the confusion has to do with the slipperiness of the word itself, and part has to do with the refusal of both parties to agree upon a definition. It is understandable that throughout the trial any conclusions using the term "obscene" were open to challenge.

In your writing, be sure that you do not shift the meaning of a term from one statement to another. If you think that you have shifted the meaning of a term, reread your paper keeping the single meaning you intend in mind. This technique will help you to see if and where you have been guilty of equivocation.

THE EITHER/OR FALLACY

This fallacy assumes that there are just two sides to a question when actually there are more. "Either you are for me or against me," the old cliché goes. Most questions simply do not have one right or wrong answer. Often many alternatives exist, defying reduction to a simple "black or white" formula.

You commit the either/or fallacy when you present a complex situation as if there were just two alternative explanations, interpretations, or solutions. You might write a paper inquiring into the performance of a quarterback. If you ask, "Did the quarterback play well or did he play badly?" you admit only two possibilities, ruling out all others. Perhaps he played a mediocre game, or played superbly at times and abominably at others. You can avoid this fallacy by acknowledging the complexity of an issue. Don't fall into the trap of misrepresenting issues by limiting options.

Of course you can draw valid conclusions from *some* either/or situations. In mathematics, for instance, an answer is either correct or incorrect. In chemistry lab, the white substance you synthesized is either aspirin or something else. To be valid, an either/or statement must cover *all* possible alternatives. The premise "Either Judy went to class or she didn't" is valid. There are no other possibilities. If, however, you say "Either Judy went to class or she stayed home," you commit the either/or fallacy. To prove your premise wrong, all someone has to do is point out that Judy went to the library, to the movies, or to the store.

HASTY GENERALIZATIONS

When charging a jury, a judge cautions jury members not to jump to false conclusions. They must base their decision only on the evidence placed before them, and they must be sure beyond a reasonable doubt that a defendant is guilty. Of course everyone jumps to conclusions at one time or another. You might assume that two people walking together are dating. Actually they could be friends, cousins, or strangers who have just met. Hasty generalizations often occur when one draws conclusions from inadequate evidence. Sometimes only one or two examples do lead to a valid conclusion: just one case of the flu convinces most people that the disease is debilitating. At other times, though, you must examine more evidence to arrive at and support a conclusion. A scientist claiming that DNA recombinant research is safe would have to offer many examples to convince his colleagues that his general conclusion is valid.

When you write, you may not have the time or space to provide an exhaustive list of examples. One is constantly in danger of basing conclusions on too little evidence. If you say that because the two Hondas you bought were defective, all Hondas are defective, anyone could undercut you by pointing out that two examples do not warrant such a conclusion. Furthermore, your two cars may represent only one model and not the entire line.

You must always think about how many facts you need to support an argument. Hasty generalizations are usually extremely vulnerable and easy to refute.

POST HOC, ERGO PROPTER HOC

Post hoc, ergo propter hoc is Latin for "after this, therefore because of this." That one event follows another closely in time does not mean that the first one caused the second one. When actress Valerie Harper says that she was born on December 7, 1941, and for years thought she was responsible for World War II, she is making fun of our tendency to indulge in this fallacy. When heavy rains fell in the northwestern United States after the first moon landing took place, many people assumed in error that one event had somehow caused the other.

Make sure that you establish the true causes of the events that you discuss. Cause-and-effect relationships are difficult to prove, and often you have to rely on experts to establish your claim. (For a more detailed look at causal relationships, see page 68, "Cause and Effect")

BEGGING THE QUESTION

This fallacy occurs when you state an arguable premise as if it were true. By doing so, you allow readers to assume that something has been proved when it hasn't. Simple cases of begging the question don't fool many people.

> Children act the way they do because they are young.
> Babylon interests historians because it is ancient.
> Thieves should be punished because they break the law.

These sentences restate an issue without proving it: they simply end where they begin.

But often arguments that beg the question are more difficult to spot. Academic writing offers many opportunities for unintentionally committing this fallacy. In defining terms and differentiating between points, students often beg the question. Here is an example from a history midterm exam.

> Import quotas are dangerous because they restrict free trade.

This says nothing. Import quotas by definition involve restriction of free trade. Whether they are dangerous has yet to be established.

Look out for this fallacy when you revise your arguments. Whenever you encounter it, you have failed to confront the real issue at hand.

ARGUMENT *AD HOMINEM*

Arguments *ad hominem*—or attacks against the person—place the focus on the person arguing an issue rather than on the issue itself. By casting aspersions on an opponent, you turn attention away from the facts of a case.

> What good is this person's advice about water pollution? After all, he is a known Marxist.
> Mrs. Perlman thinks that women should have equal pay. What do you expect from someone who is a housewife?
> I don't know how we can listen to this person's comments about censorship. She has admitted owning the very books we are trying to ban.

When emotions run high or an issue is extremely controversial, this tactic can be quite persuasive. But although you may sway some readers, others will recognize this fallacy for what it is and shift their support to your opposition.

RED HERRING

When you commit this fallacy, you change the subject in order to distract your audience from an issue. For example, "Well, what if Bert Jackson was arrested for drunk driving? Everyone takes a drink now and then." The issue is not that some people occasionally take a drink, but that one person was driving while drunk.

Many people call on this tactic when they are at a loss for evidence or when they feel backed into a corner. By switching the subject, they attempt to change direction and begin the argument on safer ground. Here is an example from a student essay.

> The proposed law allowing a moment of silence in schools should be passed. It mandates no prayers and forces no student to pray. One can only wonder if the legislators who are blocking this law don't have better things to do. Surely they would serve the people better by trying to lower the high rate of unemployment in their state.

This argument avoids what it promises to prove. The writer should supply evidence to support his assertion that the law should be passed. Instead he switches to an irrelevant issue, unemployment.

EXERCISE

Identify the fallacies in the following statements. Explain the error, and suggest a way of correcting the problem.

a. The two pieces of property I bought in this area increased in value dramatically. I don't think you can go wrong with this property.

b. Three Mile Island was a disaster. Why should we allow a nuclear plant to be built in this area?

c. The last two standardized tests I took I did badly on. I just don't do well on standardized tests.

d. The last time Venus and Mars were in line, I had extremely good luck.

e. The chief scientist in the American space program worked for the Nazis. The American space program is a Nazi idea.

f. It is difficult to take seriously the ideas of a person who favors rewarding sloth.

g. The present tax laws may be equitable. But what about those who lie on their tax returns?

h. The immoral are punished because they are immoral.

i. Last year I threw a penny in the fountain and was lucky. This year I am going to throw a quarter in and see what happens.

j. What else can you expect from someone like that?

k. The elderly are frequently victimized by criminals because they are old.

l. Writing a research paper was a problem for me last year. I am sure I won't do well on this research paper either.

m. "How would a normal person react to this book?"
"What is normal?"
"What do you mean? Everyone knows what normal is."

n. The people of this town got what they deserved when Bill Watson was elected mayor.

o. After using Crest my child got fewer cavities this checkup. Crest must be better than my former toothpaste.

WORKING WITH DATA

Read this newspaper article carefully.

Library in Town Without Wheelchairs
Douglas E. Kneeland

RUDD, Iowa, Oct. 28—The Rudd Public Library has run afoul of the Federal and state bureaucracies. It did not mean to, but it has found that that does not seem to make any difference.

The library's sin is that it does not have ramps for people in wheelchairs. That is because none of the 429 residents of this farming community 14 miles east of Mason City in north central Iowa are confined to wheelchairs.

"Why should we do it if nobody's going to use it?" asked Joyce Navratil, the part-time librarian. "Why should taxpayers have to spend the money?"

"I'm all for it if it was going to be used," said Helene Wood, president of the library board, "but it's like building a house with 10 bedrooms if you live by yourself. It's silly."

But the Federal and state governments persist in their contention that Rudd must conform to the law. As one official said, "You can't ever tell when you might have a handicapped person."

What Rudd is enmeshed in is a bureaucratic conflict not unfamiliar to thousands of cities and towns across the nation that have suddenly found themselves confronted with laws and regulations that have filtered down from Washington through regional offices and state capitals to the local level for implementation.

Still, the people who dwell in this quiet village dominated by towering grain elevators amid miles of corn and soybean fields do not often find themselves on a collision course with far-off authority. The whole matter is almost more than they can comprehend.

As often happens in such affairs, the dispute may linger endlessly. But until now, this is what has happened:

In 1973, Congress passed a Rehabilitation Act that said, among other things, that any institution receiving Federal funds must be made accessible to people in wheelchairs and other handicapped persons. Last spring, Joseph A. Califano Jr., the Secretary of Health, Education and Welfare, had regulations published in the Federal Register setting forth the timetable and methods by which institutions receiving H.E.W. funds must comply with Section 504, the pertinent part of the act.

The regulation said that programs must be made accessible to the handicapped by last Aug. 3 and that any necessary "substantial modifications in existing structures" must be completed by June 3, 1980. It also said that institutions must have on file by Dec. 15 any plans for such modifications.

What that means is that libraries, hospitals, schools and other institutions receiving money from the department, even indirectly, through one program or another must provide such things as ramps for wheelchairs.

No one in Rudd argues with the good intentions of Congress or of Secretary Califano. But the Rudd public library board was stunned when it was abruptly told last month that its 28-by-30-foot, one-story building needed a ramp, or perhaps two ramps, and an outside entrance to the basement, which has none, and possibly wider doors for its two toilets.

The first thing the board did was take a survey of the town's 429 residents. That is how it learned that no one who uses a wheelchair lives in the service area of the tiny library, which is open from 2 to 5 P.M. on Tuesdays, Wednesdays and Thursdays and from 9 A.M. to noon on Saturdays.

"There's one lady with a walker," Mrs. Wood said, "and she has never been inside the library. We would be happy to take her books, but she's never checked one out."

The major problem, as far as Rudd is concerned, is that its library does not have much money. The new building with its brick front and shingled sides was put up in 1967 after a Mason City foundation contributed $8,000 and the town scraped up another $8,000.

Last year, according to Mrs. Navratil's records, the library spent $3,591. Of that, $308.70 was for books, nearly $240 of which went for a set of reference works.

"We've spent most of our money on paperbacks and second-hand books, and some of the members of our board belong to book clubs and they donate books after they're through with them," Mrs. Wood said. "It's pretty meager. We just haven't been able to buy books after we pay the heat and the librarian and everything."

Most of the money comes from Floyd County, although the town contributes $800 a year, primarily for heat. Since both the county and the town receive Federal revenue-sharing funds, the library could lose most of its income as a penalty for not conforming to the Rehabilitation Act of 1973. Moreover, its participation in an interlibrary loan program and access to research assistance from the regional library in Mason City could be cut off, since those programs are aided by Federal funds.

All the trouble started innocently enough, as Mrs. Navratil tells it, because some groups in Rudd wanted to use the library basement for activities. But the basement had always been susceptible to water seepage after heavy rains. She said she approached the regional library to see if some funds might be obtained to seal the basement and was referred to the State Library Commission in Des Moines.

Then, she went on, Neil Hampton, the state commission's building consultant, paid her a visit.

"He got here and he wasn't too interested in the basement," Mrs. Navratil said, "but he told me about the ramps we'd have to build. He told me we'd have to put one into the basement, and that's what we really went up into the air about."

She said she had been unaware of the Federal regulations until then although she learned later that the State Library Commission had mentioned them in its newsletter.

"I never did pay any attention to them," she said.

After getting the bad news from Mr. Hampton, she and Mrs. Wood wrote to Charles E. Grassley, the Third District's Republican Representative.

The newsletter had said that 92 percent of Iowa's 502 libraries would have to make structural changes to conform with the law. It estimated the average cost for each library at $6,500.

"For us to have to spend even $6,500 to make this library accessible to the handicapped who don't even exist in our town is ridiculous," Mrs. Navratil wrote.

"It makes me sick," Mrs. Wood said in her letter. "We think in terms of 'hundreds' not 'thousands.'"

"We are supposed to submit plans for remodeling by mid-December, but we can't ask a lumberyard to spend half a day on something we know we can't afford," she added. "So the only alternative is to close the library to the whole community just because we can't remodel for the nonexisting handicapped. Isn't that ridiculous?"

Mr. Grassley wrote back with what appeared to be good news. He said he had been informed by H.E.W. that if the library did not employ 15 or more persons it did not have to make the improvements.

But Barry Porter, the state librarian, later told the people in Rudd that his information from the H.E.W. Department's regional office of civil rights in Kansas City was that the number of employees did not matter so long as the building was used by the public.

In a telephone interview this week, Mr. Porter said, "There's so much in the air and we've heard so many rumors, we're all wrestling with it right now."

In Washington, Betty Burger, an aide to Mr. Grassley, said the Congressman had written to the department asking for clarification.

"As far as we're concerned, we're just waiting for a reply to the letter," she said; "then we'll take it from there."

At H.E.W. headquarters, Elizabeth H. Hughey, chief of the state public library branch of the division of library services, said:

"We are trying to work with the office of civil rights in Kansas City on that. I have said to them to be reasonable about this, that a reasonable approach is the best one. There's nothing we can do at this time. It's up to the office of civil rights."

In Kansas City, Jesse L. High, who has been dealing with the problem at the office of civil rights, said that if Rudd or the Iowa State Library Commission would put the question in writing as to whether a town without handicapped people had to conform to the act, he would seek a policy ruling.

"We're still waiting for someone to answer that in Washington," he said.

But in Washington, David Dawson, an equal opportunity specialist at the office of civil rights, said it would not be enough, as some officials have suggested, for Rudd's library to agree to deliver books to the handicapped.

"I don't doubt for a moment," he said, "that Rudd, Iowa, has any number of elderly people who have trouble with stairs. It could be a benefit."

Meanwhile, here in Rudd, Mrs. Wood concluded: "What we want is something clear-cut. I guess that's what we're saying. There seems to be a pecking order and we're at the bottom."
(*New York Times*)

Using material in this article to support your assertions, and being sure to cite your source, write an argumentative letter to the *Des Moines Register,* Iowa's largest newspaper. Take the position *either* of Helen Wood, president of the library board (who opposes the ramps), or of a wheelchair-bound reader living elsewhere in the state (who feels the ramps should be built).

CHAPTER

11

Essay Examinations

Taking examinations is a skill, one you have been practicing throughout your life as a student. By now you may know what works best for you—how to organize your answers, how to highlight portions of them, how much time to spend answering each question, whether to guess or not—but chances are you aren't doing the best you can.

You may not have had much experience with essay examinations. Short answers—matching, fill-in, true/false, multiple choice—require very different skills. Although both kinds of tests require you to study, to recall what you know, and to budget your time carefully, only essay questions ask for clear and comprehensive responses in a series of logically connected sentences.

ESSAY-LENGTH ANSWERS

Like other writing, essay answers have a prewriting, a writing and arranging, and a revising stage. Because of time pressures, you are usually tempted to skip prewriting and revising entirely. Instead you plunge in, writing in a frenzy until your time is up. This lack of strategy can result in a disorganized or even incoherent answer. Some advance planning helps you to produce a stronger response. A tightly organized, coherent answer gets a higher mark than a loose and rambling one—provided that it is correct.

In answering examination questions, you can use many of the strategies you use in writing an essay. But you gear your answer differently to your purpose, your audience, and your other boundaries.

PREWRITING FOR ESSAY EXAMINATIONS

Examinations challenge you to recall and express in writing what you already know—what you have read, what you have heard in class, what you have reviewed in your notes. When you take an examination, you need to remember information, to make connections among ideas, and to relate these to the examination question. You can prepare by carefully reviewing the material and by being sure you understand it. You can also anticipate the questions your instructor could ask. As you study, isolate key concepts and central ideas. Try to think of potential essay questions and answer them in your mind (or even in writing) to see how well you do. Try out some of these questions on classmates, and see whether you can brainstorm together on a few of the questions you think might be asked.

◻ READING THE QUESTION

When you first look at an examination question, be sure to read it very carefully. Many students find it helpful to underline key words in the question to help them focus on the topic. For example:

Music

Explain the twelve-tone system as developed by Schoenberg.

Psychology

Distinguish between inborn and conditioned reflexes, giving several examples of each.

Literature

Define what is meant by literary naturalism and give examples from the works of Norris, Crane, and Dreiser.

Be sure to read all of the instructions carefully. You may be asked to explain, compare, contrast, trace, evaluate, discuss, interpret, analyze, summarize, describe, classify, or give examples. If the question calls for a *comparison and contrast* of *two* systems of government, a *description* or *analysis* of *one* system—no matter how detailed or thought-provoking—will not do.

The wording of the question itself may also suggest which parts of the topic to emphasize. For instance, an instructor would expect very different answers to these two American history examination questions:

1.   Give a detailed explanation of the major causes of the Spanish-American War, noting briefly some of the effects of the war on the United States.
2.   Give a detailed explanation of the impact of the Spanish-American War on the United States, noting briefly the major causes of the war.

If you read these two questions carefully and underline key words, you will see that, although these questions look somewhat alike, the first question calls for an essay on *causes,* while the second asks for *results.*

The wording of the question frequently suggests a pattern of development (process, classification, cause and effect, for instance). Use this pattern to structure your answer. Paying attention to such signals saves you time and makes your writing task easier.

☐ CONSIDERING YOUR BOUNDARIES

On any examination, your *audience* is your instructor. He or she already knows the answer and a great deal more about your subject, although you may arrange the material in a new way or make your own point. Your *purpose,* then, is to demonstrate that you know your facts and understand the material, not to dazzle your reader with clever remarks or to appeal to his or her sympathy. Your instructor reads a lot of exams, trying to get through them thoroughly but efficiently. Anything you can do to ease this task will be appreciated.

On this *occasion,* you will have to budget your time carefully, apportioning it according to the relative value of the question. If an essay question is worth fifty points, with twenty-five two-point short answers making up the balance, you know that you must spend at least half and perhaps more of your time planning, writing, and proofreading the essay. The short answers, which do not require composition, may come quickly. The examination question may specify the *length* of your answer, but more likely the amount of time you have to write determines length. Brainstorming—jotting down points that seem important—will help reveal the scope of your *knowledge* and lead you toward a workable *thesis.* If you know your material well, you may even find a thesis simply by listing the points you intend to discuss.

ARRANGING YOUR ANSWER: THE PLAN

It is especially important to plan an essay answer before you begin to write. On a timed examination, you may find yourself with no time to revise. When you have read the question carefully, listed your points or brainstormed to recall relevant information, and arrived at a suitable thesis, plan your organization. A detailed outline takes too much time, but you should write out your major points.

You can use the inside cover of your examination book or the last sheet for this. Once your plan is written out, check it against the question to make certain it addresses all relevant material and emphasizes everything the question calls for. And make sure it reflects the pattern of arrangement suggested by the examination question. One student, Elias Kazanjian, prepared this plan for a response to the first of the American history examination questions (page 279):

Question

Give a detailed explanation of the major causes of the Spanish-American War, noting briefly some of the effects of the war on the United States.

Thesis

The two major causes of the Spanish-American War were the American press's sensational treatment of the conflict between Cuba and Spain, and the sinking of the battleship *Maine*; results included Teddy Roosevelt's rise to prominence, the reform of the U.S. military system, and a U.S. move toward imperialism.

Supporting points

Causes—"Yellow journalism." Circulation war between Hearst and Pulitzer led
    newspapers to exploit war atrocities.
    —"Remember the *Maine*." U.S. battleship sunk (this followed discovery of
    Spanish minister's letter). Congress pressed for war.
Effects—T. Roosevelt became prominent
    —Military system revamped
    —U.S. imperialism (most important)

This plan reveals that Elias has read the question carefully and has a good command of the material. He recognizes that causes—not effects—should be stressed, and that the answer should show a cause-and-effect pattern.

WRITING AND REVISING

Once you have a thesis and a written plan, compose your answer, referring back to both thesis and plan at regular intervals. Don't bother with stylistic attempts to engage your reader's interest or attract attention: your time is precious, and so is your reader's. A statement of your thesis is the best introduction for an in-class essay examination. (A take-home examination may call for a more elaborate presentation.) A comprehensive and carefully worded thesis clearly signals what your answer will be about.

To make sure you continue to meet your reader's expectations, you can take additional steps. Follow your plan point by point without wandering off your topic.

Indicate movement from one point to the next by clear topic sentences and transitions. Such signals—along with repeated sentence structure ("The next reason . . . "; "The final reason . . . ") and key words—make your answer easy to follow. Topic sentences also help your reader see whether you are answering the question fully.

Your essay answer should cover the question comprehensively and in detail, but it should not be padded. Not only does irrelevant material irritate your reader, it can also be wrong. Don't repeat yourself just to make your answer look longer. Don't volunteer information the question doesn't ask for just to demonstrate that you know *something*. This tactic suggests that you are short on the relevant material. And be sure to support your assertions with specific details: facts, examples, or statistics. This demonstrates that you have studied and considered the material thoroughly.

Finally, be sure to leave enough time to reread (and correct, if necessary) what you have written. Try to look at your essay with a fresh eye. Consider the accuracy of your facts and the logic and order of your ideas. Check your sentence structure, word choice, and punctuation. Make sure your thesis, topic sentences, and transitions are clear. Finally, make sure you have included everything you needed to say but no more. If you suddenly remember something relevant, don't panic. A few additional words can be inserted with a caret (∧). Another sentence, even a paragraph, can be added neatly at the end of your answer, boxed and accompanied by a brief note telling your instructor where it goes.

Elias Kazanjian structured his essay answer to the question on page 279 in this fashion. Notice how his answer refers to the question and how he emphasizes its focus by repeating the words "causes" and "effects."

Question

Give a detailed explanation of the major causes of the Spanish-American War, noting briefly some of the effects of the war on the United States.

Answer

Introduction

Thesis statement

Background

The two major causes of the Spanish-American War were the American press's sensational treatment of the conflict between Cuba and Spain and the sinking of the battleship *Maine*; effects included Theodore Roosevelt's rise to prominence, the reform of the U.S. military system, and the U.S. move toward imperialism.

Cubans had been trying since 1868 to break free of Spanish rule. U.S. citizens were generally sympathetic to Cuba, but the government's position was strict neutrality. The 1895 revolution in Cuba was a brutal struggle with cruelties on both sides. In the American press, however, the revolution was reported as if all the atrocities were being committed by the Spaniards.

Topic sentence identifies first major cause

This slanted reporting was a direct cause of the Spanish-American War. At this time, Joseph Pulitzer's New York *World* and William Randolph Hearst's New York *Journal* were engaged in a circulation war. In an attempt to increase readership, they exploited the war in Cuba, stressing sex and violence. In the tradition of what came to be called "yellow journalism," the newspapers stressed sensationalism and printed all the lurid details of the war (both real and imaginary), complete with graphic pictures. Other newspapers, and eventually the American public, believed the tales of Spanish atrocities, and pressure was placed on President Cleveland to intervene on behalf of Cuba. Cleveland, however, believed both sides were guilty of cruelties and felt the U.S. had no business interfering. McKinley, elected in 1896, also favored American neutrality. Two events changed his mind.

Topic sentence identifies a minor cause

The first of the events that led to war occurred in February 1898, when a private letter written by the Spanish minister in Washington was made available to the American press. When the New York *Journal* published the letter, which was highly critical of McKinley, American sentiment against Spain was further aroused.

Topic sentence identifies second major cause

The most immediate cause of the Spanish-American War occurred just after this, when the American battleship *Maine* was blown up in Havana harbor, killing 260. The American public assumed Spain was responsible and clamored for war, chanting "Remember the *Maine*." Although Spain had essentially agreed to an armistice, Congress passed a resolution that declared Cuba free and empowered the president to use force to expel the Spaniards from Cuba. In other words, war was declared.

Topic sentence identifies move from causes to effects

The results of this brief war were considerable. The U.S. military, not really prepared for war, was aided by volunteer cavalry regiments, notably Theodore Roosevelt's Rough Riders. One result of the war, then, was the rise to national prominence of Roosevelt, who in 1900 was chosen as McKinley's vice-president. Another related result was the application of sweeping reforms to enlarge and strengthen the U.S. armed forces. Most significantly, the Spanish-American War marked a turn in U.S. foreign policy. In winning the war, the U.S. gained control over Puerto Rico, Guam, and the Philippines, and this in turn led to increased American interest in the Far East. By the war's end it had become clear that the Spanish-American War had been not just a war to liberate Cuba from Spain but an expression of American imperialism.

A clear, detailed thesis, explicit topic sentences, and the use of specific details all strengthen this answer. With the point of the question in mind, Elias gives a full paragraph to each cause of the war. Topic sentences distinguish between major and minor causes. Then he summarizes the war's principal results in just one paragraph. Throughout the essay, transitional elements ("This slanted reporting," "The first of the events," "just after this," "The results of this brief war") give the reader clear signals to follow. Notice how closely Elias follows the thesis and plan he developed during the prewriting and arranging stages of his work (page 280).

PARAGRAPH-LENGTH ANSWERS

Sometimes a question asks not for a full essay but for a paragraph. Your instructor will specify this, both in explicit instructions and by the relative value assigned to the question. (A question worth 25 percent or less in an hour-long exam is usually paragraph length.)

Use the criteria that apply to any strong paragraph (these are discussed fully in Chapter 5). A paragraph should have a clear *topic sentence* that summarizes the information it contains. Just as an essay answer begins with the thesis statement, a paragraph answer has its topic sentence at the beginning, so the reader immediately knows what to expect. You should phrase this topic sentence so that, in general terms, it answers the examination question. The paragraph should also be *coherent*—that is, its ideas should be linked by transitions that move the reader along. Finally, the paragraph should be as *complete* as possible. You must provide enough relevant detail to convince your reader that you know what you are talking about.

A typical paragraph-length response might look like Wanda Wilks's answer on a geography midterm:

Question

In one paragraph, identify and briefly characterize each of the six main climates of the world, indicating on what factors this classification of climates is based.

Answer

Topic sentence

Supporting detail

The six main climates of the world, classified on the basis of temperature and precipitation, are tropical humid climates, dry climates, humid mild-winter climates, humid severe-winter climates, polar climates, and mountain climates. Tropical humid climates typically have constant high temperature and heavy rainfall either throughout the year or during one season. Dry climates are characterized by very sparse and uncertain precipitation and exhibit a great range of temperatures. Humid mild-winter climates have lower temperatures during part of the year than tropical humid climates and occasionally show seasonal deficiencies in precipitation. Humid severe-winter climates have longer, colder winters and a greater temperature range from season to season than humid mild-winter climates; rainfall varies a good deal in terms of distribution and amount throughout the year. The polar climates exhibit a mean temperature under 50° F during the warmest month, having virtually no summer. It is difficult to measure precipitation because of drifting snows in the icecap subcategory, and there is little precipitation in the tundra subcategory. The last climate type is the mountain climate, a complex category characterized by many variations in climate conditions within very short distances.

The question asks for a paragraph, so the answer does not present a numbered list or key facts jotted down at random. Wanda used classification to structure her answers. The question suggested this, and she resisted any temptation to compare and contrast or to describe in detail. The key words are *identify and briefly characterize* the climates, so Wanda did that. She says nothing about where each climate is found or what kind of vegetation occurs there. The question clearly indicates that this material would be irrelevant. Instead, her answer progresses in orderly fashion from one category to the next, echoing the wording of the question to gain emphasis and coherence.

SAMPLE EXAMINATION ANSWERS

Study the following examination questions. Each is accompanied by two answers, the first strong, the second weak.

1.   History of Art examination—paragraph length

Question
In a brief paragraph, give a definition and two examples of minimalist sculpture.

Answer A
Minimalists believe in reducing sculpture to its basic form, shape, or outline. They stress the way their sculptural works fit into the environment rather than emphasizing the works themselves. They prefer basic geometric forms and industrial materials like aluminum and steel. In fact, minimal art uses the methods of industry: artists draw up plans, make plywood models, and then give each model to an industrial shop where the sculpture is produced. Minimal art may appear indoors or outdoors, but it is *not* likely to be formally displayed on a pedestal. Two notable examples of minimal art are Bernard Rosenthal's *Alamo* and Tony Smith's *Smoke*.

Answer B
The twentieth century saw many new developments in art. These included abstract expressionism, cubism, neodada and pop art, conceptual and op art, serialism, kinetic art, and minimal art. Minimal art, developed in the 1960s, makes use of industrial materials like aluminum and steel.

Analysis   The first paragraph starts with a clear topic sentence that defines minimalist sculpture by stating its basic philosophy. The answer expands the definition with description, process explanation, and negation, using sufficient detail and concluding with the required two examples. The second paragraph, however, begins with a sentence that does not address the question at all. The information is all true enough, but none of it was asked for. This answer never defines minimalist sculpture, and it entirely omits the examples the question calls for.

2.   American Literature examination—essay length (1 hour)

Question

The 1890s saw the beginning of the machine age in America, as technological developments increased rapidly. At this time, major writers like William Dean Howells, Mark Twain, Stephen Crane, and Frank Norris began to respond to the realities of American life. Minor writers also began to work with more realistic themes. Choose three minor nineteenth-century writers whose works we studied this term and in an essay discuss in detail how their work addressed the social problems caused by America's new technology and increasingly diverse, increasingly urban population.

Answer A

Unlike many of their predecessors, Hamlin Garland, Ambrose Bierce, and Kate Chopin explicitly address the not-always-pleasant realities of the changing American society in their writing.

Hamlin Garland was a "local-color" writer. The intent of most of these nineteenth-century regional writers was to convey, through a sentimental picture of customs and landscape, the sense of a particular locale rather than anything more inclusively "American." Garland's setting is the Midwest, where he had been brought up on various homesteads. But unlike local-color writers who preceded him, Garland focuses not on the picturesque charm of the region, but on the social injustices which his characters—farmers—are subject to. In *Main-Travelled Roads*, his collection of short stories, he writes largely of poor, tired people, beaten down by the hard life of farming. In several stories Garland focuses on a man returning to rural life after living in the city, invariably finding misery and hopelessness on the farm of his youth; another recurring theme is the drudgery and isolation of the farmer's wife. Throughout the book, farm life is not idealized or sentimentalized but shown to be characterized by hard work, monotony, and extreme financial deprivation.

Another writer who writes about the realities of life in the 1890s is Ambrose Bierce, who had experienced brutality and violence first-hand as a soldier in the Civil War. He remained bitter and cynical in his postwar career as a newspaperman in England and San Francisco. As a reporter, he extended his anger and cynicism to the rest of American life, seeing it to be in some ways just as brutal and grotesque as the war. The Civil War stories he wrote during the 1880s depend heavily on improbable coincidences, with heroism often ironically unrecognized. The stories, such as "An Occurrence at Owl Creek Bridge" and "One of the Missing," focus on death and destruction. Rather than stressing glory and heroic acts as some other war stories did, Bierce sees the grim, violent truth. In fiction and nonfiction, war stories and others, Bierce sees life as brutal, impersonal, and full of unpleasant surprises.

Kate Chopin also departs from the typical conventions of her genre. Like Garland's focus on grim poverty and Bierce's on violence and senseless tragedy, Kate Chopin's thrust is also realistic. Chopin's mother was French and her husband was a Creole; her married life was spent in New Orleans. As a result, her stories' setting and characters seem more French than American. While many of her early stories are quite conventional, with her characters' sensuality kept under control, her novel *The Awakening,* which deals with adultery, brings it to the surface. Chopin's heroine, Edna Pontellier, is bored by her routine life as wife and mother and yearns for something more. This yearning is symbolized by the seductive murmuring of the sea at the summer resort at which she is staying. She focuses her desires on Robert Le Brun, a handsome young man, and her yearnings soon turn to sexual desire. When, after an adulterous affair, he leaves her, she commits suicide by swimming out to sea. *The Awakening* addresses modern realism by acknowledging the power of physical desire and suggesting that marriage and family do not necessarily mean complete fulfillment for a woman.

These three minor writers, unlike some of their predecessors, face the harsh realities of American society as it approached the twentieth century. Garland looks squarely at rural poverty, Bierce at violence and impersonality, and Chopin at sensuality and the role of women. While not major writers, they confront major problems and work with major themes.

Analysis   This complex and detailed question requires careful reading, but once the student has isolated the key words, she realizes that the question suggests a fairly simple organization. She needs to deal with only three writers in turn (that is, she need not compare them or evaluate their work) and to show how they used realistic themes. So her answer focuses largely on the content (not the style or form) of these authors' works. Only *minor* writers are asked for, and only those studied *in the course.*

This student begins with a thesis statement, a rewording of the question in this case, and she uses clear topic sentences, tied explicitly to the thesis. In her body paragraphs, she emphasizes how these writers departed from other writers in their respective genres, and she clearly shows how their writing addressed American social problems. Her transitional expressions—"Another writer," "Kate Chopin also departs," "These three minor writers"—help the reader to move from paragraph to paragraph.

Answer B

Many well-known American writers of the 1890s chose to face head-on the not-always-pleasant realities of the changing American society. Three of these writers are Theodore Dreiser, Ambrose Bierce, and Kate Chopin.

Theodore Dreiser, when he wrote *Sister Carrie* in 1900, was facing the grim realities of contemporary American life—labor strife, poverty, unemployment, even suicide. Frank Norris, who died at 32, was also very much the realist. In *McTeague* he treats alcoholism, obsessive greed for money, and finally murder. In *The Octopus* he reports the bitter struggle between ranchers and the Southern Pacific Railroad. Stephen Crane's *Maggie: A Girl of the Streets* is, like Dreiser's *Sister Carrie,* a tale of urban poverty and a young woman's desperation. Crane, like Norris, died young; he was only 28.

Ambrose Bierce wrote many stories about the violence of the Civil War. He found war to be bloody and gruesome, full of violence and brutality. His Civil War stories are full of improbable coincidences and ironic twists. Stories frequently depend on a twist or a coincidence for their impact. Like Stephen Crane, he did not write of glory or heroism. His stories do not show glory attained or heroic acts honored. War, for Bierce, is brutal and violent.

In Kate Chopin's *The Awakening,* her heroine, Edna Pontellier, is a wife and mother vacationing near the sea with her children. She is bored and restless and feels yearnings for something more than the life she has, and the ocean seems to echo or even encourage these vague yearnings. She becomes sexually attracted to a young man and has an adulterous affair. When he leaves her, she commits suicide.

Each of these different writers, then, faces reality in his or her writing.

Analysis   Unfortunately, the opening sentence of this answer reveals that the student has misread the question. Not seeing that only minor writers are asked for, he plunges into a discussion of Theodore Dreiser, Frank Norris, and Stephen Crane, all major writers, reserving too little time for his treatment of Ambrose Bierce and Kate Chopin. His discussion of Dreiser, besides being irrelevant, does not deal with writing of the 1890s. Norris and Crane do not appear in the thesis. The injection of irrelevant details—Norris's and Crane's ages at their deaths—is simply meant to fill up space and impress the reader.

When the student finally gets to Bierce, he rambles and repeats himself in pairs of sentences that say essentially the same thing. His treatment of Chopin, like his paragraph on Bierce, makes no attempt to relate her work to the question. The plot summary of *The Awakening* says nothing about his thesis.

The conclusion does state that these writers are realists, but the writer has done nothing to demonstrate this. The irrelevant details, the plot summary without interpretation, the topic sentences unrelated to the thesis, and the thesis which does not address the question make this an unsatisfactory answer, even though well-written and somewhat informative.

EXERCISE

In each of the following pairs of examination answers, one is clearer, more complete, and more pertinent to the question than the other. Identify the better answer, and then analyze the strengths and weaknesses of both.

1.   Business law examination

Question

In one paragraph, distinguish between a sole proprietorship and a partnership, briefly noting the advantages and disadvantages of each kind of organization.

Answer A

A sole proprietorship is a firm owned by one person, who owns all the firm's assets and is responsible for all its debts. In a partnership, two or more people voluntarily agree to become co-owners of the business. A partnership is easy to set up and dissolve, and two partners can raise more equity capital and borrow more than one. This is a disadvantage of a sole proprietorship. Another disadvantage is unlimited personal liability, which is also a drawback for a partnership. A sole proprietorship is also easy to set up and dissolve, and it has the added advantage of giving its owner the freedom to make decisions independently. A partnership is harder to terminate than a sole proprietorship, because a partner wanting to leave the business must locate an acceptable buyer for his or her interests or else sell out to the remaining owner. A sole proprietorship has one distinct advantage: the owner does not have to share the profits. Still, a sole proprietor is less free to expand or diversify because capital and borrowing power are determined by one person's assets. On the other hand, a partnership may be troubled by personal conflicts among the partners.

Answer B

A sole proprietorship is a firm owned by one person, who may or may not also manage the firm. This person owns all the firm's assets and is responsible for all its debts. The advantages are the ease of setting up and dissolving the organization, the freedom and personal satisfaction derived from being able to make decisions independently, and the fact that the proprietor doesn't have to share the profits. The main disadvantage is unlimited personal liability; another drawback is the difficulty of expanding or diversifying, because the proprietor is limited to his or her own capital and borrowing power. A partnership is a firm set up by two or more persons who voluntarily agree to become co-owners of the business. It too has the advantage of being easy to set up and dissolve. In addition, a partnership can raise more equity capital and has greater borrowing ability because all of the partners' personal wealth can contribute capital and pay debts. This is a distinct advantage over the sole proprietorship. Still, the partnership shares with the sole proprietorship the problem of unlimited financial liability. In addition, the partnership is harder to terminate than the sole proprietorship, because a partner wanting to leave the business must locate an acceptable buyer for his or her interests or else sell out to the remaining owner. Until this is accomplished, the partnership may be troubled by personal conflicts among the partners.

2.   Sociology examination

Question

Emile Durkheim and other functionalists view social institutions as performing useful social functions which at the same time preserve the society. Write an essay defining the term "social institution," identifying the major institutions in our society and explaining how each contributes to perpetuation of our society as it meets our basic human needs.

Answer A

A social institution is a kind of human group which is important in all societies; unlike associations, which are usually private and have limited purposes, institutions are likely to be public and have numerous purposes. Social institutions influence our behavior, and because they meet basic human needs, they may be indispensable to us. At different times in our lives, however, we become more or less dependent on different kinds of institutions. Similarly, at different times in a society's history, certain institutions may become more important: in medieval times, the church dominated, and today the state supplies many of the basic needs that were formerly met by the family or the church. Moreover, the different social institutions in our society are constantly interacting with one another; sometimes their goals are compatible, and sometimes they are in conflict. Today, the most important institutions can be classified as those whose primary goal is to meet emotional needs through socialization and integration—the family, the educational system, and the church—and those whose goals are to produce and distribute goods and services—the state, the military, and technology.

The family, church, and educational system all socialize people; that is, they give them the society's values, roles, norms, and skills so they can function in the society. More specifically, the principal functions of the modern family are to reproduce and raise children, to transmit status and parental values, and to give affection. At one time the family had many more functions (such as responsibility for education) which have since been taken over by other institutions. Now, as the society as a whole grows more and more impersonal, the family's role as affection giver has become increasingly important.

The functions of the educational system in our society have broadened as those of the family have narrowed. Now the educational system's specific functions include not only teaching basic skills and information, but also preparing students for the competitive larger society through organized athletics and by transmitting political values, teaching sophisticated technical skills required by the increasingly complex society, and transmitting cultural skills needed to enter upper status levels.

The church encourages a commitment to ideal values like peace and equality and also provides comfort through its appeal to tradition. Thus while it is on the one hand dynamic and even radical, on the other hand it is static and conservative. Both of these roles are needed by citizens in our society, who must keep a sense of stability while at the same time adapting to change.

Other social institutions have as their main purpose the production and distribution of various goods and services. The state, for instance, uses power to maintain social order and create a common culture among its citizens. Through the political system it legitimizes authority and sets up processes of collective decision making for the good of all. Through its laws it maintains order and controls deviants. Each of these functions serves to strengthen and preserve the society.

The function of the military is to preserve the society by defending it against aggression, maintaining enough power to discourage aggression by outside societies, engaging in offensive acts when necessary, and maintaining law and order within a society.

Technology as an institution consists not just of machines and inventions and tools but of an interrelated group of norms and values and ideas that help people develop and adapt knowledge and techniques to meet their basic needs. In its broad sense, then, technology refers to the way citizens work in an organized fashion to satisfy their basic needs. Technology—in the form of multinational corporations—can also be viewed as a power institution, as the state and the military are, and the role of technology as an institution is expanding and growing increasingly complex. Again, the institution serves basic human needs while perpetuating society's goals.

Each of the major institutions—family, church, educational system, state, military, and technology—provides a share of our basic human needs; at the same time, as shown above, each perpetuates the society by reinforcing the basic norms, values, roles, and skills that help citizens function as part of that society.

Answer B

Social institutions are very important to all of us. They influence our behavior, and they meet our basic human needs. Functionalists like Durkheim see social institutions as performing useful social functions while at the same time preserving the society. The major social institutions in our society are the family, the church, the educational system, the state, the military, and technology.

The major functions of the family are to reproduce and raise children, to transmit status and parental values, and to give affection. The major functions of the educational system are to teach basic skills and information, prepare students for the competitive larger society, transmit political values, and transmit cultural and technical skills.

The church's functions are to encourage a commitment to important values and to provide comfort. The functions of the state are complex: it maintains social order, legitimizes authority, sets up processes of collective decision making and maintains internal order.

The military is the institution that defends the society against aggression by outside societies, engages in offensive acts when necessary, and maintains law and order within the society.

Finally, technology helps to meet our basic needs. The role of technology as an institution is expanding and growing increasingly complex. In this complex society we need new ideas and inventions. These ideas and inventions can help us meet our basic needs. Consequently, technology is very important.

These six institutions—the family, the church, the educational system, the state, the military, and technology—all help us meet our basic needs and at the same time contribute to the perpetuation of society.

CHAPTER

12

Business Letters and Memos

A recent article in the *Wall Street Journal* observed that letters and memos are the mortar that holds corporate America together. At every level, the author notes, business people seem to have an overwhelming need "to put it in writing."

Many of you will need to write a letter to a business in the near future—to apply for a job or admission to graduate or professional school, to register a complaint, or to request information. A number of you, especially those in work-study programs or with part-time jobs, will write memos as well.

BUSINESS LETTERS

Although the principles of the writing process are the same, the *boundaries* of business writing make it different from academic writing. When you write a letter to a business, your purpose is usually to get action, to influence readers, or to provide information. Your audience is someone from whom you expect a response. Most businesses receive many letters daily—so many, in fact, that no one person can read them carefully. So you must always be brief and clear. Present essential information first, and include only the material that the reader needs to know. Digressions or irrelevant details make your reader stop reading. Like all the writing tasks we have discussed so far, business letters require careful planning and revision.

DRAFTING YOUR LETTER

Most business letters are about a specific problem or situation. Before you write, get the reason for your letter clearly in mind. Your purpose and your main idea help you choose what material to include. Next, make a skeleton outline, a list of your points in order. After this, write a rough draft and *set it aside*. This "cooling off" period is especially important when you write letters of complaint, where your emotions might be running high. Finally, reread your draft, making sure that what you have said is appropriate to the situation. Be careful to edit for spelling and mechanics—errors are particularly obvious when they appear in letters. After checking your draft one last time, prepare the final typed draft.

THE TONE OF YOUR LETTER

Being concise in a business letter does not mean being curt or nasty. A letter is a substitute for a conversation, and it should sound natural and flow freely. Business correspondence has no "special language," and you should use your own voice and avoid jargon like "re your letter of the 12th" or "I would like a reply forthwith." Nor does a formal style sound "businesslike." Overusing the passive voice, for instance, makes your letters cold and stuffy. Compare "please send more information" with "it would be appreciated if more information could be sent."

Sarcasm, bluntness, and hostility are almost always out of place in the business letters you write. Negative letters seldom achieve your purpose, and they can backfire, turning a friendly or neutral reader hostile. Your reader is not "the company," but a human being too: whenever possible, you should demonstrate your concern for his or her interests. You might be tempted to say, for instance, that if you don't receive a refund, you'll never use a company's product again. You might get better results, however, if you remind the reader of the company's good reputation, which you hope it will not risk losing. Remember, the manner of your presentation should be governed not only by what you feel, but by what will accomplish your purpose.

THE APPEARANCE OF YOUR LETTER

Just as your appearance influences anyone's first impression of you, the appearance of your business letter determines a reader's initial response to it. A letter neatly arranged on the page, typed well, and free of smudges and errors makes a favorable impression. A letter that is sloppy and filled with misspellings presents both you and your request in a bad light.

Writing an appealing business letter is usually not difficult; it just takes time and preparation. Make sure that your typewriter ribbon is new and that the typewriter keys are clean. Type slowly and accurately, making sure that each key makes a clear impression. Use good-quality bond paper—never the thin erasable type—and use standard-sized envelopes and paper. If you make an error that you cannot correct neatly, retype the entire letter. Decide in advance how wide your top and bottom margins should be so that you can center your letter on the page. The space between the top of the page and the top line of your heading should be about equal to the space between your signature and the bottom of the page.

THE PARTS OF YOUR LETTER

Business letters have a number of standard sections that your readers expect to see. These conventions provide important information to a reader, and you should include them in every piece of business correspondence you send.

1.   The heading   The heading consists of the *writer's* full address and the date. When you use company stationery, which already has a letterhead, you provide only the date two spaces below the letterhead.

The first line of your heading should include the street address from which you sent your letter. (Do *not* include your name; that appears at the end of your letter.) The second line gives your city, state, and Zip Code. Words like Street, Avenue, Road, Place, East, and West should be spelled in full, but you may abbreviate states using the Postal Service list of abbreviations. The date comes on the next line, with the name of the month written in full. Each line of the heading should fall directly under the one above it, aligned at the left.

```
                                        7538 Beach Boulevard
                                        Jacksonville, FL 32216
                                        March 12, 1984
```

2.   The inside address   The inside address identifies the *recipient's* name and address. As in the heading, each line is flush left under the one above it. You should always use a title before the name on the inside address and include the recipient's full address.

Use a person's previous correspondence, if you have any, as your guide. If a company abbreviates Corporation as Corp. or Associates as Assoc., then you should, too. And be careful to use correct names and titles. Don't address someone as P. K. Phelps if he signs his letters Peter K. Phelps. If a person uses a title such as Ms., Dr., or Professor, then so should you. Finally, don't follow a name with a title that is redundant: not Dr. Ralph Most, Ph.D., or Dr. Susan Geller, M.D., when Dr. Ralph Most or Susan Geller, M.D., are sufficient. Here is an example of an inside address that illustrates these points:

```
Mr. Earl B. Hamilton
Superintendent
Methods and Training Division
Philadelphia Electric Company
1060 Swedesford Road
Berwyn, PA 19312
```

3.   The salutation   Type the salutation two spaces below the inside address, full out to the left margin. In business letters the salutation is always followed by a colon. Usually the salutation uses a title (Dr., Ms., Mrs., Mr.), followed by the last name of the recipient as it appears in the inside address. If you are on a first-name basis with someone, use his or her full name and title in the inside address, but the first name in the salutation.

If you are addressing your letter to a woman, look at previous correspondence and use the title that she uses there. If you don't know the recipient's preference, use Ms., which takes the place of Mrs. or Miss. When you don't know whether you are addressing a man or a woman, J. L. Wilson, for instance, you can call the switchboard of the company and ask whether J. L. Wilson is male or female; or you can use a neutral form of address like "Dear Supervisor," or "Dear Editor."

If you are writing to an unknown person—the Director of Personnel, for example—your salutation, using the tag "Attention:" rather than "Dear . . . ," should route your letter to a specific department.

```
Bamberger's Department Store
Cherry Hill Mall
Cherry Hill, NJ 08008

Attention: Director of Personnel

I saw your advertisement for salespeople in the Sunday . . . .
```

Or you could include a subject line in your letter.

```
Hammer Products
8515 State Road
Houston, TX 77055

Subject: Request for Information

    I am a student at Wayne State University and am interested in
the process you developed . . . .
```

Keep in mind that salutations such as "Gentlemen" and "Dear Sirs" (along with "Dear Sir or Madam") are antiquated and are no longer considered standard business usage.

4.   The body   Single-space the body of your business letter and begin it two spaces below the salutation. Body paragraphs are often not indented, but when they are, they are indented five spaces from the left-hand margin. Paragraphs are separated from each other by double spaces. With very short letters you can double-space throughout and begin each new paragraph by indenting five spaces from the left.

5.   The complimentary close   More and more, business communications are assuming a personal tone, and the all-purpose "Yours truly" is gradually being replaced by the less formal "Sincerely" or "Sincerely yours." Of course, your complimentary close should agree in tone with the rest of your letter. If you are on friendly terms with the recipient, "Cordially," "Best wishes," or "Sincerely" might be appropriate. Serious matters might call for the more formal "Yours truly" or "Respectfully yours."

The complimentary close begins two spaces below the body of your letter and flush left under it or toward the right side of the page. Capitalize only the first word and end the entire expression with a comma. Leave about four spaces below the complimentary close for your signature and type your name and title in full.

```
      Sincerely yours,

      Joseph Knepper

      Joseph Knepper
      Station Manager
```

THE FORMAT OF YOUR LETTER

Business letters have two widely used formats: *full-block* and *semi-block*. The full-block letter begins every line at the left-hand margin (flush left), and this format makes it very easy to type. You usually use the full-block arrangement with letter-head stationery. With the semi-block letter, the heading and the complimentary close start toward the right side of the page, aligned with each other. The inside address, salutation, and body paragraphs align on the left-hand margin.

Most companies use a standard form for their letters. When working for a company or business, ask what style the company uses and conform to its practices. Examples of full-block and semi-block formats are on pages 298 and 299.

PARAGRAPHS IN BUSINESS LETTERS

Paragraphs in business letters are often short. The first and last paragraphs frequently run no more than a sentence or two. Be careful, however, that you don't fall into the habit of beginning a new paragraph with each sentence. As in any writing, each paragraph must contain a meaningful segment of thought.

Full-Block Letter (with letterhead)

Letterhead	***The Upjohn Company*** ***Kalamazoo, Michigan 49001 USA***
Date	February 26, 1984
Inside address	Ms. Betsey O'Hara 237 College Avenue Chicago, IL 60680
Salutation	Dear Ms. O'Hara:
Body	Thank you for your letter of February 7 in which you inquired about the vitamin tablets you have been taking. Federal law requires us to post a warning statement on every bottle of vitamins that we sell. Rest assured that the dosage of specific vitamins, especially A and D, is well below the maximum allowable dose. The package insert that we include with all our vitamin products presents information about dosage levels and vitamin products. We appreciate your interest in the Upjohn Company. If we may be of further assistance, please feel free to contact us.
Complimentary close	Very truly yours, THE UPJOHN COMPANY
Signature	
Typed name Title	William Abbott Public Relations

Although no one can prescribe what should go into each paragraph of a business letter—each letter varies according to its subject and purpose—certain paragraphs do have certain functions.

Beginnings   The first paragraph of a business letter performs three important functions:

Semi-Block Letter (without letterhead)

Heading on the right

173 Meadowfield Drive
Southampton, Pennsylvania 18966
April 12, 1984

Inside address

Mr. Walter Johnson
Plant Manager
Product Development Division
CompuSystems Inc.
6000 Wynnwood Road
Golden Valley, Minnesota 55422

Salutation

Dear Mr. Johnson:

Body

Thank you so much for allowing me to tour your plant on April 10. The information I received will help me formulate my career goals and be more specific in my choice of a major.

I especially enjoyed seeing your computer graphics division. I now feel certain that I want to become involved in some facet of this new and rapidly developing area. Any advice you could give me concerning my goal will be greatly appreciated.

Again, thank you very much.

Complimentary close also on the right

Sincerely yours,

Signature

Marty Joyce

Typed name

Marty Joyce

1. It states the subject and purpose of your letter
2. It refers to previous correspondence
3. It establishes a satisfactory tone

Most businesses receive a lot of mail. To get the attention that you want, you must announce your subject and purpose immediately. Make clear just how your message concerns the reader. A vague or irrelevant beginning gives your reader a negative impression of you and your letter. If you are responding to previous correspondence, say so. Mentioning key names, places, or dates saves your reader valuable time.

Your opening must also establish a satisfactory tone. A negative beginning or an overly formal introduction alienates your reader. Often only a word or two changes a neutral tone to a positive one.

Neutral tone

```
We received your letter of June 5, in which you asked us for
shipping fees.
```

Positive tone

```
Thank you for your letter of June 5, in which you asked us for
shipping fees.
```

Of course, too positive a tone is out of place in some situations—in a letter of complaint, for instance. Even so, you should always be polite if you want to get results.

Here are some effective sample beginnings:

```
I would like to apply for the sales position you advertised in
the Post on Sunday, October 8.
```

```
Thank you for your letter of September 28 inquiring about the
Communications Program at Stanford University.
```

```
I recently received my August bill and was surprised to find
that I was charged for an item I did not purchase.
```

Body paragraphs   The body of your letter should carry your message clearly and convincingly in terms of your purpose, audience, and scope. Body paragraphs might contain questions that you want answered or information that you wish to convey. In any case, the material should be arranged in an orderly, understandable fashion.

Endings   Because the ending of your letter stays with your reader, it is a good place to focus attention on the points you want to reinforce. If your letter solicits donations, end with a plea for funds. If it complains about a defective product, conclude with a statement of the adjustment you want. Whenever possible, the ending of your letter should attempt to ensure good will. At the end of a letter requesting information, for instance, you might say that the material will contribute to the success of your project.

The four specific purposes of the business letters you will write most often are (1) to apply for jobs, (2) to apply for further education, (3) to request information, and (4) to register a complaint.

JOB APPLICATIONS

Your letter of application is above all a letter in which you sell yourself. Your primary objective is to convince a prospective employer that you are suited for a specific job.

Many job seekers don't focus on the real function of their application letter: it does not get you a job, it gets you an interview. So, you must state your case in a way that stimulates interest and makes your reader want to talk to you in person. Avoid tired phrases and empty generalizations. Before writing make a list of your strengths and qualifications and refer to this list as you write. And make your case in interesting yet concrete terms. Don't say "I have experience" when you can discuss your experience in some detail. Don't settle for "I am a good worker" or "I have had relevant courses" when you can provide concrete examples. Above all, present yourself in a favorable way that differentiates you from other job candidates.

Your letter of application should accomplish three things:

1.   It should identify the job you are applying for as well as where you heard about it.

2.   It should list your qualifications, including relevant courses, honors, work experience, and any other information that highlights your unique qualities.

3.   It should tell when you will be available for an interview and refer your reader to your résumé.

Begin by identifying the specific job you want and where you saw it advertised. If you saw an ad in a journal or newspaper, provide the full name of the paper and the date the ad appeared. If a teacher or company recruiter recommended the job to you, mention his or her name in your letter. End your first paragraph with your own assessment of your ability to do the job.

```
     I would like to be considered for the sales-specialist
position that I saw advertised in the Los Angeles Times on
Sunday, March 23.  I feel that my academic background and my
job experience qualify me for this job.
```

The body of your letter should prove to your reader that you are a serious candidate for the job. Discuss the relevant courses you have had and expand upon your job experience. If it is a sales job, mention the product lines you know and the success you had selling them. Don't forget to address the specific concerns that the employer mentioned in the ad. If an ad for a job calls for writing experience or familiarity with a word processor, mention your experience in these particular areas.

Conclude your letter by referring your reader to your résumé and by requesting an interview. If you are or will be near the company's offices, include the dates and times you will be available. If you cannot go on interviews because of school or other commitments, let your prospective employer know this. Remember that the conclusion of your letter should be smooth and natural. You must reflect confidence without being pushy. Never use phrases like "I will expect to hear from you" or "I want to meet with you by November 23."

A student, Ann O'Connel, wrote the following letter to apply for a part-time job:

104 East Mill Road
Hartford, CT 06103
May 23, 1984

Dr. Arthur Cataldi
Department of Pathology
Mount Sinai Hospital
Hartford, CT 06112

Dear Dr. Cataldi:

I would like to apply for the position of part-time lab assistant that my organic chemistry instructor, Dr. Stuart Baker, told me about. I feel both my academic background and my work experience qualify me for this job.

I am presently a junior biology major at the University of Connecticut. During the past year I have taken courses in biochemistry, cytology, and physical chemistry. I have had experience in the laboratory and am familiar with most basic procedures. Last summer I worked for the Federal Drug Administration studying the effects of artificial sweeteners on rats. In this position, I prepared frozen sections and did computer correlations of study results.

After graduation I expect to apply to medical school and eventually become a pathologist. Working in your department would enable me to gain more insight into this field as well as contribute something to it.

I have enclosed a résumé, and I will be available for an interview at your convenience.

Sincerely yours,

Ann O'Connel

Ann O'Connel

Before she wrote her letter, Ann brainstormed and listed the strengths that would qualify her for the job. She decided to begin her letter by identifying the job and the person who told her about it. She knew that her prospective employer would only be interested in relevant experience, so she did not mention her part-time job in the library or her work for a local day-care center. She tried out different arrangements in two different drafts, eventually deciding to tell about her courses, her summer job, and her future plans. To appeal to her audience, she mentioned how working as a lab assistant could help her gain insight into her field.

A graduating senior looking for a full-time job wrote this letter.

```
                                    2742 Kent Road
                                    Columbus, Ohio 43221
                                    May 20, 1984


Mr. Gerald Fisher
Personnel Manager
Barclays American Business Credit
1000 Herrontown Road
Princeton, New Jersey 08540


Dear Mr. Fisher:


I am applying for the Management Trainee position
you advertised in the New York Times on Sunday,
May 6.  My course work in industrial and commer-
cial finance plus my work experience convinces me
that I would be a good candidate for this posi-
tion.


I am a senior marketing and finance major at Ohio
State University and will graduate this
June.  While pursuing my dual major, I have main-
tained a 3.5 average and have held several
offices in my fraternity.  I have taken advanced
courses in industrial finance and an elective in
industrial and commercial credit instruments.


During the past two summers I have worked for a
commercial bank in Columbus.  I gained experience
in revolving loans secured by receivables and
inventory and term loans secured by plant
and equipment.  I also have a knowledge of asset
analysis and lending techniques.  My experience
in this field has convinced me that I want to
pursue a career in business credit.
```

```
I have enclosed a résumé for your consideration.
You can reach me to arrange an interview any
time after my graduation on June 6.  I look for-
ward to hearing from you.

                              Yours truly,

                              Thomas Chisholm

                              Thomas Chisholm
```

Tom's purpose was to persuade his reader that he is a good candidate for the job. Before beginning his letter, he underlined the qualifications noted in the ad and wrote down his qualifications that matched the job requirements. He carefully included strengths that differentiated him from other candidates. Tom experimented with different openings, and decided to tell where he heard about the job and to promote his potential use to the company. His grade-point average and his dual major were his strongest points, so he led off with them. Then he mentioned two summers of experience at a commercial bank. He wanted to end his letter on a positive note, so he related his job experience to his choice of a business career. Giving his reader a nudge, he ended his letter with the date after which he would be available for an interview.

□ RÉSUMÉS

Your résumé accompanies your letter of application. The résumé gives a prospective employer a concise overview of your qualifications, including your educational background and your work experience. Although it does not focus on a particular job, it must be persuasive.

In order to prepare an effective résumé, you must do some soul searching. In the prewriting phase, ask yourself what kind of job you are applying for and what information a prospective employer would need. Jot down the jobs you have held and list the skills you learned there. Think about your education, too, jotting down important courses, honors, or offices that would interest someone reading your résumé. Make a list of any special skills that make you stand out. Having done this brainstorming, you are ready to prepare your résumé.

There is no single correct format for a résumé. Whatever the arrangement, effective résumés have a number of things in common. They are brief—one page for an undergraduate and no more than two for a graduate student. They are also well organized and neat. Your résumé must look open and inviting. An employer should be able to tell at a glance what your qualifications are. Most résumés contain the following sections:

1.   Heading   Put the title "Résumé" at the top of your sheet, then your name, school address, and home address and phone number beneath the title. Some people include date of birth and marital status, but you don't have to volunteer this information. Federal law prohibits employers from discriminating on the basis of age, marital status, race, or sex.

2.   Education   List the schools you have attended, starting with the highest level of education you have completed and working back. Undergraduates list high school, but graduates list only colleges. State your major field of study, and include any academic honors or special courses that might interest an employer. If your college education was largely self-financed or paid for by scholarships, indicate this too. Finally, include your cumulative grade-point average if it is high, but omit it if it is not.

3.   Experience   Start with your most recent job and work back. List your employer, his or her address, the nature of your work, and the dates you were employed. Present only jobs that relate to the job you are applying for. In applying for a permanent job, for example, you wouldn't want to clutter your résumé with the summer lifeguard or babysitting jobs you had when you were fifteen. Present enough information to let your prospective employer know that you are generally competent, but focus his or her attention on experience that applies to the job you want. You can emphasize certain entries by describing the tasks you performed and the special skills you developed.

4.   Background   Here you provide details that show you to be well-rounded. Languages spoken, hobbies, special interests, charity work, and community service can be included under this heading, but don't go overboard.

5.   References   You can give your references in full, listing names, addresses, and phone numbers, or you can say that your references are available on request. In either case, make sure you contact the people you intend to use and get their permission to do so.

6.   Format   Your résumé should be nicely typed and absolutely free of errors. Some people prefer to have their résumés prepared by a service because they think that printing gives a more professional appearance.

Here are two kinds of résumés. The first was prepared by Karl White, a sophomore applying for a sales job at a local insurance company. Notice how he emphasizes his academic background, mentioning his grade-point average in college and his extracurricular activities in high school. He also makes the most of his limited work experience, noting his sales and general business background.

Résumé

Karl White
17 Frog Hollow Road
Austin, Texas 78719
(512)733-2137

Education

1982-1984   University of Texas, Austin, Texas (sophomore).
Marketing major. Expected date of graduation
June 1986. Presently maintain a 3.2 average on a
4.0 scale.

1978-1982   George Mason High School, Fort Worth, Texas.
Cheerleader, debating society, class treasurer,
and community tutor. Graduated in the top quarter of the class.

Experience

1983-1984   University Library, Austin, Texas. Assistant to
the business librarian. Filed, typed, and
catalogued. Also coordinated library acquisitions with publishers. Earnings used to supplement college expenses.

1983, Summer   Consumer Audio Products, Fort Worth, Texas.
Salesperson. Sold audio products to the public.
Learned about promotion and person-to-person
selling. Attended two marketing seminars and one
trade show.

Background   Debating Society (University of Texas). Acting in
local plays, horseback riding, waterskiing.

References   Mr. William Binder, Librarian
Library
University of Texas
Austin, Texas 78767

Ms. Cheryl Carson
Consumer Audio Products
732 Denton Street
Forth Worth, Texas 76101

The second résumé was prepared by Constantina Doukakis, a senior civil engineering student. Because she attended a work-study school, she has eighteen
months of full-time work experience. She highlights her qualifications with a
detailed description of each job and outlines the specific skills she has acquired.

Résumé

Constantina G. Doukakis

Home Address:
331 W. 18th Street
Ardmore, PA 19073
Telephone: (215)353-0777

School Address:
3301 Race Street
Philadelphia, PA 19104
Telephone: (215)387-8140

Education:

Drexel University
5-year Cooperative Education Program
B.S.C.E. expected June, 1984
Course: Civil Engineering, Foundation
Design
Cumulative GPA: 3.5 on a 4.0 base

Honors:

Phi Eta Sigma——Freshman Academic
Honor Society
Chi Epsilon——Civil Engineering Aca-
demic Society
Tau Beta Pi——Engineering Academic
Society
Laurence P. Mains Memorial Scholar-
ship for superior academic achieve-
ment and dedication to career goals

Employment
Experience:

December 24, 1982, to June 14, 1983
——City of Philadelphia, Division of
  Aviation, Philadelphia International Airport, Philadelphia, PA
——Supervised and inspected several
  airfield paving, drainage, and
  utility projects as well as terminal building renovations. Performed on-site and laboratory soil
  tests; prepared concrete samples
  for load testing.

January 2, 1982, to June 8, 1982
——City of Philadelphia, Division of
  Aviation
——Employed as draftsman in the Design
  Office at Philadelphia Interna-
  tional Airport. Prepared contract
  drawings, updated base plans, and

```
                            designed and estimated costs for
                            small construction projects.

                            January 3, 1981, to June 9, 1981
                            --Westinghouse Electric Corp., Power
                              Systems, Lester, PA
                            --Employed as junior engineer in the
                              Plant Eng. Dept. of the Maintenance
                              and Construction Division.  In-
                              spected and supervised in-plant
                              construction; devised solutions,
                              determined costs and ordered mate-
                              rial for small construction proj-
                              ects; gathered and presented his-
                              torical data relating to the
                              function of the department.

Organizations:             American Society of Civil Engineers,
                           Student Chapter. Offices held: Junior
                           Representative, Athletics Chairman.
                           Drexel Technical Journal--Published
                           paper, Fall, 1983.
                           Act 101 Tutor.

Interests:                 Photography, music, squash, racquet-
                           ball, orienteering.

References:                Will be furnished upon request.
```

Many qualified people apply for most full-time jobs. The letter of application and résumé help a prospective employer screen the candidates before any interviewing begins. Some part-time jobs, however, involve only a telephone call and an interview. Here, too, you must consider your audience. Decide which of your qualities will interest the person you talk to. When you contact a prospective employer, be friendly and show that you are an interesting, motivated person. Answer questions directly and forthrightly. When you see a chance to mention an outstanding quality or special skill, don't be bashful: take advantage of the opportunity. And have a copy of your résumé with you at your interview.

☐ FOLLOW-UP LETTERS

It is a good idea to send a follow-up letter to a prospective employer a week or so after your interview. This letter thanks the people you saw for their courtesy and reminds them of your interest in the job. Such follow-up also demonstrates your own courtesy and professionalism.

In this letter you can emphasize what you liked about the interview and rein-force the qualifications that might help you get the job. Finally, make clear your desire for the job and your ability to fulfill the conditions of employment. (See page 299 for a good example of a follow-up letter.)

LETTERS TO GRADUATE OR PROFESSIONAL SCHOOLS

Letters that accompany applications to graduate or professional schools resemble job application letters. Graduate schools and medical, law, and dentistry schools, for example, routinely ask applicants for a letter describing why they want to enter a specific field. These personal statements are scrutinized closely, and along with letters of recommendation, grades, and standardized test scores, they play an important part in your selection. A personal statement tells so much about your goals and maturity that it often decides whether you will be accepted.

Like a job letter, your personal statement should distinguish you from others who apply. Before you write, outline the specific reasons you chose a field, the experience you have, and the long-range goals you envision. When revising your rough draft, take out the empty phrases and abstractions in your statement. Phrases like "I want to help humanity" or "I want to further the cause of justice" may sound good to you, but they give no useful information to an admissions officer. And remember, although this statement reads like a personal-experience essay, it must have a thesis. Everything in your statement must illustrate your commitment to a field and support your belief that you should be admitted to a program. This personal statement was written by a successful candidate for medical school:

> Since high school, I have tried to increase my knowledge and assume new responsibilities. I view myself as a mature, motivated, and self-disciplined person, eager to learn and apply my knowledge and skills to the medical profession to which I am committed. I am confident that I can realistically handle the responsibilities of medical school, as proven by my ability to assume many roles: wife, mother, nurse, teacher, and student.
>
> Although interested in medicine, I pursued a career in nursing, a profession women were encouraged to enter in the small town in which I was reared. After graduating from the Hospital of the University of Pennsylvania School of Nursing and working as a staff nurse, I obtained a B.S. at Temple University on a senatorial scholarship and accepted a teaching position at the Albert Einstein Medical Center School of Nursing. As a teaching institution, Albert Einstein Medical Center gave me the opportunity to work with residents and medical students and to take advantage of many teaching programs. As a result, I became more attracted to medicine and seriously considered it as a profession I would like to enter.
>
> During my seven years at Albert Einstein Medical Center School of Nursing, I was a classroom and clinical nursing in-

structor in various medical—surgical areas, including orthope-
dics, urology, care of the critically ill, emergency room
nursing, and public health nursing. I was evaluated by both
faculty and students and judged to be an enthusiastic and con-
scientious person who stressed individualized, patient—centered care.

   While I was continuing my education and teaching, my
mother was involved in forming the Welsh Mountain Clinic of
Lancaster County, a facility for the socioeconomically de-
prived of the area. As a visiting nurse, she realized that
the facility was needed, and as director, she arranged for
residents and nursing students to participate in the delivery
of health care. Whenever possible, I assisted in the clinic.
This experience increased my understanding of the role of the
physician and of the need for quality care for the underprivi-
leged. It reinforced my desire not only to become a physician, but also to specialize in family practice.

   I feel that my background has given me insight and an
awareness of my responsibility to the medical profession and
to society. My exposure to the medical field throughout the
many phases of my nursing career has provided me with the in-
centive to pursue my interest in medicine. My academic record
and my experiences in nursing and teaching make me confident
that the medical profession is a realistic goal for me.

This personal statement went through eight drafts and numerous minor revisions.
The person who wrote it asked several of her instructors and a medical doctor to
read versions of it. She incorporated their suggestions into her final draft and asked
an English instructor to check it for errors.

   The finished statement contains lots of detail. It describes how the applicant
became interested in a medical career and gives her reasons for believing she would
be successful in medicine. Her list of the skills developed as a nurse and nursing
instructor proves that she is aware of the responsibilities of her proposed career.
Her experience with her mother in the Welsh Mountain Clinic and her desire to
specialize in family medicine establish her maturity.

   The organization here emphasizes the experience that led this woman to
choose medicine as a career. Each paragraph makes a major point and backs it up
with supporting evidence. The statement begins and ends with an overview in
which the candidate assesses her skills, background, and personality. The body
paragraphs present, in chronological order, the developments that led her to apply
to medical school. It is no surprise that the applicant was accepted.

   In a personal statement, the difference between success and failure lies in
details, organization, and a clear sense of purpose. A clear and convincing presentation of your qualifications makes a good impression. A disorganized, carelessly
written statement indicates that you might not have the maturity or discipline to
pursue a professional education.

LETTERS REQUESTING INFORMATION

Students sometimes have to send letters requesting information from a person or a business. You might write to an expert in a field to gather material for a research paper. You might write to a company asking for pamphlets or research data about one of its products. Whatever you ask, some general rules apply to letters requesting information.

Your purpose in any letter of inquiry is to get the material you need within a reasonable length of time. To achieve this, your letter must be courteous, specific, and concise. Begin your letter by introducing yourself and telling your reader what information you want and why you want it. Follow this with your list of questions. Assume that your reader is busy and that he or she is doing you a favor in responding. For this reason, keep your questions to a minimum, and request only the information that you need and cannot get from library sources.

Revise to make sure that your questions are clear and properly stated. They will be easiest to deal with if you present them as a numbered list. As a courtesy, end your letter with an expression of gratitude and, if warranted, a promise to send your reader a copy of your finished paper or report.

Here are two examples of letters requesting information. In the following letter, a student asks for production information from a company.

2736 Change Bridge Road
Pine Brook, N.J. 07058
July 27, 1984

Product Development Division
Fisher-Price Toys
636 Girard Avenue
East Aurora, N.Y. 14052

Subject: Product Development

I am a student at Rutgers University and as a summer project I am doing a survey of technical firms that specialize in designing new products.

To complete my study, I would like to know what steps you take to encourage creativity and motivation in the research teams that develop consumer product lines. When I have completed my report, I will send it to the Graduate Placement Office, where I hope it will be of value to students thinking of entering the consumer products industry.

I would appreciate any help you could give me.

Sincerely,

Susan Nagar

Susan Nagar

This letter is short and asks one rather specific question. Susan eliminated a detailed description of her project and her career goals in her revision. Because she did not know to whom specifically to address her letter, she included a subject line and sent it to the Product Development Division. Susan's main problem was to make her letter direct: here she introduces herself in the first paragraph and asks her question in the second. Had she also told Fisher-Price Toys how providing the information might help them, they would have had good reason to answer her request quickly and in detail.

The next letter, by Richard Alonzo, asks for more information.

5712 Columbia Pike
Falls Church, VA 22041
November 11, 1984

Mr. John Wagner
Regional Manager
State Welfare Office
Falls Church, VA 22041

Dear Mr. Wagner:

I am a second-year student at Virginia State College, and I am doing a social work paper that examines the frequency with which welfare recipients use prescription drugs. To complete my paper, I need specific information concerning Medicaid payments and the number of prescriptions issued to people on public assistance:

1. What is the total number of prescriptions issued to Medicaid recipients since September of last year?

2. Do Medicaid recipients request excessive quantities of drugs immediately before they go off public assistance?

3. What was the total cost of prescription drugs to Medicaid recipients last year?

I would greatly appreciate any information you could give me. The finished paper could provide you with useful information, and I would be glad to send you a copy.

Sincerely,

Richard Alonzo

Richard Alonzo

Richard presents only the information that the regional manager of the state welfare office needs to understand his request. He lists his questions and ends by giving his reader a reason to send the information.

LETTERS OF COMPLAINT

Most people write letters of complaint in an effort to resolve a problem. Whatever your problem, you should make your case in a straightforward manner. Avoid sarcasm or any digression that makes you seem petty or irrational. Try to present yourself as a reasonable person who can see both sides of an issue and who expects to have a complaint taken seriously. If a rational tone is difficult to maintain, and especially if you are upset or angry, put off writing your final draft until you have calmed down. It is the logic and strength of your claim, not name calling or empty threats, that will cause a company to act. Venting your anger may feel good to you, but it gives your reader a good excuse to dismiss your complaint.

Because a letter of complaint should be sensible and well thought out, the prewriting stage of your letter is extremely important. You should list all the facts you need to support your assertions and arrange them in chronological order. In addition, make sure you have essential details, such as serial numbers, receipt numbers, warranty dates, and names. If you need to include documents with your letter, don't send the originals: make good-quality photocopies, number them, and underline the sections that pertain to your case. A few well-chosen examples are better than a flood of paper.

Write with the reader in mind. If your reader is unfamiliar with your case, begin your letter with an overview, not an intricate account of your problem. What happened to you is not yet your reader's primary concern, and he or she needs a general statement that will pave the way for the facts to follow. Often you can do this in a single sentence.

```
On Tuesday, February 23, I bought one of your color televi-
sions, model XM-1753-TW-7, and now find it to be defective.
```

Make sure you give a clear explanation of your case. Recount events in chronological order, with transitions that make sequence apparent to your reader. Make specific reference to any additional material you have included with your letter. And tell your story without editorial comment—why you think the problem occurred or who was at fault. Conclude by saying what you expect from your reader. Be firm but reasonable, and make a request that will help to resolve the problem, not make it worse. Finally, if possible, try to end on a positive note, with a statement that asserts your belief in the good will of the company. For example, here is an effective ending:

```
I feel certain that a company with your fine reputation will
want to remedy this situation as soon as possible.
```

Here are two letters, the first of which deals straightforwardly with a simple complaint.

22 Pine Road
Williamston, N.C. 27892
June 4, 1984

Manager—Consumer Services
General Electric Company
Audio Electronics Products Department
Building 5, Electronics Park
Syracuse, N.Y. 13221

Subject: Defective Tape Recorder

On April 20 I purchased a cassette tape recorder (model number
3-5005) at the Audio Barn in Williamston, North Carolina.
This machine proved to be defective, so I am returning it to
you for a new one.

Shortly after taking the tape recorder home I plugged it in
according to instructions, but nothing happened. I immediately called the Audio Barn and was told that the Barn does
not exchange damaged merchandise and that I would have to have
it repaired at the General Electric service facility in
Greensboro.

I am troubled for two reasons. First, why should I have to
settle for a repaired tape recorder when I purchased a new
one? The machine didn't work when I bought it, and I feel that
you should supply me with a new recorder that is in working
condition. Second, shouldn't the Audio Barn have resolved
this matter for me? Is it really necessary for me to have to
write to you if a situation like this develops?

I am certain that General Electric values its customers, and I
look forward to having this matter settled promptly.

Yours truly,

Ralph Windecker

Ralph Windecker

Ralph controls his tone and presents his problem clearly and concisely. His letter
has a reasonable tone and a positive conclusion. In discussing his complaint,
Ralph carefully includes the correct model number and specific information to
support his claim.

The next letter of complaint deals with a problem that involves a complex
series of events. The writer of this letter is obviously angry; even so, she objectively presents facts that she hopes will settle her difficulties.

                                          505 Pine Street
                                          Tamaqua, PA 18252
                                          June 15, 1984

Superintendent
Presbyterian Hospital
51 North 39th Street
Philadelphia, PA 19104

Subject: Hospitalization error

My name is Lee Ann Cresina (Patient Number E 32248932), and I
am writing about a statement that I received on June 11, 1984,
from Eastern Payco Inc., your collection agency. The agency
incorrectly says that I owe Presbyterian Hospital a total of
$149.65 for the X-ray and treatment of a sprained ankle on
November 21, 1983.

About one week after my treatment, my father's employers, the
Pennsylvania Power and Light Company, sent his Blue Cross and
Blue Shield numbers to your hospital and were assured that
their plan would cover my bill. For a few months I received
bills from the hospital. At my parents' advice, I telephoned
the hospital and learned that my health insurance claims had
to be sent to the Blue Cross office in Harrisburg to be pro-
cessed. I was then told that until Blue Cross paid the bill,
I would be receiving bills from the hospital, but that I
should ignore them.

On March 1, 1984, I received notification from Blue Cross that
Blue Cross had paid Presbyterian Hospital $130.15, leaving a
balance of $19.50. I am under the impression that when Blue
Cross does not cover the total amount, a partial amount may be
accepted; but if it is not, the other party involved sends a
bill for the remainder. I received no such bill from Presbyterian Hospital. Whatever the case, the total I owe is still
only $19.50, not $149.65 as stated. I have enclosed a copy of
my correspondence with Blue Cross from March 1, 1984, to support my claim.

My family has an excellent credit standing; we have never been
delinquent on any bill, Since the people at Blue Cross offered
very little help to us, I am writing this letter in hopes of
straightening this matter out once and for all.

                                     Sincerely yours,

                                     Lee Ann Cresina

                                     Lee Ann Cresina

When planning her letter, Lee Ann knew that she had to present a number of facts clearly. She revised her rough draft several times—adding details, deleting others—until she was satisfied that she had included all relevant information. Her final organization is simple. She introduces herself, gives her patient number, and describes the bill she received. Then she presents the details of her case. She ends by referring to her family's excellent credit rating, stating her hope that the hospital superintendent can resolve her problem.

EXERCISES

1. Look through the want ads of your local paper and select a job that you are qualified to apply for. Following the advice in this chapter, write a letter of application. Present yourself in a way calculated to get you an interview.

2. Make up a résumé outlining your qualifications for a job that you could now fill. Make sure you set up your résumé in a pleasing and convincing way that will increase your chances of getting an interview.

3. Assume you are doing a research project examining methods that museums use to display acquisitions effectively. Formulate a list of questions you could ask, and write a letter requesting information to:

Curator
The Smithsonian Institution
Washington, D.C. 20560

4. Five weeks have now passed since you wrote this letter. Write a follow-up letter in which you remind the Curator of the Smithsonian of your request. Be polite and make the point that you need the information quickly.

5. You live in an area where a work crew is repairing underground power lines. The day is hot and the work is hard. Eventually the workers begin talking loudly and using foul language. Write a letter to Paynow Power and Light Company complaining that such language offends you and your children. In asking the company to put an end to this behavior, take care to keep your sense of proportion and to emphasize the positive qualities of Paynow Power and Light.

6. You are a supervisor of Beach Trucking Company, located at 37 Palm Road, Los Angeles, California. A hundred-yard strip of concrete that has just been laid is deteriorating. Upon investigation, you find that the sidewalk was not reinforced as it was supposed to be. Therefore, your trucks backing up to loading docks behind your building are causing it to crumble. Write a letter to Delco Construction Company, 14 West Latham Place, Los Angeles, and ask the company for a new sidewalk. Explain the situation to them, keeping in mind that they are a reputable company that has always done high-quality work.

MEMOS

Like letters, memoranda vary in tone and purpose, but unlike letters, they are used strictly *within* an organization. Memos are usually brief, but they can be two or three pages long. You can write a short report, a proposal, or a brief note as a memo. Truly "the mortar that holds corporate America together," memos provide information, solve problems, and serve as records of daily business.

Before you write a memo, your prewriting should be thorough. Gather information, brainstorm if necessary, and arrange your material in an appropriate order. Don't forget to consider your audience and your purpose. Only when this is done do you actually write your first draft. Memos, like all writing, should be taken through several revised drafts before you consider them ready to send. Always proofread your final draft, even if someone else typed it. You are accountable for every error, especially those affecting the accuracy of your data.

Although a memo has a conventional structure, don't let its no-nonsense format fool you. Like letters, memos should be designed to address a specific audience for a definite purpose. Most memos, however, regardless of function, contain the following segments:

1.   The opening component
2.   The purpose statement and statement of plan
3.   The body
4.   Conclusions and recommendations

The opening component   In most companies the opening component is fixed and follows a format like this:

```
      To: Arthur Weinstein, Director, Audit Division
    From: Bob Raggi, Auditor
 Subject: Delays in Audit for Research Division
    Date: October 4, 1984
```

The opening component establishes, at a glance, the audience and subject of your memo. A memo may circulate beyond its intended audience, however, and its context must be easily identified. Thus the names and titles of both parties are stated in full. The subject line of your memo must always be more than a single word. For example, "Delay" means little to a reader, even one already familiar with your subject. "Delays in Audit for Research Division" gives your reader a clear idea of what your memo is about.

The purpose statement and statement of plan   People who read memos have very little time, and that is why memos begin with explicit purpose statements. If you write a memo to describe a problem you had with a customer at your part-time sales job, say so directly.

```
The purpose of this memo is to recount the events that took
place on March 7, 1984.
```

In submitting a progress report in memo form, you might say:

```
This memo presents the second progress report for our senior
project.
```

Many people like to include a brief table of contents as well as a purpose statement in their memos. Although your purpose statement tells your audience what you want to accomplish, it does not say how or in what order you intend to do so. A short paragraph (often only a sentence in length) outlining the major sections of your memo helps. It prepares readers for your message, and it helps keep them on track. These short paragraphs could follow the purpose statements above:

```
This memo outlines the situation as it occurred, presents the
steps taken to resolve the customer's complaint, and states
the customer's reactions.

Following is (1) the background of our project, (2) an outline
of what we have done so far, and (3) a list of problems which
we need more time to resolve.
```

Like the purpose statement, a statement of plan helps draw your memo together. Instead of plunging your readers into the middle of your message, you prepare them for what is to follow.

The body of the memo   The body of your memo presents material in the order listed in your statement of plan. To ensure clarity, use headings that repeat the subject designations of the plan.

```
                          Memo 1
The Situation
Steps Taken to Resolve the Customer's Complaint
The Customer's Reactions


                          Memo 2
Background
What We Have Done So Far
Problems Remaining
```

Detailed discussion falls under each heading. The headings themselves act as guides that lead readers through the body of the memo without confusion.

Conclusions and recommendations   The end of your memo, and perhaps the most important part, contains your conclusions and recommendations. Because readers remember best what comes last, end your memo with the actions that should be taken or the conclusions that should be drawn. If your account of the customer's complaint establishes that his reactions were unwarranted, say so. If you feel that you need help to complete your senior project, make your request in your closing.

When you write a memo, you have to adapt your message to your audience and your purpose. The following memos illustrate this point. In the first example, a student transmits information about fraternity pledging to the Dean of Freshmen. Because this memo is short and uncomplicated, it includes no statement of plan and no internal headings.

```
     To: Dr. John D'Alessandro, Dean of Freshmen
   From: Richard Panofsky, President, Interfraternity Council
Subject: Pledging of Freshmen
   Date: October 25, 1984

     As President of the Interfraternity Council, I would like to
inform you of the decisions the Council has made concerning the
pledging of freshmen.

     In the past you told us that because of academic pressures
you thought fraternities on campus should not accept freshmen as
pledges.  As you requested, I introduced this motion to the Coun-
cil at their October meeting.  A majority agreed with your sugges-
tion in principle but disagreed with the contention that students
should not pledge the entire freshman year.  The Council, there-
fore, voted that freshmen should not be allowed to pledge until
the second half of their first year.

     I hope you find this action satisfactory.  I will be glad to
answer any questions you might have concerning this matter.
```

In his planning, Richard was careful to answer the needs of his audience. He did not want to begin his memo telling the Dean of Freshmen that the Interfraternity Council did not agree with him. So he stressed the ways in which both he and the Council accommodated the Dean's wishes and then announced the results of the vote. He hoped to show the Dean that, at least in part, the Council followed his suggestions.

The next memo, a proposal to change the shelving system in a college library, is more complex.

```
     To: Donald Wilson, Head Reference Librarian
   From: Deborah Wolf, Reference Assistant
Subject: Implementing Open Shelves in the Reference Section
   Date: November 17, 1984

     The purpose of this memo is to recommend a new shelving
system for books in the reference section of our library.

     Following are (1) a background statement, (2) a discus-
sion of the new system, and (3) recommendations.
```

Background

    Under the present system of closed shelves, students wishing to consult reference books must fill out a requisition slip, wait in line, give the requisition to a desk person, and wait some more before receiving the desired book. This system is time-consuming, unwieldy, and ineffective. The result is that students do not like to use the reference facility of the library.

New System

    I propose that we switch to an open-shelf system at once. The transition can be made simply by eliminating the desk that forms the front of the reference section. The fear of theft that some people have voiced could be eliminated by using the magnetic detection system that is already in place. The benefits of open shelves would be a reduction in personnel and free access to a needed library resource.

Recommendations

    To implement the open-shelf system we should proceed with the following changes:

1. Eliminate the front reference desk

2. Maintain a central information desk

3. Reassign all but two students who presently work at the front reference desk

    I am certain that these changes will do much to improve the service that this section of the library provides.

The student who wrote the memo knew that her proposal would meet opposition because it challenged a procedure that people were used to. Before writing her memo, she jotted down the problems of the old system. She knew that if she led off her memo with these problems, her audience would be more likely to accept her recommendations. After outlining, the student wrote a rough draft and then revised it. She inserted the major categories of her outline as headings for her memo and brought her recommendations to her readers' attention by putting this information into list form.

EXERCISES

1.   Assume that you are the student representative on a committee established by the president of your university to study the quality of food at your university. Write a memo to the president, summarizing the feelings some of your fellow students have about the cafeteria and the food service. End your memo with several recommendations to improve the present situation.

2.   Comment upon the tone, arrangement, and directness of the following memo.

```
    From: Sally Winter
      To: Dr. Amory Brusaw
 Subject: Lecture
    Date: April 17, 1984

      According to the Faculty Administrator's Guide, all in-
 structors have the obligation to provide service for the aca-
 demic community.

      Last week our sorority decided we would like to examine
 the history of the Women's Movement in America.  Our presi-
 dent, Bettsy Grove, suggested that we consult an expert on the
 faculty and ask him or her to address our group.  After sev-
 eral days of discussion, we finally decided to ask you, since
 you have published several articles in this area.  At first we
 were not sure that you would agree, so we consulted the Fac-
 ulty Guide and realized you had to.

      Our group is interested in the roots of the American suf-
 frage movement.  We intend to invite several experts at dif-
 ferent times to examine this area.  We want you to concentrate
 on the 1920s.  The date we would like you to appear is May 1
 at Spencer Hall, Room 23.

      If you have any questions, you may get in touch with me.
```

3.   After you have analyzed this memo, rewrite it making changes to improve its effectiveness. Keep in mind that Sally Winter is the secretary of her sorority and that Dr. Amory Brusaw is a nationally recognized expert in his field.

CHAPTER

13

The
Critical
Essay

When you write a critical essay about a creative work, your primary task is to state an attitude and then to give reasons and explanations that support it. But before you begin to write a critical essay, you must analyze a text whose meaning is conveyed *indirectly, suggested* rather than explicitly stated. Therefore you have to discover the meaning or meanings of a text before you can even think about what you want to say to your audience.

When you write a critical essay, you analyze and interpret a work; sometimes you also evaluate it.

1.   When you *analyze*, you systematically consider the different elements of a work—the plot (what happens?), the characters (what are they like?) and so on—and examine the writer's techniques. You look closely at the text itself, studying words and phrases.

2.   When you *interpret,* you use your analysis to determine what the work means.

3.   When you *evaluate,* you consider whether a work succeeds or not, building on your analysis and interpretation to help you make your judgments. Before you can evaluate a work, you must understand what it means.

WHAT IS CRITICAL WRITING?

What is critical writing, and how is it different from other writing you do? Consider these two paragraphs about the Edgar Allan Poe short story "The Cask of Amontillado." Ellen Rupp, a student in an Introduction to Literature class, wrote this answer to the examination question, "Briefly explain how Montresor uses Fortunato's weakness to his advantage."

> Montresor is aware of Fortunato's pride in his taste in wines. Using this weakness, he entices him into the catacombs where the wine is stored. Drunk, Fortunato is very vulnerable to Montresor's trap. As the two men get further and further into the catacombs, Fortunato senses danger, but the wine has dulled his reflexes, giving Montresor the ultimate opportunity to make his move. Montresor, displaying his madness and cruelty, chains Fortunato to the wall and leaves him to die.

Because the question called for facts, not analysis or interpretation or evaluation, Ellen simply summarized the relevant portion of the plot. In a critical essay she would have had to do much more. Mark Dietrich, a classmate of Ellen's, also wrote about "The Cask of Amontillado" elsewhere on the examination, when he answered an essay question on the topic "Does Montresor make a convincing villain? Why or why not?"

> Montresor is a very convincing villain. Even though his motive is never revealed, he is driven by it. Poe begins the story with Montresor's desire for revenge, and the man's vindictiveness is expressed in many of his thoughts. In addition, Montresor's careful plotting and lack of remorse, well supported in the story, also make him a very convincing villain.

In his answer, Mark went on to present the reasons for his position, explaining why he felt the characterization was successful. Because the question asked students to be critical, Mark had to get across his attitude toward his material. To evaluate Montresor as a character, though, Mark first had to understand the work fully.

"Literature" is not the only subject of critical writing. Television shows, performers, films, paintings, songs, and architectural structures are all good subjects for the amateur or professional critic. In fact, you can apply a critical eye to any aspect of life: to government policies or social programs, college curricula or employee performance. And, of course, the word "critical" doesn't always imply negative judgments, although you might be used to thinking of it that way. When you "criticize" a work, you share your evaluations—favorable as well as unfavorable—with your reader.

You most often encounter critical writing in newspaper and magazine reviews—of restaurants, of books, of plays and films, of dance and music, even of record albums, as in these capsule reviews of some top pop and jazz albums of 1982. These reviews are all very short, but the reviewer, Jim Miller of *Newsweek*, carefully provides critical analysis and interpretation to support his judgments.

> ***Imperial Bedroom,*** *Elvis Costello (Columbia)*. The new wave's verbal acrobat unleashes a cascade of caustic imagery, mostly about the wreck of a marriage. The music—a mélange of pop-rock tunes, most of them mid-tempo—is densely detailed and ironically sweet.
>
> ***Tug of War,*** *Paul McCartney (Columbia)*. Don't be fooled by the Pollyanna gush of "Ebony and Ivory," this album's big hit single. Tuneful and heartfelt, the rest of "Tug of War" explores the conflicted passions behind the Beatles' prettiest face— and one of rock's great composers.
>
> ***Mirage,*** *Fleetwood Mac (Warner Bros.)*. Here's living proof that a predictably popular album can be good smart fun: gossamer ballads and gypsy croaks—fans know the formula—plus loony tunes from pop's flakiest prankster, Lindsey Buckingham.
>
> ***Nebraska,*** *Bruce Springsteen (Columbia)*. "The Boss" has never sung better. He gets a downbeat sound in these grainy new songs—sepia snapshots of our current Great Depression. What color there is on this homemade solo effort comes from the harmonica (shades of Bob Dylan) and some eerie studio echo—imagine Woody Guthrie filtered through the Chess records of Chuck Berry. Stale images abound— more of Springsteen's trademark cars and highways—but the bleak new settings evoke an American Dream running on empty.
>
> ***"Juju Music,"*** *King Sunny Adé and His African Beats (Mango)*. A light, languid, almost casual dance style, the Nigerian popular music known as Juju is built around a conversational form of call-and-response singing, a battery of talking drums and a trio of electric guitars that caroms off the beat. Sunny Adé has updated the traditional polyrhythms with an overlay of synthesizer and pedal steel guitar—a weird juxtaposition that works beautifully in this beguiling African music.
>
> ***Going Where the Lonely Go,*** *Merle Haggard (Epic)*. It is Haggard's special genius to take the hoariest cliché—say, "travelin' down this lonesome road"—and make it sound chiseled in granite. Among his six new originals are a couple of honky-tonk sudsers and a wistful twin-fiddle Texas two-step, "If I Left It Up to You." Best of all is the Jimmie Davis classic, "Nobody's Darlin' But Mine"—a stark, elegiac performance.

In each mini-review, Miller mentions specific songs, lyrics, instruments, or musical techniques that contribute to his positive impressions. Thus he demonstrates his firm grasp of his material, and he bases his judgments on this understanding.

EXERCISE

Read each of these four reviews carefully. In two or three sentences, summarize each writer's critical opinion and the principal reasons for his or her attitude.

[1] From New Game Firm, the Results Are Mixed
Michael Blanchet

The firm Games by Apollo has only been in operation one year, but it already has managed to develop and deliver seven Atari-compatible cartridges. Its most recent releases—Space Cavern, Lost Luggage, Racquetball, Shark Attack and Infiltrate—cover the entire spectrum of subject matter, and include one sure winner, one major disappointment and a good game with a serious flaw.

The winner is Space Cavern, an outer-space adventure in which a lone astronaut battles an endless stream of aliens, known as Electrosauri. Space Cavern is simple to learn, difficult to master, and should offer challenge for months to come.

The player's man is ground-based and can shift left or right to dodge the Electrosauri's bombardment. But looking straight up is not enough. Creatures called marsupods occasionally rush the spaceman from the left and right corners of the screen. You can kill a marsupod by moving the joystick up or back. This sounds easy, but it is a true test of coordination, since you must mind what's going on above you at the same time.

The graphics are colorful and realistic. When the player's astronaut is hit by an electro-molecular charge or is caught by a marsupod, his skeleton glows as his body disintegrates. This makes getting wiped out almost as much fun as racking up a big score.

Lost Luggage is the major disappointment. The title and scenario are original, but play action is nothing more than a cute revamping of Activision's Kaboom.

The action takes place at a baggage carousel at an airport. Soon after a plane touches down in the background, the conveyor belt begins to spin wildly, throwing suitcases into orbit. The object is to catch each piece before it hits the ground. This is done by sweeping a stick figure back and forth across the screen. Missed bags pop open, exposing various unmentionables (undergarments, etc.) to public view.

If you select the terrorist option, random suitcases will explode if they are missed and bring the game to an abrupt end.

Infiltrate, the flawed game, is a cross between Berzerk and Donkey Kong. Players control a secret agent who must work his way up five floors to reach a cache of documents. Once he seizes them, he must turn around and work his way back to the lowest level, where another bundle of papers awaits him. To get from one floor to the next, our pseudo-007 must hop onto one of the perpetually moving elevators.

Two mechanized assassins are out to see that his journey is not a safe one. These robots patrol the playfield, using the same elevator system as our hero. They are easily destroyed with a quick blast from the player's Laser gun, but they can and will reappear in the worst possible places. The agent can duck to avoid enemy volleys if the player pulls the joystick in a southern direction, but this provides temporary cover only. When he is in this position, he can neither run nor shoot back.

The graphics in Infiltrate are good, but they are in no way comparable with those in Space Cavern. And Infiltrate has one major drawback. After two or three cycles, the killer robots accelerate to an almost blinding speed, while the player's speed remains constant. This makes the game little more than a massacre, and can discourage even the most stalwart player. (*Philadelphia Inquirer*)

[2] Bits 'n' Bytes About Computing: A Computer Literacy Primer
Rachelle S. Heller and C. Dianne Martin
Computer Sciences Press
Rockville, MD
174 pp., $17.95

Bits 'n' Bytes About Computing is an example of good intentions gone bad. Rachelle Heller and C. Dianne Martin attempted to write a guide for teachers about teaching computer basics to elementary school children. Unfortunately, its execution is faulty because it offers only a superficial and unimaginative explanation of the history of computers, how and why they work, and what the future holds for computers.

The major problem with this book is that it is written on a third- or fourth-grade reading level which will bore, if not insult, adult readers and teachers. The book could be read aloud word for word to students to teach them all about computers, but as any good teacher will tell you, that is not the best approach. *Bits 'n' Bytes About Computing* can still be salvaged, though, if it is revised slightly. With revisions it would make a good, introductory elementary-school computer textbook.

The book's main assets are its extensive lists of additional references and resources at the end of each chapter. These lists are comprehensive and up-to-date, and include not only magazines and books, but slides and movies available for classroom reviewing. In addition, the "Teacher's Corner" projects are good, and if readers add a little extra thought of their own, they can make them even better and more interesting to students. (*Personal Computing*)

[3] The Gold Standard
1107 S. 47th St., 729-6707. D—6-10 Tues-Sat, 5-9 Sun. No cards.

The Gold Standard is located in a remodeled townhouse down at the southwest fringe of University City. The restaurant is the big living room of the old townhouse—walls painted brown, a white chair rail, brass or copper chandeliers hanging from the ceiling. The fixed price for dinner is $17 a person. Or you can order a la carte, skip a couple of courses and spend a remarkably little amount of money here. There is no bar, and no charge for corkage.

The menu is limited—three or four choices in each course—but changes every week. Peppercakes, inaptly named, are the Gold Standard's version of piperade—crêpes piled on top of one another over layers of chopped sweet red and green pepper, cheese, tomatoes and zucchini. You get a wedge cut out of this crêpe-and-vegetable layer cake and it is extremely good. Flounder mousse was an icy cold mousse with a hot flavor so pervasive and subtle it was difficult to decide if it was pepper or ginger—an extremely light and delicious appetizer.

Zuppa di vercolore was a vegetable soup made with lots of fresh green beans, lots of vegetarian vegetable stock, lots of big chunks of zucchini. Watercress vichyssoise was smaller, but loaded with good potato and leek taste, lots of cream and specks of fresh watercress.

Fixed-price restaurants always have a problem with beef—many customers expect a steak or fillet whenever they eat out, but the price of good beef is so high that the restaurant must either serve second-rate beef, or small portions—or raise prices. The Gold Standard raises its price; it will cost you $3 more to order a fillet with béarnaise sauce. This is $3 well spent—the fillet is large, tender prime, well-cooked, covered with a very very good béarnaise. Pork sauterne was explained as a mix of pork tenders and green peppers in a wine sauce—and my dinner guest did not like peppers, so the chef obligingly made another pork tender dish, this one with mushrooms and Madeira. It is, first of all, nice to have a kitchen flexible enough to make things to order—and secondly, the pork tenders were tender and delicious, the sauce superb and the dish extremely generous.

After-dinner salads are small, served with good vinaigrette, and included excellent tomatoes and fresh basil on one visit, excellent red romaine on another.

Homemade ices are extremely good—barely sweet, heavily fruit-flavored. Chocolate mousse cake was a small wedge of dark and creamy chocolate—best of all to me. This is a very competent and well-run little restaurant. (*Philadelphia* Magazine)

[4]

When Natalia Makarova takes her final curtain call in the revival of **On Your Toes** at the Kennedy Center, she caps her delicious performance with jazz-tap shenanigans and a bit of frenzied wing beating that spoofs her sublime *Swan Lake*s. The 1936 Rodgers and Hart musical is about just that—the salubrious, and hilarious, meeting of ballet and Broadway.

The plot rolls merrily along: Bumped from the family's vaudeville act for following his "lower instincts," a teenage tap whiz, Junior Dolan, grows up to be a very square music professor. One of his pupils, Frankie Frayne, is his wide-eyed, loyal girl friend. Another, Sidney Cohn, is a fellow with a genius for jazz. Junior conveys Sidney's score, *Slaughter on Tenth Avenue,* to the Russian Ballet, a tacky outfit on its last legs that is run by a fur-swathed patroness and a choreographer whose ballets in the glorious Russian tradition are unintentional burlesques.

To pique her on- and offstage partner, one Konstantine Morrosine, the company's ballerina, Vera Baronova, vamps the susceptible Junior, whose repressed dance talents surface along with his libido. When Junior steps into the male lead at the premiere of *Slaughter,* Morrosine hires a gangland killer to rub him out at the climax of his tap-solo "suicide." Needless to say, all ends cheerfully. You're not supposed to suspend your disbelief, merely to leave it home.

On Your Toes was—and is—distinguished by its songs. The romantic "There's a Small Hotel," the poignant "Quiet Night," and the wisecracking "Too Good for the Average Man" (as in cosmetic surgery—"cutting off your face to spite your nose") still elicit genuine delight, although the passage of half a century has brought us far from innocent ways and means.

In its time, the show was doubly distinguished for its dances. *On Your Toes* is a landmark in dance history. It was the first occasion on which the dance arranger—who was George Balanchine—got the more prestigious billing of "choreographer." It was also the first musical comedy in which the dance numbers furthered the action, Balanchine's *Slaughter* thus paving the way for work like Agnes de Mille's in *Oklahoma!* and Jerome Robbins's in *West Side Story.* What was important, really, was the sophistication of Balanchine's dances: *Princess Zenobia,* a kind of *Scheherazade*-iana, devilishly undermined everything that the Ballet Russe held dear, and that Balanchine knew was inimical to vital American ballet. His haunting *Slaughter* took its strength from native rhythms and an indigenous dance style. Unfortunately, though Balanchine still gets his billing in the program, his inventive work is largely lost; one must assume that Peter Martins's credit for "additional choreography" is an understatement.

In the present production, both ballet numbers fall flat. The *Zenobia* pas de deux ignores the original's sly progress from clever imitation to wicked mockery. Merely banal rather than pointedly banal, it fails to amuse. George de la Peña's offering a spin-off of his movie Nijinsky is just a symptom of the lack of focus. Worse yet, the *Slaughter* ballet has little atmosphere beyond that of Zack Brown's cabaret décor: figures in glittering black mirrored in a tilted ceiling as they move through their smoke-filled, black-and-chrome Deco cell. Makarova does her best as the stripper whom love leads to a tragic end, but she hasn't the advantage of her predecessors in the role, Tamara Geva and Vera Zorina. These were two women Balanchine loved, and for whom, apparently, he fashioned just the right movements to express a wonderful tawdry sensuality.

While the choreography itself lets her down, Makarova has the grace not to cover it with mugging. Indeed, the whole production is directed—by George Abbott, as it was in '36—with angelic seriousness and simplicity. Makarova's triumph, amazingly, is in the acted scenes, especially an on-and-off-the-bed sequence in which, a mix of Garbo and Ginger Rogers, she instructs Junior in the art of partnering. She's brought her voice to stage proportions, along with her tremolo and throaty giggle, and she maliciously exaggerates her own charming accent to suit the stock character of temperamental emigrée ballerina. Her delivery of the epithet "false-haired, big-boobed floozie" is every bit as memorable as her pristine arabesque.

Apart from Makarova's, the best contributions to the show come from Donald Saddler, who staged the musical numbers with panache; the delectable newcomer, Regina O'Malley—who can sing and act at the same time—as Frankie; and Dana Moore, a spirited tapper, who should lead a class-action suit against the amateurs who miked the stage. (Tobi Tobias, *New York Magazine*)

WRITING THE CRITICAL ESSAY

Most of your critical essays in college work will be about literature—a poem or play or, more frequently, a novel or short story. The same systematic writing process with which you are already familiar applies: you prewrite, write and arrange, and revise. But when the subject matter is literature, there are some unique guidelines.

PREWRITING

First, of course, if your instructor gives you the option, you must choose the work or works that will be your subject. Then you must decide on an attitude toward the work, the point you want to make. You start by *reading your material*—reading it several times, in fact—carefully, thoroughly, and critically. If the subject is a poem, read it aloud and—line by line—try to paraphrase it. After your first reading, reread, underlining lines or passages that seem pertinent to your assignment.

As you read, *keep your assignment in mind*. Make sure you understand exactly what it is you are to do. Your assignment may be as general as "Write a critical essay about any work or works we studied this semester," or it may suggest that you focus on a particular area—for instance, that you analyze a character in a story or consider the rhyme and meter of a poem. It may ask you to compare two works, two writing styles, or two characters. It may even specify the work and the way you are to approach it. ("Does Montresor make a convincing villain? Why or why not?") This is particularly true on an examination. In these cases, your assignment narrows your general subject for you. But if the assignment is open, allowing you to select the work and the point of view, then you have to narrow your subject on your own.

☐ BOUNDARIES

After you know your assignment, proceed to your *boundaries*. Your *audience*—your instructor in most cases—is familiar with the work, so keep plot summaries to a minimum, unless one is explicitly asked for, and refer to the author's technique without too many definitions.

Your assignment may specify *purpose*—that is, your instructor may ask you to analyze, clarify, enlighten, argue, interpret, compare, or evaluate. A critical essay can have one or many of these purposes. And always, your general purpose is to shed light on a work of literature.

The *occasion* for your writing helps determine your content. In an examination, limited time allows you to discuss only the pertinent aspects of your subject, eliminating "extras" like unasked-for comparisons with other works or biographical details. For a long paper done at home, however, such explorations may be entirely appropriate. In class you probably can't include any but the briefest quotations, even if your teacher allows you to refer to your text. At home, however, you have the time to look up quotations that illustrate your points.

The *length* of your paper also implies certain limitations. In a long paper, naturally, you can explore areas that a five-hundred-word essay cannot touch on. Five hundred words about a short story might let you examine a character, the setting, or some aspect of language, but you could not do justice to all three. A longer paper might let you treat all these elements, and others: the author's other works, his or her life, other writers who influenced the writer, or critical responses to the work, for example.

Finally, assessing your own *knowledge* helps you choose a subject. How much you now know and how much you can get to know quickly should give you a direction for your essay.

☐ ELEMENTS OF LITERATURE

As you try to reduce your subject to a workable size, you should consider, one by one, the several elements in terms of which we analyze literature.

With a novel or short story or play, begin by considering the *plot*, what happens in the work. Examine how the events relate to one another, and how single events relate to the work as a whole. You might look at how the writer has arranged events in time, and compare that with the order in which they actually happened. You could also identify the conflicts that occur in the story and consider how they move the plot along. These conflicts usually occur between the main character, called a *protagonist*, and another character who opposes him or her, called the *antagonist*. (The antagonist may also be society in general, or a force within the protagonist's own mind.) There is always more to a plot than "boy meets girl" or "whodunit" or "rags to riches." If you can speak about the juxtaposition of individual events and what they mean, you are on your way to a successful analysis of plot.

Next, consider your work's *characters*. Analyzing characters and their motivations helps you understand the plot, but this analysis isn't always easy. A particular character's traits and feelings and values may be communicated directly to you, or you may have to infer a good deal about the character from his or her actions, relationships to other characters, or what he or she *doesn't* say or do. What are the characters like? The protagonist need not be strong or brave or beautiful or even likable—he or she may be weak or greedy or foolish or indecisive. Characters may be complex and fully developed or barely sketched in. Some characters may even be easily recognizable stereotypes, characters so often encountered by readers of fiction that they are completely predictable—the wicked stepmother, the straying husband, or the helpless, lovely damsel in distress. These *stock characters* may efficiently convey a quick impression, but major characters, ones who engage our interest, must be fully developed. Do the major characters remain essentially unchanged by events or do they grow and develop and undergo significant changes in response to these events? What do they learn? How does this knowledge affect the other characters? The plot? These and other questions can lead you to material for a paper about character.

Setting, where and when the action takes place, offers other possibilities. Setting gives you the context in which to interpret what happens. The term "setting" refers not just to a specific physical place—the dining room, for example—but also to the larger geographical location and historical period of the action. Is the setting so central to the action that the story could not take place anywhere else? Or is it almost incidental to the work? Is the *absence* of setting striking? Authors choose settings carefully, and their reasons for these choices should be considered just as carefully.

Point of view is another element you must consider. In a work of fiction, a narrator, or speaker, usually tells the story to readers from his or her point of view, or perspective. Do not confuse this narrator with the work's author; the narrator has a role to play, just as the other characters do. As one of the story's characters, a narrator may speak and think in the *first person* ("I"); this first-person narrator may be a major character who is actively involved in the story's events, or a minor character who only observes much of the story's action.

Of course, when a story is told entirely in the *third person* (referring to characters as "he," "she," and "they"), you cannot identify a narrator. The author, however, assumes a point of view anyway. That is, the author, though not a character, still reveals his or her attitude toward the people and events in the story. This third-person speaker may be an *omniscient* (all-knowing) narrator, who sees into all the characters' minds, or an *objective* narrator, who reports events from the outside, seeing into no one's mind but leaving you to draw your own conclusions about the feelings and opinions of the characters. In most plays, of course, there is no narrator, but a play still has a point of view: the author always tries to get some attitude across through sympathetic or unappealing characters.

Understanding point of view can be challenging, but the writer's point of view controls how you grasp a work's meaning: it determines how much you know about the characters and events and how you perceive them.

Other elements you should consider include the work's *tone and style. Tone* varies significantly from author to author and work to work: it can be light or serious, straightforward or ironic, bitter or enthusiastic. A narrator's tone reveals approval or disapproval of characters and action and every attitude in between. If you sense any discrepancy between the narrator's stated feeling and the attitudes the author conveys more subtly through word choice and arrangement, this too helps you unlock a writer's meaning. Or the narrator may take a certain tone toward the audience. The narrator may reveal, for instance, that he or she is closely involved with the reader or may maintain some distance. Or, a work's tone can be *ironic.* Recognizing a note of irony in a writer's tone adds to our understanding of what a writer intends. *Irony* is a use of language to suggest a discrepancy or incongruity: between what a narrator says and what he or she actually means; between what a character says and what the reader actually knows; between what appears to be true and what actually is true; or between what does happen and what probably should have happened.

Analysis of a writer's *style* also deepens your understanding of a work. In Chapter 8, we saw that tone, diction, and sentence structure all work to shape style in an essay. This is even more true of "creative" or "imaginative" prose. Style in a work of literature can be terse and understated or elaborately detailed, stiff and formal or loose and conversational. A writer can use *imagery* and *symbolism* to enrich his or her meaning, so it is essential that you recognize these elements and understand why an author has chosen to use them—or not to use them. *Imagery*—figurative language—and *symbolism* enrich style and reinforce meaning because they carry a complex message in relatively few words. A well-crafted metaphor or symbol suggests meaning without stating it explicitly or explaining it heavy-handedly. Examining tone and style can be a rewarding way to analyze a work of literature.

Finally, you may learn more about a work of literature by considering its *theme.* When we refer to the theme of a novel or short story or play, we mean the point or points the author sets out to make—the "message" of the work. To understand this theme, you must consider the author's purpose in writing the work, what truth he or she is trying to convey. The theme, or central concept, often appears subtle on the surface, yet many of the story's elements may point to it.

As you consider all these elements, you will discover that certain aspects seem more promising than others for the particular text you want to work on. This should help you move from a general subject to a topic you can develop into a strong critical essay. In other words, you can move from "Write a critical essay on 'The Cask of Amontillado'" to the narrower "The character of Montresor in 'The Cask of Amontillado'" or "Point of view in 'The Cask of Amontillado'" to topics that would be suitable for a short critical paper: "Does Montresor make a convincing villain?" for instance, or "How does the point of view in 'The Cask of Amontillado' affect the reader's perception of Montresor?"

If, after you review these elements, you still can't find a workable topic, you can try something else: look for parallels between plot, character, and so on in the work you are studying and those same elements in another work with which you are familiar—or between your work and "real life." This may suggest some good paper topics: "The theme of guilt in 'The Cask of Amontillado' and 'The Tell-Tale Heart,'" for instance. If you still cannot find a topic, move on to brainstorming, keeping the individual elements of literary criticism in mind as you write down ideas.

If the subject of your critical essay is a poem, different considerations apply as you prepare to write. In addition to tone and style, point of view, and theme (and, in a narrative poem, plot and character), you should also look at rhyme and other sound patterns, meter, and the form of the whole poem. And if your subject is not a work of literature at all, your critical essay—and hence your prewriting—focuses on still other elements. As you prewrite for a review of a dramatic performance, for instance, consider the actors, costumes, and sets; when you prepare to write a critical review of a restaurant, evaluate food, service, and atmosphere. You consider acoustics for a musical performance, cinematography for a movie, graphics for a video game, composition and color for a painting. Being a good critic requires a thorough knowledge and understanding of your subject. This helps you decide on the elements to focus on—and later on, on the kind of critical language you use as you write.

When you have your narrowed topic, proceed to brainstorm to find something to say about it. You now have a literary work to consider as well as a topic, so your brainstorming list will include more material than one for an essay on what you did last summer. But keeping your narrowed subject in mind as you brainstorm should keep your list fairly specific.

In addition to brainstorming, you may do some research, talk with friends or with your instructor, or review your class notes. When you have sharpened the focus for your essay, you are ready to work on a thesis. If the wording of your assignment or the topic you have settled on is specific, your thesis may take right off from it. If your assignment asks "Does Montresor make a convincing villain?" your thesis might be "Montresor is a convincing villain because of his intense desire for revenge and his lack of remorse."

Or your thesis may emerge during brainstorming. Just as you would when planning any essay, review your brainstorming list. Select the most promising ideas, and then sort and group them into categories; after this, arrange these categories into a scratch outline. This scratch outline should suggest a tentative thesis to guide you as you write your first draft.

The purpose of your paper always determines your thesis. If your purpose is to compare—or defend or analyze—your thesis should indicate this. In addition, you can state that a work is great (or not so great), that it resembles another work, that its theme is not the one that first meets the eye, that its characters are not individuals but types—there are many possibilities. Remember, though, that your thesis must be a *specific, arguable statement*—not "Montresor is the villain of 'The Cask of Amontillado'" but "Montresor is a convincing villain because of his intense desire for revenge and his lack of remorse."

EXERCISE

Read the following story, Edgar Allan Poe's "The Cask of Amontillado," carefully. Then reread it, several times if necessary, underlining important passages. When you are sure you understand the story, complete the following tasks.

1.   Consider plot, character, setting, point of view, tone, style, and theme, one by one. Which two elements seem to suggest the most promising topics for a critical essay? Try to find a good topic for a critical paper about the story by examining these two elements in detail.

2.   Brainstorm to find material for a critical essay.

3.   Find a tentative thesis for such an essay.

THE CASK OF AMONTILLADO
Edgar Allan Poe

The thousand injuries of Fortunato I had borne as I best could, but when he ventured upon insult I vowed revenge. You, who so well know the nature of my soul, will not suppose, however, that I gave utterance to a threat. *At length* I would be avenged; this was a point definitely settled—but the very definitiveness with which it was resolved precluded the idea of risk. I must not only punish but punish with impunity. A wrong is unredressed when retribution overtakes its redresser. It is equally unredressed when the avenger fails to make himself felt as such to him who has done the wrong.

It must be understood that neither by word nor deed had I given Fortunato cause to doubt my good will. I continued, as was my wont, to smile in his face, and he did not perceive that my smile *now* was at the thought of his immolation.

He had a weak point—this Fortunato—although in other regards he was a man to be respected and even feared. He prided himself on his connoisseurship in wine. Few Italians have the true virtuoso spirit. For the most part their enthusiasm is adopted to suit the time and opportunity, to practise imposture upon the British and Austrian *millionaires*. In painting and gemmary, Fortunato, like his countrymen, was a quack, but in the matter of old wines he was sincere. In this respect I did not differ from him materially;—I was skilful in the Italian vintages myself, and bought largely whenever I could.

It was about dusk, one evening during the supreme madness of the carnival season, that I encountered my friend. He accosted me with excessive warmth, for he had been drinking much. The man wore motley. He had on a tight-fitting parti-striped dress, and his head was surmounted by the conical cap and bells. I was so pleased to see him that I thought I should never have done wringing his hand.

I said to him—"My dear Fortunato, you are luckily met. How remarkably well you are looking to-day. But I have received a pipe of what passes for Amontillado, and I have my doubts."

"How?" said he. "Amontillado? A pipe? Impossible! And in the middle of the carnival!"

"I have my doubts," I replied; "and I was silly enough to pay the full Amontillado price without consulting you in the matter. You were not to be found, and I was fearful of losing a bargain."

"Amontillado!"

"I have my doubts."

"Amontillado!"

"And I must satisfy them."

"Amontillado!"

"As you are engaged, I am on my way to Luchresi. If any one has a critical turn, it is he. He will tell me—"

"Luchresi cannot tell Amontillado from Sherry."

"And yet some fools will have it that his taste is a match for your own."

"Come, let us go."

"Whither?"

"To your vaults."

"My friend, no; I will not impose upon your good nature. I perceive you have an engagement. Luchresi—"

"I have no engagement;—come."

"My friend, no. It is not the engagement, but the severe cold with which I perceive you are afflicted. The vaults are insufferably damp. They are encrusted with nitre."

"Let us go, nevertheless. The cold is merely nothing. Amontillado! You have been imposed upon. And as for Luchresi, he cannot distinguish Sherry from Amontillado."

Thus speaking, Fortunato possessed himself of my arm; and putting on a mask of black silk and drawing a *roquelaire** closely about my person, I suffered him to hurry me to my palazzo.

There were no attendants at home; they had absconded to make merry in honour of the time. I had told them that I should not return until the morning, and had given them explicit orders not to stir from the house. These orders were sufficient, I well knew, to insure their immediate disappearance, one and all, as soon as my back was turned.

I took from their sconces two flambeaux, and giving one to Fortunato, bowed him through several suites of rooms to the archway that led into the vaults. I passed down a long and winding staircase, requesting him to be cautious as he followed. We came at length to the foot of the descent, and stood together on the damp ground of the catacombs of the Montresors.

The gait of my friend was unsteady, and the bells upon his cap jingled as he strode.

"The pipe?" said he.

---

*A knee-length cloak.

"It is farther on," said I; "but observe the white web-work which gleams from these cavern walls."

He turned towards me, and looked into my eyes with two filmy orbs that distilled the rheum of intoxication.

"Nitre?" he asked, at length.

"Nitre," I replied. "How long have you had that cough?"

"Ugh! ugh! ugh!—ugh! ugh! ugh!—ugh! ugh! ugh! ugh! ugh! ugh!—ugh! ugh! ugh!"

My poor friend found it impossible to reply for many minutes.

"It is nothing," he said, at last.

"Come," I said, with decision, "we will go back; your health is precious. You are rich, respected, admired, beloved; you are happy, as once I was. You are a man to be missed. For me it is no matter. We will go back; you will be ill, and I cannot be responsible. Besides, there is Luchresi—"

"Enough," he said; "the cough is a mere nothing; it will not kill me. I shall not die of a cough."

"True—true," I replied; "and, indeed, I had no intention of alarming you unnecessarily—but you should use all proper caution. A draught of this Medoc will defend us from the damps."

Here I knocked off the neck of a bottle which I drew from a long row of its fellows that lay upon the mould.

"Drink," I said, presenting him the wine.

He raised it to his lips with a leer. He paused and nodded to me familiarly, while his bells jingled.

"I drink," he said, "to the buried that repose around us."

"And I to your long life."

He again took my arm, and we proceeded.

"These vaults," he said, "are extensive."

"The Montresors," I replied, "were a great and numerous family."

"I forget your arms."

"A huge human foot d'or, in a field azure; the foot crushes a serpent rampant whose fangs are imbedded in the heel."

"And the motto?"

"*Nemo me impune lacessit.*" *

"Good!" he said.

The wine sparkled in his eyes and the bells jingled. My own fancy grew warm with the Medoc. We had passed through long walls of piled skeletons, with casks and puncheons intermingling, into the inmost recesses of the catacombs. I paused again, and this time I made bold to seize Fortunato by an arm above the elbow.

"The nitre!" I said; "see, it increases. It hangs like moss upon the vaults. We are below the river's bed. The drops of moisture trickle among the bones. Come, we will go back ere it is too late. Your cough—"

"It is nothing," he said; "let us go on. But first, another draught of the Medoc."

I broke and reached him a flagon of De Grâve. He emptied it at a breath. His eyes flashed with a fierce light. He laughed and threw the bottle upward with a gesticulation I did not understand.

I looked at him in surprise. He repeated the movement—a grotesque one.

*"No one provokes me with impunity."

"You do not comprehend?" he said.

"Not I," I replied.

"Then you are not of the brotherhood."

"How?"

"You are not of the masons."

"Yes, yes," I said; "yes, yes."

"You? Impossible! A mason?"

"A mason," I replied.

"A sign," he said, "a sign."

"It is this," I answered, producing from beneath the folds of my *roquelaire* a trowel.

"You jest," he exclaimed, recoiling a few paces. "But let us proceed to the Amontillado."

"Be it so," I said, replacing the tool beneath the cloak and again offering him my arm. He leaned upon it heavily. We continued our route in search of the Amontillado. We passed through a range of low arches, descended, passed on, and descending again, arrived at a deep crypt, in which the foulness of the air caused our flambeaux rather to glow than flame.

At the most remote end of the crypt there appeared another less spacious. Its walls had been lined with human remains, piled to the vault overhead, in the fashion of the great catacombs of Paris. Three sides of this interior crypt were still ornamented in this manner. From the fourth the bones had been thrown down, and lay promiscuously upon the earth, forming at one point a mound of some size. Within the wall thus exposed by the displacing of the bones, we perceived a still interior crypt or recess, in depth about four feet, in width three, in height six or seven. It seemed to have been constructed for no especial use within itself, but formed merely the interval between two of the colossal supports of the roof of the catacombs, and was backed by one of their circumscribing walls of solid granite.

It was in vain that Fortunato, uplifting his dull torch, endeavored to pry into the depth of the recess. Its termination the feeble light did not enable us to see.

"Proceed," I said; "herein is the Amontillado. As for Luchresi—"

"He is an ignoramus," interrupted my friend, as he stepped unsteadily forward, while I followed immediately at his heels. In an instant he had reached the extremity of the niche, and finding his progress arrested by the rock, stood stupidly bewildered. A moment more and I had fettered him to the granite. In its surface were two iron staples, distant from each other about two feet, horizontally. From one of these depended a short chain, from the other a padlock. Throwing the links about his waist, it was but the work of a few seconds to secure it. He was too much astounded to resist. Withdrawing the key I stepped back from the recess.

"Pass your hand," I said, "over the wall; you cannot help feeling the nitre. Indeed it is *very* damp. Once more let me *implore* you to return. No? Then I must positively leave you. But I must first render you all the little attentions in my power."

"The Amontillado!" ejaculated my friend, not yet recovered from his astonishment.

"True," I replied; "the Amontillado."

As I said these words I busied myself among the pile of bones of which I have before spoken. Throwing them aside, I soon uncovered a quantity of building stone and mortar. With these materials and with the aid of my trowel, I began vigorously to wall up the entrance of the niche.

I had scarcely laid the first tier of the masonry when I discovered that the intoxication of Fortunato had in a great measure worn off. The earliest indication I had of this was a low moaning cry from the depth of the recess. It was *not* the cry of a drunken man. There was then a long and obstinate silence. I laid the second tier, and the third, and the fourth; and then I heard the furious vibrations of the chain. The noise lasted for several minutes, during which, that I might hearken to it with the more satisfaction, I ceased my labours and sat down upon the bones. When at last the clanking subsided, I resumed the trowel, and finished without interruption the fifth, the sixth, and the seventh tier. The wall was now nearly upon a level with my breast. I again paused, and holding the flambeaux over the mason-work, threw a few feeble rays upon the figure within.

A succession of loud and shrill screams, bursting suddenly from the throat of the chained form, seemed to thrust me violently back. For a brief moment I hesitated, I trembled. Unsheathing my rapier, I began to grope with it about the recess; but the thought of an instant reassured me. I placed my hand upon the solid fabric of the catacombs, and felt satisfied. I reapproached the wall. I replied to the yells of him who clamoured. I reechoed, I aided, I surpassed them in volume and in strength. I did this, and the clamourer grew still.

It was now midnight, and my task was drawing to a close. I had completed the eighth, the ninth and the tenth tier. I had finished a portion of the last and the eleventh; there remained but a single stone to be fitted and plastered in. I struggled with its weight; I placed it partially in its destined position. But now there came from out the niche a low laugh that erected the hairs upon my head. It was succeeded by a sad voice, which I had difficulty in recognizing as that of the noble Fortunato. The voice said—

"Ha! ha! ha!—he! he! he!—a very good joke, indeed—an excellent jest. We will have many a rich laugh about it at the palazzo—he! he! he!—over our wine—he! he! he!"

"The Amontillado!" I said.

"He! he! he!—he! he! he!—yes, the Amontillado. But is it not getting late? Will not they be awaiting us at the palazzo, the Lady Fortunato and the rest? Let us be gone."

"Yes," I said, "let us be gone."

"*For the love of God, Montresor!*"

"Yes," I said, "for the love of God!"

But to these words I hearkened in vain for a reply. I grew impatient. I called aloud—

"Fortunato!"

No answer. I called again—

"Fortunato!"

No answer still. I thrust a torch through the remaining aperture and let it fall within. There came forth in return only a jingling of the bells. My heart grew sick; it was the dampness of the catacombs that made it so. I hastened to make an end of my labour. I forced the last stone into its position; I plastered it up. Against the new masonry I re-erected the old rampart of bones. For the half of a century no mortal has disturbed them. *In pace requiescat!**

WRITING AND ARRANGING

Once your work-in-progress has a tentative thesis, you can begin shaping your ideas into a rough draft with a beginning, a middle, and an end. Write this first draft quickly, without paying much attention to style. You may follow your scratch outline or use sections of your brainstorming list as your guide.

As you proceed, use *present tense* verbs. These indicate that the literary work

*May he rest in peace.

has an existence outside your paper—"Lessing's short stories *focus* on different themes at different stages of her career . . . ," "Both Lady Gregory and Chekhov *arrange* their one-act plays to highlight the pattern of separation and reconciliation between the main characters." But when you refer to biographical data, use the *past tense*—"Plath's unresolved conflicts with her father *led* her to portray him as a Nazi."

As you write, you should cast yourself as an *objective narrator*. Avoid feeble phrases like "In my opinion" and "I feel." If your evidence demonstrates that a judgment is valid, why suggest that it is true only because you say so? Keep your point of view professional and your paper will take on more credibility.

Although your rough draft is guided by your tentative thesis and your scratch outline, your material may still emerge in a fairly shapeless form. As you reread your rough draft, then, see how you can rework it to give it a strong thesis-and-support structure. First, make sure your tentative thesis is a strong one and that the facts and examples in your draft support it. Then concentrate on adding necessary information and deleting what is irrelevant. Finally, arrange your material so that your essay has an *introduction* that expresses your attitude toward the work you are evaluating, a *body* that gives reasons and explanations for your attitude, and a *conclusion* that reaffirms your position. Here is one possible essay structure:

1.   *Begin* with a paragraph or two introducing your paper. If you are responding to a specific question, be sure to echo the wording of the question. Here, too, you want to present some background for your subject, information about the author, perhaps, or about comparable works that have relevance to the work of literature you are discussing. You might describe the work, review its most striking features, *briefly* summarize its plot, or place it in its historical context. Your beginning paragraphs exist simply to give your readers an overview of the work and a clear idea of your thesis.

2.   The *middle* of your essay moves on to elaborate on your specific points. It may be necessary to analyze in detail some or all of the elements—plot, character, theme—that apply to the work you are writing about. Here you support your critical judgments with specific references to the work under discussion. Be sure to use plenty of evidence to support your assertions; when you make a judgment, back it up with pertinent examples from the text itself. You may recount events, quote dialogue, describe character or setting, or paraphrase ideas, but you must supply a sufficient number—and a sufficiently wide range—of examples if your readers are to accept your conclusions. You cannot just assert that a story's theme depends on a Biblical allusion or that a pattern of imagery exists; you must explain the allusion, and you must list the related images that make up the pattern.

Use a direct quotation where you must—where a writer says something important or unusual in a way that is special or unique. *Don't overdo it,* however, or your essay will wind up just a string of quotations. And be sure that your quotations actually illustrate your points. In general, be sure that a quotation is necessary. Could a paraphrase be equally effective, or are the author's actual words really crucial to your point?

Your familiarity with different patterns of arrangement should guide you as you shape your essay. You can give your critical paper an underlying structure by comparison and contrast ("Compare the plot structures of Lady Gregory's *The Workhouse Ward* and Chekhov's *The Marriage Proposal*"); by cause and effect ("Trace the influence of Zen on the later works of J. D. Salinger"); by classification ("Discuss the feminist, leftist, and apocalyptic themes that dominate Doris Lessing's short stories"); or by any other pattern or combination of patterns.

3.   At the *end* of your paper, you review your main points, perhaps reaffirm and clarify your thesis, and close your essay gracefully yet emphatically. The last paragraph may include comparisons with other works, a particularly apt quotation from the work or a statement by the author or a literary critic, or simply a summary of the work's significance: its contribution to its literary genre, to its historical era— or to you as a reader.

EXERCISES

1.   Students in a communications class wrote critical essays in which they were assigned to evaluate a popular television program and account for its success. Two of these essays follow. Read both carefully, evaluate them, and decide which is the superior critical essay. Then write out two lists: first, list the features that make the stronger essay a good piece of criticism; then, list the weaknesses of the poorer essay.

All My Children

Agnes Nixon created "All My Children" in 1970, and a few years later I started watching it. Every school holiday, every time I was sick, and all summer long I watched my favorite "soap." The story revolved around two families—the wealthy Tylers and the upper-middle-class Martins—in the fictional town of Pine Valley, Pennsylvania. Today those two families are still at the center of many of the plots—and I'm still watching.

When the show began, Lincoln and Amy Tyler were at center stage. Lincoln was a prosperous attorney and Amy, his wife, had a secret in her past: an illegitimate son, Philip, raised by her sister Ruth Brent. (By the time I started watching, Amy had left town.) Also central were the aristocratic Phoebe Tyler, Lincoln's mother, and her husband Charles Tyler, a physician. Charles and Phoebe were also responsible for raising their teenaged grandson Chuck, best friend of Philip Brent. For years the primary focus of "All My Children" was a love triangle between Chuck, Phil, and Tara Martin, daughter of Dr. Joe Martin. Phil went off to Vietnam, leaving Tara pregnant; when Phil was declared missing in action, Tara married Chuck. (Naturally, Phil eventually returned to Pine Valley.)

Another interesting story line revolved around Donna Beck, a former streetwalker whom Chuck, by that time a doctor, wound up marrying. Donna and her best friend Estelle were abused by their pimps—Donna was sterilized without her knowledge and both were beaten and threatened. Both eventually achieved respectability—Donna when she married Chuck, and Estelle when she married Benny Sago, Phoebe Tyler's chauffeur. But both paid a price—Donna was never really accepted by the Pine Valley aristocracy she tried so hard to please. Even today, whatever she does is wrong, and Phoebe never lets her forget it. And Estelle was forced into a nightmare marriage with her pimp, Billy Clyde Tuggle, and eventually died in a car crash.

Erica Kane is another fascinating character. Erica, a high school friend of Chuck, Phil, and Tara, spends most of her time getting married and divorced. First she tricked Jeff Martin (Tara's brother) into marrying her, then she seduced (and married) Phil Brent, and finally (so far) she charmed Tom Cudahy, the local pro football star—but she divorced all of them. In between marriages she was involved in steamy love affairs: with Nick Davis, Phil Brent's natural father; with Jason Maxwell, a man Erica's mother murdered; with Brandon Kingsley, a married man with grown children; and with Kent Bogard, for whose murder Erica was tried and acquitted. (Erica also tried to seduce one Mark Dalton, but she found out just in time that he was her half-brother.)

"All My Children" is my favorite show. Ever since I was a little kid I have been following the stories of Phil and Tara, Phoebe and Charles, Donna and Chuck, and Erica and her man of the moment. These characters, and the town in which they live, have been an important part of my life.

All My Children

From the time it first appeared in 1970, Agnes Nixon's popular daytime drama "All My Children" has managed to stay at or near the top of the ratings by doing something no other soap has been able to do as well: staying timely. Although the story line still revolves around the well-to-do Tylers and the somewhat less well-to-do (but still comfortable) Martins, new characters keep the plot developments socially relevant as well as interesting. It is this constant updating, this attention to current topics, that separates "All My Children" from its competitors.

One of the show's earliest innovations was the introduction of the complex Amy Tyler. Wife of attorney Lincoln Tyler—son of Dr. and Mrs. Charles Tyler, the town's most solid citizens— Amy was a rebel from the start. In typical soap opera fashion, she had a skeleton in her closet— an illegitimate son, Philip Brent, raised by her sister Ruth. Philip, the result of an affair between sixteen-year-old Amy and the infamous Nick Davis (later owner of the Pine Valley dance studio), had no idea that Amy was his real mother. So far, the character may seem very familiar: an upper-class woman threatened by a seedy past. But Amy had another side, too: she insisted, despite the disapproval of her snobbish mother-in-law, Phoebe Tyler, on taking part in protests against the Vietnam War. Amy, a respected, middle-class, suburban housewife, was taking a still-unpopular stand on a controversial issue; millions of viewers must surely have felt her conflicting emotions and, perhaps, respected her decision to stand up to Phoebe and to others who disapproved of her actions.

Another character who has kept pace with the times is the show's "villainess," Erica Kane Martin Brent Cudahy. A popular soap opera type, Erica mistreats her long-suffering mother, engages in serious social climbing in choosing friends and husbands, and desperately craves money, social position, and attention. But Erica's struggles reflect not just soap opera stereotypes but also current social trends. She and her husbands invariably break up because Erica insists on a splashy career—as a TV "weather girl," as a model, as owner of a disco, as an actress—while her husbands want her to stay home and have children. Erica even had television's first legal abortion—for which she was duly punished by a life-threatening case of septicemia and the loss of her next child.

Other regular characters also have experiences that parallel "real life" situations, and it is these experiences that keep viewers watching. Phoebe Tyler struggles with alcoholism, Ellen Shepherd's husband abandons her for a younger woman (and she, in turn, marries a much younger man), Ruth Martin is raped, Paul Martin fights in Vietnam, Anne Tyler Martin gives birth to a retarded child, Charles Tyler needs a hearing aid, Benny Sago has a gambling problem, Nina Warner is a diabetic. Minor characters, too, are victims of child abuse and wife abuse, infertility and unwanted pregnancies.

Yes, the stereotypical soap opera situations do, for the most part, prevail: gentle Mary Kennicott Martin, dying of leukemia, is shot in a robbery; "little Philip" Tyler is really Phil Brent's illegitimate son. Yes, many current topics—euthanasia, incest, the loneliness of the nation's elderly, the recession—are still apparently too controversial for the writers of "All My Children" to consider. And yes, other soap operas also pay attention to timely topics. But somehow "All My Children" is different. Maybe it is because the station flashes local phone numbers for child abuse and Gamblers Anonymous hot lines during relevant programming. Maybe it is because many important social issues appear on the soap opera almost as soon as they become serious concerns in the "real world." Or maybe it is because we see our own familiar soap opera characters reacting to the changing, threatening world around them, just as we are. Whatever it is, it works: by keeping up with the times, "All My Children" keeps its place in the ratings.

2.   Write a draft of a critical essay on Poe's "The Cask of Amontillado" using the thesis you have already developed (page 334) as a guide.

REVISING

Once your first draft is completed, you begin to focus on revision. Here you reconsider the soundness of your ideas, the phrasing of your thesis, the number and suitability of your supporting examples, and the logic of your organizing pattern. Consider too your tone and your style, your sentence construction, and your choice of words.

You may use any of the revision strategies discussed in Chapter 9—peer criticism, outlining, or checklists—to help you revise your critical essay. When you are satisfied with your essay's basic content, logic, structure, and style, it is time to review your mechanics and do some editing and checking. Are spelling and punctuation correct? Have you quoted your sources accurately? Have you remembered to include the page number (for fiction), line number (for poetry), or act and scene number (for drama) parenthetically after each quotation, and given credit for each idea which is not your own? Is the paper arranged, presented, and typed neatly, and according to the format required by your instructor?

EXERCISES

1.   Read this sonnet and the student essay that discusses it. Then answer the questions that follow.

Shall I Compare Thee to a Summer's Day?
(Sonnet 18)
Shall I compare thee to a summer's day?
Thou art more lovely and more temperate.
Rough winds do shake the darling buds of May,
And summer's lease hath all too short a date.
Sometime too hot the eye of heaven shines,
And often is his gold complexion dimmed;
And every fair from fair sometimes declines,
By chance, or nature's changing course, untrimmed.
But thy eternal summer shall not fade,
Nor lose possession of that fair thou ow'st;
Nor shall Death brag thou wand'rest in his shade;
When in eternal lines to time thou grow'st.
    So long as men can breathe or eyes can see,
    So long lives this, and this gives life to thee.

A Sonnet for All Time
1   Shakespeare's sonnet 18 is a concise, effective expression of the mutability theme. I would define this theme as "time flies so we must take advantage of it while we can." In the poem, the speaker compared the one he loved to a summer's day. He attempted to deny the inevitability of death by suggesting that in this poem's "eternal lines" his love could live forever.
2   The poem is a carefully crafted example of the Shakespearean sonnet form. This kind of sonnet has fourteen lines, divided into an octave (the first eight lines) and a sestet (the remaining six lines). The meter is iambic pentameter (five units per line, each unit—or foot—consisting of an unstressed syllable followed by a stressed syllable).
3   In the octave, the speaker shows a day in the summer to be short-lived, easily damaged, and generally inferior to the person the poem is addressed to. He goes on to show the inevitability of the decline of nature's beauty, using a nautical image to further underscore the idea of time's inability to stop in its course to extinction. Lines 9–13 introduce the emphatic phrases "thy *eternal* summer," "possession" and "ow'st," suggesting the speaker's loved one to be indeed eternal, with youth and life not merely "leased" to him. The final couplet lends support to these lines and at the same time sums up the entire poem, by quietly explaining that the speaker's love can live forever while summer cannot, because he has immortalized his love in his poem.
4   Figurative language (metaphors, similes, and other figures of speech) enriches nearly every line of the sonnet. One example is line 3's "darling buds of May." By contrasting these buds with the "rough winds" that shake them, the speaker shows their fragility. These flowers should keep the season young and alive by decorating it with buds that signify new life; however, the mention of only one month and the contrast between the tender buds and the rough winds help stress the fact that the buds will soon disappear. "Summer's lease" (line 4) is another effective

image which lends support to the concept of summer's temporary quality. The phrase refers to the amount of time summer has borrowed or "rented" to live in. The "eye of heaven" is the sun, a single orb which gives light and sees all. The image helps to emphasize once more summer's evanescent quality by associating summer with the sun, which rises only to set at night. Finally, "thy eternal summer" expresses a paradox (an apparent contradiction). This encourages the reader to examine the entire poem's meaning, as the speaker suggests his love will remain young forever, something the reader and speaker both know is impossible.

5   I feel that the poem's effective use of imagery, especially its many contrasts, strengthens the central contrast between summer and the speaker's loved one. Its equally effective structure and orderly meter and rhyme scheme help deliver the poet's message clearly and unambiguously. In conclusion, it is my opinion that the speaker's playful exaggeration sets just the right tone in view of the essentially impossible claim the poem makes.

    a.   What is this essay's thesis? Where is it stated?

    b.   What attitude does the writer have toward the work she is evaluating?

    c.   Are the writer's judgments based on opinion or on analysis and interpretation? Explain.

    d.   Consider the writer's audience. Are the number and kind of definitions and explanations suitable? Explain.

    e.   Does the writer use enough examples?

    f.   Are the style and tone of the essay appropriate for the writer's audience and purpose?

    g.   Suggest any revisions you feel the writer of this essay should make.

2.   Revise your essay on "The Cask of Amontillado."

SUPPLEMENTARY EXERCISES

---

1.   Read this poem and the brief student evaluation that follows. Then answer the questions.

Constantly Risking Absurdity
Lawrence Ferlinghetti
    Constantly risking absurdity
                 and death
      whenever he performs
             above the heads
                   of his audience
     the poet like an acrobat
          climbs on rime
             to a high wire of his own making
 and balancing on eyebeams
          above a sea of faces
       paces his way
          to the other side of day

performing entrechats
                  and sleight-of-foot tricks
and other high theatrics
                  and all without mistaking
        any thing
                  for what it may not be

    For he's the super realist
                  who must perforce perceive
        taut truth
              before the taking of each stance or step
  in his supposed advance
              toward that still higher perch
where Beauty stands and waits
          with gravity
             to start her death-defying leap
    And he
        a little charleychaplin man
                who may or may not catch
    her fair eternal form
            spreadeagled in the empty air
      of existence

The Poet-Acrobat

In Ferlinghetti's poem "Constantly Risking Absurdity" the speaker compares the poet to an acrobat. He says poets and acrobats are alike for a number of reasons. This comparison gives the audience insight into the poet's problems.

Both poets and acrobats look for beauty and reach high to get it. Both depend on their audience's reaction to keep their performances sharp. In both cases the audience depends on the poet/acrobat to catch (and hold on to) beauty and to perform perfectly. And both audiences expect the poet/acrobat to make it all look easy.

But it *isn't* easy. Like a skilled acrobat, the poet works hard. The poet may seem like a silly comedian, but he or she is actually a skilled technician as well as an artist. A poet needs the grace of a dancer, the insight of a realist, the balance of a tightrope walker, the tricks of a magician, and the timing of a trapeze artist. The poet, like the acrobat, sets challenges for himself or herself—and those challenges may or may not be met. If they are, the poem is a success. If not, the poet can make a fool of himself or herself.

Most people have seen acrobats and trapeze artists perform at the circus. We know how hard they work. Now we also understand how hard poets work.

    a.   What is the essay's thesis? What is the student's attitude toward the poem?
    b.   What points does the student make to support her thesis? Can you, after rereading the poem, add any other supporting points?
    c.   The student does not quote any of the poet's words. Indicate places where she should quote, and choose relevant quotations that could illustrate her points.
    d.   The essay's conclusion is weak. See if you can strengthen it.

e.   The student rightly devotes most of her brief essay to explaining how the poet is like an acrobat, but the focus of the essay needs to be sharper. Rewrite paragraph 1 to achieve this.

2.   Reread the Ferlinghetti poem on page 344 and the poem below. Write a critical essay comparing their themes. (Note: Both poems are about poetry, but each has a different theme.)

Poetry
Nikki Giovanni

poetry is motion graceful
as a fawn
gentle as a teardrop
strong like the eye
finding peace in a crowded room

we poets tend to think
our words are golden
though emotion speaks too
loudly to be defined
by silence

sometimes after midnight or just before
the dawn
we sit typewriter in hand
pulling loneliness around us
forgetting our lovers or children
who are sleeping
ignoring the weary wariness
of our own logic
to compose a poem
    no one understands it
it never says "love me" for poets are
beyond love
it never says "accept me" for poems seek not
acceptance but controversy
it only says "i am" and therefore
i concede that you are too

a poem is pure energy
horizontally contained
between the mind
of the poet and the ear of the reader
if it does not sing discard the ear
for poetry is song
if it does not delight discard
the heart for poetry is joy
if it does not inform then close
off the brain for it is dead

if it cannot heed the insistent message
that life is precious

which is all we poets
wrapped in our loneliness
are trying to say

3.   Read the following two poems written on the same subject. The first poem is by
E. A. Robinson (1869–1935), a Pulitzer Prize-winning poet who spent most of his life
in poverty. He was also an alcoholic and frequently wrote poems about lonely, isolated
people who had trouble adjusting to life in Tilbury Town, the setting he created for
them. The second poem was written as a song by Paul Simon, the well-known composer and performer. In his poem, Simon expands the story of Richard Cory by having a
worker in Cory's factory respond to the news of his death. Using both poems as
sources, make a list of facts about Richard Cory and significant events in his life and
write a five-hundred-word obituary for the *Tilbury Times*. (You might want to read
some obituaries in your local paper before beginning your writing.) Giving a narrative
account of Cory's life, try to invent problems or situations that could have led to his
suicide.

To help you infer details about Cory's life, consider some of these questions about
both poems. Who is Richard Cory? Who might the speaker be? How is he different
from Cory? What qualities and possessions does Cory have? What doesn't he have?
What is the implied thesis of the poem? Can you tell how much time passes in the
poem? Look carefully at E. A. Robinson's poem and notice how many of the words
suggest royalty. Why do you think Robinson chose those words?

Richard Cory
Edwin Arlington Robinson
Whenever Richard Cory went down town,
We people on the pavement looked at him:
He was a gentleman from sole to crown,
Clean favored, and imperially slim.

And he was always quietly arrayed,
And he was always human when he talked;
But still he fluttered pulses when he said,
'Good-morning,' and he glittered when he walked.

And he was rich—yes, richer than a king—
And admirably schooled in every grace:
In fine, we thought that he was everything
To make us wish that we were in his place.

So on we worked, and waited for the light,
And went without the meat, and cursed the bread;
And Richard Cory, one calm summer night,
Went home and put a bullet through his head.

Richard Cory
Paul Simon
With Apologies to E. A. Robinson

They say that Richard Cory owns
One half of this old town,
With elliptical connections
To spread his wealth around.
Born into Society,
A banker's only child,
He had everything a man could want:
Power, grace and style.

Refrain:

But, I, I work in his factory
And I curse the life I'm livin'
And I curse my poverty
And I wish that I could be
Oh I wish that I could be
Oh I wish that I could be
Richard Cory.

The papers print his picture
Almost everywhere he goes:
Richard Cory at the opera,
Richard Cory at a show
And the rumor of his party
And the orgies on his yacht
Oh he surely must be happy
With everything he's got.   *(Refrain)*

He really gave to charity,
He had the common touch,
And they were grateful for his patronage
And they thanked him very much,
So my mind was filled with wonder
When the evening headlines read
     "Richard Cory went home last night
     And put a bullet through his head."   *(Refrain)*

4.   Read the following short story carefully and write up a quick analysis of each of its elements in turn. Be sure to look up any unfamiliar words you encounter in the story. Then complete one of the three tasks described at the end of the story.

THE FURNISHED ROOM
O. Henry (William Sydney Porter)

Restless, shifting, fugacious as time itself is a certain vast bulk of the population of the red brick district of the lower West Side. Homeless, they have a hundred homes. They flit from furnished room to furnished room, transients forever—transients in abode, transients in heart and mind. They sing "Home, Sweet Home" in ragtime; they carry their *lares et penates* in a bandbox; their vine is entwined about a picture hat; a rubber plant is their fig tree.

Hence the houses of this district, having had a thousand dwellers, should have a thousand tales to tell, mostly dull ones no doubt; but it would be strange if there could not be found a ghost or two in the wake of all these vagrant guests.

One evening after dark a young man prowled among these crumbling red mansions, ringing their bells. At the twelfth he rested his lean hand-baggage upon the step and wiped the dust from his hat-band and forehead. The bell sounded faint and far away in some remote, hollow depths.

To the door of this, the twelfth house whose bell he had rung, came a housekeeper who made him think of an unwholesome surfeited worm that had eaten its nut to a hollow shell and now sought to fill the vacancy with edible lodgers.

He asked if there was a room to let.

"Come in," said the housekeeper. Her voice came from her throat; her throat seemed lined with fur. "I have the third floor back, vacant since a week back. Should you wish to look at it?"

The young man followed her up the stairs. A faint light from no particular source mitigated the shadows of the halls. They trod noiselessly upon a stair carpet that its own loom would have forsworn. It seemed to have become vegetable; to have degenerated in that rank, sunless air to lush lichen or spreading moss that grew in patches to the staircase and was viscid under the foot like organic matter. At each turn of the stairs were vacant niches in the wall. Perhaps plants had once been set within them. If so they had died in that foul and tainted air. It may be that statues of the saints had stood there, but it was not difficult to conceive that imps and devils had dragged them forth in the darkness and down to the unholy depths of some furnished pit below.

"This is the room," said the housekeeper, from her furry throat. "It's a nice room. It ain't often vacant. I had some most elegant people in it last summer—no trouble at all, and paid in advance to the minute. The water's at the end of the hall. Sprowls and Mooney kept it three months. They done a vaudeville sketch. Miss B'retta Sprowls—you may have heard of her—Oh, that was just the stage names—right there over the dresser is where the marriage certificate hung, framed. The gas is here, and you see there is plenty of closet room. It's a room everybody likes. It never stays idle long."

"Do you have many theatrical people rooming here?" asked the young man.

"They comes and goes. A good proportion of my lodgers is connected with the theatres. Yes, sir, this is the theatrical district. Actor people never stays long anywhere. I get my share. Yes, they comes and they goes."

He engaged the room, paying for a week in advance. He was tired, he said, and would take possession at once. He counted out the money. The room had been made ready, she said, even to towels and water. As the housekeeper moved away he put, for the thousandth time, the question that he carried at the end of his tongue.

"A young girl—Miss Vashner—Miss Eloise Vashner—do you remember such a one among your lodgers? She would be singing on the stage, most likely. A fair girl, of medium height and slender, with reddish, gold hair and a dark mole near her left eyebrow."

"No, I don't remember the name. Them stage people has names they changes as often as their rooms. They comes and they goes. No, I don't call that one to mind."

No. Always no. Five months of ceaseless interrogation and the inevitable negative. So much time spent by day in questioning managers, agents, schools and choruses; by night among the audiences of theatres from all-star casts down to music halls so low that he dreaded to find what he most hoped for. He who had loved her best had tried to find her. He was sure that since her disappearance from home this great, water-girt city held her somewhere, but it was like a monstrous quicksand, shifting its particles constantly, with no foundation, its upper granules of to-day buried to-morrow in ooze and slime.

The furnished room received its latest guest with a first glow of pseudo-hospitality, a hectic, haggard, perfunctory welcome like the specious smile of a demirep. The sophistical comfort came in reflected gleams from the decayed furniture, the ragged brocade upholstery of a couch and two chairs, a foot-wide cheap pier glass between two windows, from one or two gilt picture frames and a brass bedstead in a corner.

The guest reclined, inert, upon a chair, while the room, confused in speech as though it were an apartment in Babel, tried to discourse to him of its diverse tenantry.

A polychromatic rug like some brilliant-flowered rectangular, tropical islet lay surrounded by a billowy sea of soiled matting. Upon the gray-papered wall were those pictures that pursue the homeless one from house to house—The Huguenot Lovers, The First Quarrel, The Wedding Breakfast, Psyche at the Fountain. The mantel's chastely severe outline was ingloriously veiled behind some pert drapery drawn rakishly askew like the sashes of the Amazonian ballet. Upon it were some desolate flotsam cast aside by the room's marooned when a lucky sail had borne them to a fresh port—a trifling vase or two, pictures of actresses, a medicine bottle, some stray cards out of a deck.

One by one, as the characters of a cryptograph become explicit, the little signs left by the furnished room's procession of guests developed a significance. The threadbare space in the rug in front of the dresser told that lovely women had marched in the throng. Tiny finger prints on the wall spoke of little prisoners trying to feel their way to sun and air. A splattered stain, raying like the shadow of a bursting bomb, witnessed where a hurled glass or bottle had splintered with its contents against the wall. Across the pier glass had been scrawled with a diamond in staggering letters the name "Marie." It seemed that the succession of dwellers in the furnished room had turned in fury—perhaps tempted beyond forbearance by its garish coldness—and wreaked upon it their passions. The furniture was chipped and bruised; the couch, distorted by bursting springs, seemed a horrible monster that had been slain during the stress of some grotesque convulsion. Some more potent upheaval had cloven a great slice from the marble mantel. Each plank in the floor owned its particular cant and shriek as from a separate and individual agony. It seemed incredible that all this malice and injury had been wrought upon the room by those who had called it for a time their home; and yet it may have been the cheated home instinct surviving blindly, the resentful rage at false household gods that had kindled their wrath. A hut that is our own we can sweep and adorn and cherish.

The young tenant in the chair allowed these thoughts to file, softshod, through his mind, while there drifted into the room furnished sounds and furnished scents. He heard in one room a tittering and incontinent, slack laughter; in others the monologue of a scold, the rattling of dice, a lullaby, and one crying dully; above him a banjo tinkled with spirit. Doors banged somewhere; the elevated trains roared intermittently; a cat yowled miserably upon a back fence. And he breathed the breath of the house—a dank savour rather than a smell—a cold, musty effluvium as from an underground vault mingled with the reeking exhalations of linoleum and mildewed and rotten woodwork.

Then suddenly, as he rested there, the room was filled with the strong, sweet odour of mignonette. It came as upon a single buffet of wind with such sureness and fragrance and emphasis that it almost seemed a living visitant. And the man cried aloud: "What, dear?" as if he had been called, and sprang up and faced about. The rich odour clung to him and wrapped him around. He reached out his arms for it, all his senses for the time confused and commingled. How could one be peremptorily called by an odour? Surely it must have been a sound. But, was it not the odour that had touched, that had caressed him?

"She has been in this room," he cried, and he sprang to wrest from it a token, for he knew he would recognize the smallest thing that had belonged to her or that she had touched. This enveloping scent of mignonette, the odour that she had loved and made her own—whence came it?

The room had been but carelessly set in order. Scattered upon the flimsy dresser scarf were half a dozen hairpins—those discreet, indistinguishable friends of womankind, feminine of gender, infinite of mood, and uncommunicative of tense. These he ignored, conscious of their triumphant lack of identity. Ransacking the drawers of the dresser he came upon a discarded, tiny, ragged handkerchief. He pressed it to his face. It was racy and insolent with heliotrope; he hurled it to the floor. In another drawer he found odd buttons, a theatre programme, a pawnbroker's card, two lost marshmallows, a book on the divination of dreams. In the last was a woman's black satin hair-bow, which halted him, poised between ice and fire. But the black satin hair-bow also is femininity's demure, impersonal, common ornament, and tells no tales.

And then he traversed the room like a hound on the scent, skimming the walls, considering the corners of the bulging matting on his hands and knees, rummaging mantel and tables, the curtains and hangings, the drunken cabinet in the corner, for a visible sign, unable to perceive that she was there beside, around, against, within, above him, clinging to him, wooing him, calling him so poignantly through the finer senses that even his grosser ones became cognisant of the call. Once again he answered loudly: "Yes, dear!" and turned, wild-eyed, to gaze on vacancy, for he could not yet discern form and colour and love and outstretched arms in the odour of mignonette. Oh, God! whence that odour, and since when have odours had a voice to call? Thus he groped.

He burrowed in crevices and corners, and found corks and cigarettes. These he passed in passive contempt. But once he found in a fold of the matting a half-smoked cigar, and this he ground beneath his heel with a green and trenchant oath. He sifted the room from end to end. He found dreary and ignoble small records of many a peripatetic tenant; but of her whom he sought, and who may have lodged there, and whose spirit seemed to hover there, he found no trace.

And then he thought of the housekeeper.

He ran from the haunted room downstairs and to a door that showed a crack of light. She came out to his knock. He smothered his excitement as best he could.

"Will you tell me, madam," he besought her, "who occupied the room I have before I came?"

"Yes, sir. I can tell you again. 'Twas Sprowls and Mooney, as I said. Miss B'retta Sprowls it was in the theatres, but Missis Mooney she was. My house is well known for respectability. The marriage certificate hung, framed, on a nail over—"

"What kind of a lady was Miss Sprowls—in looks, I mean?"

"Why, black-haired, sir, short, and stout, with a comical face. They left a week ago Tuesday."

"And before they occupied it?"

"Why, there was a single gentleman connected with the draying business. He left owing me a week. Before him was Missis Crowder and her two children, that stayed four months; and back of them was old Mr. Doyle, whose sons paid for him. He kept the room six months. That goes back a year, sir, and further I do not remember."

He thanked her and crept back to his room. The room was dead. The essence that had vivified it was gone. The perfume of mignonette had departed. In its place was the old, stale odour of mouldy house furniture, of atmosphere in storage.

The ebbing of his hope drained his faith. He sat staring at the yellow, singing gaslight. Soon he walked to the bed and began to tear the sheets into strips. With the blade of his knife he drove them tightly into every crevice around windows and door. When all was snug and taut he turned out the light, turned the gas full on again, and laid himself gratefully upon the bed.

.   .   .

It was Mrs. McCool's night to go with the can for beer. So she fetched it and sat with Mrs. Purdy in one of those subterranean retreats where housekeepers foregather and the worm dieth seldom.

"I rented out my third floor, back, this evening," said Mrs. Purdy across a fine circle of foam. "A young man took it. He went up to bed two hours ago."

"Now, did ye, Mrs. Purdy, ma'am?" said Mrs. McCool, with intense admiration. "You do be a wonder for rentin' rooms of that kind. And did ye tell him, then?" she concluded in a husky whisper, laden with mystery.

"Rooms," said Mrs. Purdy, in her furriest tones, "are furnished for to rent. I did not tell him, Mrs. McCool."

"'Tis right ye are, ma'am; 'tis by renting rooms we kape alive. Ye have the rale sense for business, ma'am. There be many people will rayjict the rentin' of a room if they be tould a suicide has been after dyin' in the bed of it."

"As you say, we has our living to be making," remarked Mrs. Purdy.

"Yis, ma'am; 'tis true. 'Tis just one wake ago this day I helped ye lay out the third floor, back. A pretty slip of a colleen she was to be killin' herself wid the gas—a swate little face she had, Mrs. Purdy, ma'am."

"She'd a-been called handsome, as you say," said Mrs. Purdy, assenting but critical, "but for that mole she had a-growin' by her left eyebrow. Do fill up your glass again, Mrs. McCool."

a.   Choose one element to focus on and create a topic for a critical essay about "The Furnished Room." Brainstorm, make a rough plan, and find a thesis. Then write the essay.
b.   Write a creative paper based on this story. For instance, write a news article reporting on the two deaths. Or write a section of the young woman's diary, or a letter from her to someone else. Or, you may write a story depicting a scene between the man and woman. Finally, you can write a story that is set after this one: create new characters and show how the events of "The Furnished Room" affect them.
c.   Read another story by O. Henry and write a critical essay comparing some aspect of the two.

SUGGESTED TOPICS FOR WRITING ABOUT LITERATURE

1.   Choose one of the following topics and write a critical essay on it.
    a.   Write a book review evaluating a novel or nonfiction book you have read for pleasure.
    b.   Write a critical essay in which you analyze the lyrics of a popular song. Show why those lyrics make the song memorable.

c. Write a study of the use of types instead of individuals in a soap opera, of plot structure in a TV sitcom, or of setting in a Western or science fiction program; or write on a similar topic which focuses on *one* element of drama.

d. Write a detailed analysis, element by element, of a movie.

e. Choose any two stories, poems, or plays by the same author and write an essay in which you demonstrate that one is superior to the other.

f. Compare a novel and a film based on it.

2. Choose one of the following topics and write a creative paper about it.

a. Write a story or a one-act play using characters, setting, or plot of a story or novel you have read. Try putting the author's characters in a different setting, or adding a new character who changes the plot.

b. Retell a play or a narrative poem as a short story.

c. Write a continuation of a story or play you have read, or write a story describing a scene or events that might have preceded the story.

d. Write a letter from one character to another, or write an excerpt from a character's diary.

e. Write a news article reporting on an event described in a story or play.

f. Write a fable or fairy tale using the plot and/or characters of a short story.

CHAPTER

14

The Library Research Paper

Y ou approach a library research paper much the way you do other essays. In planning it, you consider your boundaries, limit your topic, find something to say, formulate a thesis, and decide upon an effective arrangement for your materials. You also write several drafts of your paper, revising as you go. The difference, however, is that you base these activities on research materials from the library and elsewhere. You do this research in waves: you gather enough information to start writing; then as you write, you go back and do more research. The following schedule shows you one orderly way to proceed:

Prewriting

Step 1: Choosing a topic
Step 2: Preliminary research
Step 3: Assembling a preliminary bibliography

Step 4:   Concentrated reading and note taking
Step 5:   Deciding on a thesis

Writing and arranging

Step 6:   Making a working outline
Step 7:   Writing the first draft

Revising

Step 8:   Revising the first draft
Step 9:   Documenting
Step 10: Preparing the final draft
Step 11: Final editing

Prewriting takes the most time in this process. To set up a realistic schedule, then, you should allot at least half of your time to steps 1 through 5—two to four weeks, let us say. If you do this, you can eliminate much of the last-minute tension routinely associated with a research paper.

PREWRITING

STEP 1: CHOOSING A TOPIC

☐ NARROWING YOUR SUBJECT

Usually your research topic begins as a specific assignment from your instructor. Some instructors give a list of topics to choose from, while others list a number of general subject areas that are acceptable. In the latter case, you must narrow your general subject to a workable topic. You do this the same way you do when working on a short essay. You brainstorm and use questions for probing or the journalistic questions. The main differences are that you use the time to investigate the full potential of a subject and that you choose a topic that requires research. (See "Getting Started," page 25.)

The subjects in the list below are no more than general ideas. The narrowed topics, however, are specific questions that suggest guided research.

Subject	Topic
Medical research	How are research priorities of the American Cancer Institute set?
Paris in the 1920s	What effect did the Lost Generation have on the American literary tradition?
Nutrition	What are the benefits and drawbacks of a macrobiotic diet?

School desegregation since 1954	How has the 1954 Supreme Court decision on desegregation affected the Boston parochial schools?
Women in the military	How have opportunities for women in the U.S. Army changed since World War II?
Harry Truman and Thomas E. Dewey	What were the major political differences between Harry Truman and Thomas E. Dewey?
Palimony	How has "palimony" influenced recent rulings on distribution of property among divorced couples in California?

☐   TOPIC SUITABILITY

Whatever your topic, it must be suitable for *research,* not based exclusively on your personal experience or value judgments. The questions "Was Richard Nixon a criminal?" or "Is James Michener a better novelist than Herman Wouk?" might interest you, but they are weak topics because neither research nor expert testimony can resolve these issues.

Nor should your research paper just report information or rehash issues already established beyond any doubt. Your topic must be debatable, phrased as a question that your research will answer. "How is meat preserved?" is not debatable. It does not require you to weigh evidence and reach conclusions. "Do nitrates in preserved meats pose a threat to the consumer?" does work because you can locate data, consider a variety of opinions, and draw a conclusion based on evidence.

Finally, your topic must fit within the boundaries of your assignment. The question "How is the Holocaust dealt with by the press?" is far too broad for a ten-page, or even a hundred-page, treatment. But how the Holocaust was dealt with during one year in three specific newspapers might work very well.

EXERCISE

Which of the following would be suitable topics for a ten-page library research paper? Be prepared to discuss why those you rejected could be poor choices.

    a.   Should the government have relocated Japanese Americans during World War II?

    b.   Law School: how to apply.

    c.   What ethnic groups were represented on the western frontier?

    d.   Fantasy fiction: literature or trash?

    e.   What were the advantages or disadvantages of the monarchy during the eighteenth century?

    f.   Who was the most influential politician of the twentieth century?

g.   What is the best way of investing money?

h.   Are today's teenagers more or less moral than their parents?

i.   How are automobiles manufactured in Japan?

j.   The history of the submarine.

STEP 2: PRELIMINARY RESEARCH

More than one person has said that the key to successful research is knowing what questions to ask. Don't start your preliminary research with a preconceived conclusion in mind. Let the results of your investigation determine what you say about your topic. Don't be afraid to look at a wide range of material, even some that seems unrelated to your subject. Accidents, wrong turns, and unexpected sources sometimes lead to the most exciting results. Remember that as you do your preliminary research you will probably continue to narrow your topic, or even change it.

You do two kinds of reading for a library research paper: preliminary and concentrated. In your *preliminary reading,* you check a topic, first to make sure that your library has enough information on it, and second to see whether (and how) it might be further modified. At this point you want to assess the workability of a topic, not to gather a lot of specific information. Your notes at this stage will be sketchy, primarily bibliographic.

Even now you should proceed in an orderly fashion. For the greatest efficiency, check your topic in the following sources:

1.   The card catalog

2.   Reference books

3.   Periodical indexes

If most of the materials you need are not in your library, change your subject. On the other hand, if the amount of information on your topic is overwhelming, narrow it further to a more manageable size. Incidentally, a meeting with your college librarian during your preliminary research stage can save you hours of hit-or-miss investigation on your own.

Recently a number of libraries have installed computerized systems that allow students to call up catalog entries on terminals. Other libraries have transferred catalog cards to microfiche, and you can quickly locate and scan material on a viewing device. Most, however, will continue, at least for the near future, to register their holdings in card-catalog drawers.

Using the card catalog   First of all, find out whether your library has a single catalog that interfiles author, title, and subject cards or two separate catalogs, one for author-title cards and the other for subject cards. If it has a single file, you can do all your work in one area. With separate files, you have to decide whether to look up particular books or your general subject first. This decision isn't hard. At a preliminary stage, you probably don't have specific titles in mind, so usually you start by looking up your topic.

Let us say that you are thinking of doing a paper on crime in the Old West. After doing some preliminary thinking you decide to investigate the topic, "How Common Were Gunfighters in the Old West?" Now you want to look this up in the card catalog. Entries are arranged alphabetically, just as they are in a dictionary or an encyclopedia. If you find a general subject listing—"Gunfighters"—for your topic, then you are in luck. If you don't, don't give up hope. Books on "gunfighters" may appear under a different heading. You can find out by consulting the index volume, *Subject Headings Used in Dictionary Catalogs of the Library of Congress*, which is kept at the reference desk. Looking at the index, you find that "gunfighters" appears under the general heading of "Crime and Criminals—The West." Under this heading in the catalog you find the following card.

Subject card

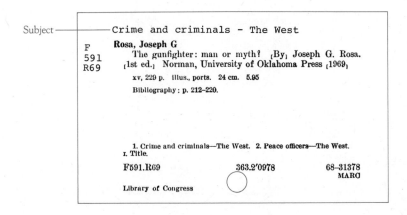

Many times your subject catalog has cross-reference cards that refer you to related subject headings. Under "Crime and Criminals—The West," for instance, you find this cross-reference card:

Cross-reference card

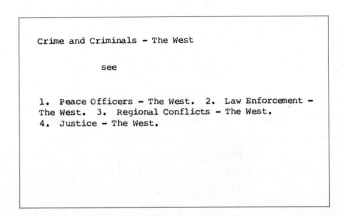

You can find material that you might otherwise miss under these headings. If, for example, you wanted information on Wild Bill Hickok, the colorful frontier marshal, you would find his biography, by Joseph G. Rosa, listed only under "Peace Officers."

You could also find the book *The Gunfighter: Man or Myth?* under "Rosa, Joseph G.," or under the title, in the author-title catalog. Notice that all the cards listing this book carry the same call numbers in the upper left-hand corner. The title card is the same as the subject card except it has the *title* typed across the top. The author card is the same as the other two except for the *author's name* at the top.

Title and author cards

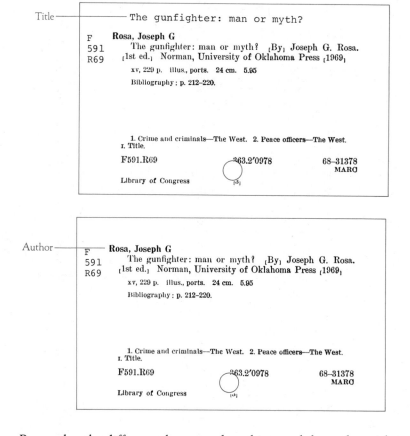

Remember the difference between the subject and the author-title cards. If you look up an author, Hart Crane for instance, in the subject index, you find books *about* the author and his works—for instance, R. W. B. Lewis's *The Poetry of Hart Crane.* If you look up an author in the author-title index, you will find books written *by* the author. Under "Hart Crane" are all Crane's works that the library owns.

Interpreting the catalog card   Besides telling you whether your library has a book, the card catalog gives you other useful information. It not only tells you where to find a book in the library, it also helps you see whether a book contains the information you want.

Assume you want to do a paper on methods of flood control in use in the United States. As part of your preliminary research you locate this subject card:

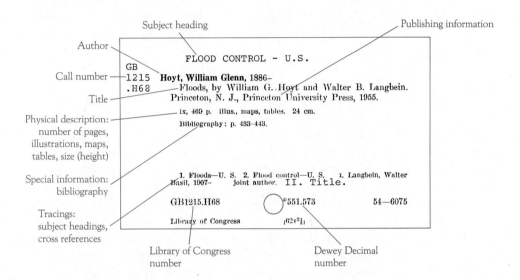

Once you learn to read the notations, the card is surprisingly easy to understand. The call number tells the subject category under which the book *Floods* is shelved. Most college libraries use the Library of Congress classification system, which combines numbers and letters to identify books by subject area. Many public libraries and some college libraries index books by the Dewey Decimal system, using numbers to designate subject headings.

In addition to the call number, the catalog card gives biographical information about the author and publishing data about the book. From the card above, you can tell that William Glenn Hoyt wrote the book *Floods* with a coauthor, Walter B. Langbein, and that it was published in 1955. From the notations on the card, you see that *Floods* is a substantial work: 469 pages, with illustrations, maps, tables, and an 11-page bibliography that you might use for your research. This material *could* be outdated, but old does not automatically mean bad. You would have to look at the material to see how useful it is.

Sometimes called "tracings," the Arabic numerals at the bottom of the catalog card indicate subject headings that reflect the main focus of the book. The Roman numerals show under what headings you can find other cards for the same book. You can find *Floods*, for example, by looking under the name of its coauthor, Walter Basil Langbein, or the title.

The card catalog provides you with enough data to make preliminary judgments. A 64-page book published in 1940 with no bibliography might or might not be worth looking at. But a book of 250 pages, published in 1984 and written by an expert in your subject, with a 14-page bibliography, would most certainly be worth a special look.

One final word of advice. If you cannot find a book, don't give up. Go to the librarian for help. The book may be out, on reserve, or held in a different section of the library. If it has been checked out, the librarian will tell you when it is due back and, in many cases, will notify the borrower that someone else is waiting for it.

□ REFERENCE BOOKS

Reference books give you an overview of your topic. These works include general encyclopedias, encyclopedias and dictionaries in special subjects, unabridged dictionaries, special dictionaries, yearbooks and almanacs, atlases, general bibliographies, and biographical dictionaries and indexes. The following list only suggests the vast amount of reference material available. Many college libraries hand out "pathfinders" that provide additional reference sources for specific academic fields.

Encyclopedias   A *general encyclopedia* gives information on all branches of knowledge. Articles are arranged alphabetically and are often written by experts in a particular field. Because they are easy to use and available in all college libraries, encyclopedias can give you a good overview of your subject and help you narrow your subject to a workable topic. They are, however, *no substitutes* for further research. Even the best general encyclopedias make no attempt to be comprehensive, and you should consider them only as sources of introductory information.

Not all general encyclopedias, however, are suited for college-level research. The *World Book,* although interesting and informative, aims primarily at high-school students. It does present complex issues and concepts in simple and easily understood articles, but your college instructors will probably want a richer explanation of a subject. The *Encyclopedia Americana,* on the other hand, is written for a college audience. It contains articles on a great number of subjects and includes an index volume that lists main entries as well as cross references. Its major disadvantage is that it stresses North American subjects—articles on American places, organizations, and institutions, for instance—and does not give uniform coverage to other subjects.

Perhaps the most respected multivolume encyclopedia is the *Encyclopaedia Britannica,* now in its fifteenth edition. Unlike previous editions, the 1974 edition is divided into three sections: the *Propaedia,* a one-volume general subject index; the *Micropaedia,* a ten-volume index containing brief articles; and the *Macropaedia,* a nineteen-volume detailed discussion of many of the subjects listed in the *Micropaedia.* Although it takes some getting used to, the *Britannica* is invaluable in providing an overview of your topic. You can begin your preliminary research by consulting the *Propaedia,* then read the brief articles in the *Micropaedia,* and finally focus on the in-depth discussions in the *Macropaedia.* These comprehensive articles, written by internationally recognized scholars, frequently are illustrated and are accompanied by briefly annotated bibliographies.

A one-volume encyclopedia can give you a quick sense of a subject. Two of the best are the *New Columbia Encyclopedia* and the *Random House Encyclopedia.* Both contain a surprisingly large number of short entries. They list subjects in alphabetical order, but they do not offer the cross-referencing and in-depth bibliographic information that the multivolume encyclopedias do. Using them, therefore, does not excuse you from consulting the *Encyclopedia Americana* or the *Encyclopaedia Britannica* if you decide to proceed with a topic.

Encyclopedias and dictionaries in special subjects   Many reference works concentrate on particular subjects. Called either "encyclopedias" or "dictionaries," they examine one subject area thoroughly. Your reference librarian can help you locate these specialized reference books in your school library. The following list of special reference works only suggests the variety of sources available:

Art

Encyclopedia of World Art, 15 volumes. Scholarly articles, detailed bibliographies, and many plates. Covers art of all periods and countries.

Oxford Companion to Art. A one-volume encyclopedia devoted to the visual arts.

Biology

Gray, Peter, ed. *The Encyclopedia of the Biological Sciences.* Directed at students and experts reading outside their fields. Includes bibliographies, biographical articles, and illustrations.

A Dictionary of Genetics. Comprehensive information about genetic research, including definitions of terms.

Business and economics

The McGraw-Hill Dictionary of Modern Economics. Extended definitions of terms. Also includes bibliographies.

Heyel, Carl, ed. *The Encyclopedia of Management.* Definitions and explanations. Includes references for further reading.

Munn, Glenn Gaywaine. *Encyclopedia of Banking and Finance.* Defines and explains pertinent terms.

Chemistry

Encyclopedia of Chemistry. Articles about distinguished chemists, various chemical associations, and chemicals themselves.

Chemical Technology: An Encyclopedic Treatment. Focuses on the applied uses of chemical technology.

The Merck Index of Chemicals and Drugs. Formulas, properties, and uses of drugs and chemicals. References to relevant literature.

Drama

The Oxford Companion to the Theatre. A one-volume encyclopedia of the theater.

McGraw-Hill Encyclopedia of World Drama, 4 volumes. Comprehensive coverage of all aspects of drama from ancient to present times.

Education

Dictionary of Education. A scholarly dictionary with extended definitions of terms.

The Encyclopedia of Education, 10 volumes. Covers all aspects of the field. Emphasizes theory and history.

Engineering

Engineering Encyclopedia. A concise encyclopedia and mechanical dictionary. Includes definitions of engineering terms and some historical material.

McGraw-Hill Encyclopedia of Science and Technology. Not specifically geared to engineering, but includes articles of related interest.

History

Cambridge Ancient History. Egypt to the fall of Rome. Each chapter is written by a specialist; each volume includes a full bibliography.

Cambridge Medieval History. Reference history of the Middle Ages prepared by experts in the field.

New Cambridge Modern History. Authoritative and comprehensive general modern history, covering the Renaissance through World War II, with an emphasis on Europe.

Dictionary of American History. Brief articles on many topics on American history and life. Does not include biography.

Oxford Companion to American History. Short articles on American history.

Literature

Oxford Companion to American Literature. Short articles dealing with the literature of Canada and the United States. Entries cover a wide range of subjects: authors, specific works, historical figures.

Oxford Companion to English Literature. Concise articles on English authors and on characters and allusions encountered in English literature.

Oxford Companion to Classical Literature. Handbook of information on classical Greek and Roman literary works, authors, history, institutions, and religion.

Spiller, Robert E., and others. *Literary History of the United States*, 2 volumes. A detailed literary history of the United States from colonial times to the present. Volume I concentrates on specific periods; Volume II has bibliographical essays and a detailed index.

Cassell's Encyclopedia of World Literature, 3 volumes. Volume I includes brief definitions of literary terms and essays on literary history. Volumes II and III contain biographical sketches.

Princeton Encyclopedia of Poetry and Poetics. A comprehensive work dealing with history, prosody, and terminology. No biographies.

Mathematics

The Universal Encyclopedia of Mathematics. Alphabetically arranged articles on topics from arithmetic to calculus. Over two hundred pages of formulas and tables.

The International Dictionary of Applied Mathematics. Defines terms and describes methods of applying math to various fields of physical science and engineering.

Music

Grove's Dictionary of Music and Musicians, 9 volumes. Covers the field from 1450 to the present. Includes biographies; musical history, theory, and practice; definitions of terms; analyses of songs and operas. Emphasis on English subjects.

Apel, Willi. *Harvard Dictionary of Music*. A one-volume dictionary with articles based on scholarship; numerous definitions; no biographies. Emphasizes historical point of view.

Physics

Encyclopedic Dictionary of Physics, 9 volumes. A scholarly dictionary of physics. It also deals with astronomy, geophysics, biophysics, and related subjects. Articles are signed; many have bibliographical references.

Encyclopedia of Physics, 54 volumes. Covers the field comprehensively.

Political science

The American Political Dictionary. Includes definitions and explanations of terms, laws, and cases pertaining to civil liberties, the Constitution, and the legislative process.

Dunner, Joseph, ed. *Dictionary of Political Science*. Compact encyclopedia treats important people, places, terms, and events.

Theimer, Walter. *Encyclopedia of Modern World Politics*. Brief articles on current political issues and figures of all periods and countries; also covers current political terms.

Psychology

Encyclopedia of Psychology, 3 volumes. Contains both short and long entries.

Encyclopedia of Human Behavior: Psychology, Psychiatry and Mental Health, 2 volumes. Contains long articles as well as definitions and case histories.

Contemporary Psychology. Collection of current reviews in the field.

Religion and philosophy

Concise Encyclopedia of Living Faiths. In-depth articles on the world's religions.

Encyclopedia Judaica, 16 volumes. Gives a comprehensive view of Jewish life, customs, religion, history, and literature.

New Catholic Encyclopedia, 15 volumes. Examines the teachings, history, organization, and activities of the Catholic Church in detail.

Oxford Dictionary of the Christian Church.

A collection of historical and biographical articles and definitions of ecclesiastical terms and customs.

Burr, Nelson R. *A Critical Bibliography of Religion in America*. Bibliography of books, articles, and reviews. Includes social and cultural aspects of religion.

The Concise Encyclopedia of Western Philosophy and Philosophers. A one-volume work including brief articles on thinkers and ideas of all time periods.

Sociology, social work, and anthropology

Encyclopedia of Social Work. Articles on social work history, theory, practice, and policy.

Encyclopedia of Sociology. Articles by experts covering a wide variety of subjects.

Winick, Charles. *Dictionary of Anthropology*. Brief articles identify prominent early (pre–1900) anthropologists and their contributions.

Work, Monroe Nathan. *Bibliography of the Negro in Africa and America*. Scholarly bibliography covering periodicals and books published before 1928.

Dictionary Catalog of the Schomberg Collection of Negro Literature and History. Reprints nearly 200,000 author, title, and subject catalog cards from the New York Public Library's collection.

Unabridged dictionaries   Unabridged dictionaries are comprehensive works that give detailed information about words.

Webster's New International Dictionary of the English Language, 2nd ed. (1934). Unusually clear definitions, given in historic sequence (the oldest meaning appearing first). Contains over 600,000 words and includes obsolete words and antonyms as well as synonyms. Considered more reliable for questions of usage and status of words than the third edition. Includes biographical dictionary, abbreviations, and other supplementary lists.

Webster's Third New International Dictionary (1971). Includes 100,000 new words or new meanings of older words. Over 200,000 quotations illustrate current usage and meaning.

Funk and Wagnalls New Standard Dictionary (1959). Emphasis on current meaning, spelling, and pronunciation. Newest meaning of each word appears first.

Oxford English Dictionary, 15 volumes (1884–1928; supplements 1933, 1972, 1977). The most scholarly and comprehensive English language dictionary. Includes the history of every word used in England since 1150. Information is provided about when and how each word entered the language and about changes in spelling, meaning, and usage. Each word history is illustrated by quotations.

Special dictionaries These dictionaries focus on particular characteristics of language.

Fowler, Henry Watson. *Dictionary of Modern English Usage,* 2nd ed. Authority on problems of grammatical usage.

Nicholson, Margaret. A *Dictionary of American-English Usage.* Simplified version of Fowler, designed to meet current American needs.

Evans, Bergen, and Cornelia Evans. *Dictionary of Contemporary American Usage.* Lively treatment of questions of usage. Treats words, idioms, style, punctuation, and the like with humor.

Partridge, Eric. *Dictionary of Slang and Unconventional English,* 5th ed. Defines English slang terms and gives approximate date each word first appeared.

Webster's Dictionary of Synonyms. Lists words with similar meanings and discriminates among them.

Roget's International Thesaurus, 3rd ed. Lists synonyms, groups words into categories; detailed index.

Yearbooks and almanacs Yearbooks and almanacs are useful places to find facts or statistics. A yearbook is an annual publication that brings information on a subject up to date. An almanac provides lists, charts, and statistics about a number of subjects.

World Almanac. Includes statistics about government, population, sports, and many other subjects. Includes a chronology of events of the previous year. Published annually since 1868.

Information Please Almanac. Supplements the *World Almanac* (each work includes information unavailable in the other) and is somewhat easier to read. Published annually since 1947.

Facts on File. A news digest with index.

Covering 1940 to the present, this work offers digests of important news stories from metropolitan dailies. Published weekly, *Facts on File* serves as a kind of current encyclopedia.

Editorials on File. Reprints important editorials from American and Canadian newspapers. Editorials represent both sides of controversial issues and are preceded by a summary of the principles involved.

Atlases An atlas contains maps and charts and often a wealth of historical, cultural, political, and economic information.

Rand McNally Cosmopolitan World Atlas. A modern and extremely legible medium-sized atlas.

Encyclopedia Britannica World Atlas. Uses *Rand McNally Cosmopolitan* maps and includes geographical summaries and information on world distribution.

Times, London. *The Times Atlas of the World,* 5 volumes, John Bartholomew, ed.

Considered one of the best large world atlases. Includes inset maps for many cities. Very accurate and attractive maps throughout.

Shepherd, William Robert. *Historical Atlas,* 9th ed. Covers period from 2000 B.C. to 1955. Excellent maps showing war campaigns and development of commerce.

General bibliographies   General bibliographies list books available in a number of fields.

Books in Print. A helpful index of authors and titles of every book in print in the United States. *The Subject Guide to Books in Print* indexes books according to subject area. *Paperbound Books in Print* is an index to all currently available paperbacks.

The Bibliographic Index. A tool for locating bibliographies, this index is particularly useful for researching a subject which is not well covered in other indexes. Provides references to long bibliographies in books and brief ones in periodical articles.

Biographical dictionaries and indexes   Specialized biographical reference books provide valuable information about people's lives and times and sometimes contain lengthy bibliographic listings.

Living persons

Who's Who in America. Published every other year, this dictionary gives very brief biographical data and addresses of prominent living Americans.

Who's Who. Concise biographical facts about notable living English men and women.

Current Biography. Informal articles on living people of many nationalities; articles often include portraits.

American Men and Women of Science. Information about prominent Americans in the physical, biological, social, and behavioral sciences.

Twentieth Century Authors. Informal biographies of contemporary authors of many nationalities. Portraits and lists of authors' writings included.

Deceased persons

Dictionary of American Biography. Considered the best of American biographical dictionaries. Offers articles on over thirteen thousand deceased Americans who have made contributions in all fields.

Dictionary of National Biography. The most important reference work for English biography.

Webster's Biographical Dictionary. Perhaps the most widely used biographical reference work. Includes people from all periods and places.

American Authors 1600–1900; European Authors 1000–1900; British Authors Before 1800. These works provide biographical data on authors who wrote before the twentieth century.

Who Was When? A Dictionary of Contemporaries. A reference source for historical biography; covers 500 B.C. through the early 1970s.

Who Was Who in America 1607–1896. Entries on deceased Americans; supplemented by *Who Was Who in America 1897–1960.* These volumes, though useful, do contain some inaccuracies.

□ PERIODICAL INDEXES

Articles in newspapers, magazines, and journals are not indexed in the card catalog but in bound volumes located on specific tables or shelves in your library's reference section. Learning how to use these indexes requires only a bit of effort.

Books take a year or more to get into print, and in some fields—computers, engineering, medicine—rapid change is the rule. Periodicals also present subjects too limited for book-length treatment but possibly very pertinent to your research. The only way to find this material is to search the periodical indexes.

Using a periodical index   A periodical index lists, by subject, articles from a selected group of magazines, newspapers, or scholarly journals. Some are annual; others are monthly or biweekly supplements that are bound together at the end of each year. Most such indexes have similar formats: they arrange entries according to subject and use abbreviations to save space. The key to the abbreviations at the front of the volume not only enables you to use the index; it also provides all the information that you will need to assemble your list of works cited at the end of your paper.

When you see a promising entry, copy all the information that you will need to find your article: author; article title; periodical title; volume; date; pages. Here is a sample entry from the *Humanities Index*.

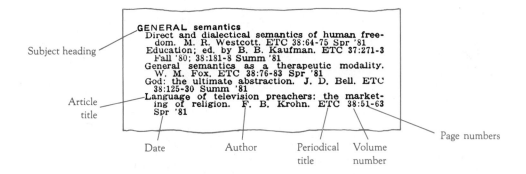

Subject heading

Article title

Date

Author

Periodical title

Volume number

Page numbers

Once you have this information, find out if your library has the periodical. Many libraries have separate catalogs, computer terminals, or microfiches listing their periodical holdings. (A periodical catalog is like the card catalog except that, instead of books, it lists the journal, newspaper, and magazine holdings of the library.)

Periodical card

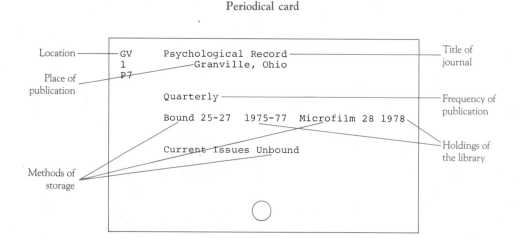

Location

Place of publication

Methods of storage

Title of journal

Frequency of publication

Holdings of the library

As the card shows, libraries house periodicals in a number of ways. You can find them in yearly bound volumes or in current paperbound supplements. Cards that say *"microfiche," "microprint,"* or *"microfilm"* tell you that the material has been stored photographically. You usually cannot take periodicals out of the library, so you will have to copy by hand or photocopy all the material you need.

Useful indexes   Indexes are classified in terms of the audience of the periodicals they list: general readers or experts in different fields. Here are several indexes that many college students find useful.

Readers' Guide to Periodical Literature

The *Readers' Guide* lists articles that appear in over 150 magazines for general readers. Good for current views of history, social science, and some scientific topics, it does have limitations. Popular articles tend to oversimplify complex issues, leaving out data you might need. You should supplement this material with information from more scholarly works.

Appearing in yearly volumes and paperbound supplements, articles are listed and cross-referenced under subject headings. For a paper on grown children who move in with their parents, look up the general subject "Parent-child relationship" in the latest volume. Under this heading is this list of cross references and articles:

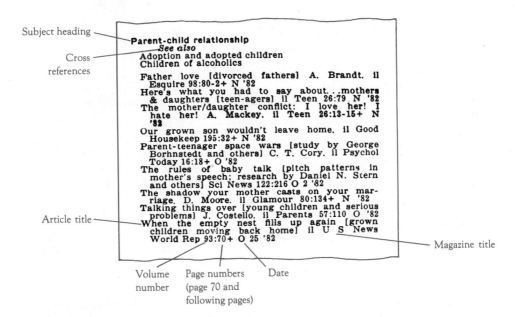

The *New York Times Index*

The *New York Times* is an excellent and reliable record of current events. In addition to news, it contains feature-length articles on issues of general interest. The *New York Times Index* lists major articles and features

of the *Times* since 1851 by year or years. To find articles on a subject, locate the volume for the appropriate year. Articles are listed alphabetically by subject with short summaries. Supplements are published every two weeks. If your library subscribes to the *New York Times* microfilm service, you have access to every issue of the *Times* back to 1851. Articles give a contemporary view of a wide variety of subjects—everything from business and politics to literature and the arts.

For a paper on economic conditions in Communist China, under the general subject "China," you would find a number of articles under the subheading "Economic Conditions and Trends."

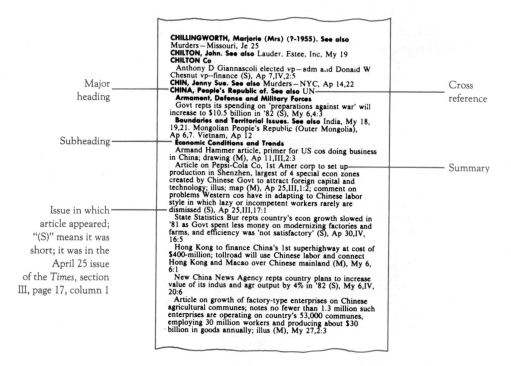

Major heading

Subheading

Issue in which article appeared; "(S)" means it was short; it was in the April 25 issue of the *Times*, section III, page 17, column 1

Cross reference

Summary

CHILLINGWORTH, Marjorie (Mrs) (?-1955). See also Murders—Missouri, Je 25
CHILTON, John. See also Lauder, Estee, Inc, My 19
CHILTON Co
  Anthony D Giannascoli elected vp—adm and Donald W Chesnut vp--finance (S), Ap 7,IV,2:5
CHIN, Jenny Sue. See also Murders—NYC, Ap 14,22
CHINA, People's Republic of. See also UN
  Armament, Defense and Military Forces
  Govt repts its spending on 'preparations against war' will increase to $10.5 billion in '82 (S), My 6,4:3
  Boundaries and Territorial Issues. See also India, My 18, 19,21. Mongolian People's Republic (Outer Mongolia), Ap 6,7. Vietnam, Ap 12
  Economic Conditions and Trends
  Armand Hammer article, primer for US cos doing business in China; drawing (M), Ap 11,III,2:3
  Article on Pepsi-Cola Co, 1st Amer corp to set up production in Shenzhen, largest of 4 special econ zones created by Chinese Govt to attract foreign capital and technology; illus; map (M), Ap 25,III,1:2; comment on problems Western cos have in adapting to Chinese labor style in which lazy or incompetent workers rarely are dismissed (S), Ap 25,III,17:1
  State Statistics Bur repts country's econ growth slowed in '81 as Govt spent less money on modernizing factories and farms, and efficiency was 'not satisfactory' (S), Ap 30,IV, 16:5
  Hong Kong to finance China's 1st superhighway at cost of $400-million; tollroad will use Chinese labor and connect Hong Kong and Macao over Chinese mainland (M), My 6, 6:1
  New China News Agency repts country plans to increase value of its indus and agr output by 4% in '82 (S), My 6,IV, 20:6
  Article on growth of factory-type enterprises on Chinese agricultural communes; notes no fewer than 1.3 million such enterprises are operating on country's 53,000 communes, employing 30 million workers and producing about $30 billion in goods annually; illus (M), My 27,2:3

Book Review Digest

To determine whether a book is a reliable source, look at *Book Review Digest*. Containing selected excerpts from reviews of books when they were published, annual volumes list entries according to title and author. Look up a book in the volume with the same year of publication or the next year's volume in case the book was not reviewed in its year of publication.

Book Review Digest lets you see the initial reactions of critics to books published as far back as 1905. This gives you some insight into the critical climate of a book's times, and it also helps you judge whether a book is informative and accurate.

How would these excerpts from *Book Review Digest* help you do a paper on the politics of nuclear energy?

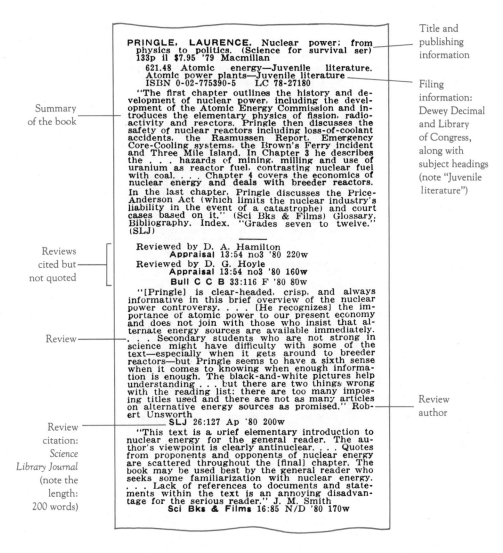

Title and publishing information

Filing information: Dewey Decimal and Library of Congress, along with subject headings (note "Juvenile literature")

Summary of the book

Reviews cited but not quoted

Review

Review author

Review citation: *Science Library Journal* (note the length: 200 words)

PRINGLE, LAURENCE. Nuclear power; from physics to politics. (Science for survival ser) 133p il $7.95 '79 Macmillan

621.48 Atomic energy—Juvenile literature. Atomic power plants—Juvenile literature. ISBN 0-02-775390-5 LC 78-27180

"The first chapter outlines the history and development of nuclear power, including the development of the Atomic Energy Commission and introduces the elementary physics of fission, radioactivity and reactors. Pringle then discusses the safety of nuclear reactors including loss-of-coolant accidents, the Rasmussen Report, Emergency Core-Cooling systems, the Brown's Ferry incident and Three Mile Island. In Chapter 3 he describes the . . . hazards of mining, milling and use of uranium as reactor fuel, contrasting nuclear fuel with coal. . . . Chapter 4 covers the economics of nuclear energy and deals with breeder reactors. In the last chapter, Pringle discusses the Price-Anderson Act (which limits the nuclear industry's liability in the event of a catastrophe) and court cases based on it." (Sci Bks & Films) Glossary. Bibliography. Index. "Grades seven to twelve." (SLJ)

Reviewed by D. A. Hamilton
  Appraisal 13:54 no3 '80 220w
Reviewed by D. G. Hoyle
  Appraisal 13:54 no3 '80 160w
  Bull C C B 33:116 F '80 80w

"[Pringle] is clear-headed, crisp, and always informative in this brief overview of the nuclear power controversy. . . . [He recognizes] the importance of atomic power to our present economy and does not join with those who insist that alternate energy sources are available immediately. . . . Secondary students who are not strong in science might have difficulty with some of the text—especially when it gets around to breeder reactors—but Pringle seems to have a sixth sense when it comes to knowing when enough information is enough. The black-and-white pictures help understanding . . . but there are two things wrong with the reading list: there are too many imposing titles used and there are not as many articles on alternative energy sources as promised." Robert Unsworth
  SLJ 26:127 Ap '80 200w

"This text is a brief elementary introduction to nuclear energy for the general reader. The author's viewpoint is clearly antinuclear. . . . Quotes from proponents and opponents of nuclear energy are scattered throughout the [final] chapter. The book may be used best by the general reader who seeks some familiarization with nuclear energy. . . . Lack of references to documents and statements within the text is an annoying disadvantage for the serious reader." J. M. Smith
  Sci Bks & Films 16:85 N/D '80 170w

The filing information and the summary indicate that *Nuclear Power: From Physics to Politics* is appropriate for high school students who want a general introduction to this subject. The reviews reinforce this, pointing out specific problems with the author's bibliography and with his lack of references. Having seen this, you would most likely disregard this book as a source for a college paper.

For a paper on the role of factory workers in Japan before World War II, the following entry would confirm your hunch that Misiko Hane's book was worth a look. Not only are the reviews favorable, but both summary and reviews tell you the book is relevant to your topic. Even if you couldn't find the book on your library shelf, then, it might be a good idea to see if you could reserve the book or look for it in another library.

HANE, MIKISO. Peasants, rebels, and outcastes; the underside of modern Japan. 297p maps $20.50; pa $9.95 1982 Pantheon Bks.

952 Japan—Social conditions. Japan—History—1868-1945

ISBN 0-394-51963-9; 0-394-71040-1 (pa)

LC 81-18912

Using diaries, memoirs, fiction, trial testimony, personal recollections and other accounts, the author, a professor of Japanese history who was born in California in 1922 and lived in Japan until 1940, describes the problems of several social groups in Japan between 1868 and 1941. These include farmers, rural women, outcastes, factory textile workers, prostitutes, and coal miners. Index.

"[Hane seeks] to explore the human dimension in Japan's modernization during the late 19th and early 20th centuries. He links the economic and social changes in village and city with the costs as well as the new possibilities affecting the lives of ordinary Japanese. . . . The result is a vivid supplement to the picture of Japanese economic growth found in textbooks. This book will attract those interested in comparative questions as well as in the Japanese case." E. S. Rawski

Library J 107:727 Ap 1 '82 90w

"[The author] sets out to tell us about 'the actual experiences of "ordinary" people' during the extraordinary process of Japanese modernization from the Meiji Restoration to World War II. [His book] consists of a series of chapters, some overlapping. . . . The material is overwhelmingly drawn from Japanese publications and thus most of it will be quite unfamiliar to Western readers. . . . [However,] a surprising amount of it is familiar to any historian of common folk during the transition to industrial capitalism. . . . What justifiably impresses the reader is the sheer depth of poverty in which so many (rural) Japanese lived as late as the 1930s. . . . The most heart-rending of the testimonies collected by Hane come from women and are about women. . . . [But] in spite of the title of [his] book, there are few 'rebels' in it, and, after the 1870s, few rebellions of any size except the famous 'rice riots' of 1918." E. J. Hobsbawn

N Y Rev of Books 29:15 Ap 15 '82 1950w

Humanities Index and *Social Sciences Index*

Before 1974 these two indexes appeared under one title as the *Social Sciences and Humanities Index*. Now a separate publication, the *Humanities Index* lists articles from 259 *scholarly* journals in areas such as archaeology, history, language, literary and political criticism, and religion. The *Social Sciences Index* lists articles from 265 scholarly journals that focus on economics, environmental science, education, medicine, psychology, and sociology, for example. Both indexes follow the same format as the *Readers' Guide*. Entries are arranged alphabetically according to author and subject in the volume corresponding to the year in which the article appeared.

For the topic, "How has the women's movement affected the status of women in medicine?" you could start under "Women" in the *Humanities Index* and find the appropriate subheading.

The 17-page article in the *American Quarterly* (see page 373) is likely to contain useful case histories, statistics, and further references. Sources like this can give you a deeper, more detailed treatment of a subject than those from indexes like the *Readers' Guide*.

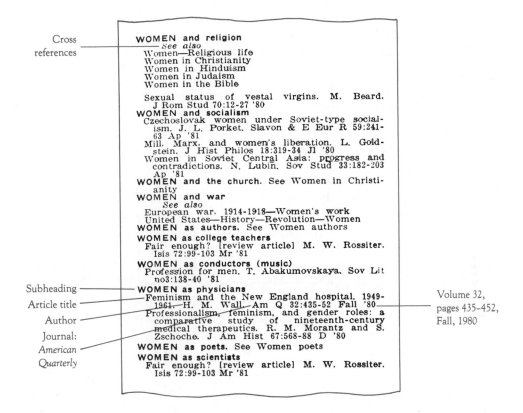

Cross references — WOMEN and religion

Subheading — WOMEN as physicians

Article title — Feminism and the New England hospital, 1949-1961.

Author — H. M. Wall.

Journal: American Quarterly — Am Q 32:435-52 Fall '80

Volume 32, pages 435–452, Fall, 1980

WOMEN and religion
See also
Women—Religious life
Women in Christianity
Women in Hinduism
Women in Judaism
Women in the Bible

Sexual status of vestal virgins. M. Beard. J Rom Stud 70:12-27 '80
WOMEN and socialism
Czechoslovak women under Soviet-type socialism. J. L. Porket. Slavon & E Eur R 59:241-63 Ap '81
Mill, Marx, and women's liberation. L. Goldstein. J Hist Philos 18:319-34 Jl '80
Women in Soviet Central Asia: progress and contradictions. N. Lubin. Sov Stud 33:182-203 Ap '81
WOMEN and the church. See Women in Christianity
WOMEN and war
See also
European war, 1914-1918—Women's work
United States—History—Revolution—Women
WOMEN as authors. See Women authors
WOMEN as college teachers
Fair enough? [review article] M. W. Rossiter. Isis 72:99-103 Mr '81
WOMEN as conductors (music)
Profession for men. T. Abakumovskaya. Sov Lit no3:138-40 '81
WOMEN as physicians
Feminism and the New England hospital, 1949-1961. H. M. Wall. Am Q 32:435-52 Fall '80
Professionalism, feminism, and gender roles: a comparative study of nineteenth-century medical therapeutics. R. M. Morantz and S. Zschoche. J Am Hist 67:568-88 D '80
WOMEN as poets. See Women poets
WOMEN as scientists
Fair enough? [review article] M. W. Rossiter. Isis 72:99-103 Mr '81

Other specific indexes For a more detailed view of the scholarly work done in a specialized area, you must consult an index devoted entirely to that field. Many of the articles listed in such indexes assume expert knowledge, but some are accessible, and these could be valuable. Here are several useful specific indexes:

Applied Science and Technology Index

A monthly publication that lists articles from over three hundred periodicals.

Biological Abstracts

An abstract journal that summarizes selected articles in subjects like microbiology, immunology, public health, and basic medical sciences. *BASIC (Biological Abstracts Subjects in Context)*, a computer-made subject index to each issue, is also available.

Business Periodicals Index

A monthly publication covering business and related topics from 1958 to the present. Lists under subject or company name.

Chemical Abstracts

Includes abstracts of current periodical articles. Excellent indexing system.

Education Index

Contains listings for articles in 230 journals.

Essay and General Literature Index

Indexes essays and articles in periodicals and books by author, subject, and sometimes by title.

General Science Index

Lists articles pertaining to all scientific subjects; a basic tool for general information on the sciences.

Historical Abstracts

Lists articles in over two thousand periodicals and tells where to find source material.

MLA International Bibliography of Books and Articles on the Modern Languages and Literature

Lists articles and books on language and literature. Published by the Modern Language Association.

Psychological Abstracts

Abstracts of books and articles in the field published since 1935. Includes subject and author index.

Computer searches   Many libraries now have the facilities to offer computer searches of various topics. This eliminates the time-consuming task of poring over many index volumes yourself. The data bases for scientific and technical material are more extensive than those for the humanities and social sciences. But the situation is rapidly changing, so you might want to ask your librarian if a computer search of your topic would be worthwhile. Also ask how much this service costs—many libraries charge for it. The product is a printout of citations and, depending on the data base, entire abstracts that summarize articles. Here is part of a printout on the topic "teaching science fiction."

```
? т 3/5/1-18
3/5/1
EJ178584  S0506288
   Beyond  Flash  Gordon  and "Star Wars":  Science Fiction and History
Instruction
   Cooper, B. Lee
   Social Education, 42, 5, 392-7   May 78
   Reprint Available (See p. vii): UMI
   Historical concepts  can  be  taught  through  analysis  of  science
fiction.   Offers  a  class  outline with science fiction resources to
examine the boundaries of historical inquiry;  six themes for  student
investigation  based  on  specific  resources;  and a bibliography of 44
additional anthologies and books. (AV)
   Descriptors: *Social Studies/ *History Instruction/ *Instructional
Innovation/  *Science  Fiction/  *Reading  Materials/  Instructional
Materials/  Concept Teaching/  Teaching Methods/  Elementary Secondary
Education

3/5/2
EJ174256  SE520516
   Children Create Fiction Using Science
   Cacha, Frances B.
   Science and Children, 15, 3, 21-2   Nov/Dec 77
   Reprint Available (See p  vii): UMI
   Describes how a variety of science topics could be used to encourage
elementary  school  children  to write creatively   A list of books to
stimulate discussion is provided. (CP)
   Descriptors:  *Creative  Writing/  *Elementary  School  Science/
*Reference  Materials/  *Science  Activities/  *Science  Fiction/
Elementary Education/  Instructional  Materials/  Science  Education/
Teaching Methods/ Writing
```

The computer search turned up twenty-seven abstracts, work the student would have had to do manually. But she still has to see if her library has these periodicals, go to the shelves to find them, and read the articles.

EXERCISES

1. What research sources would you consult to find information on the following subjects?

    a. A book review of Ernest Hemingway's *The Sun Also Rises*.

    b. Biographical information about Ernest Hemingway.

    c. Books about Hemingway and his works.

    d. Information about the theories of Johannes Kepler, the seventeenth-century scientist.

    e. Whether your college library has the book *On Death and Dying* by Elisabeth Kübler-Ross.

    f. How many pages there are in the Kübler-Ross book and how long its bibliography is.

    g. Where you could find other books on the subject of death and dying.

    h. Where you could find other books by Elisabeth Kübler-Ross.

    i. General information about physics.

    j. A detailed discussion of research in particle physics.

    k. A detailed discussion of the author Herman Melville and his works.

    l. Articles about Herman Melville's *Moby Dick*.

    m. Whether Melville's novel *White-Jacket* has been published in paperback.

    n. Information about the whaling industry in the nineteenth century.

    o. Whether your library has the *Yale Review* 35 (September, 1945).

    p. The reaction of the country to the sinking of the *Titanic* in April 1912.

    q. An article on the government's antitrust suit against American Telephone and Telegraph Corporation.

    r. Information on the Philadelphia Poisoning Ring of 1939.

2. Use your library's resources to answer the following questions. Try not to ask your librarian for help until you are sure you can't find the answer on your own.

    a. Who designed the Brooklyn Bridge?

    b. What were the previous names of Zaire, Zimbabwe, Sri Lanka, and Hawaii?

    c. Where was the last game of the 1919 World Series played?

    d. What was George Orwell's real name?

    e. Why was Jim Thorpe stripped of the medals he won at the 1912 Olympics? When and why were they restored?

    f. How long was John Kennedy's inaugural address?

    g. What is Alzheimer's disease?

    h. What was the *Andrea Doria*?

    i. What books did Jean Toomer write?

    j. Who was Molly Pitcher?

    k. When was the first issue of *Discover* magazine published?

    l. What do hemophilia and color blindness have in common?

m.   What was the original meaning of the word "hussy"?

n.   Which radio show was on the air longer, "Fibber McGee and Molly" or "One Man's Family"?

o.   What is Germaine Greer's nationality?

p.   What is transformational grammar?

q.   Who won the Academy Award for best actress in 1960?

r.   Who wrote the song "Stairway to Heaven"?

s.   What nation is directly south of Poland?

t.   When did *Tobacco Road* open on Broadway? Were the reviews generally favorable or unfavorable?

3.   Use a research source to write a biographical or historical paragraph on any one of the following.

    a.   Elvis Presley

    b.   Bing Crosby

    c.   Linus Pauling

    d.   Coretta Scott King

    e.   William F. Buckley, Jr.

    f.   Ronald Reagan

    g.   The Ford Motor Company

    h.   ENIAC

    i.   The Civilian Conservation Corps

STEP 3: ASSEMBLING A PRELIMINARY BIBLIOGRAPHY

Once you know that your library has what you need to do your research, you can compile the working bibliography you need for concentrated reading and note-taking. There is nothing complicated about this: you simply look at the sources you have found so far, see whether they will be useful, set aside those that are, and eliminate those that aren't.

☐ JUDGING YOUR SOURCES

Don't waste time reading irrelevant material. To evaluate a source's usefulness you might first consider its *scope*—how comprehensive a treatment of your subject the source offers. Study the table of contents and index quickly for major discussions of your topic. To help with a paper on the Battle of Britain, for example, a book should have a chapter or so on this subject, not simply a footnote. A long article in the *Atlantic* on "Literary Censorship in Church-Related Schools" will have more information than a short treatment of the same subject in *Reader's Digest*.

The *date of publication* tells you whether the information in a book is current. A discussion of solid-state technology published in 1962, for instance, is probably obsolete. Scientific and technological subjects require that you consider up-to-the-moment developments. Even in the humanities, new discoveries and research force scholars to reevaluate and change their thinking from time to time.

Some classic books and articles, however, never lose their usefulness. *Cybernetics: or Control and Communication in the Animal and the Machine,* by Norbert Wiener, deals with computers. Written in 1948 and revised in 1961, it is still required reading for anyone doing research in this area. If a number of your contemporary sources refer to certain works, you should consult those works, regardless of their publication dates. Be careful, however, to examine the data to see what information has become obsolete.

Another factor to consider is the *reliability* of your source. Is it a book or article intended to inform or to persuade? Does the author have a personal axe to grind? An account of the dropping of the atomic bomb on Hiroshima and Nagasaki written by then-Secretary of War Henry L. Stimson may try to justify the author's actions as well as to set the record straight. One way to judge the objectivity of a work, then, is to see what you can find out about the authors of your most important sources. Check the source itself for biographical information, and perhaps even consult a biographical dictionary. Read the book's preface to see whether the author explains his or her purpose. What do other sources say about the author: is he or she well known? highly respected? considered to be fair? reliable? biased? misinformed? Check a few statements against an encyclopedia or textbook or see if you can find a contemporary review of your source. Consider the source of a periodical article. Lightweight pieces from popular sources should probably be discarded.

Finally, your working bibliography must represent a reasonably wide *variety of viewpoints.* Your research paper should not depend on one or two sources or the work of one or two people. Testimony by a number of experts adds depth and balance to your presentation. Tracking down sources that you come across during your reading is of great help. Bibliographies, footnotes, and references in a text are excellent sources of reliable further information about your topic.

EXERCISE

Read the following paragraphs, paying close attention to the information provided about their sources and authors as well as to their content. Decide which sources would be most useful and reliable for a paper on "Why do people join the Ku Klux Klan?" Which sources, if any, should be disregarded? Which sources would you examine first? Be prepared to discuss your choices.

1. . . . the Klan summed up within itself, with precise completeness and exactness, the whole body of the fears and hates of the time, including, of course, those which were shared with the rest of America and the Western world. That is why, somewhat modified for the purpose (particularly in leaving out the anti-Yankee bias which was quite plainly present in its Southern form), it eventually spread far beyond the borders of Dixie. It was, as is well known, at once anti-Negro, anti-Alien, anti-Red, anti-Catholic, anti-Jew, anti-Darwin, anti-Modern, anti-

Liberal, Fundamentalist, vastly Moral, militantly Protestant. (W. J. Cash, *The Mind of the South*, Random House, 1941).

In the Preface, Cash says he sees the South as "another land, sharply differentiated from the rest of the American nation"; *Time*, the *New York Times*, the *American Historical Review*, and other publications gave *The Mind of the South* favorable reviews.

2. There's been a whole lot of let's-kick-the-Klan going on—jabs, jokes, putdowns. While I don't approve of Klan actions, I do think it's easy to forget that any organization is still made up of individuals. I knew two men, two fine, gentle, humane people who at one time in their lives were members of the Ku Klux Klan. Both men were nonviolent and deeply caring about their country and their fellow human beings. (Ruth Moose, "Decent Klansmen," *New York Times*, March 3, 1980)

3. What the Klansman says next becomes a blur . . . but like in the old cartoons, his words seem to gather over his head in black clouds of hate and violence and ugliness. I can see them filling the room, pressing against the walls, staining them. Is it moral to house and feed a man who has "Resettle All Negroes in their African Homeland" stickers in his suitcase? I feel unclean. I should stand up, talk back, but I am too frightened. (Anonymous, "Bigotry Incarnate," *New York Times*, March 3, 1980)

4. The Fergusons were the liberals of the 'twenties, at least in Texas. The standards of liberalism change as public attention shifts, from one public question to another. When prohibition was a subject of controversy, the liberal was wet. When the Klan rides, those who oppose it are liberal . . . . In the 1924 gubernatorial campaign the issue was the Klan. To their everlasting credit, the Fergusons were against it. (V. O. Key, Jr., *Southern Politics*, Random House, 1949)

Key, a Texan, was a professor of political science at Harvard and Johns Hopkins universities. *Southern Politics* won an award from the American Political Science Association.

5. There has been an increase in Ku Klux Klan activity across the country in the last few years. The Klan, even with its new recruits, is still small in numbers. But still, an increase in Klan activity—with its anti-black, anti-Semitic and anti-Catholic propaganda—should not be ignored.

Teachers across the country have reported Klan activities in and around their schools. These activities include the distribution of racist literature as well as efforts to recruit students. Both national teacher organizations, the American Federation of Teachers and the National Education Association, responding to the requests of members across the country, decided to prepare materials for use in the classroom to teach students about the Klan, its history, its objectives. (Albert Shanker, "How Not to Teach About the KKK," *New York Times*, September 1, 1981)

Shanker is president of New York City's United Federation of Teachers.

6. Ku-Klux Klan is a secret organization in the United States, especially associated with the South. The original Klan was formed to maintain white supremacy in the South after the Civil War. A subsequent organization, active during the 1920's, considered itself a guardian of religion, morality, and patriotism as well. After World War II, as the Negro civil rights movement gained momentum, the Klan reasserted itself in the South. Acts of violence attributed to the Klan resulted in widespread public and official condemnation of the organization and its activities . . . .

The Ku-Klux Klan started innocently when, in May 1866, a group of former soldiers of the Confederate Army organized at Pulaski, Tenn., a club with intentions scarcely more significant than those of the many fraternal orders common in the United States . . . . The new organization was bound to secrecy and adopted the habit of nightly parades in ghostly disguises . . . .

The second Ku-Klux Klan was organized on Stone Mountain, near Atlanta, Ga., in October 1915 by Col. William Simmons and 14 associates. Although the new organization adopted the costumes and ritual of the first Klan, it was inspired by an exaggerated nationalism growing out of World War I and the protest against the apparent letdown in morals after that struggle. The second Ku-Klux Klan used intimidation and violence to enforce the ideals of the less tolerant segment of the American people. (*Encyclopedia Americana,* 1978, Vol. 16. Article on Ku-Klux Klan, pp. 549–551)

7. The Ku Klux Klan was founded so that white people could keep together and the colored could keep together. They're beginning to find out up North that it's the only way—because God had his own good reasons to make some of us white and some dark, and who is anyone to go disagreeing. (One-time Klan member, quoted in Robert Coles, *Farewell to the South,* Little, Brown, 1972)

Coles, a child psychiatrist, has studied and written about families in the South and elsewhere, producing journalistic documentaries. He has written many well-received books noted for their accuracy and insights.

8. The "climate" was right. America was disillusioned by the war. Isolationism, America-for-Americans, was in the air. Attorney General Palmer's hysteria about Reds; the depression of 1920–21; the rural discontent; unemployment; the strikes; the race riots in Eastern cities—all these created a perfect climate and soil for Klan development. (Ralph McGill, *The South and the Southerner,* Little, Brown, 1959)

McGill, a southerner, was editor of the *Atlanta Constitution;* his book won the 1962 *Atlantic* nonfiction award.

□ MAKING BIBLIOGRAPHY CARDS

When you find a suitable source, make up a 3 × 5″ card for it, including the following information:

Book	Article
Author(s)	Author(s)
Title (underlined)	Title (quotation marks)
Call number (for future reference)	Title of journal (underlined)
City of publication	Volume
Publisher	Date
Date	Page numbers
Short note about the book	Short note about the article

You need not follow the format that you will use in your final paper now, but you must make sure that your notes are *full* and *accurate*. If they aren't, you will be in trouble later. Following are two sample bibliography cards.

Bibliography card for a book

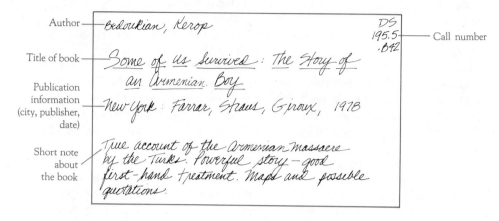

Author — Bedoukian, Kerop
Title of book — Some of Us Survived: The Story of an Armenian Boy
Publication information (city, publisher, date) — New York: Farrar, Straus, Giroux, 1978
Call number — DS 195.5 .B42
Short note about the book — True account of the Armenian massacre by the Turks. Powerful story — good first-hand treatment. Maps and possible quotations.

Bibliography card for an article

Author — Burhaus, C.S.
Title of article — "Hemingway and Vonnegut: Diminishing Vision in a Dying Age,"
Title of journal — Modern Fiction Studies, 21 (Summer, 1975) 173-91
Publication information
Short note about the article — Good comparison of Hemingway and Vonnegut. Concentrates on The Sun Also Rises and Slaughter-House Five

These cards form a complete record of your sources. Make sure that your entries are accurate and complete because it may be impossible to find a source again once you have returned the book to the library.

STEP 4: CONCENTRATED READING AND NOTE TAKING

With useful sources selected, you are ready to begin your concentrated reading and note taking. Your reading should be concentrated, focusing only on those sections of a work that pertain to your topic. Before you begin reading any book or article, survey it, checking the headings and subheadings in the table of contents, and especially the index, for subjects you need to read carefully or to skim. As you read, take notes on index cards: this is the information you will boil down for use when you plan and write your paper. Concentrated reading helps you narrow your topic further and enables you to lay claim to your subject and develop ideas about it. As you read and take notes, you will move toward a tentative thesis.

☐ MAKING NOTE CARDS

Using index cards may seem cumbersome, but their advantages become obvious when you go about arranging and rearranging material. Often you don't know where a particular piece of information goes or whether you will use it at all. You should be constantly rearranging ideas, and index cards make adding and deleting information and experimenting with different sequences possible. Students who take notes in a notebook or on a tablet find that they spend as much time untangling their notes as they do writing their paper.

At the top of each card, *include a short heading* that relates the information on your card to your topic. Later, this heading will help you make your outline.

Each card should *accurately identify the source* of the information you are recording. You need not include the complete citation, but you must include enough information to identify your source. "Wilson, p. 72," for example, would send you back to your bibliography card carrying the complete documentation for *Patriotic Gore* by Edmund Wilson. For a book with more than one author, or for two books by the same author, you need a more complete reference. "Glazer & Moynihan, p. 132," would suffice for *Beyond the Melting Pot* by Nathan Glazer and Daniel Patrick Moynihan. "Terkel, *Working*, p. 135" would be necessary if you were using more than one book by Studs Terkel.

Here is one good note-card format:

Note card

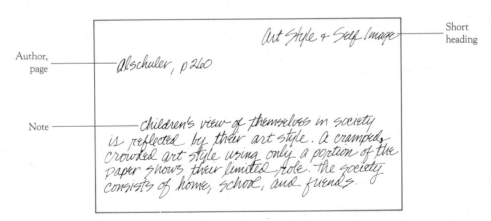

Author, page

Short heading

Note

Alschuler, p 260

Art Style & Self Image

children's view of themselves in society is reflected by their art style. A cramped, crowded art style using only a portion of the paper shows their limited role. The society consists of home, school, and friends.

☐ TAKING NOTES

Even at this stage of your research you can do several things to make the actual writing of your paper easier.

Put only one note on a single card. If you don't, you lose the flexibility that you gained by choosing this method of note taking in the first place.

Include everything now that you will need later to understand your note. You might think, for instance, that this makes sense:

Peyser—four important categories of new music.

But in several weeks you won't remember what those categories were. They should have been listed on your card.

Indicate what kind of information is on your note card. If you copy an author's words, use quotation marks. If you use only an author's ideas, do not use quotation marks. Finally, if you write down your own ideas, enclose them in brackets ([]). This system helps you avoid mixups.

Put an author's comments into your own words whenever possible. Word-for-word copying of information is probably the most inefficient way anyone can take notes. Why copy two pages when all you need is a one-paragraph summary? You may use quotations in your final paper, but for the most part, you will summarize and paraphrase your source material, adding your own observations and judgments. Putting information into your own words now prevents your final paper from turning into a patchwork of other people's words.

☐ SUMMARY

A summary is always shorter than the original; it highlights important information in a source. After you read a passage, write down what you remember in your own words. Then check your summary against the original to make sure that you have not distorted the author's meaning or accidentally used his or her exact words.

For a research paper on "What has the effect of recessions in the 1980s been on the American middle class?" you might want to summarize a paragraph such as this one from *The Real America* by Ben J. Wattenberg.

Original

It should come as no surprise, then, that the new middle class has further demands and deeper demands—demands not dissimilar from those made by the earlier, narrower, middle class. Americans today from all walks of life have, in the phrase of pollster Daniel Yankelovich, "a psychology of entitlement." They feel they are entitled to college educations for their children, and entitled to a meaningful or interesting job and entitled to feel alienated—just like the earlier, more narrowly based middle class. When reality rubs up against this sense of entitlement, when, for example, workers at Lordstown and elsewhere find themselves still glued to hard and boring jobs (albeit for fewer hours, fewer weeks, fewer years and more money than earlier), they feel entitled to bitch about it and seek redress. Bitch they do—blue-collar blues—and redress of grievances they get—flotillas of commissions about job redesign, a few of which may produce amelioration, and tough union demands, most of which will be effectuated.

Summary

Middle Class Desires

Wattenberg, p. 49

    Wattenberg says that the middle class feels entitled to certain things like a college education and a good job. When they find they can't achieve these things, they feel entitled to complain.

Notice that this summary gives a general sense of Wattenberg's paragraph. It does not, however, include the specific information you might need to rely heavily on it for support. To capture that, you would have to do a paraphrase.

☐ PARAPHRASE

When you paraphrase, you present the author's points in your own words, often including the order and emphasis of the original. Paraphrase is sometimes almost as long as the passage it is based on. This technique helps you capture a fairly complete sense of an author's ideas without using his or her exact words. When you paraphrase, however, be careful *not* to interpret, analyze, or evaluate your material.

The following paragraph appears in *Comedy High and Low* by Maurice Charney.

> Comic paranoia could be demonstrated biographically from the lives of the great comedians, or even from the lives of the second- and third-rate comics who figure in Phil Berger's *The Last Laugh: The World of The Stand-up Comic*. Woody Allen is in a long tradition of sad, neurotic, defensive clowns—schlemiels, nebbishes, misfits—whose wit is the only thing that keeps them going. These are the oppressed anti-heroes, beaten down by bureaucracy, baffled by the intricacies of The Machine Age, nonplussed by the mysteries of women and sex, who find it difficult to perform the simplest acts, but who nevertheless have feverish fantasies of their suppressed heroic potential, as Woody Allen recreates machismo roles in the style of Humphrey Bogart in *Play It Again, Sam*. There are similarly inflated dream sequences in most of Woody Allen's movies.

A student doing a paper on "The Comic Hero in Woody Allen's Films" paraphrased it in this way:

> Charney, p.67   *Play it Again, Sam*
>
> Charney says that Woody Allen is one of a long line of "schlemiels, nebbishes, misfits" who are confused by the modern age. In spite of not being able to cope with life, Allen's charades maintain a vivid fantasy life. In *Play it Again, Sam* Allen assumes the style of a Humphrey Bogart. Many of his films have similar macho fantasy sequences.

The student captures Charney's sense here, but he writes down only material that is for his paper. He does not include Charney's term "comic paranoia" or his reference to the book *The Last Laugh*. Nor does he quote the phrase "suppressed heroic potential." The student does include the phrase "schlemiels, nebbishes, misfits" because it gives the flavor of Charney's paragraph and because it can't be paraphrased.

□ QUOTATION

You will want to quote an author exactly on either of two occasions:

1. *Quote when an author's words are especially memorable.* Use a quotation when an author's words are so well chosen that to summarize or paraphrase would be to destroy them. An author's words can be so concise that paraphrasing them would result in an awkward or incorrect restatement. Consider the following paragraph from Alexander Leighton's essay "That Day at Hiroshima."

> The destroyed heart of Hiroshima consisted of 4.7 square miles, and the best estimates indicate that the mortality rate was 15,000 to the square mile. For many days funeral processions moved along the roads and through the towns and villages around Hiroshima. The winds were pervaded by the smell of death and cremation. At night the skies were lit with the flares of funeral pyres.

These lines clearly evoke the scene in Hiroshima after the bomb. In such cases, it is better to let the author speak for himself. If you must comment, do so later in your paper.

2. *Quote when an author's words lend authority to your presentation.* If an author is a recognized expert on your subject, his or her words will add authority to your points. Using quotations well can be like bringing expert testimony into a trial. In a paper contrasting Grant and Lee, for example, the following quotation by Bruce Catton, the Civil War expert, could help you make your point that the two generals stood for contrasting styles of American life:

> So Grant and Lee were in complete contrast, representing two diametrically opposed elements in American life. Grant was the modern man emerging; beyond

him, ready to come on the stage, was the great age of steel and machinery, of crowded cities and a restless burgeoning vitality. Lee might have ridden down from the old age of chivalry, lance in hand, silken banner fluttering over his head. Each man was the perfect champion of his cause, drawing both his strengths and his weaknesses from the people he led.

When you copy out quotations, make sure you include quotation marks on your note cards. You may even circle the quotation marks to be sure you won't overlook them. If you do mistake the author's words for your own, you may unintentionally plagiarize when you write your paper. And make sure that you copy your source material exactly, paying careful attention to spelling, capitalization, and punctuation.

☐ YOUR OWN OBSERVATIONS

You can also record your own observations and reactions on note cards. Often some of your best insights come as you read your sources. Get into the habit of writing these ideas down—if you don't, you'll probably forget them. But be sure to bracket your observations so you won't confuse them with the author's material. Remember *your* ideas and judgments are just as important and should be recorded just as carefully as those from your source material.

The student who wrote this note card was exploring the way the press portrayed President Richard Nixon during the Watergate crisis. His comments are included in brackets after his summary of his source.

> Bernstein + Woodward, Washington Post
> p. 366
>
> The authors say that by the summer of 1973 both Alexander Haig and Henry Kissinger urged Richard Nixon to cut his ties with his *aides*. [Is there any evidence of this? What sources support this? Seems doubtful.]

☐ PLAGIARISM

"Plagiarism" comes from a Greek word meaning "kidnap." It occurs when you take another person's words or ideas and present them as yours. Recently, Princeton University denied a student a diploma when she was found to have plagiarized a paper. A candidate for Education Commissioner of New Jersey was denied the post because he had plagiarized sections of his doctoral dissertation. And in 1979 a Yale medical researcher tried to pass off another person's studies as his own. As these people found out, plagiarism is stealing.

One rule of research, and for that matter of all writing, is that you always give credit to the authors whose work you use. All sources must be accounted for— ideas as well as quotations. In the following passages, notice how a student uses words and phrases from the original:

Original

The Amish community tends to be self-sufficient in its social and educational functions; the social needs of the individual are met within it. The Amish have no schools of higher learning, but they have built elementary schools in some places to avoid the external influence that comes with the centralized school system. As soon as the law will allow, Amish children are taken out of school for work at home.

John A. Hostetler, *Amish Society*

Plagiarism

The Amish community is self-sufficient. It meets the social needs of the individual. The Amish do not have schools of higher learning, but they have built elementary schools in some places. In most cases as soon as the law will allow, Amish children are taken out of school to work at home.

The student who plagiarized this paragraph could just as easily have quoted or paraphrased Hostetler's remarks. Of course, he would also have had to document his source (see "Documenting," pages 399–415).

Paraphrase

Hostetler says that the Amish are educationally and socially independent. In some communities they have constructed their own elementary schools to avoid the centralized school system. Usually the Amish will remove their children from school as soon as the law lets them.[5]

Some students plagiarize deliberately. If they are found out, they are severely punished. Some students plagiarize accidentally. They forget that a note they took is a quotation or that an idea they are using is someone else's. This accidental plagiarism is often dealt with equally harshly. There are just no good excuses for plagiarism. It *can be avoided* if you follow a few simple rules:

1.   Take accurate notes, including page numbers and titles.

2.   Be sure to differentiate between your ideas and the ideas of others on your note cards, clearly identifying all quotations.

3.   Do not include words or phrases from original sources unless you say that they are not your own.

When you document your sources, make sure you identify all material that is not yours—concepts as well as direct quotations. *Remember: Plagiarism is no problem if you take careful notes and give credit where credit is due.*

EXERCISE

Read the following passage from the book *Simple Justice* by Richard Kluger. When you think you understand the author's points, make a set of three note cards for a paper on the topic "What social, political, and economic conditions in Topeka, Kansas, preceded the 1954 *Brown v. Board of Education* decision which declared the city's 'separate but equal' schools illegal?" One card should include a *summary* of pertinent ideas, one should *paraphrase* a point, and one should include a *quotation*. Add your own observations where you have questions or comments about the author's ideas.

Whatever else it was in 1951, Topeka was also a Jim Crow town. It had been one as long as anyone could remember.

There were no separate waiting rooms at the train and bus stations, and Negroes did not have to ride in the back of the local buses, but in most other ways it was segregated by law and, more effectively, by custom. There were eighteen elementary schools for whites and four for blacks. There was one colored hotel, the Dunbar, and all the rest were for whites. Almost no restaurants downtown served colored customers. Before the Second World War, a number of the better beaneries in town had a sign in the window reading: "Negroes and Mexicans served in sacks only," meaning they could take out food in bags but not eat on the premises. One movie theater in town admitted colored people to its balcony. Another, called the Apex, was for colored only. The other five movie houses were for whites only. The swimming pool at Gage Park was off-limits to colored, except one day a year when they were allowed in for a gala picnic.

Worse yet was the employment picture. Blacks had won some jobs at the Santa Fe shops during a strike in the early Twenties, but there were few black union members in Topeka and fewer held white-collar positions of any kind. A black clerk at a retail shop or a black stenographer at an insurance company was almost unknown. Mrs. Inza Brown, who had been a legal secretary to the only black lawyer in town for thirteen years in the Twenties and Thirties, won a civil-service job at the State Department of Health, where, as she remembers, "They didn't know what to do with a black woman, so they lent me out to the city health department. In two years there, I was never offered a cup of coffee from the office coffee wagon. I had to go around the corner to get some. Topeka was one prejudiced town then, let me tell you."

Unwelcomed by most white employers, Topeka blacks retreated into their own world and tried to make do. The principal black businesses in town were beauty and barber shops, barbecue restaurants, after-hours bars, and whorehouses. A black-owned drugstore started up and, serving black clientele only, folded after a year. Few colored retailers could command credit from the banks; few could get management experience at any white-owned store. A hundred or so professionals made a living in town—black teachers teaching black children, black preachers serving black churches, a few physicians tending the black sick. The only other work blacks had a corner on in Topeka was the most menial sort: the janitorial jobs in the statehouse, the mop-up work at the hotels, the maids and laundresses and cooks and gardeners and chimneysweeps of the white people. A black laborer was much more likely to find an honest day's work in Detroit or Pittsburgh or back South.

Until the Second World War, black Topeka took it all quietly. Things were worse elsewhere, they said. The head of the local NAACP branch, who had been a lieutenant in the First World War and was the first Negro to work in the Topeka post office, was no firebrand. "We've got to learn to crawl before we can walk," he was wont to say with the solemnity of Booker Washington. The war, though, began to change things on both sides of the color line. Says Tom Lee Kiene, a native Topekan who served seventeen years on the staff of the Topeka *Capital-Journal* before becoming its executive editor in 1959: "Blacks who participated in civic drives selling war bonds or raising money for the Red Cross began to come to banquets—it seemed the patriotic thing to ask them—and we whites started remarking to each other that it didn't seem to spoil our dinners."

In the black community, a few enlightened discontents began to emerge, like Lucinda Todd, an ex-schoolteacher who had been forcibly retired by the then common rule that married women could not teach. Mrs. Todd was especially sensitive to the education her daughter, Nancy, received and was increasingly disturbed when she found that it was not as rich as that offered white youngsters. She had wanted her daughter to play the violin, for example, but there was no musical instruction at any of the black schools. Then one day she saw a notice in the newspaper about a concert by the grade-school orchestra representing all eighteen schools in town, and she exploded. "I got on the phone to the music supervisor," she remembers, "and told him there were twenty-two grade schools in town, not eighteen, and why weren't the black children offered music instruction?" She was directed to the coordinator of black schools in Topeka, who assured her that colored folks did not want music instruction and could not afford to buy the instruments. She brought her case to the Board of Education and won it. There was another time—in 1944, she places it—when Mrs. Todd bought a ticket to the Grand movie theater, the one that admitted Negroes to a section of the balcony, and when she climbed up there the two dozen or so seats reserved for colored were filled, so she took a seat right across the aisle in the white section. A policeman came and told her that she could not do that and would have to sit in the colored section or nowhere. They gave her her money back. "They did things like that all the time," Lucinda Todd recalls. Soon she became active in the NAACP, was elected secretary of the branch, and once had Walter White as an overnight guest in her residence.

But there were few such proud and angry Negroes in Topeka who were ready to do something about their degraded standing in the community. Things would pick up after the war, everybody said. It was no time to rock the boat. In fact, though, very little opened up after the war. Remembers Negro attorney Charles Scott, who went to Washburn Law School after military service prior to joining his father's firm: "You'd look up and down Kansas Avenue early in the morning, and all you could see were blacks washing windows. That wasn't anything, but at least it was work. There was still no chance for a black man to become a bank teller or a store clerk or a brick mason. The few blacks with union jobs at Goodyear almost never advanced, and people were retiring from the Santa Fe shops after holding the same job for twenty or twenty-five years. A lot of hopes got dashed."

The 1950 U.S. Census documents the job plight of Topeka Negroes:

	White	Non-white
Bookkeepers (female)	541	2
Stenographers, secretaries and typists	2,225	16
Bus drivers	86	1
Electricians	215	1
Salesmen and sales clerks in retail trade	2,158	11
Accountants and auditors	425	1
Plumbers and pipefitters	197	4

Compositors and typesetters	214	2
Pharmacists	71	2
Dentists	57	2
Managers, officials, proprietors (self-employed)	1,600	30
Managers, officials, proprietors (salaried)	1,684	32
Janitors, porters, charwomen	293	318
Private household workers (living out)	320	347
(living in)	120	14

What did the black children of Topeka have, then, to look forward to as adults in their own community?

STEP 5: DECIDING ON A THESIS

Even after you have finished your concentrated reading and note taking, you may not yet have an obvious thesis. If you have phrased your topic as a question, however, your answer to the question could be your thesis.

Topic	**Possible thesis**
What was the role of private fire companies in colonial America?	Private fire companies, such as the ones that existed in colonial Philadelphia, served a social function in the community and contributed to the formation of the professional companies that developed later.
What are the long-range effects of microwave radiation?	Although scientists have reached no definite conclusions, they suspect that the long-range effects of microwave radiation could be hazardous.

Some writers find that free writing helps them focus their thoughts and formulate a tentative thesis. Sometimes, you may have to try out different ways of grouping ideas or do a scratch outline before you find a thesis. More often, however, you probably think about several possible thesis statements as you read and take notes. The thesis you finally decide on depends on your own preference and the kind and amount of material you have found.

Let's say your research topic is "Are the SATs culturally biased?" As you read, you consider these possible thesis statements:

1. The SATs are culturally biased.
2. Today's SATs are less culturally biased than those of the 1960s.

3.   The SATs are slanted in favor of upper-middle-class students.

4.   SATs should be given in a student's native language.

When you have completed your reading and note taking, you examine these possible thesis statements one by one. The first seems too broad; it needs much more detail than you can give it in a ten-page paper. The second is also extremely broad; besides, you haven't found much material on SATs twenty years ago and you don't have time to do additional research. That leaves the third and fourth thesis statements. Now you can make your decision on the basis of which thesis appeals to you more and which you have more useful information about.

EXERCISE

Read these three passages from Jerre Mangione's book *The Dream and The Deal,* a history of the Federal Writers' Project (1935–1943). Imagine you are writing a library research paper on the topic "Should the Federal Writers' Project be revived?" What possible thesis statements could be supported by the information below?

The official birthday of the Federal Writers' Project was July 27, 1935, but its period of gestation began some five years earlier with the arrival of the nation's worst economic calamity, the Great Depression. To appreciate how so bold an enterprise as the Project could have been fathered under governmental auspices, one needs to understand the desperate circumstances of the era. More than one third of the country's labor force was thrown out of work, and millions of Americans began to worry about going hungry. Far more telling than the statistics on the sharp decline of the Gross National Product were the breadlines, the shanty towns called Hoovervilles, the thousands of homeless men and women sleeping in subway stations and public parks, the anarchistic reactions of conservative farmers to the loss of their lands. These were but a part of the gross evidence that underlined the black anxiety permeating the American people.

.   .   .

An inconspicuous but significant clause in the [Emergency Relief Act of 1935] authorized "assistance to educational, professional, and clerical persons; a nation-wide program for useful employment of artists, musicians, actors, entertainers, writers . . . and others in these cultural fields."

.   .   .

In less than four years the Project had produced some three hundred twenty publications, of which about one hundred were full-sized books. Besides state, city, small town, and highway guides, the list included works on subjects as diverse as ethnic studies, place names, folklore, and zoology. More than six hundred other books were in various stages of completion. It made quite an impressive record, especially when one considered the difficulties of conducting a project made up largely of workers with little or no writing experience, most of whom had to qualify as paupers before they could be employed.

WRITING AND ARRANGING

STEP 6: MAKING A WORKING OUTLINE

After you have settled on a tentative thesis, it is time to structure your paper. Making up a working outline can help you put your research into focus and isolate any problems.

Jeff Tuckwood decided to do his paper on the topic "Does the law adequately protect abused children?" Jeff arrived at a thesis and an arrangement as he did his research. His preliminary outline looked like this:

Thesis: Even though laws in a number of states have addressed child abuse, abused children and their parents are still largely ignored.

    I.   Dimensions of the problem
   II.   Limitations of recent legislation
 III.   Social services
 IV.   Difficulty of further action

Jeff next laid his note cards out and rearranged them. Guided by the topics in the upper right-hand corner of his note cards, he made this more detailed working outline.

Thesis: Laws protecting abused children are inadequate.

Introduction: Even though laws in a number of states have addressed child abuse, abused children and their parents are still largely ignored.

    I.   Dimensions of the problem
       A.   Statistics on abused children
       B.   Physical abuse
           1.   Child labor
           2.   Family abuse
       C.   Psychological abuse
           1.   School-related
           2.   Parental
       D.   Arlene Skolnick's position
           1.   Family dynamics
           2.   Psychology of abuse

   II.   Limitations of recent legislation
       A.   New Jersey
           1.   Public policy
           2.   Recent legislation
       B.   California
           1.   Enlightened legislation
           2.   Compliance

    C. Florida
        1. Runaways
        2. State funding

III. Social Services
    A. Physician's responsibility
        1. Hospital emergency rooms
        2. Mandatory reporting
    B. School's responsibility
        1. School nurse
        2. Teachers
        3. Counselors
    C. Law enforcement agencies' responsibility
        1. Criminalization
        2. Role of the police
    D. Role of social agencies
        1. Foster homes
        2. Family therapy
        3. Custody

IV. Difficulty of further action
    A. Position of the courts
    B. Position of legislators
        1. Sanctity of the family
        2. Paternalism
    C. Leontine Young's comments
        1. Trends
        2. Handicapped children

V. *Conclusion:* Although much has been done for abused children, much more still has to be accomplished.

Jeff's evidence supports his thesis that abused children and their parents don't receive much help from the courts or state legislatures. Under each heading he indicates critical opinion and draws conclusions.

    Before writing his first draft, Jeff should review his working outline to make sure that all his entries reinforce his thesis. Anything off the subject should be recast or deleted. Jeff might also decide that he lacks material under some headings. The single source under IV.C, for example, may not give him a cross-section of opinion. He probably has to go back to the library and find another source for support. As a matter of fact, Jeff did do further research and found a book which gave him the perspective he wanted in his final section.

STEP 7: WRITING THE FIRST DRAFT

When you write your first draft, your primary purpose is just to get ideas down on paper. Most research papers are long, and you probably won't be able to complete a rough draft in a single sitting. Try dividing your writing up into segments that you can complete—covering a major subject heading from your outline, for instance, is a realistic goal for one morning or afternoon of writing.

Many students find it very difficult to get started. Once you get going, you'll be surprised how easily your rough draft flows. The time you spent taking notes and roughing out an outline now pays dividends. If you do have trouble, try free writing for a short period, a technique which can get you off the mark and into your paper. Sometimes leaving your paper for only five or ten minutes lets you see your material in a new way and gives you a fresh start. Just don't give up. You will begin to move eventually.

Like most essays, the research paper has an introduction, a body, and a conclusion, but these elements take a somewhat more expanded form.

□ INTRODUCTION

Beginning with an overview, your introduction identifies a broad subject area and establishes what aspects of it you will discuss. You could, for example, survey previous research in a field or give the background of a problem to be solved. You also state your thesis here, the question you will answer or the statement you will support in the rest of your paper. Your introduction should take no more than a paragraph or two, and it is a good idea to end your introduction with your thesis because this makes a smooth transition into the body of your paper.

□ BODY

The body of your paper follows your tentative outline. As you write, be sure to indicate your pattern of organization with strong topic sentences,

> Recent legislation has had a limited effect on child abuse.

or with section headings, such as

> *Limitations of Recent Legislation*
> New Jersey is one state that has recently passed laws aimed at curbing child abuse . . . .

Even in your first draft, headings or topic sentences help you keep your discussion under control.

Use the patterns of arrangement discussed in Chapter 4 to construct the individual sections of your paper. Remember that the principles that apply to short essays also apply to research papers.

□ CONCLUSION

Restate your thesis in your conclusion. This is especially important in a long paper—by the time your reader gets through it, he or she may have forgotten your thesis. After this restatement, you can end your paper with a summary, a call for action, or an apt quotation. In the paper on child abuse, you could say that your discussion covers laws presently in force but that several state legislatures are considering laws which might remedy the problems you identify. You could express your hope that these laws will go into effect or recommend that further work be done on how the state can help combat child abuse. Just remember that your conclusion must be based on your data. If you have done a good job, your reader will be persuaded to accept your thesis.

☐ DOING THE DRAFT

When preparing to write, lay out your note cards in the order in which you intend to use them. As you write, move from one entry on your outline to the next, using your note cards as you need them. Keep track of your sources on your rough draft by indicating the source and page number in brackets in the text. Opposite is a page from a student's first draft. (This material corresponds to point II.A, 1 of the outline on page 391.)

Don't think you can fill in source information later. It is easy to get confused when you try to recall fifteen to twenty citations. If you're not sure a piece of information needs documentation, put the source in anyway, and make your final decision when you revise.

REVISING

STEP 8: REVISING THE FIRST DRAFT

Once you have your first draft, check your thesis to make sure that it still fits your paper accurately. If it does not, you will have to fine-tune it. Students often find that the research paper they actually write does not exactly match the paper they planned. To identify discrepancies, make an outline of your rough draft and compare it with your working outline. If you find significant differences, you will have to modify your thesis or redo sections of your paper. New ideas do occur to you as you write, so changes may be improvements. Make sure, however, that the rest of your paper and your thesis are consistent with any revisions.

Next you should check your paragraphs. Is your introduction effective? Does it establish the context of your discussion? What about your conclusion? Does it restate your thesis? Do you need a summary or a call for action? Read the body of your paper and ask yourself if you have supported your thesis with enough material. Is more research necessary to support certain points? Must you reorganize your discussion? Should you rearrange points to construct stronger sections? Do you need section headings?

Everyone in New Jersey is required to report suspected child abuse to the Division of Youth and Family Services. Statistics ~~show~~ reveal that the number of child abuse cases ~~in~~ throughout ~~Jersey~~ New Jersey has ~~grown~~ increased 119 percent from 1973 to 1974 and the trend is still rising. ~~The New Jersey Statutes~~ ~~Between 1974 and 1977~~ ~~in the state of New Jersey~~ In the state of New Jersey between 1974 and 1977 child abuse increased 148 percent, and between 1976 and 1977, 60 percent. It is estimated that the 24,523 reported cases are only 5 percent of the actual number of child abuse cases. [Mahoney, p. 25]

New Jersey medical statistics estimate that one ~~of~~ out of every four children die from injuries caused by an abusive parent. At least ~~20~~ 25-30 percent of the abused children ~~are physically~~ remain physically or emotionally disturbed for life. These statistics ~~seem to show~~ indicate that the New Jersey Child Abuse Laws are not adequate. [Mahoney p. 23]

The New Jersey Statutes ~~which~~ establish the public policy for child abuse. ~~It~~ They ~~says~~ say that children who ~~are~~ have been abused by their parents should be protected. ~~It~~ They also say that doctors and hospitals that act to protect children should be immune ~~for~~ from legal ~~suit~~ action. The statutes also require that doctors must write out a report ~~of~~ of possible child abuse and ~~in at one~~ immediately send it to the Division of Youth and Family Services and notify the local police. [Statutes, p. 93]

Does it make sense to consider these issues at this stage of your paper? Absolutely. Most writers find that only after they see their ideas in a rough draft can they put them into an effective final form.

☐ WORKING SOURCE MATERIAL INTO YOUR PAPER

One of the biggest problems students have is taking control of their sources. Even though you can use the ideas, and sometimes the words, of your sources, the framework of your paper must be your own. When you revise, make certain that you have drawn your own conclusions from your sources to create an original paper.

Kathy Downey drafted the following paragraphs for her paper "Censorship in the Movies."

> The first protest against a movie came in Atlantic City, New Jersey. A nickelodeon peep show called "Dolorita in the Passion Dance" was shown on the boardwalk just two weeks after the invention of Thomas Edison's kinetoscope on April 14, 1894. [Randall, p. 11]
>
> The earliest type of movie restraints came in the form of licensing fees. Movie house owners were required to pay stiff annual fees in order to stay open for business. [Randall, p. 11] In Deer River, Minnesota, a $200 license fee was not considered outlandish for a town of 1,000. [Randall, p. 12]
>
> In 1907 stronger regulations were imposed in Chicago and New York. All films would be censored before public viewing. In Chicago the chief of police was made the chief censor. His job was to withhold films determined to be immoral or obscene. [Randall, p. 12]

When Kathy reviewed her rough draft, she saw that she had not made good use of her information. She had copied material from her note cards without drawing any conclusions. In her next draft, she tried to assimilate her sources, reworking three paragraphs into one effective one.

> Apparently movies had earned a bad reputation right from the beginning. The first recorded protest came in Atlantic City, New Jersey, as a result of a nickelodeon peep show called "Dolorita in the Passion Dance." Interestingly, this film was showing on the boardwalk just two weeks after Thomas Edison invented the kinetoscope on April 14, 1894. Soon to follow these protests came restraints, first in the form of licensing fees and then actual censorship. In 1907 films were censored in New York and Chicago before public viewing. In Chicago the chief of police could withhold a film that he determined to be immoral or obscene. [Randall, pp. 11–12]

Kathy's research now supports her own observations. She doesn't weaken her presentation with phrases like "I feel" or "In my opinion." Crisp and straightforward, her assertions portray her as an objective critic using evidence to reach conclusions. She begins with her main idea that movies apparently had a bad reputation from the start. She supports this with an example from her research, the 1894 protest against "Dolorita in the Passion Dance." Then she evaluates the results of these protests—first license fees, then censorship. Most of the facts in the first version appear in the second. Simply by reworking, she gave her material new shape and eliminated the sense that she was using someone else's words.

□ USING QUOTATIONS

We have said that you should quote only when something vital would be lost by using other words. When you do use quotations, they must be woven smoothly into the fabric of your discussion. Consider the following passages:

> Advertisers use subliminal stimuli to manipulate the emotions and to direct buying behavior of the public. "Goals may appear simple, but the psychological expertise and the media technology employed are incredibly sophisticated and subtle—tricky enough to bypass your every natural defense." [Packard, p. 72]

With some revision, the student tailored the quotation this way:

> Advertisers use subliminal stimuli to manipulate the emotions and to direct buying behavior of the public. At least one researcher has shown that the goals of advertisers "may appear simple, but the psychological expertise and the media technology employed are incredibly sophisticated and subtle—tricky enough to bypass your every natural defense." [Packard, p. 72]

Sometimes a quotation does not fit neatly into a sentence. When confronted by a change of tense or subject, you can edit the quotation, leaving out words or changing and bracketing them.

Awkward

The Italian family was so strongly bonded that it became the most powerful unit for the individual. "The Italian family is a stronghold in a hostile land." [Gallo, p. 152]

Revised

The Italian family was so strongly bonded that it became the most powerful unit for the individual. It was "a stronghold in a hostile land." [Gallo, p. 152]

Awkward

No sooner does Usher speak than "I become aware of a distinct, hollow, metallic, and clangorous, yet apparently muffled reverberation." [Poe, p. 238]

Revised

No sooner does Usher speak than the narrator "[becomes] aware of a distinct, hollow, metallic, and clangorous, yet apparently muffled reverberation." [Poe, p. 238]

When you want to call attention to the author's name as well as his or her words, you can write the name into the text.

> According to Rousseau, "There is no soul so vile, no heart so barbarous as to be insusceptible to some sort of affection." [p. 71]

If you want to emphasize the words and not their author, you identify the source in a note.

> Earl Kenneth Hines has been called the father of modern jazz piano because he, "more than anyone else, emancipated it from the lingering restrictions of rag-time thought and principle." [Garraty, p. 554]

Here the student incorporates the quotation into his sentence. In his final draft, he will cite the author in a footnote.

Occasionally you may want to use long quotations, of four lines or more. These give your audience more insight into your sources, but they break the flow of your paper. They also force your reader to do work that, perhaps, you should have done. In any event, use long quotations sparingly.

Long quotations should be introduced in your own words. Start a new line, indent ten spaces from the left, and double-space the material.

```
As anyone who has ever worked with a computer on campus knows,

there are students, called ''hackers,'' who compulsively work with

computers. In her article ''Computer Addicts,'' Dina Ingber exam-

ines this phenomenon:

            What do they do at the computer at all hours of the day

            or night?  They design and play complex games; . . . like

            ham radio operators they communicate with hackers in

            other areas who are plugged into the same system. . . .

            One hacker takes his terminal home with him every school

            vacation so he can keep in touch with other hackers.

            And at Stanford University, even the candy machine is

            hooked up to a computer . . . to disperse candy on credit

            to those who know the password.  [Ingber, p. 97]
```

The writer introduces the quotation into her draft in order to present the author's list of examples. With the quotation set off, quotation marks are unnecessary. (For typing directions, see "Preparing the Final Draft," page 417.)

You can reduce the length of a quotation by inserting three dots, called ellipsis points, for the words or phrases you have eliminated. At the end of a sentence you use three spaced periods plus the final punctuation (. . . ? or . . . .). The following example shows how to use ellipsis points:

Original

The Scientific Revolution can be held to begin in the year 1543 when there was brought to Copernicus, perhaps on his deathbed, the first printed copy of the book he had finished about a dozen years earlier.

Jacob Bronowski, *Science and Human Values*

Deletion of nonessential information using ellipsis points

The Scientific Revolution can be held to begin in the year 1543 when there was brought to Copernicus . . . the first printed copy of the book he had finished about a dozen years earlier.

Here "perhaps on his deathbed" can be eliminated without distorting the author's meaning. But never delete words that convey distinctions essential to a passage.

□ CHOOSING A TITLE

Your title must tell your readers what your paper is about. Just because your paper is academic, however, does not mean that its title has to be dull. Consider how these authors have tried to find titles with some appeal:

Richard Gamble, "Hitch Your Wagon to a Star: Confessions of a Postacademic Job Seeker," *Profession 80*, pp. 20–23.
Dean Memering, "Forward to Basics," *College English*, 39 (Jan. 1978), 554–561.
Peter F. Greenberg, "The Thrill Seekers," *Human Behavior*, April 1977, pp. 16–21.

You may not always want to use clever or humorous titles—you would hardly want to joke about the death penalty or starvation, for example. Still, your titles can be engaging and to the point. "Hunger in Chad" might be descriptive, but "Chad: A Picture of Third-World Hunger" makes your point more dramatically.

STEP 9: DOCUMENTING

With your first draft revised and your source material smoothly integrated into your paper, you must acknowledge the material you borrowed from your sources. Not all fields, however, use the same style of documentation. This section explains the formats most commonly used in the humanities, the social sciences, and the sciences. Before doing a research assignment for one of your courses, find out what form your instructor requires and consult the appropriate guide sheet and follow it to the letter.

☐ WHAT TO DOCUMENT

Documentation enables your readers to identify your sources and to judge the quality of your work. It also encourages them to look up the books and articles you cite. Therefore, you should carefully document the following kinds of information:

1. All direct quotations
2. All summaries or paraphrases of passages from your sources
3. All opinions, judgments, and insights of others
4. All tables, graphs, and charts that you get from your sources

Be careful, however, not to overdocument. Inexperienced writers often feel that the more notes, the better the paper. This is quite wrong. Too many notes and references distract a reader. If, in a single paragraph, for example, you cite information from two pages of a book, document it with one note, not two, at the end of the paragraph.

☐ WHAT NOT TO DOCUMENT

Common knowledge, information that you would expect most educated readers to know, need not be documented. You can safely include facts that are widely available in encyclopedias, textbooks, newspapers, and magazines, or on television and radio. Even if the information is new to you, as long as it is unchallenged and generally accepted, there is no need to indicate your source. Information that is in dispute, however, or that a particular person has discovered, should be documented. You can usually assume that information which appears in several of your sources is generally known. You need not, for instance, document the fact that the Declaration of Independence was signed on July 4, 1776, or that Josiah Bartlett and Oliver Wolcott signed it. You do have to document a historian's analysis of the document, or a particular scholar's recent discoveries about Josiah Bartlett.

When to document is largely a matter of judgment. As a beginning researcher, you had better document any material you have questions about. That way you avoid any hint of plagiarism.

☐ PARENTHETICAL DOCUMENTATION

In May 1982 the Modern Language Association (MLA) proposed that documentary references in the humanities no longer appear as endnotes or footnotes (See page 409 for a discussion of endnotes and footnotes.).* Instead, references are inserted parenthetically within the text and keyed to a list of works cited at the end of the paper.

---

*Parenthetical documentation follows the guidelines set in the *MLA Handbook for Writers of Research Papers*—second ed.

□   MLA FORMAT

MLA documentation consists of the author's last name and a page number. If you
use more than one source by the same author, include a short title. If any of these
elements is stated in the text, omit it in the parenthetical reference.

```
The colony's religious and political freedom appealed to many ide-

alists in Europe (Ripley 132).
```

```
Penn's religious motivation is discussed by Joseph P. Kelley in

his work Pennsylvania, The Colonial Years, 1681-1776 (44).
```

Note: Because the author's name is mentioned in the text, only a page reference is necessary.

```
Penn emphasized his religious motivation (Kelley, Democracy 93).
```

Note: More than one work by Kelley is cited; therefore, a shortened title is included.

Place each parenthetical reference as close as possible to the material it documents. Keep in mind that you punctuate differently for (1) indirect references;
(2) direct quotations in the text; and (3) double-spaced quotations set off from the
text.

Parenthetical documentation for indirect references should appear *before* all
punctuation marks.

```
Degler believes Penn's writings epitomize seventeenth-century re-

ligious thought (72).
```

Parenthetical documentation for double-spaced quotations that are set off from
the text should appear *after* the final punctuation at the right-hand margin.

```
As Ross says, "Penn followed his conscience in all matters" (127).
```

Parenthetical documentation for double-spaced quotations that are set off from
the text should appear *after* the final punctuation at the right-hand margin.

```
. . . . a commonwealth in which all individuals can follow God's

truth and develop according to God's will.                    (314)
```

Sample references   Parenthetical references provide a straightforward and easy
method of documentation. Even so, the following situations call for special attention:

Citing a work by more than one author

One group of physicists questioned many of the assumptions of relativity (Harbeck and Johnson 31).

Citing a volume and page number

In 1912 Virginia Stephen married Leonard Woolf, with whom she founded the Hogarth Press (Woolf 1:17).

Citing a work without a listed author

Television rating wars have escalated during the past ten years ("Leaving the Cellar" 102).

It is a curious fact that the introduction of Christianity at the end of the Roman Empire "had no effect on the abolition of slavery" ("Slavery").

Note: Omit a page reference if you are citing a one-page article.

Citing an indirect source

Wagner said that myth and history stood before him "with opposing claims" (qtd. in Winkler 10).

Note: You should always try to get material from the original source, but sometimes you will have to use an indirect source. Indicate that the material is from an indirect source by using the abbreviation *qtd.* for the word *quoted.*

Using explanatory notes with parenthetical references Explanatory notes—providing bibliographic comments or offering remarks that are necessary but do not fit into the text—may be used along with parenthetical documentation. These notes are indicated by a raised number in the text and are listed on the first full page following the text, entitled "Notes."

Use explanatory notes to cite more than one source in a single reference. Multiple references in a single pair of parentheses distract readers and should be avoided.

Both researchers emphasize the necessity of having dying patients share their experiences.[1]

Notes

[1]Elizabeth Kübler-Ross, <u>On Death and Dying</u> (New York: Macmil-

lan, 1973) 27; Charles R. Stinnette, <u>Anxiety and Faith</u> (Greenwich,

Conn.: Seabury, 1955) 43.

Note: See "Endnotes and Footnotes" (page 409) for the proper format for explanatory notes that refer to books and articles.

Use notes to provide comments or explanations that are needed to clarify a point in the text.

The massacre of the Armenians by the Turks during World War I

is an event that the survivors cannot forget.[3]

Notes

[3]For a first-hand account of these events, see Kerop

Bedoukian, <u>Some of Us Survived</u> (New York: Farrar Straus Giroux,

1978) 17-81.

Listing the works cited   The list of sources that you have used in your paper is called the "Works Cited" section. If your instructor tells you to list all the sources you read, whether you actually cite them or not, use the title "Works Consulted."

Begin the list of works cited on a new sheet, after your explanatory notes, or after the last page of text if you have no explanatory notes. Number the list of works cited as the next page of text. (If the paper ends on page 8, the works cited page is page 9.) List items in alphabetical order according to the authors' *last* names. If one of your sources is unsigned, as is the case with many magazine and newspaper articles, use the first main word of the title as your guide. The first line of each entry should be flush against the left-hand margin, and subsequent lines should be indented five spaces from the left. The list of works cited is double-spaced throughout, within and between items.

An item in a list of works cited usually has three divisions, each separated by a period.

Works cited format

Name: last name first   The three sections end with periods

Dyson, Freeman. <u>Disturbing the Universe.</u> New York: Harper and

Row, 1979.

Sample entries: books   The following entries illustrate the format for citing books:

A book by one author

Barsan, Richard Meran. <u>Non-Fiction Film</u>. New York: Dutton, 1973.

A book by two or more authors

Feldman, Burton, and Robert D. Richardson. <u>The Rise of Modern</u>

   <u>Mythology</u>. Bloomington: Indiana UP, 1972.

Note: Only the first author's name is entered in reverse order. The second and third authors are listed in normal order. Authors' names should be listed in the order in which they appear on the title page. For books with more than three authors, list the first author followed by ''et al.'' or ''and others.''

Spiller, Robert E., et al. <u>Literary History of the United States</u>.

   New York: Macmillan, 1974.

Two or more books by the same author

Kingston, Maxine Hong. <u>China Men</u>. New York: Knopf, 1980.

----------. <u>The Woman Warrior</u>. New York: Vintage, 1977.

Note: Books by the same author can be listed in alphabetical order or in order of publication. Ten hyphens followed by a period take the place of the author's name after the first entry.

An edited book

Melville, Herman. <u>Moby Dick</u>. Ed. Charles Feidelson, Jr. Indian-

   apolis: Bobbs-Merrill, 1964.

An essay appearing in a book

Forster, E. M. "Flat and Round Characters." In The Theory of The

   <u>Novel</u>. Ed. Philip Stevick. New York: Free Press, 1980.

   223-231.

Note: The inclusive pages on which the *full* essay appears are shown, even though your paper may cite only one page. If you were using several essays from this book in your paper, you would list the book itself in the works cited section.

Stevick, Philip, ed. <u>The Theory of The Novel</u>. New York: Free

   Press, 1980.

A multivolume work

Raine, Kathleen. Vol. 1 of <u>Blake and Tradition</u>. 2 vols. Prince-

ton: Princeton UP, 1968.

The foreword, preface, or afterword of a book

Beauvoir, Simone de. Preface. <u>Treblinka</u>. By Jean-François

Steiner. New York: Mentor, 1979. xix-xxiii.

An encyclopedia article

"Liberty, Statue of." <u>New Encyclopaedia Britannica: Macropaedia</u>,

1974 ed.

Note: You enter an unsigned article's title in the way that it is listed in the encyclopedia. For a signed article, you enter the author's name (last name first) and then follow it with the article's title using normal word order.

Fellman, David. "Academic Freedom." <u>Dictionary of the History of</u>

<u>Ideas</u>, 1973.

A reprint

Greenberg, Daniel S. <u>The Politics of Pure Science</u>. 1967, rpt.

New York: New American Library, 1971.

A pamphlet or bulletin

United States, Department of State. <u>International Control of</u>

<u>Atomic Energy: Growth of a Policy</u>. Washington: GPO, 1946.

Sample entries:

An article in a scholarly journal with continuous pagination through an annual volume

LeGuin, Ursula K. "American Science Fiction and The Other."

<u>Science Fiction Studies</u> 2 (1975): 208-210.

Note: Citations for articles give the pages on which the full article appears. The abbreviations "p." and "pp." are not included in the page reference.

An article in a scholarly journal that has separate pagination in each issue

Farrell, Thomas J. "Developing Literate Writing." <u>Basic Writing</u>

2.1 (1978): 30-51.

Note: For a journal that has separate pagination in each issue, add a period and the issue number after the volume (e.g., 2.1 for volume 2, issue number 1).

An article from a weekly magazine

Seiberling, Dorothy. "The New Masculinity." New York 31 Jan.

    1977: 54–55.

Note: The date is put in parentheses only when a volume number is mentioned.

An unsigned article in a weekly magazine

"Solzhenitsyn: An Artist Becomes an Exile." Time 25 Feb. 1974:

    34–36, 39–40.

Note: The page listing of this article is not continuous. After being interrupted on pp. 37–38 by an advertising supplement, the article continues on pp. 39–40.

An article in a monthly magazine

Williamson, Ray. "Native Americans Were The First Astronomers."

    Smithsonian Oct. 1978: 78–85.

Gaspen, Phyllis. "Indisposed to Medicine: The Women's Self–Help

    Movement." The New Physicians May 1980: 20–24.

An article in a daily newspaper

Boffey, Phillip M. "Security and Science Collide on Data Flow."

    New York Times 24 Jan. 1982, late ed.: B6.

An editorial

"Yes, There Is a Better Income Tax." Editorial. New York Times 6

    June 1982, late ed.: C12.

Sample entries: nonprint sources

Computer software

Atkinson, Bill. Macpaint. Computer software. Apple, 1983.

Note: This citation contains the writer of the program, the title of the program, a descriptive label ("Computer software"), the distributor, and the date of publication.

Material from a computer service

Baer, Walter S. "Telecommunications Technology in the 1980's."

    Computer Science June 1984: 137–45. ERIC ED 184 568.

Note: Enter material from a computer service—such as BRS, DIALOG, or ERIC—just as you would other printed material, but mention the information service and the identifying number at the end of the entry.

A lecture

Abel, Robert. "Communication Theory and Film." Communications

    Colloquium, Department of Humanities–Communications, Drexel

    University, 20 Oct. 1983.

A letter

Davidowicz, Lucy. Letter to the author. 7 May 1983.

An interview

Fuller, Buckminster. Personal interview. 17 Dec. 1980.

A film

Lucas, George, dir. Return of the Jedi. With Mark Hammill, Har-

    rison Ford, Carrie Fisher, and Billy Dee Williams. Twentieth

    Century Fox, 1983.

A television or radio program

Nothing to Fear: The Legacy of F.D.R. Narr. John Hart. NBC.

    KYW, Philadelphia. 24 Jan. 1982.

"The Greening of the Forests." Life on Earth. Narr. David At-

    tenborough. PBS. WGBH, Boston. 26 Jan. 1982.

Other parenthetical documentation formats

☐ APA FORMAT

The American Psychological Association (APA) documentation style is used extensively in the social sciences. As in MLA documentation, short references in parentheses appear within the sentence in which the source is mentioned.

```
One study of the family (Zimmerman, 1980) shows a close connec-
tion . . . .
```

Note: The last name followed by a comma and the date of publication are put in parentheses.

```
In his study Zimmerman (1980) shows a close connection . . . .
```

Note: When the name appears in the text, only the date of publication is needed.

```
In his 1980 study, Zimmerman shows a close connection . . . .
```

Note: When both the name and date of publication appear in the text, no reference is needed.

```
When he completed his next study (Zimmerman, 1981b) . . . .
```

Note: If you are using two publications that are by the same author and that also appeared in the same year, you designate the first one ''Zimmerman, 1981a'' and the second ''Zimmerman, 1981b.'' You should also use this format in the reference list that follows the text of your paper.

```
Many historical differences between city and farm families seem to
be diminishing (Rainwater & Freedman, 1982).
```

Note: With two authors, both names are cited. If a work has three or more authors, mention all names the first time, and in subsequent references, cite the first author followed by ''et al.'' and the year.

```
These theories have an interesting history (Lee, 1966, p. 53).
```

Note: When you are citing a book, you should include page numbers.

At the end of your paper, list all the sources you cited on a separate page headed "References." Arrange each item in alphabetical order, giving the author's last name and initials (never the full name). Next comes the title, date of publication, and, with journals, volume number and pages. With books you give the city of publication, publisher, and date of publication. Underline all book or journal titles to indicate italics. When you finish preparing your reference list, edit for underlining, capitals, punctuation, and sequence.

A book with one author

```
Bott, E.  Family and social network.  London: Tavistock Publica-
    tions, 1957.
```

Note: Separate the three sections of a reference with periods. Capitalize only the first letter of the first word of a book title or the title of an article. For journal titles, capitalize the first letter of each major word. Underline all titles.

A book with more than one author

Lantz, H. R., & Snyder, E. C. Marriage: An examination of the

man—woman relationship. New York: Wiley, 1962.

Note: Both authors are cited last name first.

A journal article

Wilson, J. Q. The police and their problems: A theory. Public

Policy, 1963, 12, 173—201.

Note: Titles of articles are not enclosed in quotation marks. Journal volume numbers are underlined to indicate italics.

An article in an edited book

Miller, W. Violent crimes in city gangs. In M. E. Wolfgang,

L. Savitz, & N. Johnston (Eds.), The sociology of crime and

delinquency (2nd ed.). New York: Wiley, 1970.

☐ NUMBER-REFERENCE SYSTEM

The number-reference system is used in a number of the sciences. Instead of parenthetical name and year citations, numbers in the text refer to a reference list at the end of a paper. References are listed in alphabetical order or in the order in which they appear in the paper.

This method of radiocarbon dating was applied to several hundred

samples (1). The results . . .

(1) Libby, W. F. Radiocarbon dating. Chicago: Univ. of Chicago

Press, 1952.

☐ ENDNOTES AND FOOTNOTES

Since some instructors prefer endnotes (notes following the whole paper) or foot-notes (notes at the bottom of each page) for documentation, we present these formats here.* There are two parts to this documentation: (1) the number in the

---

*Endnote and footnote forms follow the guidelines set in the *MLA Handbook for Writers of Research Papers,* second edition.

text that refers to your note, and (2) the note itself. The number directly follows the material you are documenting and is typed slightly above the line. Notes are numbered consecutively throughout the paper and placed *after* all punctuation.

```
. . . . a double helix."³
```

The number is not followed by a period, asterisk, or other symbol.

First references: books   If your endnote is a first reference to a book, it will contain the following information.

1.   A number that matches the number in the text

2.   Author (name as it appears on the title page)—first name, middle name or initial, and last name

3.   Book title (underlined)

4.   City of publication ⎱
5.   Publisher   ⎰ enclosed in parentheses
6.   Year of publication ⎰

7.   Page reference

Indent the first line of each note five spaces, and begin it with a number (typed slightly above the line) corresponding to the note number in the text. After the first line, type all the lines that follow flush with the left margin. Endnotes are double-spaced within notes as well as between notes. (Footnotes are single-spaced within the note and double-spaced between notes.)

Sample endnote

```
¹William Appleman Williams, The Roots of American Empire (New

York: Random House, 1969) 359.
```

Sample footnote

```
¹Norman Mailer, The Executioner's Song (New York: Little,

Brown, 1979) 125.
```

With endnotes and footnotes, insert punctuation exactly as it appears in these sample references.

The following endnotes corresponding to the sample entries in "Listing the works cited" (page 403), illustrate many of the situations you will encounter.

A book by one author

```
¹Richard Meran Barsan, Non-Fiction Film (New York: Dutton,

1973) 62.
```

Note: To conserve space you should not include "incorporated," "publishers," or "company" after the name of the publisher. Thus, E. P. Dutton and Company, Inc., is shortened to "Dutton."

A book by two or more authors

[2]Burton Feldman and Robert D. Richardson, The Rise of Modern Mythology (Bloomington: Indiana UP, 1972) 102.

Note: For books with three authors, you should list the authors in the order in which they appear on the title page with "and" before the last name. For books with more than three authors, list the first author followed by "et al." or "and others."

[3]Robert E. Spiller, et al., Literary History of the United States (New York: Macmillan, 1974) 217.

An edited book

[4]Herman Melville, Moby Dick, ed. Charles Feidelson, Jr. (Indianapolis: Bobbs–Merrill, 1964) 51.

An essay appearing in a book

[5]E. M. Forster, "Flat and Round Characters," in The Theory of the Novel, ed. Philip Stevick (New York: Free Press, 1980) 225.

A multivolume work

[6]Kathleen Raine, Blake and Tradition, 2 vols. (Princeton: Princeton UP, 1968) 1:117.

The foreword, preface, or afterword of a book

[7]Simone de Beauvoir, Preface, Treblinka by Jean–François Steiner (New York: Mentor, 1979) xx.

An article in an encyclopedia

[8]"Statue of Liberty," New Encyclopaedia Britannica: Macropaedia, 1974 ed.

Note: Entries appear in alphabetical order, so a volume number is not needed. If an article is signed, then begin your reference with the author's name.

[9]David Fellman, "Academic Freedom," Dictionary of the History of Ideas, 1973.

A reprint

[10]Daniel S. Greenberg, The Politics of Pure Science (1967,

rpt. New York: New American Library, 1971) 51.

A pamphlet or bulletin

[11]United States, Department of State, International Control

of Atomic Energy: Growth of a Policy (Washington: GPO, 1946) 128.

First references: articles Endnotes for articles are similar to those for books. There are differences in form, however, that have to do with the serial nature of publication. First references to articles contain the following information:

1. A number that matches the number in the text

2. Author (name as it appears in the article)—first name, middle name or initial, and last name

3. Article title (full title in quotation marks)

4. Title of journal or magazine (underlined)

5. Volume number (in arabic numbers)

6. Date of publication (in parentheses when preceded by volume number)

7. Page reference

Like endnotes for books, endnotes for articles are double-spaced throughout. (Footnotes are single-spaced.)

An article in a scholarly journal with continuous pagination through an annual volume

[1]Ursula K. LeGuin, "American Science Fiction and The Other,"

Science Fiction Studies 2 (1975): 209.

An article in a scholarly journal that has separate pagination in each issue

[2]Thomas J. Farrell, "Developing Literate Writing," Basic

Writing 2.1 (1978): 33.

An article in a weekly magazine

[3]Dorothy Seiberling, "The New Masculinity," New York 31 Jan.

1977: 54.

Note: Notice that dates for articles follow military format with the day preceding the month.

An unsigned article in a weekly magazine

[4]"Solzhenitsyn: An Artist Becomes an Exile," Time 25 Feb.

1974: 35.

An article in a monthly magazine
[5]Ray Williamson, "Native Americans were the First

Astronomers," <u>Smithsonian</u> Oct. 1978: 80–81.

[6]Phyllis Gapen, "Indisposed to Medicine: The Women's Self-

Help Movement," <u>The New Physicians</u> May 1980: 21.

Note: In the first reference to the above article, you must include a *full* title, not just "Indisposed to Medicine."

An article in a daily newspaper
[7]Philip M. Boffey, "Security and Science Collide on Data

Flow," <u>New York Times</u> 24 Jan. 1982, late ed.: B6.

An editorial
[8]"Yes, There Is a Better Income Tax," editorial, <u>New York</u>

<u>Times</u> 6 June 1982, late ed.: C12.

First references: nonprint sources Sources other than those in print must also be documented.

Computer software
[1]Bill Atkinson, <u>Macpaint</u>, computer software, Apple, 1983.

Material from a computer service
[2]Walter S. Baer, "Telecommunications in the 1980's," <u>Computer</u>

<u>Science</u> June 1984: 138 (ERIC ED 184 568).

A lecture
Robert Abel, "Communication Theory and Film," Communication

Colloquium, Department of Humanities and Communications, Drexel

University, 20 Oct. 1983.

A letter
Lucy Davidowicz, letter to the author, 7 May 1983.

An interview
Buckminster Fuller, personal interview, 17 Dec. 1980.

A film

⁵George Lucas, dir., <u>Return of the Jedi</u>, with Mark Hamill, Harrison Ford, Carrie Fisher, and Billy Dee Williams, Twentieth Century Fox, 1983.

Note: The citation should include the title *(underlined)*, distributor, and date. Other information, such as the director, writer, and performers, can also be given.

A television or radio program

⁶<u>Nothing to Fear: The Legacy of F.D.R.</u>, narr. John Hart, NBC, KYW, Philadelphia, 24 Jan. 1982.

⁷"The Greening of the Forests," <u>Life on Earth</u>, narr. David Attenborough, PBS, WGBH, Boston, 26 Jan. 1982.

Note: Because ''The Greening of the Forests'' is one part of the thirteen-part series *Life on Earth,* it is placed in quotation marks.

Subsequent references   After the first reference to a *book,* you no longer have to provide full bibliographic information. The author's last name and the page reference for the citation are sufficient.

First reference

¹Maxine Hong Kingston, <u>The Woman Warrior</u> (New York: Vintage, 1977) 37.

Subsequent reference

²Kingston 40.

If your paper refers to two or more books by the same author, subsequent references to each book should include a shortened form of the title or the full title if it is already short.

⁶Kingston, <u>The Woman Warrior</u> 93.

⁷Kingston, <u>China Men</u> 31.

Subsequent references to *articles* follow the same format. Here, too, if you use two or more sources by the same author, include titles in your references.

First reference

¹¹Maurice Beebe, "What Modernism Was," <u>Journal of Modern Lit-erature</u> 3 (1974): 1068.

[12]Beebe 1072.

If you have been using "Ibid." ("in the same place") when a note refers to the same source as the one above it, don't. This once popular abbreviation, along with "op. cit." ("in a work cited recently") and "loc. cit." ("in the place cited"), is now outdated.

Bibliography   The list of sources at the end of a paper, called the bibliography, follows the form of the "works cited" section discussed above. Begin your bibliography on a new sheet, after your endnotes (or after the last page of text if you use footnotes) and list items in alphabetical order according to the authors' last names.

Here are the major differences between notes and bibliographic entries for books:

Endnote form

Marker — Name: normal order — Comma — Title — Parentheses

[1]David McCullough, The Great Bridge (New York:
Simon and Schuster, 1972) 49-50.

Publication information

Page reference

Bibliography form

Name: last name first

The three sections of the entry end with periods

McCullough, David. The Great Bridge. New York:
Simon and Schuster, 1972.

No parentheses

EXERCISE

This student paragraph integrates material from three sources, but the student author has neglected to cite those sources. Read the paragraph and the three excerpts that follow it. Then:

1. Identify material which has been quoted directly from a source. Check the wording against the original for accuracy and enclose the quote in quotation marks or paraphrase the words of the source.

2. Add proper documentation for each piece of information that requires it. Use the form your instructor requires.

Student paragraph: Oral History

Oral history became a legitimate field of study in 1948, when the Oral History Research Office was established by Allan Nevins. Like recordings of presidents' fireside chats and declarations of war, oral history is both oral and historical. But it is more: oral history is the creation of new historical documentation, not the recording or preserving of documentation that already exists. Oral history also tends to be more spontaneous and personal and less formal than ordinary tape recordings. Nevins's purpose was to collect and prepare materials to help future historians to better understand the past. Oral history has enormous potential to do just this, for it draws on people's memories of their own lives and deeds and of their associations with particular people, periods, or events. The result, when it is recorded and transcribed, is a valuable new source.

Source 1

. . . when Allan Nevins set up the Oral History Research Office in 1948, he looked upon it as an organization that in a systematic way could obtain from the lips and papers of living Americans who had led significant lives a full record of their participation in the political, economic, and cultural affairs of the nation. His purpose was to prepare such material for the use of future historians. It was his conviction that the individual played an important role in history and that an individual's autobiography might in future serve as a key to an understanding of contemporary historical movements. (From page 71, Volume 28, number 1 of *The American Archivist.* The article, written by Saul Benison, is called "Reflections on Oral History." It appeared in January 1965.)

Source 2

Typically, an oral history project comprises an organized series of interviews with selected individuals or groups in order to create new source materials from the reminiscences of their own life and acts, or from their association with a particular person, period, or event. These recollections are recorded on tape and transcribed on a typewriter into sheets of transcript. . . . Such oral history may be distinguished from more conventional tape recordings of speeches, lectures, symposia, etc., by the fact that the former creates new sources through the more spontaneous, personal, multitopical, extended narrative, while the latter utilizes sources in a more formal mode for a specific occasion. (This excerpt is from an article called "Oral History: Defining the Term" by Elizabeth Rumics. It appeared in 1966 in Volume 40 of the *Wilson Library Bulletin,* on page 602.)

Source 3

. . .oral history, as the term came to be used, is the creation of new historical documentation, not the recording or preserving of documentation—even oral documentation—that
already exists. Its purpose is not, like that of the National Voice Library at Michigan State
University, to preserve the recordings of fireside chats or presidential declarations of war or
James Whitcomb Riley reciting "Little Orphan Annie." These are surely oral and just as
surely the stuff of history; but they are not oral history. For this there must be the creation
of a new historical document by means of a personal interview. (Norman Hoyle wrote this
in the July 1972 issue of *Library Trends*. The excerpt is from p. 61 of the article "Oral
History.")

STEP 10. PREPARING THE FINAL DRAFT

A typed research paper is always preferable. It is easy to read, and when done
right, has an attractive, professional appearance. Handwritten papers, no matter
how carefully done, look less polished. If you must submit handwritten copy, use
wide-lined paper and write or print on every other line in blue or blue-black ink.
Your final draft, whether typed or written, should be clear and free from smudges.
Never cross out words. If you have made a mistake that you cannot correct neatly,
redo the page.

Materials   When typing your manuscript, use 8½-by-11-inch 20-pound white
bond paper. Do not use erasable bond (it smudges) or onionskin paper (it is hard to
handle and to read). Always use a black ribbon and a standard typewriter face—
fancy types, like italic or script, distract your readers.

Typing   Your paper, including notes and bibliographic pages, should conform to
the following specifications.

◦ Type your text double-spaced.

◦ Type footnotes single-spaced; double-space between notes. Type endnotes entirely double-spaced. A list of works cited and APA references are double-spaced.

◦ On the first page of your paper, place your title two inches down from the top
margin.

◦ Capitalize the first letter of each word in the title, except for prepositions,
conjunctions, and articles. Never underline it, put it in quotation marks, or use
capital letters throughout.

◦ Double-space twice (four spaces) below your title before you begin your text.

◦ Use a 1-inch margin left and right on all pages.

◦ Indent the first word of each paragraph five spaces from the left-hand margin.
Begin long indented quotations ten spaces from the left-hand margin.

First page of your paper

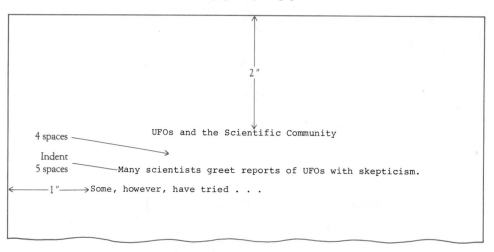

Page numbers   Number the pages of your paper consecutively. The first page of your text does *not* carry a page number, even though those pages count in the page numbering. Put numbers on all other pages in the upper right-hand corner. You may add your last name in front of each page number to prevent misplaced pages. (Do *not* punctuate numbers with periods, hyphens, or dashes.)

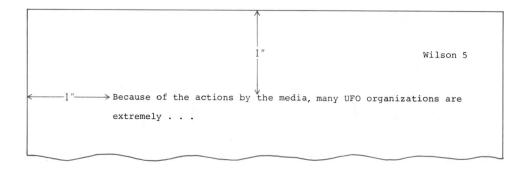

The title page   Put all identifying information double-spaced in the upper left-hand corner of the first page of your manuscript.

Manuscript without a title page

```
Susan Wilson
English 102-5
Professor Hall
March 9, 1985


               The Hidden Message:

     Subliminal Advertising in American Magazines


     The use of subliminal language in American magazine

advertisements affects millions of . . .
```

Many instructors, however, still like a separate title page, and one appears with the paper at the end of this chapter (page 421). It carries the title; your name, course, and section number; your instructor's name; and the date you submitted your paper. When you use a title page, don't forget to repeat your title on the first page of your manuscript.

The outline   Your instructor may also want you to include your formal outline. Be sure that it reflects all the changes that you made when you revised your paper.

Preparing the paper   Papers do occasionally get misplaced or lost, and you can avoid a host of problems by making a spare copy of your paper for your file.

The best way to fasten the pages of your typed manuscript is by placing a large paper clip at the upper left corner or a single staple diagonally across that corner. Don't staple your paper down the side or make it difficult in any way for your instructor to turn the pages.

STEP 11: FINAL EDITING

At this point you probably want to throw down your books and never see your research paper again. Stay with it just a bit longer. Before you hand in your manuscript, read through it one last time to look for any grammar, spelling, or typing mistakes you may have missed. Pay particular attention to documentation. We don't mean to harp on this, but every error takes away from the credibility of your whole paper. Once you are satisfied that your manuscript is as accurate as you can make it, put it in a folder or envelope and hand it in.

A SAMPLE RESEARCH PAPER

On the following pages is a sample research paper that conforms to the style outlined in the 1982 *MLA Handbook.*

About ⅓ down page

Civilian Control of Atomic Energy: } Title

Scientists' Bridge into Politics

                                                      } 2"

                            by

                     Jeanne Parker   Name

                                                      } 2"

Double-space {   English 102, Section 12   } Course
                       Dr. Richard Elias   Instructor
                        March 8, 1983   Date submitted

Heading centered ————————

Thesis statement precedes body of outline ————————

Double-space throughout* ————————

Margins on both sides ══════════

Follow correct outline form with consistent indentions and parallel listings ————————

No page number if outline runs one page; if outline exceeds one page, number with Roman numerals.

*The spacing in this outline has been reduced to fit it on one book page.

→ Outline

→ Thesis: The atomic bomb motivated scientists to enter post–World
War II politics.

I. End-of-war attitudes of scientists toward control of atomic
energy
   A. Franck Report: international agreement
   B. Einstein and others: world government
II. Postwar activities of ~~scientists~~
   A. Ability to influence public policy
      1. Had greatest knowledge of bomb
      2. Enjoyed great public prestige
   B. Drawbacks of influencing public policy
      1. Reluctant to get involved in politics
      2. Temperamentally unsuited for role as lobbyists
III. The May–Johnson Bill
   A. Provisions of the bill
      1. Military control
      2. Nine-member commission
   B. Objections of scientists
      1. Wanted to resume prewar lives
      2. Wanted freedom from regimentation
      3. Opposed military secrecy
      4. Feared limits on equipment and personnel
IV. Actions of scientists against military control
   A. Opposed May–Johnson Bill
      1. Organized the Federation of American Scientists
      2. Lobbied despite reluctance
      3. Convinced Truman to withdraw support
   B. Supported McMahon Bill
   C. Opposed Vandenberg Amendment
V. Conclusion
   A. Scientists entered politics
      1. Learned to influence public opinion
      2. Learned to influence government policy
   B. Scientists helped determine the future of atomic energy

¶ 1:   Introduction, presenting background information _____

Thesis _____

Quotation woven into last sentence _____
Original source:
"When Hans Bethe was recently asked whether the impact of Los Alamos had been
important his reply was simple: 'It *changed everything; it took scientists into politics.*'"
Bethe's words succinctly express and reinforce Jeanne's thesis.

Parenthetical documentation includes a short title because the student uses two
books by the same author.

¶ 2:   Introduces discussion of outline point I: scientists' end-of-war attitudes toward _____
control of atomic energy.

Inserted definition of important term, set off by commas _____

No page number on opening page

Civilian Control of Atomic Energy:

Scientists' Bridge into Politics

1   In 1939 a group of physicists who had fled to the United
States from Hitler's Germany persuaded President Roosevelt to
begin work on an atomic bomb. Six years later, on August 6,
1945, the United States dropped an atomic bomb on the Japanese
city of Hiroshima and a second bomb on Nagasaki three days
later. The world was stunned, mainly because no one, except for
a handful of political and military leaders, knew we were working on an atomic weapon. Also, its power surprised everyone,
even the scientists who built it. For most of these scientists,
however, the greatest shock came with the realization that in
the new atomic age which their efforts had created, they could
no longer remain aloof from politics. Having urged the creation
of the atomic bomb, many scientists felt obligated to take steps
to ensure that the governments of the world used atomic energy
for the good of mankind, not for its destruction. Thus, in the
words of Hans Bethe, a leading physicist, the atomic bomb
"changed everything; it took scientists into politics" (qtd. in
2   Smith, "Los Alamos" 40).

Even before the end of the war, many scientists foresaw the
need for some form of governmental control over atomic energy.
As scientists, they knew that the atom was potentially a source
of enormous, even unlimited power. Working on the Manhattan
Project, as the American effort to build the atomic bomb was
called, they were attempting to liberate this power for use in a
weapon. They realized, however, that because the basic physics
of nuclear reactions, the kind that caused an atomic bomb to
explode, was widely known, the American monopoly on nuclear

Documentation refers to three pages of source material, summarized here to convey —————
general sense rather than specific detail.

¶ 3: Outline point I.A —————

Direct quotation introduced by colon captures flavor of report. To clarify the original —————
statement, "the atomic bomb" is used for "a weapon as indiscriminate as the rocket
bomb and a million times more destructive." Square brackets indicate that phrnot from Jeanne's source.
Original source:
"It may be very difficult to persuade the world that a nation which was capable of
secretly preparing and suddenly releasing a weapon as indiscriminate as the rocket
bomb and a million times more destructive, is to be trusted in its proclaimed desire of
having such weapons abolished by international agreement."

Informational note 1 follows parenthetical documentation.

¶ 4: Outline point I.B —————

Page numbers are arabic, typed at upper right, beginning with second page of text.

weapons would not last long (Jungk 171–73). Once another nation acquired an atomic bomb, so the scientists reasoned, the world would be locked into a spiraling arms race.

3   Most scientists concluded that the only way to prevent this was some form of international control. Probably the most important statement of these concerns is the Franck Report, written by a committee of scientists at the University of Chicago in June 1945. A month before the first atomic bomb was tested, these scientists peered ahead into a future filled with dangers. Their immediate concern was to argue that the bomb should not be used against the Japanese. Like many other scientists, the Franck Committee saw no alternative to international control of nuclear weapons. The problem, however, was whether using the bomb against the Japanese would make it virtually impossible to get other nations to join us in some form of international agreement. "It may be very difficult to persuade the world that a nation which was capable of secretly preparing and suddenly releasing [the atomic bomb] is to be trusted in its proclaimed desire of having such weapons abolished by international agreement" (Smith, Peril 377).[1]

4   Some scientists went even further. Like the scientists who wrote the Franck Report, they foresaw that an arms race was inevitable unless the nations of the world agreed not to build atomic bombs. But they did not believe that a mere agreement was sufficient to eliminate the threat. A few of them argued that a world filled with atomic weapons was so dangerous that the nations of the world would have to surrender their sovereignty to some form of international government if mankind were

Einstein quote illustrates scientists' arguments in favor of world government. Over four lines, it is typed as a block, indented ten spaces, double-spaced, with no quotation marks. Einstein's words carry weight, but long quotations break the flow of a paper and make demands on readers. A block quotation is not just dropped into text but prepared for with an introductory phrase followed by a colon. Notice the placement of the parenthetical reference followed by a raised number that refers to an informational note.

Implications of Einstein's words are summed up in paragraph's last sentence. ——

Refers to previous material ——

¶ 5: Transitional paragraph, summarizing discussion and anticipating point II of outline ——

Points forward to discussion in next paragraph ——

Documentation indicates that material does not represent the writer's original ideas. ——

to avoid destroying itself.   Probably the best-known advocate
of world government was Albert Einstein, who, in November 1945,
published an article arguing that a world government was necessary.   The alternative, he declared, was nuclear war sometime
in the future:

> Do I fear the tyranny of a world government? Of
> course I do. But I fear still more the coming of an-
> other war. Any government is certain to be evil to
> some extent. But a world government is preferable to
> the far greater evil of wars, particularly when viewed
> in the context of the intensified destructiveness of
> war. If such a world government is not established by
> a process of agreement among nations, I believe it
> will come anyway, and in a much more dangerous form;
> for war or wars can only result in one power being
> supreme and dominating the rest of the world by its
> overwhelming military supremacy.   (349)[2]

In other words, the nations of the world could either join together now in a world government or wait for one nation to
emerge victorious over the rest of the world after a nuclear
holocaust.

5   Many atomic scientists, then, saw no alternative to some
form of international control, although few went so far as to
advocate world government. The enormity of their discoveries
forced them to conclusions like these. However, the failure of
their efforts to influence the decision to use the bomb against
Japan convinced many scientists that they would have to organize
in order to lobby more effectively for their views (Jungk 221-23).

¶ 6: Outline point II.A ———————————

Parenthetical references indicate direct quotations. ⟍

Two separate points are introduced by "First" and "Second." ⟋

Here is Jeanne's note card for Jungk 236. Her own comments appear in brackets:

Scientists' prestige
JUNGK, p. 236
        One scientist said —
"Before the war we were supposed to be
completely ignorant of the world and inexperienced in its ways. But now we are
regarded as the ultimate authorities on all
possible subjects, from nylon stockings to
the best form of 'international organization.'
    [RELATE TO LANG QUOTATION ABOUT
            "GLAMOUR BOYS"   ]

¶ 7: Outline point II.B ———————————

Transitional phrase relates this discussion to preceding quotation. ———

6   After the war, therefore, scientists at the major sites of
the Manhattan Project—Los Alamos, New Mexico; Oak Ridge, Tennes-
see; and Hanford, Washington—organized into groups whose purpose was "to promote the attainment and use of scientific and technological advances in the best interests of humanity" (Strickland 38). In the closing months of 1945, many scientists felt
they were in a unique position to influence the outcome of contemporary debates over control of the atom. First, unlike the
general public and nearly all government and military leaders,
scientists at Los Alamos, Oak Ridge, Hanford, and especially at
the University of Chicago had had a long time to contemplate the
consequence of their discoveries since they were virtually the
only ones who knew anything at all about the bomb until August
6, 1945 (Jungk 115–17).[3] Second, after the war they enjoyed
great public prestige. Once the secret was out, the popular
press was filled with accounts of the Manhattan Project, its
scientific director, J. Robert Oppenheimer, and the secret cities of Los Alamos and Oak Ridge that the army had erected for
the purpose of creating the bomb. Writing in 1945, Daniel Lang
noted that "atom" had become "a magic word in Washington" and
that the atomic scientists, the only ones who fully understood
its meaning, were looked upon as "glamour boys" (58). "Before
the war," as one scientist remarked, "we were supposed to be
completely ignorant of the world and inexperienced in its ways.
But now we are regarded as the ultimate authorities on all possible subjects, from nylon stockings to the best form of international organization" (qtd. in Jungk 236).

7   As the tone of these comments suggests, the scientists
themselves were often unsure of how to use their new prestige.

Paragraph 7 lists reasons why scientists were unsure of how to use their status. Parallel structure ("First . . . " "Second . . . " "Finally . . . ," each supported by a documented example) helps to keep track of these reasons.

¶s 8 and 9:   Outline point III. A

¶ 8:   Identifies bill ————————

It was one thing to know what, in their judgment, the government ought to do; it was quite another matter to get the government to do it. First, they had to overcome the traditional reluctance of scientists to involve themselves with politics. According to Daniel S. Greenberg, the "war-born relationship" between American science and politics seemed to reverse nearly two centuries of "mutual aloofness between the federal government and the most influential and creative segments of the scientific community" (51). Second, most scientists were temperamentally unsuited to their new roles as lobbyists:

> They were accustomed to objectivity. An experiment worked or it didn't, data were correct or incorrect; there was no middle ground. They found it difficult to adjust themselves to the give-and-take way of getting things done in Washington, and they were unable to understand why everybody couldn't see at once how right they were. (Lang 60)

Finally, many leading scientists cautioned their colleagues to refrain from any sort of public comment or political action which might jeopardize the chances of getting some form of control. For example, Robert Oppenheimer warned the Association of Los Alamos Scientists that one of their proposed public statements might be calamitous to a new bill being written by the Truman administration (Strickland 40).

8   But that new bill, the May-Johnson Bill, quickly forced the scientists to overcome all of their prejudices against political involvement and doubts about their political effectiveness. The

¶ 9:   Gives specific provisions of bill.

Documentation indicates source of information in paragraphs 8 and 9.

¶ 10:   Outline points III.B, 1 and 2

Topic sentence introduces three-paragraph discussion of reasons for scientists' objections to military control of atomic research.

Note card for (Jungk 227):   Paragraph 10 uses material from 3 sources:

Scientists' Objections to
Military Control
Jungk, p. 227

      "But when the rejoicings came to an end
it was found that for the present everything was
to go on as before. The world might be under
the impression that peace had come again.
But so far as the people in research at
Los Alamos, Oak Ridge, Hanford, and Chicago
were concerned, the same strict rules of
secrecy prevailed as had been in force during
the war."

Note card for (United States 128):

Scientists' Objections to Military Control
      U.S. Dept. of State International Control of
Atomic Energy, p. 128
      Oppenheimer's testimony for May-Johnson
Bill!
      "... scientists are not used to being controlled;
they are not used to regimentation, and there are
good reasons why they should be averse to it, because it is in the nature of science that the individual is to be given a certain amount of
freedom to think, and to carry on the best he
knows how."
[OPPENHEIMER + OTHERS FEARED MILITARY CONTROL OF
THEIR RESEARCH-CONFLICT BETWEEN NATURE OF SCIENTIST
AND NATURE OF MILITARY.]

May—Johnson Bill was the first legislation proposed to deal with
the domestic control of atomic energy. Although the atomic scientists still hoped that the administration would propose a plan
for international control, they were greatly upset by several
provisions of this bill, notably its proposal to continue military control over atomic research. Thus most scientists quickly
switched their effort from proposing different schemes for international control of atomic energy to blocking the passage of
the May—Johnson Bill.

9

The May—Johnson Bill proposed a part-time commission of
nine members selected by the president with the Senate's consent. These nine members would then choose their own administrator and deputy administrator, and any of these positions
could be held by military officers. The commission would be
given broad power over nearly all aspects of atomic energy, including scientific research (Hewlett and Anderson 428–31).

10

The scientists opposed continued military control over
atomic research for a number of reasons. After the hard years
at Los Alamos and other project sites, they were looking forward
to freedom from military discipline. Even before the bill was
proposed, the scientists had had enough of the military involvement in their lives. Although the war was finally over, they
soon discovered that "everything was to go on as before" (Jungk
227). These scientists wanted to go back to their research,
their universities, and their homes to live as they had before
the war. Moreover, their experience on the Manhattan Project
convinced some of them that their freedom to dream up new ideas
would be curtailed by continued military control. Testifying

Note card for (Goodchild 72–73):

Scientists' Objections to
Military Control
Goodchild, pp. 72-73

    Disagreement between Oppenheimer
and Groves over issue of scientists'
wearing uniforms – Oppenheimer
resisted and won. Shows basic conflict between scientific freedom
and military control.

¶ 11: Outline point III.B, 3 ——————

Transition links discussion to previous paragraph.

Quotation by expert in field sums up scientists' views and lends authority and credibility to Jeanne's summary.

Indicates discussion concludes in this paragraph.

¶ 12: Outline point III.B, 4 ——————

for the May–Johnson Bill, Robert Oppenheimer admitted that
"scientists are not used to being controlled; they are not used
to regimentation, and there are good reasons why they should be
averse to it, because it is in the nature of science that the
individual is to be given a certain amount of freedom to think,
and to carry on the best he knows how." (United States 128).
Oppenheimer spoke from experience; as director of the Los Alamos
laboratory, he had successfully resisted pressure from General
Leslie Groves, military head of the Manhattan Project, to enlist
project scientists into the army (Goodchild 72–73).

11   In addition, they felt the need to inform the public about
the facts of this new and mysterious weapon. They soon found
that the strict secrecy regulations were also "to go on as before" and under the May–Johnson Bill would continue indefinitely
with regard to foreign policy. There was much concern by
the administration that the "secret" of the atom bomb would
escape to other countries. This position infuriated the scientists because they argued that there was no secret. They felt
that the only secret was the procedure, but within a few years
any country could experiment, as the United States had, and discover that very same secret. The scientists also felt that secrecy would hurt the United States' atomic project. Robert Cush-
ner summed up the scientists' views on this subject when he
said, "It would be calamitous to shut off the broad and free
discussion of the basic points involved, since it is only by
such free discussion that we can hope to increase our wisdom and
inform public opinion with respect to the vital questions of
policy which must be faced" (Cushman 58).

12   The last reason the scientists disapproved of military con-

First example in support of topic sentence: incident at Metallurgical Lab ——————

Second example in support of topic sentence: quotation ——————

¶ 13:   Outline points IV.A, 1 and 2 ——————

trol of atomic energy was that they had reason to fear that the

military would restrict the equipment and personnel they needed.

These scientists remembered too well what it was like during

the war. They used as an example to support their disapproval

an event that occurred at the Metallurgical Lab. A request was

sent in for linoleum flooring to go under a sensitive piece of

equipment being used, but the army did not accept it at first,

because they did not see the necessity of it. One man involved

said, "You had to lose your temper--they wouldn't take your word

for it otherwise" (Strickland 101). Furthermore, the army's

detailed examinations and investigations might reject a fully

qualified scientist who would aid the project. They felt that

this would inhibit the natural growth of knowledge acquired on

atomic energy.

13   The majority of scientists, then, opposed the May-Johnson

Bill and supported the concept of civilian control. In an ef-

fort to defeat the bill, they began organizing themselves into

the Federation of Atomic Scientists--later to be changed to the

Federation of American Scientists (Lang 55).[4] Their strategy

for action was to change public opinion and to lobby directly in

Washington. At first the scientists were somewhat reluctant to

lobby because they felt that "science should not be dragged

through the political arena" (Hewlett and Anderson 448). But

they still saw the necessity of action. Their attitude began to

change as they got more involved with the legislators and offi-

cials. Everyone in Washington and all over the country was hun-

gry for information on atomic energy, so the scientists had to

force no one to listen to their views.

¶ 14:   Outline point IV.A, 3 —————————

Introduces next paragraph's discussion of the McMahon Bill. —————————

¶ 15:   Outline point IV.B —————————

¶ 16:   Outline point IV.C —————————

14   Their lobbying efforts, although time-consuming, were successful; at the beginning of December, President Truman withdrew
his support of the May-Johnson Bill, and its argument collapsed
under the pressure exerted. The scientists had good reason for
rejoicing, but their work was not yet finished. Although the
threat of May-Johnson had been eliminated, there was no acceptable bill to take its place. On December 20, such a bill, the
McMahon Bill, was introduced (Hewlett and Anderson 439-43).

15   Just as the May-Johnson Bill proposed military control of
atomic energy, the new McMahon Bill proposed civilian control.
It created a five-member, full-time, civilian commission that
would report directly to the president. It would have broad
powers to supervise and regulate atomic research and fissionable
materials and to study social and health effects of experiments
and uses (Hewlett and Anderson 714-22).[5] Because of its emphasis on civilian control, the scientists felt that the McMahon
Bill was an acceptable alternative to the May-Johnson Bill. The
scientists openly supported the McMahon Bill, using the techniques they had used to attack the May-Johnson Bill.

16   Things were beginning to look optimistic for passage of the
bill until, during the McMahon hearings, from January 22 to
April 8, 1946, the Vandenberg Amendment was proposed. This
amendment suggested that a military liaison, who would have some
influence on all the decisions dealing with national security,
be attached to the commission. The amendment infuriated the
scientists because they felt that it was "a clear declaration to
the world that the people of the United States will put their
faith only in military might" ("Army" 333-34). They also feared

Note card for ("Civilian" 494):

> Scientists opposed Vandenberg
> Amendment
> "Civilian Atomic Control,"
> _New Republic_, 15 April 1946
>
> Defeat of Vandenberg Amendment
> credited to McMahon, scientists, and
> public opinion which caused
> Vandenberg and his supporters on
> Senate Committee to back down.

Paraphrase of source

Source for ("Civilian" 494):
"Vandenberg and his colleagues on the Senate committee backed down, not because they were suddenly overcome by sweetness and light, but because they were trounced by McMahon, the scientists, a great number of civic organizations and the newly formed National Committee for the Civilian Control of Atomic Energy."

¶ 17: Conclusion: Summarizes results of scientists' entry into politics and long-range significance of their involvement.

Indicates impact of scientists' efforts.

Focus on May-Johnson and McMahon Bills reinforces their importance to scientists, politicians, and general public.

that the liaison would take away the powers of the commission but leave the responsibilities. Opposition to this amendment renewed the protests of the scientists and the public shown during the fall of 1945, and it was through this intensity of action that the Vandenberg Amendment was defeated. An article in the New Republic credited the scientists' lobby with the victory, saying that McMahon, the scientists, and public opinion caused Vandenberg and his supporters on the Senate Committee to back down ("Civilian" 494). On June 1, 1946, the McMahon Bill was passed by the Senate and was soon to be passed by the Senate-House Conference Committee. It was signed by the president on August 1 and became law as the Atomic Energy Act of 1946 ("Army" 334).

17   By taking an active part in politics, the scientists had learned that they could affect public opinion and influence government policy. Their success indicates they learned this lesson well: during the last few weeks of the Senate committee investigations, 70,972 letters were received, with 24,851 expressing views opposing the Vandenberg Amendment, 35,000 opposing the May-Johnson Bill, and only a dozen opposing the McMahon Bill ("Thousand" 6). Petitions were sent in with thousands of signatures. If the scientists had not felt the need to actively oppose the May-Johnson Bill and support the McMahon Bill and the decision had gone the other way, it would have meant a change in national policy with respect to atomic energy. However, these two bills are important not only in themselves but also because the controversy they engendered made scientists, politicians, and the general public aware of the perplexities and problems of life in the Nuclear Age.

Note 2 is an informational note that provides supplementary information to the reader.

Note 4 is a bibliographic note that comments on and evaluates sources.

1″

Center Notes

2 spaces

Indent
5 spaces → ¹Smith prints the complete text of the Franck Report in Appendix A, 371–83.

Use
superscript → ²Other notable advocates of world government included Norma Cousins, editor of the <u>Saturday Review</u>, and Robert M. Hutchins, president of the University of Chicago.

Double-
space all
entries → ³Here Jungk discusses the secrecy at Los Alamos and other project sites.

⁴For a full discussion of the foundation of the FAS and its early goals, see Lang 54–65 and Jungk 235–38.

⁵Hewlett and Anderson reprint the McMahon Bill on these pages.

First page of works cited: number consecutively

The first two entries illustrate the correct form for an unsigned journal article; the
Cushman entry shows the form for a signed article in a journal. Note that all three
provide inclusive pagination (the *New Republic* article is just one page long).

Entry refers to one article in an edited book of Einstein's writings.

Entry denotes a book with a single author.

Entry indicates that the book the student consulted was a reprint of an earlier edition.

Entry indicates work is a translation.

1"

Center Works Cited

2 lines

Use alphabetical order

"The Army and the Atom." Nation 23 May 1946: 333–34.

"Civilian Atomic Control." New Republic 15 April 1946: 494.

Cushman, Robert E. "Civil Liberties in the Atomic Age: Threat

Indent 5 spaces

of Military Control." Annals of the American Academy of

Political and Social Sciences, 249 (Jan. 1947), 54–60.

Einstein, Albert. "Atomic War or Peace." Einstein on Peace.

Double-space

Eds. Otto Nathan and Heinz Norden. New York: Schocken, 1968.

Goodchild, Peter. J. Robert Oppenheimer: Shatterer of Worlds.

Boston: Houghton Mifflin, 1981.

Greenberg, Daniel S. The Politics of Pure Science. 1967; rpt.

New York: New American Library, 1971.

Hewlett, Richard G., and Oscar E. Anderson, Jr. The New World,

1939–46. 2 vols. University Park, Pa.: Pennsylvania State

UP, 1962.

Jungk, Robert. Brighter Than a Thousand Suns: A Personal History

of the Atomic Scientists. Trans. James Cleugh. New York:

Harcourt Brace, 1958.

Lang, Daniel. From Hiroshima to the Moon: Chronicles of Life in

the Atomic Age. New York: Simon & Schuster, 1959.

"70 Thousand Letters Back the McMahon Bill." Bulletin of the

Atomic Scientists 15 April 1946: 6.

The list of works cited includes two works by Alice Kimball Smith. The first is an article by Smith in a collection edited by Lewis and Wilson. (If Jeanne Parker had consulted other articles in the collection, her entry would cite the collection itself, not the article.) The second work is a complete book written by Smith. Note that the author's name is not repeated; instead, ten unspaced hyphens, followed by a period, are used.

This entry refers to a publication of the U.S. Government Printing Office. —————

Smith, Alice Kimball. "Los Alamos: Focus of an Age." Alamogordo Plus Twenty-Five Years. Ed. Richard S. Lewis and Jane Wilson. New York: Viking, 1971.

----------. A Peril and a Hope: The Scientists' Movement in America, 1945-47. 1965; rpt. Cambridge, Mass.: MIT P, 1970.

Strickland, Donald A. Scientists in Politics: The Atomic Scientists' Movement, 1945-48. Lafayette, Ind.: Purdue Research Foundation, 1968.

United States, Department of State. International Control of Atomic Energy: Growth of a Policy. Washington: GPO, 1946.

"Richard Cory" by Paul Simon. Copyright © 1966 Paul Simon. Used by permission.

Excerpt from *Reversals: A Personal Account of Victory Over Dyslexia* by Eileen Simpson. Copyright © 1979 by Eileen Simpson. Reprinted by permission of Houghton Mifflin Company.

Excerpt by David Swanger from *Change* reprinted with permission from *Change* Magazine, Vol. 7, No. 7 (September 1975). Copyrighted by the Council on Learning, P.O. Box 2023, New Rochelle, New York 10802.

Excerpt from "Television's Hottest Show." Copyright 1981 by Newsweek, Inc. All rights reserved. Reprinted by permission.

Excerpt from "Why Women Are Paid Less Than Men" by Lester C. Thurow. Copyright © 1981 by The New York Times Company. Reprinted by permission.

Dance column by Tobi Tobias. Copyright 1983 by News Group Publications, Inc. Reprinted by permission of *New York* Magazine.

Excerpts from "The First Ten Men in Space" from *The Book of Lists* by David Wallechinsky, Irving Wallace, and Amy Wallace. Copyright © 1977 by David Wallechinsky, Irving Wallace, and Amy Wallace. By permission of William Morrow and Company.

Excerpts from "Ten Medical Breakthroughs by Non-Doctors" from *The Book of Lists* by David Wallechinsky, Irving Wallace, and Amy Wallace. Copyright © 1977 by David Wallechinsky, Irving Wallace, and Amy Wallace. By permission of William Morrow and Company.

"The Good Things: Duke on America" from *John Wayne: America, Why I Love Her.* Copyright © 1977 by Devere Music Corporation and Batjac Music Company. Reprinted by permission of Simon and Schuster, a division of Gulf and Western Corporation.

Excerpt from "What the Game Is All About." Copyright 1981 by Newsweek, Inc. All rights reserved. Reprinted by permission.

Excerpt from "A Wraith Among the Goons." Copyright 1982 by Newsweek, Inc. All rights reserved. Reprinted by permission.

Index

NOTES

NOTES

NOTES

NOTES

NOTES